THEOLOGICAL TERRITORIES

DAVID BENTLEY HART

THEOLOGICAL
TERRITORIES

A David Bentley Hart Digest

University of Notre Dame Press
Notre Dame, Indiana

Published by the University of Notre Dame Press
Notre Dame, Indiana 46556
undpress.nd.edu

Library of Congress Cataloging-in-Publication Data
Names: Hart, David Bentley, author.
Title: Theological territories : a David Bentley Hart digest / David
   Bentley Hart.
Description: Notre Dame, Indiana : University of Notre Dame Press, [2020] |
   Includes index.
Identifiers: LCCN 2019054882 (print) | LCCN 2019054883 (ebook) | ISBN
   9780268107178 (hardback) | ISBN 9780268107185 (paperback) | ISBN
   9780268107208 (adobe pdf) | ISBN 9780268107192 (epub)
Subjects: LCSH: Theology. | Philosophical theology. | Bible. New
   Testament—Criticism, interpretation, etc. | Bible—Theology.
Classification: LCC BR118 .H3646 2020 (print) | LCC BR118 (ebook) | DDC
   230—dc23
LC record available at https://lccn.loc.gov/2019054882
LC ebook record available at https://lccn.loc.gov/2019054883

for

John and Laura Betz

CONTENTS

ACKNOWLEDGMENTS

My thanks to all the persons and institutions (recorded in the Introduction below) who originally provided the occasions for—and usually the topics of—these pieces. My gratitude also to the Notre Dame Institute for Advanced Study and its four permanent denizens over the three years of my association with it—Brad S. Gregory, Donald Stelluto, Carolyn Sherman, and Grant Osborn—for granting me the time and space in which to pursue my work and to join in a great many of the conversations that generated a number of these pieces; and many thanks to the McGrath Institute for Church Life for a semester's hospitality during my tenancy at Notre Dame. I am grateful as well to Roberto de la Noval for preparing the index to this volume, a task for which I am temperamentally and probably morally unsuited.

INTRODUCTION

The large preponderance of the pieces gathered here are texts of live addresses delivered in various settings, and so have never before been published. The few that remain have appeared in print previously but are given here in alternative (and more authoritative) form, restoring material that originally had to be omitted for reasons of space; their claim to a place in this collection is that they, like the others, were written as occasional meditations, on topics usually assigned by others, without footnotes, and almost all of them were also at various points delivered as lectures or private talks; and yet, curiously enough, they fill in certain crucial dimensions of my thinking over the past several years. Like most scholars who have been at their work for any appreciable stretch of years, I find that I have committed a great many of my ideas—even some of the better ones, I think—only to public lectures, or to public remarks on the work of other scholars. In many cases, moreover, those ideas are expressed more concisely and with greater clarity than they might have been in the context of a large written text. A single address written to be delivered live belongs to a special genre, one that imposes certain exigencies on its author. One does not enjoy the liberty of extending one's exposition beyond the scope of, say, an hour (or forty-five minutes, if one is merciful), but neither can one curtail one's remarks before reaching some kind of satisfying conclusion. It is a usefully severe discipline, especially if one hopes to say anything of consequence in the time allotted. The result, if one succeeds in one's aims, can be a degree of economy and lucidity that the greater freedom of a longer text might actually discourage or thwart. But for the pitiless relentlessness of the clock on the wall, one might never strive for the kind of crystalline exactitude that becomes necessary when one can say no more than what *must* be said to communicate one's meaning within an unforgivingly fixed span.

All of this having been noted, the first chapter in this collection was in fact written initially as an essay and was published as an article in a symposium on Rowan Williams's darkly scintillating book *The Tragic Imagination*, in *Modern Theology* (April 2018), in a somewhat shorter version than the text given here; only in a revised form was it delivered as a public lecture (at Canisius College in Buffalo, New York, in March 2018). I like to think that it is a fairly accomplished piece, structurally and stylistically at least, and that it makes an argument of some subtlety. That does not mean, however, that I can claim that its argument has proved quite as clear to every reader or listener as I might have hoped. In general, this has been my experience whenever I have addressed this topic. When I wrote on the relation of tragedy and theology in my first book, some years ago now, I found myself on more than one occasion being accused of disliking tragedy as a dramatic form. In point of fact, I am, if anything, excessively attached to it. My objection to "tragic theology," back then and in this present piece, is partly the result of my belief that this style of theology has the effect of distorting and even obscuring something strange, crucial, and unprecedented in the Christian story; but it is no less the result of my indignation at the ways in which some of the tragic theology I have encountered in the past has almost invariably (as far as I can see) stripped tragic art of its true mystery, variety, and beauty and contracted it to a banal set of platitudes regarding hope despite uncertainty, hope despite suffering, hope despite the impenetrable darkness, hope despite . . . Happily, Williams's book breaks from that reductive pattern. Like everything he writes, it is marked by an extraordinary degree of tact and penetrating intelligence. My essay is in one sense a reaction to his book, and partly to certain mild remarks it directs toward my earlier writing on the matter (as well as remarks not quite as mild made by Williams in a public lecture that I watched online); but it is more essentially a larger meditation on the nature of the Christian story, and on the relevance of tragic art to our understanding of that story. My approach to the matter might be said to be more or less the opposite of Williams's, but I prefer to think of it as complementary. As I say in my essay, my concern is not so much to contest his claims regarding what tragedy has the power to reveal about reality but rather to ask whether he neglects adequately to consider what tragedy has the power to conceal. And, I confess, his sympathy for Hegel's reading of Attic tragedy is one I cannot share; I have always found Hegel's treatment of, say, *Antigone* deeply depressing, for the admittedly petty reason that it spoils the play for me, by turning it into what looks to me like a bourgeois morality tale, and thus robbing it of its terrifying pagan grandeur (but I deal with that in the essay).

I should note, by the way, that Williams offers some responses to my essay—and to several others also concerned with his book—in that same issue of *Modern Theology*; his remarks are well worth consulting and are probably wiser than my cavils regarding his argument. Here I will mention only that he arraigns me for perhaps falling prey to a certain "essentialism" regarding tragedy. He may be right. As a rule, that would not be a charge that would bother me very much, since it is one that can usually be deflected with little more than a languid wave of the hand and a surly *tu quoque*; anything to which we apply a general name—anything we situate in a particular category—is likely to be something we identify by certain *essential* qualities, and none of us can wholly escape his or her own generalizations. As far as I know, however, apart from some specific observations on the cultic context of Attic tragedy, my only intentional general characterization of tragedy as a genre or natural kind is in terms of the special affective power that it possesses: it excites a peculiar kind of pathos, one that occupies a particular place along the emotional spectrum. Ideally, tragedies are sad, comedies amusing, and so forth. Admittedly, I also advert to a certain somnifacient virtue in tragedy well performed, but that seems like a harmless rhetorical conceit to me. Even so, I do not dismiss Williams's criticism, and I fully grant that nothing I say in my essay should be taken as the sole "correct" account of the tragic, and I definitely do not mean to suggest that Williams's account is somehow objectively "wrong." His is a rich and somewhat troubling meditation upon this most mysterious of dramatic forms, and one of considerable originality. It has made me think many issues over again (but still, so to speak, on the obverse).

Most of the remaining pieces collected here, fortunately, require less by way of preface. Chapter 2 was originally delivered at the University of Chicago in May 2017, under the auspices of the Lumen Christi Institute; it was one of two addresses (the other being by Cyril O'Regan) made to Jean-Luc Marion on the occasion of the (oddly incomplete) publication of his Gifford Lectures, and Marion replied to both with great grace and aplomb. Chapter 3 consists in remarks made to the great Czech philosopher Msgr. Tomáš Halik in November 2015, as part of a large colloquium on a research project he had undertaken when he and I were both fellows at the Notre Dame Institute for Advanced Study. Chapter 4 consists in comments on books by two extremely gifted scholars, Jennifer Newsome Martin and Brandon Gallaher, that I delivered while participating in a panel at the annual convention of the American Academy of Religion in Boston in November 2017. Chapter 5 consists in remarks made at the University of Notre Dame in April 2018, in response to a lecture by Bruce McCormack.

Chapter 6 is an essay that has been published previously ("The Devil's March: *Creatio ex Nihilo*, the Problem of Evil, and a Few Dostoyevskian Meditations," in *Creatio ex Nihilo*, edited by Gary Anderson, University of Notre Dame Press, 2017), albeit in somewhat different form.

Chapter 7 is the text of a lecture delivered at a conference on the idea of tradition (Jewish, Christian, and Muslim) in the modern world, held at Valparaiso University in April 2018. Section III was omitted from the live reading, for reasons of length. The unabridged version will also be published in a volume comprising the full proceedings of the conference at some time in the future. This essay comes with a warning. For those with a mercilessly sober sensibility—and especially those of clericalist inclination—the experience of reading the first part of the text may be more jarring than interesting, and I would not blame them for avoiding it altogether. In a previous book, published not very long ago, I pledged that in future I would attempt a more emollient tone in my future theological writings. My resolve has already abandoned me, however. Life is short and generally tedious, so why make a virtue of blandness? And, truth be told, the savagery of the lecture's humor is intended principally to distract the reader from the subversiveness of its more serious arguments (or what will look like subversiveness to anyone who cherishes an idyllically uncomplicated picture of dogmatic history). I should probably not admit that, of course, so please neglect to read the sentence directly preceding this one.

Chapter 8 is the text of a lecture delivered at the University of Notre Dame in April 2017 at a conference called "The Quest for Consonance: The Sciences and Theology," directed by Prof. Celia Deane-Drummond and the Center for Theology, Science, and Human Flourishing. Chapter 9 is a lecture originally delivered to the American Maritain Society at a conference held at Providence College in February 2014.

Chapter 10 is an article published previously ("The Illusionist," on Daniel Dennett's *From Bacteria to Bach,* in the *New Atlantis,* Summer/Fall 2017), though—once again—in somewhat different form.

Chapter 11 is a lecture delivered at Marquette University in May 2017 at the annual convocation of the Lonergan Society—a conference with the rather cumbersome and enigmatic title "At the Level of Our Time: Lonergan between Today and Tomorrow."

Chapters 12 and 13 are related to one another and have both been published previously ("Christians and the Death Penalty: There Is No Patron Saint of Executioners," on Edward Feser and Joseph M. Bessette's *By Man Shall His Blood Be Shed: A Catholic Defense of Capital Punishment,* in *Commonweal,* December 1, 2017; "Further Reflections on Capital Punishment [and on Edward Feser]," in the *Institute for Church Life Journal,* December 19, 2017), with some differences. Both are extremely harsh in the judgments they pass upon the book, and I have no inclination to revise my remarks now. I do not like altering the record after the fact; and, as it happens, my opinion of the book's biblical, patristic, historical, theological, philosophical, and pragmatic arguments remains entirely unfavorable. I have to say, however, that in the course of private exchanges with one of the authors, the philosopher Edward Feser, he assured me that the callousness that I and other critics believed we had discerned in the book's arguments is an appearance rather than the reality and is the unintended consequence of the somewhat forensic style the authors had chosen to adopt. I take his word on this unreservedly, am relieved to be corrected on the matter, and regret any impression I may have given that I think I can read the authors' souls. And, to be honest, I cannot claim perfect purity of heart in this regard. I believe that Christian faith absolutely forbids the normal judicial application of the death penalty, and that any Christian who thinks otherwise simply has never understood the teachings of Christ or the example of the earliest Christians. The record of the first three centuries of the faith is clear and uncompromising on this matter. To me, there is not even an interesting argument to be had here. Moreover, I find the draconian American penal system and the brutality of its "justice" abhorrent. But I am not offended by those who argue for the justice of capital punishment in certain particular cases where one cannot deny the presence of absolute evil. In fact, I think one would have to be inhuman not to feel the desire for a final retribution in certain cases. So I ought not presume to understand or judge the motives of others.

Chapter 14 is the text of an address delivered at Fordham University in September 2017, as that year's Archbishop Demetrios Orthodoxy in America Lecture.

Chapter 15 contains remarks on an address by the redoubtable Reinhard Hütter, delivered at the University of Notre Dame in October 2015. Chapter 16 is a lecture delivered at Duke University, also in September 2017, as a keynote address at the divinity school's annual theology graduate students' conference. Chapter 17 is the oldest text here, being a lecture whose first version was delivered in 1998 at the University of Virginia, and which has been delivered in ever shifting forms at many venues since then (I have probably delivered some version of it nearly a dozen times). Given its age, some of its phrases have also over the years insinuated themselves into my books and articles. Chapter 18, by contrast, is the most recent piece contained herein, though it resumes many of the themes of the preceding chapter and carries them in another direction. It is a plenary address made to the Society of Christian Ethics at that organization's annual conference in January 2019 in Louisville, Kentucky. As I am not a member of the society, it was something of an honor to be invited to deliver the lecture, one for which I am sincerely grateful.

Chapters 19 through 21—though written as essays on particular writers—all appeared in different form, trimmed to the dimensions of book reviews, in various issues of *First Things* (respectively, "The Shock of the Real," on Victor Segalen's *Journey to the Land of the Real*, November 2017; "Empson in the East," on William Empson's *The Face of the Buddha*, May 2017; "The Lost Modernist," on David Jones, March 2018). I have since severed all connections with that journal and really should have done so sooner; so these represent my last contributions to its pages.

Chapter 22 was originally written as a foreword to Cluny Media's reprint of Léon Bloy's *The Pilgrim of the Absolute* (2017). This version contains a few sentences judiciously omitted from the previously published version.

After my translation of the New Testament appeared late in 2017, I was invited to give a great many interviews and to write a great many short articles on the project. Chapters 23 through 27 are all examples of the latter (in order: "Are Christians Supposed to Be Communists?" in the *New York Times*, November 4, 2017; "Everything You Know about the Gospel of Paul Is Likely Wrong," in *Aeon*, January 8, 2018; "The Word Made Fresh," in *The Tablet*, January 13, 2018; "The Spirit of the Text," in *Yale Books Unbound*, November 3, 2017; "A Prayer for the Poor," in the *Institute for Church Life Journal*, June 5, 2018), reproduced here with a few changes and additions, as well as the titles I gave them when I wrote them. Chapter 28, on the other hand, has never appeared in print before at all; neither was it ever delivered live, at least not as a lecture. Rather, it is a distillate of various remarks I made regarding my translation in the course of a number of radio and podcast interviews.

Given the nature of this collection, I should note, it is inevitable that certain arguments appear more than once, albeit not in an identical context. Some phrases and some passages resemble one another, because no lecturer should be obliged always to think of an entirely new way of saying the same thing. Even so, I ask the reader's patience.

All reprinted pieces appear here with permission.

PART ONE

Theology and What May Be Said

The Gospel According to Melpomene

Reflections on Rowan Williams's
The Tragic Imagination

πολλῶν ταμίας Ζεὺς ἐν Ὀλύμπῳ,
πολλὰ δ᾽ ἀέλπτως κραίνουσι θεοί:
καὶ τὰ δοκηθέντ᾽ οὐκ ἐτελέσθη,
τῶν δ᾽ ἀδοκήτων πόρον ηὗρε θεός.
τοιόνδ᾽ ἀπέβη τόδε πρᾶγμα.
—Euripides, *Medea*

I

The ghastliest performance of *Tristan und Isolde* I ever attended was at the Metropolitan Opera in March 2008. It was one of that creakingly venerable institution's rare, touchingly awkward ventures into the avant-garde (of the sort that would have seemed quite innovative in Berlin circa 1934 or 1954), and everything about it was excruciatingly ill-conceived: the sets, the props, the costumes, the precipitously forward-slanting stage floor, even the stage machinery (a malfunction in which created a long delay in the final act by sending the hapless and supine *Heldentenor*, Gary Lehman sledding down the boards on his pallet to crash headfirst into the prompter's box). But the most egregious offense came only at the very end, when Isolde (Deborah Voigt) stepped to the front of the stage and sang the *Liebestod*, quite ravishingly really, and then inexplicably failed to die; the lights simply dimmed and, after a moment's perplexed silence, polite applause rippled through the audience and only after several seconds swelled to full appreciative exuberance. Not much of a *Liebestod* at all, at that point, really—more a *Liebesangst*. Of course, one can somewhat sympathize with the director here. There is something so annoyingly idiotic about the tendency of Wagnerian heroines to keel over dead at the drop of a strong emotion—Isolde, Elizabeth, Elsa, Kundry; apparently, Wagner was under the impression that women have the physical constitutions of houseflies. But I was indignant. As far as I was concerned, having paid the price of admission, I was entitled at opera's end to one dead soprano. After all, the entire reason for following the sinuous, interweaving currents of all those gorgeous *Leitmotiven* for four and a half hours, and even for enduring the ordeal of an almost parodically obnoxious production, is the ecstatic release of that intoxicating consummation, when Isolde takes her final leave of both the Tristan chord and life and briefly becomes our psychopomp, leading us along with her down into the shades below and across the dark waters, serenely adrift for a few lingering moments in an opium trance of perfect resignation. Then the lights come up, we gather our things, we go home, and we enjoy uncommonly peaceful dreams. This is how one knows that Wagner's "music-dramas" were the works of a true tragedian, after all: the infallible mark of the tragic is that it helps one sleep well.

Then again, I take something of an antinomian aesthete's approach to tragedy. For me, its greatest virtue as an art is more "musical" (in the classical sense) than discursive, and I am suspicious of any didactic reduction of its power to something easily grasped—most especially to a species of moral tutelage (which can be a dangerously protean thing). I tend to think tragedy's unity as an aesthetic form is almost entirely affective rather than conceptual, consisting in a certain overwhelming mood, and that any attempt to say what tragedy as such means or what lessons we might derive from it is an exercise not so much in objective hermeneutics as in personal testimonial. This is not to say that the great tragedies do not abound in "messages"; many fine things are said by the characters, many incisive aphoristic exchanges challenge us with their piercing insights, many moral depths are sounded. But I assume that all of that is merely part of the decorative design, clothing the architecture of the plot in rich textures and darkly sparkling hues. It is not what tragedy *means*. Really, as aesthetic experiences go, tragedy is probably among the least intellectual, and this is why it can so often encompass plots of such exorbitant stupidity (of a sort that no well-crafted comedy could tolerate) without the least impairment to its total effect. I assume, moreover, that this effect is largely uniform for all of us, while any lessons we take from the drama are chiefly those we took with us into the theater. Much of the virtuosity of a great tragedian lies in the ability to bedizen obvious truths and silly tales with a grandeur and a pathos far in excess of their native properties. I object to (for instance) the opulent confection of Hegel's reading of Attic tragedy not because I find its anachronism preposterous or doubt its brilliance or think it "wrong"—what would that mean?—but because I suspect it of philistinism: a crude subordination of the aesthetic to the theoretical, and of something splendidly mysterious to a system of rather ordinary ideas. As understandings of the tragic go, I far prefer the narcotic to the speculative.

And yet, all this said, I have to concede that, in long retrospect, my reaction to Isolde's impertinent durability that night raises certain questions for me of a distinctly moral nature. Why, out of that whole cosmic cataclysm of a production, should this have been the insult that stung me most deeply? Why, after all, should I have wanted her to die? Hers was hardly a happy life to begin with, what with her dreadful marriage and that final horribly thwarted romance, and it is hard to find an ethically wholesome explanation for the emotional satisfaction that I hoped to derive from watching her killed by a surfeit of love. The curious thing is not that we can take pleasure in tragedy but that this pleasure would be palpably diminished if at the last moment the drama were to reverse itself and end happily. Nor do I think this is simply because we would then think that the drama is not true to life, since that is something we demand of no art and that, blessedly, no art offers us. When I think about it, of all the innumerable lives squandered by tragic drama down the centuries, there is only one whose loss I find totally intolerable: Cordelia's. And it seems to me clear that the reason for this is that *King Lear* is a tragedy that somehow exceeds the customary boundaries of the tragic, precisely because right in the middle of its final descent into the darkness it provides an impossible glimpse of an entirely different ending to the story—not, that is, a mere false dawn, a dramatic trick or penultimate twist, one last unanticipated peripety cheaply amplifying the suspense, but rather a sudden radiant interruption of the narrative by a wholly different narrative, one from outside the logic of the play altogether, filled with the eschatological light of another world. As a result, when the inevitable comes, it is simply shattering. That night, one does not sleep well at all.

II

Which brings me to *The Tragic Imagination*. I have to say, I will read anything by Rowan Williams—or would do if I could read as fast as he writes—because I know that it will be brilliant, subtle, absorbing, and probably right, and that I will profit from it. This is true even in the case of a book, like this one, in which I think I find certain of my own arguments somewhat misrepresented and truncated, and in which a case is made that I think ever so slightly (but ever so persistently) off the mark. But I should also confess that this particular book runs afoul of some of my more stubborn prejudices. It comes perilously close to a genus of literary criticism to which I am temperamentally adverse. Actually, I find quite a lot of art criticism suspect, no doubt on account of a few fairly heathen superstitions on my part regarding some special mana or numinous magic in the arts. I tend to think that all great artistic accomplishments occur on the far side of a mysterious threshold where propositional or analytic discourses fail because they are infinitely inadequate to what lies beyond. Every true work of art is an indissolubly singular event whose intricacies can be approached only by a language in which the most tactful poetic phenomenology—of the delicate and of the sublime and of all the beautiful medians in between—has displaced every form of explanation, whether technical, social, economic, moral, psychological, philosophical, theological, or other. When we try to reduce the work to the lesser languages of those fragmentary disciplines, all we do is retreat from the incomparable to the conventional, and from visions to platitudes. It is rather like attempting to understand the flight of a swallow by attaching anchors to its wings. And, in the case of tragic drama, I am not even sure there is in any meaningful sense a single genre here, comprising the dramas of the Attic Dionysia, Seneca's storm-wracked banquets of blood, the wild farragoes of Spain's and England's Golden Age dramas, the glimmering gloom of France's, Sarah Kane's extravaganzas of inadvertently Monty-Pythonesque gore, and so on. The critic's frequent need to proceed as if there is such a thing can yield formulations of positively vacuous generality. And it seems to me that, in sometimes playing by the rules of that kind of criticism, Williams allows himself to be drawn toward a few of these: for instance, Stanley Cavell's assertion that tragedy "is about what we *know* and do not acknowledge" (31). (Well, yes. And no. Sometimes. Rarely ever, really. Often quite the reverse.) Or even, perhaps, Gillian Rose's fascinating suggestion that "it is the flight from sadness that precipitates tragedy" (35). (Again, yes, occasionally. Often, vaguely speaking. Not quite so often, speaking more precisely.) And, of course, the *literary* critic in particular is all too likely to invent rationales for the actions of fictional characters, in order to reduce the intractably mercurial poetic illusion of living personality to the banal clinical consistency of psychological character—as in the case of Cavell's reading of *Othello*, which Williams accords considerable respect, but which seems to me to involve the ascription of motives to an Othello who somehow exceeds the letter of the text. Othello really exists, however, only as a tissue of words; his entire being consists in 887 lines of verse; Iago is precisely 211 lines more real. The number of equally plausible alternative readings is incalculable.

Misgivings aside, however, the best literary scholarship, of which Williams's text provides many exemplary passages, is not merely the kind of criticism that I find problematic; and obviously we cannot help but talk about the arts, if only for the sake of a deeper experience of the delight they afford us, and there are certainly better and worse ways of doing this. But none is authoritative or free from arbitrariness. Naturally, we all want the arts we love, like tragic drama, to be elevating, and *serious* in ways we think important, which for most of us means *morally* serious. We certainly do not want to imagine, for instance, that a taste for tragedy resembles voyeurism or sadism (though, for some viewers, it probably does) or arises simply from an instinct toward nothingness that the drama allows us to discharge vicariously (although that too, it seems reasonable to suppose, is the case for many). And, so, we choose what to think. To me, it seems obvious that Hegel's treatment of Attic tragedy has nothing much to do with the arts of ancient Athens and everything to do with his genius in converting all interesting cultural artifacts into motifs illustrative of his own philosophy. Conversely, the reflections of the young Nietzsche (who, curiously, receives not a single mention in Williams's text) are immeasurably truer to the aesthetic and religious verities of the Dionysia, even if Nietzsche himself later, for philosophical reasons, somewhat distanced himself from *The Birth of Tragedy*. To Williams, with his pronounced Hegelian sympathies, it seems plausible to entertain the suggestion that "the classical audience is supposed to be learning how to let its own partial rationality be suspended in the excess of the Dionysian liturgy so as to have its dangerously limited certainties challenged, changed, and absorbed in a more solid and 'lawful' reasoning" (34). To me, with my very different understanding of the economies of Attic cult, it seems that this is more or less objectively false, an unhistorical imposition of post-Christian notions on a society to which they are irrelevant, and that it might in some ways be truer to say that the chief purpose of the suspended rationality and general amnesty that obtained during the season of Dionysian misrule was to have those "dangerously limited certainties" confirmed and fortified.

Then again, it may be that I find Williams's understanding of Attic tragedy strange largely because it is so thoroughly a literary interpretation, a treatment principally of texts, abstracted from the historically concrete realities of both the aesthetic form and the religious context of the plays. Not that he entirely ignores these things; but they are fairly secondary concerns in *The Tragic Imagination*. And, of course, inasmuch as most of the plays still extant have been separated from the rest of the cycles to which they belong, and none of them is still performed within the setting of the civic liturgy of the Dionysia, the literary approach is largely inevitable for us. But the occasional inattention to cultural context allows Williams to make some fairly extraordinary (even perhaps incredible) claims for what Attic tragedy in particular teaches, and for what the genre of tragedy as a whole has the power to reveal to us: the receptive act of silently watching tragedy disabuses us of certain kinds of fantasy, isolates us from forms of false and trivializing solidarity that lead to corporate practices of exclusion and violence, confronts us with intractable human otherness, obliges us to recognize what allows us to listen and respond to others, shows us how to start thinking about what a 'self' is, changes us, even perhaps "converts us" (159). Confronted by claims as rapturous and rhapsodic as these, my first impulse is not in fact to dismiss them; Williams is a powerful thinker and is quite capable of discerning his own experience of tragic art. But I have to question the degree to which these are objective observations as opposed to private reactions—not so much truths that tragedy imparts as prior convictions that tragedy provides the unsurpassable occasion for recalling. This latter is no mean thing, of course. One of the most marvelously "prophetic" of great art's powers is that of apprising us of who we already are. But one must take care scrupulously to distinguish between that power, with its inexhaustibly multifarious consequences, and anything as rigidly definite and uniform in effect as a mere "meaning."

III

There is a real danger in assuming that one's moral or metaphysical interpretation of an aesthetic experience is something intrinsic to its object, rather than simply one's own personal mode of receiving it. And it seems to me that Williams sometimes writes as if this is indeed his assumption, and that consequently he too easily ignores other equally—and sometimes more—plausible interpretations, and that hence, while he is often ingenious in describing what tragedy can reveal, he pays far too little attention to what it can hide. Even so, his is a compelling picture, one that combines a great variety of views with immense virtuosity (even if, to my mind, he accords the Hegelian an unmerited preponderance). He sees tragic art as having, if not a *unique*, at least a *singular* power to demystify social violence and to enlarge the moral imagination. For him, as for Hegel, Attic tragedy repeatedly discloses the insubstantiality, contingency, and delusion of the hieratic self-identifications of its characters, the false polarities and conflicts they create by their fiercely sanctimonious partial perspectives, the ruin they visit on the personal and civic orders by their refusal to entertain opposing perspectives, the ways in which their sufferings point toward the universal vantage of a more rational and lawful order, one in which seemingly antithetical visions of the holy are peacefully reconciled. In *Medea*, for instance, the catastrophic disruption of the fragile social compacts of society, however much of a probation of the negative it may be, aids reflection's advance toward a true order of justice. Tragedy of every epoch reveals both the necessity and the perilous friability of civil order. It offers us no *cure* for suffering, but rather *healing;* by narrating the seemingly unspeakable it shows us that we are not rendered speechless; and, if suffering can be spoken, we can begin again to think, about our self-representations, and about the process of our thinking itself. And to acknowledge, narrate, and transcend the past is to inaugurate mourning. Tragedy informs us, moreover, that the result of seeking to know other minds, and of being governed by the torment of being unable to do so, is frequently destructive. It demands from the audience instead a willing recognition of the real, indissoluble separateness of other persons. It reminds us that we shall always be confronted with suffering we cannot control, and forbids us from denying it by explaining it away as somehow secretly good and just, and disenchants us of any belief that reconciliation cancels out the past. By forcing us to watch the drama silently, prevented from intervening, it convicts us of both our habitual inaction in the face of unjust suffering and our habitual complicity in the disastrous misrecognitions that create it. And so on.

Obviously, it is hard to do justice to a text as rich as Williams's by attempting to distill it into a single paragraph. I cannot possibly enumerate all the brilliant insights and provocations this book contains. Suffice it to say, the claims are numerous and sometimes grand, and I take issue with none of them. But they too represent only partial perspectives, which should not be allowed to obscure other perspectives. To begin with, it may be true that tragedy tells us that we can speak about suffering and so are not destroyed by it; but it also teaches us to speak in a very particular way—which is to say, beautifully. Williams does address the moral question raised by the practice of casting abysmal misery in exquisite language and grand spectacle, but only briefly; and, on the whole, he devotes very little space to the consideration of tragedy as an aesthetic event. It is possible, after all, that the form of the drama encourages us to speak of unjust suffering too damned well. What else are we to learn from the wild canorous solemnities of Sophocles, or Shakespeare's elemental organ tones, or the fluent quicksilver gleam and genuinely alarming elegance of Racine's alexandrines? If I were to guess at what I may have learned from tragedy over the years (and I am a rapt lover of the form), I might have the temerity to believe that the truths Williams says tragedy teaches were largely known to me before I entered the theater, from other, less splendid sources, and that I had to know them already in order to understand what I was seeing as more than a celebration of despair. What, however, I could never have known but for the experience of the drama itself was that all these terrible truths could somehow, by the application of sufficient art, be made beautiful, hypnotic, gorgeously grave, and stupefying. Surely that is more distinctive of tragic drama than any kind of "information" it might provide; why else would the greatest tragedies be also the most ecstatic and darkly melodious poems? And, so, a willfully vulgar skeptic might well ask whether, if it is moral lessons about the sufferings endured by real persons we are seeking, these might not better be imparted by a discourse devoid of the distracting glitter of all those sweet obliquities and swelling sonorities and fluttering embellishments. Perhaps good journalism, purged of artificial pathos and free from the mediations of poetry, might do a far better job at awakening us from our comfortable fantasies and ethical inertias and at forcing us to recognize the concrete particularities of human anguish and the destructive social practices in which we ourselves are involved—the way in which, for instance, a single photograph of a naked child, running in terror and crying out in agony from napalm burns, might alter an entire nation's consciousness regarding a war it is waging abroad. Granting the emotional power of great tragedy, the cutting edge of its well-honed verse, the grave attentiveness it requires of its audience, if its special purpose were truly moral illumination, one would have to ask what the aesthetic form adds that a direct, unadorned acquaintance with simple facts could not offer. Yes, of course, great art draws us in in a way simple reporting does not. But converting the knowledge of human suffering into an occasion of aesthetic rapture seems an altogether peculiar way to stir the conscience.

Even so, I do not doubt that an encounter with great tragedy can, in many individual cases, be an occasion of moral enlightenment or even of the birth of sympathy. But I do not believe that this is what makes tragedy distinctive as an art. At least, I think it plausible, and considerably more plausible than Williams seems willing to grant, to argue that great tragedy, far from encouraging us to ponder human calamity deeply, instead invites us to cease thinking about it at all, precisely because by the end of the play it has successfully borne us not only beyond all answers but even beyond the desire to ask any questions. Perhaps for a great many of us, by way of a special power no other art possesses, it reconciles us to inevitability and even teaches us that this can leave us in a deeply soothing condition. Tragic pathos perhaps offers a unique liberation from the burdens of a reflective conscience. The "all passions spent" understanding of the experience, of which Williams is rather dismissive (76), is simply an aesthetic fact; and catharsis (to use the traditional term) is a precious thing; but we should not mistake therapy for deep thought. In tragic drama, after all, we never for a moment directly confront the brute reality of human suffering; we see everything through a shimmering veil of beauty. Even when tragedians attempt to tear the veil away by making the spectacle more brutal, grim, and graphically violent—as, say, in *Titus Andronicus* or *The Duchess of Malfi*, to give the most distinguished examples—the result is that the Dionysia merely dissolves into the Grand Guignol, and tragic gravity is replaced by titillating horror. Real suffering, in its unadorned concreteness, simply overwhelms artistic representation. But, then, perhaps that is the point: tragedy is the art that allows us to avert our gaze from the grimmest truths while imagining we have, in fact, bravely exposed ourselves to them. The extraordinary passivity endured by tragedy's audience, on which Williams places such stress, may serve for most of us as a tutelage in habitual passivity. Perhaps what the drama really tells me is that, if I am willing to grieve for the shadows passing before my eyes for an appointed period of time, with of course the aid of fine verse and perhaps some moving music, I shall by that transitory surrender have discharged the debt of tears I owe the world and now need not grieve for the far more solid but immeasurably less interesting figures that pass me on the street. Not only does tragedy inaugurate mourning, as Williams says; it brings it ceremoniously to a close and seals it with a lustrous black silk bow. And all of this occurs within a contained ritual space from which I can afterwards emerge emotionally unscathed but secure in conscience, knowing that I must be a capital fellow, quite sensitive and compassionate, even while remaining sadly aware that many things are beyond all remedy. Life goes on. Again, a good night's sleep awaits.

IV

Seen this way, tragedy—at least, in a culture capable of tragedy, which sadly ours probably is not—inevitably serves certain political and even religious purposes. Attic tragedy in particular served the religious and political mythos of Athens; but all tragedy is at least potentially an endorsement of resigned consent to the orders that preserve us against the elemental powers we cannot subdue. This in no way diminishes the magnificence of tragedy's most glorious expressions. Great art invariably transcends the local conditions of its origin. Still, what it *beautifully* recommends to our sensibility—though not really to our thinking—is the vision of a place where the distinction between freedom and necessity is meaningless, a boundary where hope can relent and the soul find release from false expectations. There thought, following emotion, disappears in an equanimity that "wisely" recognizes the fragility of order, the accommodations necessary to preserve it, the losses that are beyond all recovery, and the consolations of dignified lamentation. Rather than a training in moral discernment, it can serve as a rite of absolution. Then comes the Satyr play or masque, because the work of mourning has been completed, and now we may laugh and resume our normal distance from the divine catastrophe of life. Nietzsche was correct about the genius of Attic tragedy's aesthetic form: it combines seemingly irreconcilable sacred truths in a perfect choreography of (to borrow a later phrase) force and structure. The audience never simply encounters the irrecuperable surd of unredeemed suffering but in fact finds all things in perfect balance because everything, even the chaos of life at its most primal, has been translated into the beautiful dream-images of the drama. Apolline representation makes the Dionysian *agōnia* bearable, even delightful and life-affirming. Whatever imbalance of justice befalls the protagonists of the drama, it is more than compensated for by the harmonious integration of form, and the consequent sense of harmony this awakens in those looking on. And this magnificent aesthetic reconciliation of seemingly antinomous divine orders, with its mysterious power to extract spiritual peace from personal desolation, is very much an achievement of the *religious* genius of ancient Athens. It is a reconciliation achieved not by a higher synthesis of forces, however, but only by their finely preserved equilibrium.

Williams really does pay too little serious attention to the actual religious context of the Attic dramas. Even when speaking of "the Dionysian liturgy," he studiously avoids a host of traditional themes—tragedy as religious consolation, as apotropaic rite, as ritual appeasement, as sacrificial spectacle, as catharsis, as an acknowledgment of the occasionally irresoluble conflict between different sacred spheres (such as city and family)—that clearly were dimensions of the drama in its original sacral setting. The Dionysian festivities were, after all, a civic act of propitiation, a way of honoring, containing, and drawing upon the power of "the wild god" of the orgy while keeping the most destructive expressions of his power at bay, and were thus also a way of affirming once again the necessary order of the polis (and specifically Athens) as the only place where the contending energies of the divine achieved harmony. But Williams tends to resist the notion of irreconcilable conflicts between different regions of the sacred in Attic tragedy. He claims, for instance, that "*Medea* makes little sense in terms of clashing imperatives" (24), and *maybe* he is right. It was not necessary that every Attic tragedy exhibit an explicit conflict between precisely delineated realms of divine obligation. The religious logic of the drama was a broad picture of reality, not a set of didactic narrative rules. Nevertheless, in the case of *Medea* the story fairly clearly involves, if nothing else, contending divine *forces*. Medea is obviously a wronged woman, and the chorus mostly takes her side. But she is also definitely an agent of destructive numinous powers, of the sort whose presence the polis probably could not long abide even had Jason and Creon of Corinth not conspired to annul Jason's wedding oaths or Creon's sacred pledge of hospitality. She calls on the justice of Zeus, but to no avail. The chorus explicitly regards Apollo and the muses as being on the side of Jason, and of men in general, and blames Medea's misfortunes on the malice of some god. So she places herself under the protection of Artemis (avenger of betrayed women) and Hecate (goddess of sorcery); and then she is aided by Helios (her grandfather, as it happens). But, while her complaint may be just, her actions are not. She murders a young girl; she commits regicide, thus violating holy law; she perpetrates the ultimate abomination of murdering her own children. And yet, rather than suffer the condign wrath of Zeus, she undergoes a kind of apotheosis at the end, spirited away in the divine chariot of Helios (to Athens, of course), uttering prophecies in a state of divine enthusiasm. It is as though Euripides were saying that all of this too—sorcery, vengeance, implacable jealousy, strange Asiatic mysteries, even dragons from Colchis—belongs to the divine. This, in fact, is the message explicitly conveyed by the play's final choral lines. As ever, each of the gods brings blessing and curse, healing and contagion, love and violence; and all must be served and revered.

Even when Williams grants the presence of divisions between sacred spheres in the plots of certain tragedies, he is still loath to admit that these are anything more than apparent. He takes, for example, very much the Hegelian line in regard to *Antigone*: the central drama concerns the conflict between two characters equally inflexible in their commitment to and self-identification with one dangerously isolated aesthetic image of the divine; their unreasoning obstinacy thwarts every possibility of truthful thinking or openness to a more universal perspective; they have not yet learned to think past this primitive stage of self-knowledge, to recognize the real subjectivity of others, to find their own full recognition in a free spiritual community of lawful relations. Hence, for Williams, Creon and Antigone have falsely set the sacred in opposition to itself, by having mistaken their projected sacred identities as unconditional and so having failed to grasp that their ethical passions are not truly at odds; but this very tension points toward a more truthful reasoning that would transcend these static fictions (62–70). Now, needless to say, Hegel was perfectly free to use *Antigone* as an allegory of his own tale of personal emergence and legal recognition; but, as an actual interpretation of the play, it is merely the imposition of a modern, "ethical," unitary logic on a religious culture for which one of the deepest of divine truths was ungovernable plurality. And Williams's is also a deeply moral, and deeply monotheist, approach to Attic tragedy. This is fair enough. We who are or have been Christians are accustomed to thinking of our ultimate encounter with the divine in terms of an eschatological horizon, one that we cannot quite see from our present position, but one whose undoubted reality exposes and ironizes all our conflicts as in essence provisional, illusory, and sinful. And the Hegelian story translates this prospective habit of thought into a law of historical development. Williams is quite right, moreover, that the plays themselves frequently—usually in the voice of the chorus—call attention to the folly and wickedness that precipitate calamity, and raise earnest prayers to the heavens, and lament the sufferings borne by unoffending victims and culpable perpetrators alike; the dramas do in fact expose partial perspectives as partial; they really do contain deep interrogations of the meaning of lawfulness; and, yes, Creon and Antigone are both inflexible and sanctimonious. But that does not mean, as Williams believes, that the plays treat these contending perspectives as arising from mere mistakes of judgment. The dilemmas are not illusory. Often differences cannot be reconciled because their origin lies in the realm of the gods; the sacred truly is often opposed to the sacred, especially when the fierce, jealous, mysterious sanctity of the family comes up against the grandiose, garish, pompous, and finally invincible sacrality of the state. And those who die on stage as a result of these contradictions are the victims not so much of misunderstandings as of inevitably conflicting divine truths. At a certain point, only the death of the agent of contention can eliminate the impasse and allow peaceful mourning to replace perilous discord. Many of us may here see, and recoil from, the "Girardian mechanism" of the scapegoat, the bearer of contagion who must be excluded as ontologically guilty; we may protest the injustice and do so far more forcibly than the chorus ever could, and may lament the avoidable contingencies that destroy this or that particular protagonist, and may assume that a more universal and comprehensive order of divine truth is available either to the characters in the play or to the audience, if only they will set aside their hideously narrow commitments; but that is because we are—or have been—Christians.

After all, had the chorus's entreaties softened Creon's heart only a little sooner, and had Antigone been saved from death, and had mercy triumphed over judgment in ideal Christian fashion, the result would have been—from the perspective of the drama itself—altogether disastrous. Only two things could have happened: *either* Creon's failure to have upheld the law of the city would have provoked divine retribution against him and Thebes; *or* (perhaps worse) it would have provoked absolutely no response whatsoever, which would have revealed all at once that the law itself was no more than an arbitrary human convention, without any true basis in divine justice. Only Antigone's death spares the polis either of these two devastating eventualities. And there could be no other outcome. The sacred allegiances of family will always, when the conflict comes, fall before the dictates of the state; someday, after all, the state may require your children for waging war. Each side has a legitimate divine claim, but there is no question which must end in silence. For Hegel, the tragedy points *forward* from itself toward a higher truth. For the cultic logic of the Dionysia, however, it points *backward*, away from that sacred limit where the city's delicate harmonization of the divine's often countervailing forces breaks down, and back toward the city— ideally, perhaps, toward the house of the Eumenides. And the beauty of the drama, in all its rich ritual cadences, teaches us to accept this as the

place to which we belong. To his credit, Hegel preserved some of the innate sacrificial logic of Attic tragedy. He may not, like certain denizens
of the ancient Peloponnese, have believed in perennial conflicts within
the divine; but he still assumed that the spiritual dynamism of history
advances only by way of concrete negation, followed by speculative recu-
peration, and that therefore in a sense Antigone really did have to die,
even if it was all folly in the end, just as the Battle of Jena (or something
like it) had to be fought. The price of achieving civil society's lawfulness,
and of discerning the rationality of history, is still reckoned in blood.
And for him, in the end, the universality of the civil state remained supreme over the particularities of the local attachments of family or native
affinity. As always with Hegel, the concrete particular is indifferent in its
very particularity, its dispensable and scandalous specificity: the single
human life whose destruction is like the harvesting of a head of cabbage
or a coil of smoke rising into the sky from a sacrificial pyre. To that
degree, most certainly, Hegel was faithful to the sacred verities of the
Dionysia.

V

None of this constitutes some kind of condemnation of Attic tragedy, or
of tragedy as a whole. I mean it as praise. But I object to the imposition
of our cherished moral truths on a dramatic tradition that emerged from
an entirely different cosmic vision, as I do also to any demand that great
art justify itself by proving its moral profundity. I object as well to mis-
taking our recognition of the contingencies of the sufferings of tragic
protagonists for the intrinsic message of "the tragic" *tout court*. And, I
must confess, I object with special vehemence to the Hegelian reading
of Attic tragedy, if only on aesthetic principle: I dread the loss of a certain
ominous and shadowy beauty unique to those plays, and I deplore Hegel's presumptuous unwillingness to leave that beauty intact, and his
eagerness to dissolve it into what often looks like a boring bourgeois moralism and idolatry of the modern civil state. There is a dark majesty in
the vision of reality that the dream-images of the Dionysia figure forth,
and there is a kind of gorgeous grandeur in the power of the drama to
encompass so much that is irresoluble, chaotic, and pitiless in existence

with such consummate artistic grace and moral calm. But for Hegel, in a very real sense, Attic tragedy is meaningful only as the overcoming of the tragic. For him, everything truly numinous and terrible and splendid in the drama—everything irreconcilably contradictory and indomitable and wild in the divine, everything at once holy and baneful in the depths of reality, everything simultaneously life-giving and devastating—is really, ultimately, just a metaphysical, moral, and aesthetic error, an exaggeration of partial perspectives in need of correction. It will all prove to have been an inevitable misunderstanding at the last, one that in some sense had to be subjected to the probations and terrors of the tragic in order to be transcended; but the tragic itself, in its essence, is only propaedeutic to a higher spiritual science and belongs to a rational historical process that will finally cause all of its apparent tensions and contradictions to vanish in the ever clearer light of ethical reflection. At the level of the individuals whose stories pass before our eyes, the end may be death; but, at the level of the absolute, the end is the institution of ethical substance. The tragic is rescued from itself by a redemptive futurity, one that conjures away all those threatening shadows and tempestuous sorrows with the promise of final reconciliation of all conflicts in a perfectly rational order. How very dreary. Surely it would be more enlightening—and even more surely a sign of good taste—not to intrude on the Dionysian liturgy with our rationalist (or, for that matter, Christian) sanctimonies but instead to allow Attic tragedy to express its own metaphysical, religious, and aesthetic vision of things. It may be true that Attic tragic drama mesmerizes us and mystifies violence; I suspect it does. On the other hand, however, it may at the same time offer a truer picture of existence than we are generally prepared to abide, and the particular kind of resignation it encourages may in fact turn out to be the highest wisdom, strength, and piety. If it is an opiate, it may also be a medicine we require. It is as well to keep our options open, in any event, if only to test our own convictions. The oldest pagan tragic vision is, after all, a disturbingly plausible one, quite congruent with our usual experience of life in this world, and so—if we are willing to allow it to do so—it can provide an especially powerful challenge to our complacencies. Rather than attempt to subsume it into our rationalist (or, again, Christian) narratives—to dilute it with philosophy or corrupt it with theology—we would perhaps be more honest and reap greater profit if we were simply to allow it to bear witness to the understanding of being from which it naturally emerged. But, again, this is merely a matter of my own aesthetic preferences; all of it is open to debate.

What, however, I regard as unarguable is that the use of tragic categories to illuminate the story of the life, death, and resurrection of Christ is an error of judgment—not because tragedy is too grim or "pessimistic" an art but because it is not yet terrible enough to account for what the gospel brings into human reflection. To some extent, I happen to agree with Williams (and Terry Eagleton) that tragedy is a "hopeful" art. That is in part the problem. I do not wish what is most radical and subversive in the Christian story to be obscured by the misapplication of even the highest of wisdoms or noblest of arts, or even by the "wrong" kind of hope. And it seems to me that, in using tragedy as he does, Williams does not adequately emphasize where the deepest differences lie. Sometimes, of course, this is simply a matter of differing aesthetic judgment. There is a touch of genius in Williams's "tragic" reading of John's Gospel, but to my sensibility that text's often frighteningly dark tale of cosmic conquest sounds far too many chords that cannot be modulated into a genuinely tragic key; the stark confrontation between eternal heavenly light and unyielding cosmic darkness is not matter for tragedy. Then again, we may simply be destined to disagree here. Williams suggests that, in my own treatments of Attic tragedy (from many years ago), I seem "to be working with just the model of Greek tragedy that Hegel so consistently objected to—tragic drama as a story of the conflict between noble humans and cruel external necessity" (111). Well, that certainly is not so (especially if I am right in assuming that by "noble" Williams means the character, rather than merely the class, of the protagonists), though I may have expressed myself sufficiently ineptly to have given that impression. On the issue of "necessity," however, I grant this much: whereas Williams endorses Hegel's rejection of the central role of fate in Attic tragedy, I cannot imagine how one can read, say, the *Oresteia*, or the Oedipus plays, or the *Bacchae* (or even just the closing words of *Medea*) without granting that fate is one of the deepest themes of the form. Then again, this is clear only if one does not regard fate as some kind of mechanical predetermination wholly external to the free personal agency of mortals. Rather, fate—especially in the sense of *tychē*, which like "fortune" means at once both "destiny" and "chance," but also in the sense of *moira* or *heimarton,* an "apportioned" doom, or of *anankē,* "necessity"—is always depicted in the plays as being both consequence and cause, according to the direction from which one looks at it. It is, one might say, a kind of dark providence operating through independent secondary causes (such that even free human choices accomplish fixed destinies), as well as an unalterable law of cause and effect (such that even deeds done in ignorance can be a source of pollution). In *tychē* (as in Hegel's philosophy), there is an ultimate coincidence of contingency and necessity. And to deny that Attic tragedy was in part a way of reconciling human beings to the inevitability of the fated limits of life is to refuse to acknowledge part of the very essence of the art. It would border on perversity not to grant that tragedy necessarily consoles every bit as much as it disenchants (otherwise, no tragedy would ever have been performed). Tragic catharsis, after all, is hardly a novel critical doctrine. And yet that very consolation is precisely the one that the gospels withhold.

Such, at least, I suppose, is the burden of my hostility to "tragic theology." My original complaint, of which Williams in turn somewhat complains, was against the arguments of D. M. MacKinnon and Nicholas Lash that Attic tragedy in particular, and then also tragedy in all its more venerable forms, provides a way of viewing the gospel narratives that forbids "optimistic" misconstruals and glib trivializations of their contents, or a flight from the raw reality of the cross and tomb to a "metaphysical consolation" that might conjure away the testimony of Christ's eternally indelible wounds. And, again, my claim was that this is to get the matter backwards, because it is precisely the very real "metaphysical comfort" that tragedy offers that renders it, despite the magnificence of its most perfect realizations, impotent to illuminate the full range of the gospel's assault upon all our best attempts to make sense of suffering. (And here I find my objection to—in particular—MacKinnon's treatment of Attic tragedy to be practically the reverse of my objection to Hegel's: where Hegel refuses to leave the drama unmolested in the purity of its vision of irreconcilable divine forces, MacKinnon seems so to reduce the tragic to its power of bleak, brutal disenchantment as to ignore entirely its own intrinsic logic of "redemption" in the life of the polis. Again, it is a very literary approach to the texts, and one that takes no account of their festal setting.) Clearly, of course, as one moves away from the Attic exemplars toward the later dramas of Christian Europe, the more one finds that those elements of the plays conformable to the terms of Christian moral scrutiny—the contingency of human malevolence, the victims' blamelessness or (at least) extenuating circumstances, the unqualified injustice of many tragic fates—come to predominate, and render the stories more intelligible in Christian terms. Even then, of course, the tragic form still has the power to "beautify" the calamity and to make it an occasion of ambiguous comfort, in a way quite inapposite to the story of Christ. There is, for instance, a disturbing inexactitude in MacKinnon's repeated assertion that (as a tragic reading of the gospel supposedly helps us to see) Christ's resurrection does not negate, but rather vindicates, the Crucifixion. This is both uncontroversially true and dangerously false, and MacKinnon does not consistently differentiate between the two ways in which it might be taken. Yes, of course, Easter affirms the self-offering of Christ in his dauntless faithfulness to the Father, even unto death; but at the same time it absolutely negates and even reverses the sacrificial logic and unjust violence of Christ's supposedly *necessary* death (a necessity to which both Caiaphas and Pilate attest). Two quite different kinds of offering coincide on the cross, which might be—and often have been—confused with one another, but between which in fact the light of Easter absolutely and irrevocably discriminates. Here, then, a surfeit of tragic profundities can only obscure the new thing announced about God in Christ.

In a sense, taking the matter in long historical perspective, I find it hard not to feel that MacKinnon and Lash are wrestling with phantoms. I am not sure I do not occasionally suspect both of them of a very British fear of seeming overly impressed by good news, and of a consequent desire to temper the Mediterranean extravagance of the gospels with a salutary dose of chilly northern reserve, by cultivating a certain sardonic distance from their own deepest spiritual hopes; after all, British phlegm is often just a palliated case of the "sickness unto death." But, even if I am wrong to harbor such suspicions, it seems an odd notion that most Christians need to be disabused of a glibly "optimistic" picture of their faith, unless one thinks someone who dares to hope that two or three fortunate survivors might escape from a burning city could be called an optimist. What most Christians down the centuries have needed to be liberated from is the crushing weight of moral imbecility visited upon them by versions of the faith that convert the glorious good tidings of

God incarnate, and of humanity called to union with him, into a grim calculation of the limits of the divine will or power to save, or into a morbid tale of the merciless demands of divine wrath. Frankly, as far as I can see, Christian theology has suffered from too God-damned much of a certain kind of tragic wisdom—too much of a resigned sense of the losses that must be borne or the exchanges that must be made, too much sacrificial economy, too much healing without cure—and all with monstrous results: the notion that Christ's death is a necessary appeasement of the Father's wrath, as well as the outpouring of that wrath upon sin, apart from which the Father could not forgive; double predestination, or single predestination set off from an irresistible dereliction (if one prefers the more speciously reasoned version), for the sake of an edifying display of divine sovereignty or glory; visions of a final beatitude reserved for only the tiny number of the elect; theories of limited atonement; the idea of a universal inherited guilt that presumptively condemns every soul to eternal torment, actual personal innocence notwithstanding; the very idea of a literal state of eternal torment, in fact, imposed or countenanced by God (easily the single most degenerate and diseased idea ever invented by the religious imagination); and so on. As I have said, part of the genius of the tragic imagination is its power to make idiotic stories seem plausible.

In another sense, though, I understand some of MacKinnon's and Lash's anxiety. Obviously, the empty tomb ought not to be regarded as a simple happy ending that makes all the unpleasantness preceding it somehow unimportant or unreal. But, then again, within the ambit of a tragedy, what else would it be? The gospels may at times seem to invite a tragic reading. Certainly the accounts of the events leading to the cross have many of the ideal elements: a protagonist identified as the bearer of destruction for the city, brought before the tribunal of human and divine justice, with us perhaps cast in the role of the chorus; searching interrogations of moral ineptitudes and false ideals; absurd contingencies, bootless supplications for divine deliverance, darkness and terror; misunderstandings, hesitations, one possibility of averting the disaster disappearing after another; a dénouement—contingent, foreseeable, and yet also inevitable—in which, lamentably, the agent of contradiction is rejected and destroyed and then the peace of the city is restored (after a decent period of mourning). These things are regrettable, but sometimes a victim must be offered up to the divine, in exchange for the blessings of order. There is loss but also a higher compensation. A truly tragic theology would be the story of Golgotha as told by Pilate. And that is the story the world usually tells. And yet it turns out that the story God tells is just the reverse. All at once, and quite contrary to both dramatic and religious good order, Easter exposes the entire splendid drama of necessary sacrifice as a fantasy. Not only does the divine not accept the offering that the religious and political orders offer in exchange for a higher good; God overturns all the verdicts passed upon Jesus by the authorities of this world. Quite contrary to those defective forms of Christianity that see Christ's death as a price that must be paid to secure the Father's favor, the story of the gospels is of the Father accepting the faithful love of the Son but decisively rejecting and reversing his death at our hands. All at once, a certain economy of rational hope has been abandoned; a certain sacred social vision has been forsaken. And no sooner has mourning been inaugurated than it is rudely curtailed by the command to rejoice— even if it is an illicit rejoicing that will cut like a sword or burn the earth like fire or carry Christ's followers to ends to which they would not be led. This is not a comfortable situation. After all, life is full of tragic necessities that cannot be evaded, and it requires real equanimity to endure them. Williams is right that a tragic contemplation of our fragility can "protect us in some measure not against suffering and loss but against the terror that loss is necessarily the end of meaning or hope" (154). This, though, is the terror that the Christian story restores. By the gospel's logic, no exchange is possible; the entire prudential social, political, and religious calculus of inevitable loss and higher gain is exposed as a lie. And, if the loss is irrecoverable, meaning and hope are lies too. The only true answer to the scandal of this blood-soaked cosmos is the restoration of the very *One* who was destroyed. Balance is forsaken. Now the stakes are all or nothing. This is a mad and quite imprudent vision of divine truth, and in its austere, pitilessly literalist light the only horizon of hope is that of the humanly impossible; and the only peace for which the city can now properly long is not that which can be bought by a victim's blood, which is a plentifully available coin, but that which can be given solely by that *One* who has borne the consequences of human violence and falsehood all the way to the end and then miraculously returned, still able and willing to forgive (as is so brilliantly discussed in Rowan

Williams's early masterpiece *Resurrection*). And, of course, once this is understood, each one is *the one* whose loss cannot be borne.

VI

In a sense, tragedy is "profounder" than the gospel. As those clever Athenians who laughed at Paul on the Areopagus knew, the doctrine of resurrection is a poignant inanity—a foolishly fond, in fact *childish* refusal to look away from the poor perishable individual toward a higher and enduring universal truth. Adults understand that as a rule one cannot get back what one has lost; true adulthood is the death of the innocent, hopeless hope that one can. We must learn to temper our expectations, make our peace with death. The child, however, lacks that wisdom, that profundity. She simply wants back what has been taken away: the adored pet, the prized toy, the long lovely day . . . the earthly paradise . . . the loved one who has died. She has no desire for some other good of supposedly equivalent or higher value, some sane compensation, let alone any species of "hope despite . . ." She truly desires—and knows only—the concrete, the specific, the irreplaceably singular. And Christianity is childish in just that way. Perhaps that is why some of the most successful and remarkable literary expressions of the Christian sense of reality have been fairy tales. Tragedy's narratives are profound; they are able to reach down into the deepest depths of human despair precisely because they are willing to release their grip on what cannot be saved. By comparison, the gospel story suffers from an incorrigible superficiality; it refuses to take leave of the things that a truly tragic wisdom knows how to let go of. But, again, this can be a shattering superficiality.

Which brings me back to Cordelia. As I say, she alone represents to my mind an instance of loss in a tragic drama for which no compensation—emotional or speculative—seems possible. And, again, I think that this is because, on the verge of her death, something has been revealed that cannot quite be comprehended within the logic of the tragic. In that dreamlike, "eschatological" interlude when Lear and Cordelia are reunited—with all its talk of unmerited forgiveness, unqualified reconciliation, even resurrection, and the brief, unimaginable glimpse it affords of Cordelia as already "a soul in bliss"—all the portentously "truthful" shadows of the drama are momentarily dispelled, and we realize with an absolutely crystalline clarity that she, and *only* she, is redemption. Thus, when she is stolen away again, this time forever, it proves impossible to return to the tragic illusion that there is any hope at all beyond her, without her. Cordelia's death is so devastatingly, crushingly beyond our capacity for emotional resignation or speculative wisdom that no compensation, no consoling pathos of resignation, can rescue us from a final vision of perfect meaninglessness. When her death comes, moreover, it tells us that in fact this is what every death truly is. It is as if Shakespeare had broken the tragic open from within and gone beyond the horizon of the tragic itself. It is tempting to imagine that he himself recognized that something had happened here that could not be contained by tragic form alone, and that this is why he continually revisited the same tale of estrangement, death, and impossible reconciliation in the Romances or "problem plays," but in inverted form, so that the "resurrection" arrives as a dénouement even more terrible and overwhelming than tragic loss: somewhat bleakly and hesitantly in *A Winter's Tale*, wildly and fantastically in *Cymbeline*, fabulously and almost like a dream in *Pericles*. Who can say, though? What is certain is that in *Lear* he produced a tragedy that exceeds the capacity of tragedy, and that reaches out to that still further horizon of the impossible that Easter opened up, without lapsing into fatuous optimism, and without compromising the power or unity of his art. It is a feat of uncanny inspiration. But, then again, perhaps it is unsurprising that Shakespeare alone should have written a tragedy that transcends the merely tragic. He also wrote *A Midsummer Night's Dream*, after all.

2

Remarks Made to Jean-Luc Marion regarding *Revelation and Givenness*

I

It may be that the most crucial task incumbent upon theology today is that of finally overcoming the overcoming of metaphysics. For roughly five centuries now, theological reasoning has found itself assailed by the same tedious but persistent refrain: the ringing imperative that it strip itself of philosophical tradition's glitteringly gorgeous but cumbersome panoply of categories and concepts, so that it might again rush with youthful lightness of limb—chastened, humbled, naked, but finally free—into the embrace of the God who reveals himself only to the eyes of faith. Over the years, the intonations of the demand have gone through predictable cycles of alteration, continually oscillating between the extremes of mournful resignation and grandiose sanctimony while sounding every note along the way and modulating themselves ever anew in accord with each succeeding epoch's special intellectual prejudices; but the essential injunction never changes, however expressed—the Reformation era's disdain for "the God of the philosophers" and the obscurantisms of the "Schoolmen," Kantian or Kantianesque prohibition of all conjectures that exceed reason's transcendental limits, Heideggerean warnings against the oblivion of the ontological difference and the "double founding" of "onto-theology," popular Barthianism's turgid and vapid dialectics, the dour linguistic mysticism of American Protestants corrupted by Wittgenstein, postmodern cries of histrionic terror at the colonializing "violence" of all essentialisms (and so on). Granted, not entirely without cause: there are any number of metaphysical regimes inimical to whatever Christians believe God may have revealed in Christ, and naturally any of them can burden theology with defective models of divine transcendence. To take an obvious example, in the whole long tradition of Catholic theological reasoning there has been no school of thought more incoherent and hideous than the early modern manualist Thomism that enjoyed such preponderant authority from the time of Bañez and Alvarez right up to that of the dismal Garrigou-Lagrange; and all of that system's most egregious offenses against both faith and reason—*praemotio physica*, "irresistible permissive decrees," *duplex beatitudo, natura pura*, the possibility of a rational spirit finding its satisfaction in a purely natural end—were merely inevitable consequences of the corrupt metaphysical premises underpinning it: its inadvertently mechanistic understanding of the nature of all causality (divine and natural alike), its doctrinaire adherence to a principle of perfect proportionality between "natural" ends and "natural" capacities (which is utterly inapplicable to rational spirits created in the divine image and called to union with God), and so on. And, of course, it would be positively impious to deny that metaphysics is not sufficient for knowledge of God, and that the soul's truest vision of God can be found only in an intimate union that transcends every finite concept. Nor can anyone who is properly aware of this be insensible, for example, to the prim pomposity of Kant's *Die Religion innerhalb der Grenzen der bloßen Vernunft*. And so, yes indeed, any philosophy that presumes to decide in advance what *may* or *may not* be revealed by God is in all likelihood an artifact of human self-delusion. And I have myself, in fact, written in the past of the "tragic" nature of Western metaphysical tradition when unredeemed by its "Christian interruption." So, for appearance's sake at least, I know that one has to exercise a certain degree of delicacy here.

Even so, and all this having been said, I find myself unable to credit the notion that there is any proper *general* definition of "metaphysics" that names an entire dimension of discourse that somehow proleptically precludes or distorts the genuine apocalyptic novelty, the *semper novum*, of God's manifestation of himself to us. And I can imagine no more disastrous alternative to metaphysical reasoning than the attempt to confine revelation within the severe limitations of phenomenological reasoning—most especially a phenomenology of saturation and intuitional excess that would condemn theology forever to the false profundity of paradox, and the voice of theology to a monotonous register of perpetual surprise. Frankly, as far as strictly phenomenological investigations go, once the methodological *epochē* has discharged its essentially preliminary and prolegomenal role, any phenomenology that will not surrender itself to a metaphysical deduction and secure itself within a metaphysical structure must instead inevitably dissolve into interminable, ever more impressionistic rhapsodies of pure description, pure exuberant *ekphrasis*, which can do little more than beguile us with their enchanting vacuity: ever more precise and so ever more trivial, ever more exacting and so ever more vague, constantly dissipating in the inconclusiveness of a willful refusal to think. Every attempt at "pure phenomenology" is, at the close of day, an act of elective mystification, the systematic suppression of a certain metaphysical memory that is always threatening to rise up again out of the depths of forgetfulness. Phenomenology *as such* always invokes a prior metaphysical deduction, because it always already presumes a metaphysical premise: that there is a real correlation between the givenness of the phenomena and the intentionality of the perceiver that cannot be reduced to some kind of happy chance or bizarrely persistent occasionalism; there is an inseparable liaison between the objective and subjective poles within any experience, and hence an indissoluble nuptial intimacy between Being and mind that urges reason toward the thought of some more eminent source of unity, where the act of being and the act of knowing coincide as *one*. The very act of any finite intention is already contingent upon a more primordial intentionality of the mind toward a transcendental object of rational desire, Truth as such, and so we already attest to a metaphysical horizon in our intentional grasp of every discrete *noema*. There simply is no escape from the metaphysical. Even the rejection of a metaphysical deduction made from the evidence of phenomena entails a thoroughly metaphysical decision regarding the relation between Being and knowing; even the distinction between phenomenology and metaphysics is a metaphysical distinction, made on the basis of some presumed higher vantage from which it is possible to survey and demarcate the exact boundary between experience and speculation. And so, simply said, the phenomenological and metaphysical dimensions of theological discourse cannot constitute opposed approaches to revelation, since neither enjoys any perfect warrant for its exercise or discoveries apart from its complementary relation to the other; and this complementarity merely reflects the necessarily inverse relation that obtains between the *ordo cognoscendi* and the *ordo essendi*, which can never be alienated from one another in theological reflection (doctrinal or speculative) without producing gibberish. So, when Marion poses his plangent question—"Does God reveal himself in order to make himself known and take a place within our rationality? Or does he instead reveal himself in order to allow himself to be loved, and to love us?" (29)—the only answer I can think to give, or to regard as coherent, is "Yes."

II

Of course, I may be prone to see mere false dilemmas where Marion sees truly crucial oppositions simply because we are using the word *metaphysics* in starkly different ways. When Marion asks us to shape our understanding of revelation by choosing between *alētheia* (understood in a principally Heideggerean fashion) and *apokalypsis* (understood principally in terms of the "saturated phenomenon"), or between the priority of love and the priority of knowledge (as though intellect and will actually functioned as discrete faculties), or between the horizon of beings and the horizon of charity, or between theology *de Deo uno* and theology *de Deo trino*, or even between phenomenological and metaphysical responses to revelation—well, to be frank, I find myself merely looking about for what I take to be a host of inexplicably excluded middles. Rather than feeling the need to choose, I am predisposed to think that all we are talking about are various modalities by which God reveals himself in every dimension of our natural capacities and supernatural yearnings. Where Marion sees oppositions, I think I might see only different moments within the nuptial mystery of God's condescension to us and our elevation into him.

But I suppose I know what he means. At least, I assume that by *metaphysics* he means what Heidegger called "onto-theology," which grants to thought only the "God" of the "double founding"—the grounding of beings in Being and of Being in a supreme being—which reduces all of reality (including divine reality) to a closed totality of ontic causal forces from which the mystery of being has been fully exorcised. This is the "God" of the *causa sui*, that merely "supreme" principle before which "kann der Mensch weder aus Scheu ins Knie fallen, noch kann er . . . musizieren und tanzen." And, indeed, if by *metaphysics* one means only the philosophical systems of early modernity—Suarezian, Cartesian, Leibnizian-Wolffian—and their sequelae, then why quibble over terms? And yet, for Heidegger these philosophical enormities do not merely represent a general defection from classical models of thought but instead disclose a pervasive pathology discernible at least as far back as Plato's "apostasy of the gaze," the turning of the philosopher's eyes away from beings in their "presencing" and toward a realm of lifeless ideas that, in their very static impalpability, afford him rational control over the mystery of Being. And Heidegger's epochal story of this ontological "forgetfulness," and of its termination in the "age of the world picture" and the technological *"Ge-Stell,"* embraces the whole of Western intellectual history, including patristic and mediaeval Christian metaphysics. And this is a problem. Granting the power and occasional acuity of Heidegger's narrative, his treatment of ancient, late antique, and mediaeval philosophy is so defective and reductive, and so soaked in ignorance of classical Christian thought, that it seems not only idiosyncratic but positively perverse to allow this essentially fabulous narrative to dictate how we use the word *metaphysics* or how we understand the labor of reason in the light of God's revelation. Heidegger needed to tell a monolithic story about "metaphysics" (so that in this the moment of highest risk, or so the sibyl of the Schwarzwald tells us, when the nihilistic destiny of metaphysics has become explicit, there might also appear a possibility of healing, one that will allow the "thinker" to try to retrieve and reflect upon that story, and thereby to avoid the primordial error, and instead simply let the world *be* in its worlding, and learn to await another dawn, and . . .), but we do not. Whenever we pronounce the word *metaphysics* with Heideggerean inflections, we allow the shadow of the *causa sui* to fall backward over ages of thought that were largely innocent of its evil and that in fact possessed the best resources for resisting its advent.

We also risk falling prey to an intolerably dialectical picture of divine revelation. Marion is quite right, of course, that the existence of "revelation" as a special theological category is a modern development, arising from the ever more impermeable partitions erected between philosophy and theology—or between natural and supernatural knowledge—at the end of the Middle Ages; and he is right also that, as a consequence, revelation suffered a kind of "epistemological" reduction, as though revealed truth were merely another body of information that, precisely because it is revealed rather than deduced, "irrationally" supplements the knowledge that natural reasoning can discover on its own. Thus, too, faith comes to be seen as an entirely supernatural capacity graciously bestowed, rather than the fullest expression of the natural intentionality of intellect toward Truth, and so becomes by definition something also essentially irrational. In this sense, the concept of revelation in early Catholic thought (for instance) followed the pattern established by the debased, "two-tier" theology of Baroque Thomism, in which grace is by definition an extrinsic superimposition upon and superelevation of nature. This is surely not what, say, Paul meant by the γνῶσις of God revealed in Christ by the Spirit who "knows the depths of God." And it is this simultaneous continuity of kind and discontinuity of content between natural and supernatural knowledge that ultimately leads to the estrangement of philosophy (including natural philosophy) from theology, as though they constituted two competing systems of "information" (univocally understood). But surely, having seen this, we only exacerbate the problem if we then widen this chasm by insisting upon some ultimate heterogeneity between natural forms of thought and supernatural *apokalypsis,* or between "metaphysical" and "phenomenological" approaches to revelation. This is, after all, the folly of so much popular Barthian theology: in rejecting the metaphysics of the *analogia entis,* supposedly in order to safeguard the transcendence of God against the presumptuous claims of creatures, it accomplishes exactly the opposite, reducing God to an *aliud,* a "Wholly Other" who can actually be posed "over against" creation, and who must therefore logically be contained within some neutral medium of relation and alienation that encompasses both him and creation severally, as discrete "entities." The tendency of the greatest Christian thought of the last century—Maurice Blondel, Henri de Lubac, Erich Przywara, Sergei Bulgakov—was to reject the dialectical in favor of a genuine metaphysics of participation, which alone allows us to recognize nature as more originally creation, and human nature in particular as more originally the *imago Dei*, and divine revelation as a deepening and consummation of natural vision and intentionality. Created spirit is constitutively open to transcendence—is indeed, as de Lubac wrote in a letter to Blondel, *nothing but* the insatiable desire for God. For precisely this reason, our rational and even conceptual intentions do indeed in some sense "constitute" the phenomena of revelation. But they can do this, in their limited and corrigible way, because (as Blondel argues with special brilliance) all movements of natural intellect and will toward finite ends are sustained within a prior and inexorable orientation of the mind toward the infinite horizon of Being's fullness in God. In the terms of Maximus the Confessor, the gnomic will's wanderings are animated by and embraced within the natural will's inalienable longing for God. Revelation quickens this primitive movement of love, yes; but, apart from this active capacity—which necessarily includes natural intentions, concepts, anticipations, even a few indispensable metaphysical predispositions—there could be no revelation at all. But for this primordial relation of the natural will to the whole of Being—which, far from limiting or frustrating the apocalyptic freedom of revelation, is in fact its womb within nature, the *fiat mihi* where the Logos condescends to be made manifest—the appearance of the divine within creation (including that of the incarnate Logos) would be neither enlightenment nor redemption but merely either a magical transition or a monstrous amalgamation: either nature's destruction and replacement by something alien or an extrinsic and hence chimerical alliance of nature and supernature.

III

Now, I recognize that Marion has striven heroically to open a path to a renewed receptivity to revelation that never risks crystallizing—or rather, petrifying—into the sort of grotesque and monstrous metaphysical systems that characterized early modern thought; and I admit that, if the only alternative to his path were something on the order of the manualist Thomism whose moldering remains are grotesquely preserved in the writings of Garrigou-Lagrange, or of the Leibnizian-Wolffian system of predications and principles, then this sort of rapt, dilatory, perpetually astounded phenomenological encounter with the sheer, unanticipated event of revelation would certainly be the more attractive and more civilized option. But I question whether it is really a path that theologians or Christian philosophers should be eager to tread, as there truly are far better alternatives. At one point in one of his lovely readings of Paul, Marion speaks engagingly of "God's right to overstep the distinction between being and non-being" (68)—which presumably no one doubts—but then adds, "The difference between being and non-being is cancelled out because God excludes himself from Being, and thus from the very difference between Being and beings." Now, on a first reading I take this claim to be, not false, but merely meaningless; at second glance, however, I fear it may prove to be deeply perverse. Surely the better and more theologically coherent way of saying what I presume Marion means to say is that God *transcends* the difference between beings and nonbeing—that is, between existence and nonexistence—*precisely because of* the difference between Being and beings. Precisely because he is not himself an entity among other entities, comprised within the fold of beings in their finite existence, but is instead absolute Being as such—the infinite and supereminent plenitude and wellspring of all reality, the unconditioned "to-be" upon which all beings are dependent—he is eternally and infinitely *absolved* of all ontic distinctions, as well as of the ontological contingency manifested in the difference between finite existence and nonexistence. As Maximus says, infinite Being cannot be negated, nor can it have nonexistence as its contrary. God is not modally qualified by any relation to nonbeing, because he is himself the "is" both of "it is" and of "it is not." He is the creator *ex nihilo*, because for him the difference between beings and nonbeing is literally nothing at all.

Marion, however, confines all talk of "Being" within a remarkably narrow ambit of philosophical options. He does not, for instance, hesitate to speak of "the essentially *finite* horizon of Being and beings" (70). This, however, is surely completely backwards. At least, here the language of Thomas and others is more precise: every created essence is by nature finite, and yet for this reason the distance between its existence and nonbeing is qualitatively infinite. In itself, any finite thing is impossible; insofar as it exists, it has arrived (so to speak) from across an infinite distance that it never had the power to traverse from its "side." Marion's language, by contrast, clearly invokes Heidegger's insistence on

"the finitude of Being" and on an economy of the *Ereignis* in which possibility ultimately presides over actuality. But is it not the case that this
was little more than a symptom of Heidegger's ontological purblindness?
For, in the end, both the *Sein* and the *Seiendes* of Heidegger's thought
turn out to be only distinct aspects of a wholly ontic process of arising,
"whiling," and passing away, and so to differ from one another only as
finite possibility and finite actuality. Both actually lie on this side of the
"difference." The true difference between Being and beings, which alone
makes any finite economy of existence possible—the difference between
the transcendent actuality of divine being and the contingency of finite
becoming—is something Heidegger singularly failed to grasp (in large
part by blunderingly confusing it with the "onto-theology" of early modernity). Hence the ever more nebulous inconclusiveness of his attempts
to articulate an ontology without metaphysical premise. Heidegger's true
distinction as a philosopher was not to have recalled the ontological difference but to have forgotten it more completely than anyone else. It
seems a pity, then, cavalierly to dispense with the language of Being,
which Christian tradition addressed with such richness and exquisite
subtlety, out of deference to a philosopher who addressed it with such
unprecedented incompetence.

Perhaps, though, I am assuming too much. Perhaps Marion's eye is
turned only to the Aristotelian definition of metaphysics as the science
of ὂν ᾗ ὄν, *ens in quantum ens*. But, if so, this too raises many questions.
Certainly metaphysics in this sense is not yet properly aware of what, say,
later Christian thought understands by such terms as τὸ ὄντως ὄν or τὸ
εἶναι or *esse ipsum* or *actus essendi subsistens* (and so forth). The best way
of rendering the Aristotelian formula would not be "being qua being" but
rather something like "entity qua (the condition of) entity": that is, the
science of entities not as specific kinds of things but solely in the abstract,
as individuated substantial forms in action. Here, then, philosophy is still
preoccupied with the realm of beings, in relation to which the divine
realm is always of course ἐπέκεινα τῆς οὐσίας, *super substantiam* or *super
essentiam*. But, while a distinct concept of "Being itself" has not emerged
here, or arguably at any point in pre-Christian Western philosophy, it is
clearly adumbrated, as the answer to a question that metaphysics had to
ask but had not yet properly posed. And it was, arguably, the special
achievement of Christian thought both to elucidate that question and to

provide its answer, and to do so specifically in light of revelation. In part, this was because the notion of a *creatio ex nihilo* obliged it (unlike pagan philosophy) to think through the absolute difference between Being and nothingness and so more properly to conceive of God's transcendence of contingent existence and nonexistence. But it was also the result of that most mysterious aspect of Christian thought, Trinitarian doctrine.

In the three centuries before Nicaea, in the Eastern half of the empire especially, the philosophical grammars of most schools of religious thought—pagan, Jewish, and Christian alike—encompassed what we might call a "Logos metaphysics," inasmuch as nearly all systems concurred in thinking that the liaison between the divine and this world took the form of what one might call a "subordinationist" hierarchy. In Alexandria, most Christian factions conceived of the Trinity in terms of one God Most High, the Father, who in his inaccessible transcendence could express himself *ad extra* only in a derivative or secondary divine principle; they accepted the common premise that, to overcome the measureless disproportion between the immanent and the transcendent, there must be some intermediary reality or realities inhabiting the interval, the μεταξύτης, constituting at once a hypostatic continuum and a qualitative disjunction between the One or the Father there above and the realm of unlikeness here below. The second "moment" of the real—*Logos, Nous,* or what have you—was understood as a sort of economical embassy, sufficiently reduced in nature to enter into contact with the realm of discrete beings, yet capable of translating some of the power of the supreme principle into finite effects. For everyone in this tradition, of every religious adherence, this disproportion between the supreme principle of reality and every secondary principle of manifestation was absolute. This meant that any revelation of the divine could never be complete, or even really a revelation; it could be only the paradoxical manifestation of a transcendence that could never become *truly* manifest—perhaps even to itself, as it possessed no Logos immanent to itself. We see this in the metaphysical language of Plotinus, for instance, according to which the first metaphysical moment of intellectual reflection and knowledge "there above" is already of its nature a departure from unity. Nous contemplates the One but in so doing inevitably does so under the form of a duality that already belies the simple light of the One, and that acts as a kind of ontological prism refracting that light into endless multiplicity. As for the One itself, though it can be said to "know itself" not as an object but by a kind of knowing "beyond intellection"; in itself it has no "specular" other, it infinitely exceeds "reflection," and so anything we might think of as self-manifestation or self-contemplation. In this scheme, the difference between Being and beings, in a sense recognizable to later Western thought, simply remains as yet unaddressed. How, after all, could that which absolutely transcends intuition, conceptualization, and knowledge, even within itself, be said to exist at all? Being *is* manifestation, in this tradition, and to the degree that anything is wholly beyond thought, and hence is not "rational," it does not "exist" in the proper sense. So, with unwavering consistency, later Platonist tradition placed "being" second in the scale of emanation: as the purely unmanifest, unthinkable, transfinite unity that grants all things their identities, the One admits of no inner distinctions, no manifestation *to* itself, and so in some sense *is* not (though it is not simply *not*). And, on the whole, none of these late antique systems was so much ontological in its logic as "henological." None had any real concept of "Being" as truly distinct from beings; each had some notion of a "being principle," but only as a kind of "hypostasis" or intermediate entity, subsisting as part of the hierarchy of emanations, occupying a particular station within the larger structure and inventory of reality, a discrete principle situated among other discrete principles. In regard to all these late antique systems, without question, it is perfectly correct to speak of the metaphysical structure of reality as a "hierarchy within totality," secured at its apex by a principle so exalted that it was effectively also the negation of the whole of finite reality, while yet also paradoxically constituting only the highest part of a larger universal continuum. Still, even then, none of these systems can really be described as a form of "onto-theology"; while each of them "grounded" being in its highest principle, none reciprocally "grounded" that principle in "Being"; they always preserved a sense that the Most High is beyond all "ground." Still, nowhere did this tradition clearly descry any real "ontological difference" or "analogy of being," because on the whole it had failed to grasp the true *ontological* nature of divine transcendence. Hence, when "Being" did become conceivable as infinite source rather than as a discrete principle among others, far from being mistaken for the "ground" of a God who was no more than a supreme being among lesser beings, it was recognized as one of the proper names of God in his transcendence.

   The advent of Nicene theology, however, radically altered the conceptual world of late antiquity, especially as regarded the relation between God and world, and thus slowly forced Christian thinkers to conceive that relation in a properly "ontological" fashion. With the defeat of subordinationist theology, and the final definition of the coequality of the Trinitarian Persons, an entire metaphysical economy had implicitly been abandoned (even if it took some time for this to express itself explicitly in a new metaphysical language). Not only is the Logos of Nicaea *not* a lesser manifestation of a God who is simply beyond all manifestation; it is in fact the eternal reality of God's manifestation of his own essence to himself, and therefore the eternal act whereby God is. This perfectly proportionate convertibility of God with his own manifestation of himself to himself is God's own act of self-knowledge and self-love in the mystery of his transcendent life. Thus his being is an infinite intelligibility; even his hiddenness—his transcendence—is always already manifestation too. This movement of infinite disclosure is nothing less than his "essence" as God. And, if it is correct to understand "being" as in some sense convertible with manifestation or intelligibility, then the God who is also always Logos is also eternal Being: not *a* being, that is, but transcendent Being, beyond all finite existence. More to the point, once the earlier notion of a graduated hierarchy of hypostases mediating between the world and its absolute principle had been abandoned, and it had become possible to understand true transcendence not merely as dialectical supremacy, it became necessary to affirm that it is the transcendent God alone who makes creation to be, and directly: not, that is, through an economic reduction of his power in lesser principles, but by his immediate presence. He is at once *superior summo* and *interior intimo*. Rather than merely the supreme being set atop the summit of the hierarchy of beings, he is the one who is transcendently present in all beings, the infinite act within and beyond every finite act, the immediate source of the being of the whole who is at the same time infinitely beyond the reach of the whole, even in its highest principles. It is precisely here, in the discovery that God is not situated within any kind of ontic continuum with creation, as some other "thing" mediated to the creature by his simultaneous absolute absence *from* and dialectical involvement *in* the totality of beings, that Christian thought also discovers him to be the truly ontological cause of creation. The true difference of Being from beings becomes visible for the first time as nothing less than God's true transcendence of and intimacy to creation. But this *metaphysics* (that is the proper word) of *Being* (that too is the proper word) did not enter thought merely as a paradox that overturns *all* prior concepts; rather, it at once completed and corrected (and so preserved) earlier metaphysical conceptions by detaching the thought of Being from the mythology of a hierarchy of essences and so helped to complete God's revelation in Christ *as revelation*. And so the metaphysical and the apocalyptic are here inseparable—indeed, are as one. This metaphysics prepares us to receive what God reveals, and to respond to it, precisely because it forbids us to imagine that anything can limit or condition what appears within the horizon of Being; τὸ ὄντως ὄν, *esse ipsum*—what is this but the aptitude for everything? And it is because Being's infinite actuality, purged of all ontic determinations, constitutes the proper horizon of rational spirit's natural intentionality—so much so that the givenness of Being and the natural orientation of mind are teleologically one and the same event— that within the realm of finite experience it is possible for one to experience in any phenomenon a surfeit of meaning, an excess of intuition over concept, that does not dissolve into mere unintelligibility but that instead summons the soul to an ever higher and deeper knowing.

IV

There is in Marion's thought an obvious, if intentionally ambiguous, reciprocity between his phenomenology of "the Gift" and his understanding of phenomenological givenness as such; and I cannot begin to summarize the reflections and conversations that this has provoked. So I shall simply observe that, as far as I am concerned, Marion's language of the Gift is probably irreparably defective: not only phenomenologically incoherent but dangerously close to being morally distasteful. On his account, the Gift—any true gift, that is—must be not merely given but also in some sense abandoned, with so austere a disinterest that absolutely nothing remains of the gesture of donation but pure release. A true gift, supposedly, is one given without any hope or expectation of return, as that would fatally compromise its gratuity; the giving must actually efface the giver and, in fact, the recipient. It is pure surrender, a donation without term or reciprocity, an infinite passage from an entirely hidden origin toward an entirely hidden end. But, conceived thus, it is very hard indeed to distinguish the act of giving from the purest expression of nihilism. It is also a nonsensical picture. A gift is a gift when, and only when, it is given with a hope and an expectation of return. Not, of course, an immediate or equivalent return: as Pierre Bourdieu would note, a gift instantly returned and in identical form would be in effect merely the rejection of the initial giving; so the return must come with difference and delay. But return there must be; otherwise, there is no difference between the act of giving something to someone and the act of contemptuously disposing of something by flinging it away in the general direction of no one in particular. A gift given without a craving for recognition on the giver's part is little more than violence against the recipient, as it declares the recipient in his or her particularity to be a matter of indifference to the giver, someone whose regard and gratitude is not worth seeking. To give in this way is the most imperious and patrician of insults. Moreover, it is a gesture that, by requiring nothing of the recipient, declares the recipient to be a thing outside the realm of reciprocity and so beneath the status of a moral being. There could scarcely be a more infernal kind of largesse, or one more contaminated by demonic pride: the absolute refusal to submit to gratitude, to become dependent upon another's recognition and regard, to bear and acknowledge one's own indigence in requiring a response. The true form of the Gift is quite the reverse. One gives a gift only if one gives with a desire for that *commercium mirabile* by which a token of regard becomes an invitation to communion.

And so it is, also, in the case of the gift of revelation: it is God's kenotic gift to us precisely because it demands of us a response, a return of the gift, but one given with difference and delay—the light of revelation returned upward to its source in the form of a pious act of intellectual interpretation, the constant and probably interminable offering of moral and metaphysical speculation, guided by prayer. The labor of metaphysics is merely one of several vital dimensions of the reverent thanksgiving required of us when we are the beneficiaries of the gracious generosity of revelation. And, really, the more-than-Kantian rigorism in Marion's account of the Gift is of a piece with his hyperbolic abstention from ontology. The sort of phenomenological reduction he recommends, in its very metaphysical reticence, looks suspiciously like a late expression of a pathology common to modern thought, from Descartes to Heidegger: the priority of the subjective vantage, the unwillingness to defer to the "objectivity" of metaphysical deduction. For Descartes, of course, the authority of the phenomenal is so thoroughly indistinguishable from the intentionality of the reasoning self who attempts to reconstruct reality from the subjective position that, at the last, the "metaphysical god" of the *causa sui* is positively required as an adventitious support for the entirety of true knowledge, *logically* deduced but still always absent, beyond the furthest horizon of that meager phenomenal order that is immediately available to thought. Subsequent philosophers would expend ever greater energy in securing that distant boundary against the invasions of this god—Kant, for instance, by erecting the Great Wall of his antinomies and further reducing God to a postulate of practical reason, or Heidegger by contracting ontology into the insipid immanence of "Being's finitude." Marion, to his credit, is perfectly content to abandon all those forms of metaphysical prejudice that would prevent the event of God's self-manifestation from violating those boundaries; and yet, quite oddly, he is at the same time entirely *unwilling* to abandon modern philosophy's equally metaphysical prohibition upon reason's power to receive transcendent truths within the embrace of its *natural* intentionality toward the divine—reason's power, that is, to transcend the limits of the phenomenal. The result, as could scarcely be otherwise, is a kind of mysticism of the incoherent.

So, I have to say, I am not sure what to make of Marion's accounts of the "saturated phenomenon." At times, at least when speaking in qualitative and quantitative terms, he seems simply to be describing cognitive dissonance, which is (at least, potentially) no more than a corrigible failure of intentionality. At other times, he seems to be speaking of the excess of meaning over intuition in certain experiences, but in unwarrantably dialectical and static ways. And, when applied to the question of revelation (understood in a solely phenomenological fashion), the concept of phenomenal saturation seems to generate formulae more rhetorically stirring than conceptually solvent. Granted, I can go so far as to say that the phenomenon of *apokalypsis* ought not *simply* be reduced to an object already predetermined by prior concepts, "based on the gaze," but should *also* be allowed to "appear based on itself" (47)—even though I find the actual danger here vanishingly tiny—but I cannot imagine how I could agree to the notion that we are confronted here by an either-or. And I certainly cannot get from there to the concept of "the *paradox* that brings about counter-experience" or that "defines [phenomena] that do happen (like events) only by *contra*-dicting the conditions of my experience" (55), or that "extends experience . . . by allowing us to describe an experience that is non-objectifiable and thus all the *more* manifest in that it comes from phenomena that manifest themselves in themselves, because they give themselves from themselves" (57). Yes, of course, revelation surprises us, overturns our common expectations, exceeds our normal ability to articulate what we have seen with our eyes and felt with our hands, offers us ever more than we can comfortably comprehend, and so on. But this is very different from saying that it simply contradicts the conditions of experience—which would be to say that it is not an experience of anything at all. There is a clear difference between the apophatic and the incoherent. The word *paradox* quickly becomes largely worthless unless it is scrupulously confined to its most proper meaning: a *seeming* contradiction that is really no rational contradiction at all. But much of Marion's language comes perilously close to speaking of paradox as a thing in itself, an ultimate contrariety *never* dissoluble into a higher order of rational vision. Is revelation really revelation at all if our experience of it remains frozen in that initial moment of phenomenality, of surprised expectations? And how can any phenomenon give itself if there is no prior realm of rational intentionality where it shows itself? No phenomenon proceeds from itself alone, at least not if it really is a *phenomenon*. True, finite intention can be thwarted or overwhelmed at the level of the empirical self. But would it not be a kind of crude psychologism to imagine that this exhausts the intentional conditions of experience? Or that experience cannot extend itself further from its initial phenomenal moment in the form of a further logical deduction? And would it not be an even cruder obscurantism to claim that one can experience anything for which one does not possess *any* natural intentional capacity? At that aforementioned level of the empirical self, perhaps, given the psychological self's "gnomic" wanderings of attention, the limits of intentionality can be reached well before experience has been exhausted. At the level of the *natural* will, however, in its pure and transcendental state, there is only a primordial orientation toward—and openness to—the infinite, an orientation that is not constituted by, but that instead constitutes, the psychological self as a phenomenon; and within the full scope of this orientation any phenomenon can make its appearance, and any seeming contradiction can be resolved. This does not mean that that highest intelligibility can be reduced to calculative and quantitative cognition; final knowledge is unitive, not merely cognitive, and must ultimately go beyond the limits of concepts and formulae. Still, this means that even that first moment of surprise must be experienced as a vocation of the mind to waken in its love for Truth and to seek to follow the phenomenon—led by the inextinguishable love sustaining every movement of thought—back to its most original principles, and perhaps even to that original act of Being from which all things flow. And this corresponds to that one undoubted "saturation" that we can all experience in any phenomenon, in those rare moments when we become all at once aware of the uncanny inexplicability of all that is—when we experience, in addition to even the commonest object of attention, the mysterious fortuity of its existence, the infinitely irreducible interval of the surfeit of Being over beings. In that moment, we discover also an intentional range within ourselves capable of that interval, and so capable of going beyond the finite occasion of experience toward the inexhaustible source of its event, the whole horizon of Being. We awaken also, however briefly, to the first stirrings of metaphysical consciousness within ourselves, and to the knowledge of a deeper natural intentionality within us whose end is convertible with the whole of Being's infinite fullness, allowing us to discern the invisible difference of Being from all beings and to respond to it by, in part, our metaphysical conjectures. The event of any essence appears within the infinite horizon of Being's gratuity, the interval of an analogical act of synthetic thought, moving from the conditions of beings to the unconditionality of Being, *analogia entis ad esse ipsum*, and so also within a natural capacity within us that is always open to God. Here we find that the fullest reality of supernatural faith is only another name, granted from the inverse perspective, for the natural intentionality of the rational intellect toward Truth. And this returns me to where I began.

Some of Marion's most brilliant reflections on the "saturated phenomenon" are those on events that seem somehow to precede or exceed their causes. And I certainly do not want in any way to detract from the originality and precision of those reflections. But I do have to ask whether in some sense this precedence and this excess are not conditions of *every* phenomenon, *every* experience, in the actual moment of its event.

I do not say this merely because I believe in final causality, and therefore in real causes that would remain invisible to any inventory of a phenomenon's antecedent causes (though indeed I do believe this); I say it also because I believe that the priority of *every* event over its causes is the very nature of experience *as phenomenal*. It is all a matter of perspective. In temporal terms, all causes and their effects are simultaneous, just as ancient and mediaeval tradition asserts, even in the case of causes that "arrive" from past or future. And in the *ordo essendi*, obviously, all causes are logically prior to their effects. But in the *ordo cognoscendi* just the reverse is true: all causes are posterior discoveries, preceded by a sheer event that is a phenomenal experience *before* it is an intelligible truth; the event comes first for us, while its causes lie only at the end of the wakened intellect's journey toward a reality that the event has already made manifest but has not yet rendered wholly intelligible. For every truth that, *sub specie aeternitatis*, might be characterized as a *metaphysical* truth, is for the time-bound soul at first sheer *apocalypse*, utter novelty breaking in upon the patient capacity of the rational will. And this, of course, is simply the noetic expression of the basic structure of participated being: for us, whose very existence is always already a gift ceaselessly granted us from a source beyond ourselves, every moment of being's advent is a pure *novum*, calling us out of ourselves toward the *novissima* of the divine nature, which summons us to itself from nothingness and to our last end. Just so, even in the most ordinary experience, the fortuity of the phenomenon precedes its meaning; and in *extraordinary* experiences the normally entirely tacit surprise of the phenomenal is amplified into shock, alarm, delight, confusion, or what have you. In either case, however, nothing is known or even truly experienced so long as the mind remains fixed in that initial moment of the unexpected; and here the desire to eschew or go "beyond" metaphysics can amount to nothing more than the desire to be fixed forever in the most infantile condition of thought, that delightful or terrific state of guileless wonder before the wholly unexpected. But, of course, when childish innocence is artificially prolonged it becomes mere perversion. Thought *must* respond to the event of surprise as to an irresistible vocation to understand, because the irrepressible desire of the natural will seeks to ascend to the source of the phenomenon and reach that which in the *ordo cognoscendi* is most ultimate precisely because in the *ordo essendi* it is that which is most original. In that most extraordinary event of all, the disclosure of the divine within the created, this means an ascent of the mind to God, the infinite source of all; and this certainly must involve every power of the rational spirit, including its capacity for speculative deduction. It is this second movement—this response to the provocation of the unanticipated event of God's revelation and its power to surpass our existing concepts—that translates any φαινόμενον into γνῶσις. And it is in just this way, also, that phenomenology must ultimately be rescued from banality by metaphysics, and by the latter's ceaseless and pious labor truly to discover the correct inverse proportion between the orders of knowledge and of Being, thereby demonstrating that these two orders are, in the end, one and the same.

3

What Is Postmodern Theology?

Reflections for Tomáš Halík

I

I might, I suppose, confine myself—or, at the very least, de-vote the better part of my energy—to observations on all the ways in which it is profitable for theology today always to begin from what might be called a postmodern position. After all, my first reaction when asked for my thoughts on the concept of "postmodern theology" is rather like Gandhi's reaction on being asked about "Western civilization": it would be a good idea. For a truly *post*-modern theological grammar would be one no longer confined within, constrained by, or defined in terms of Western modernity's understanding of itself. Such a theology would be one already situated on the far side of the recovery of a more classical conception of God and of revelation from *both* the metaphysics of early modernity (say, God conceived as the *causa sui* of "onto-theology") *and* *also* the supposedly "postmetaphysical" dogmas of late modernity. I might also, I imagine, talk sympathetically about certain philosophers of the last half century who have much to contribute (at least, critically) to a theology so conceived. I might even pay tribute to a small handful of thinkers who could vaguely be identified as postmodern and who have provoked me to think more deeply about the task of theology: Badiou, Agamben, and so on. But I fear all of that would quickly devolve into insipid testimonial, of the most boring kind. So, instead, I have elected to spend the next half-hour complaining peevishly about the things that, it seems to me, the standard "postmodern theologies" of our time get wrong. And I shall begin by confessing my suspicion of suspicion, and my consequently somewhat jaundiced view of this entire topic.

The term *postmodern theology*, of course, can be as nebulous as the term, well, *postmodern*. So let us start from the premise that modernity, understood at least as a kind of ideological project rather than just a cultural history, is a particular discourse regarding the historical fatedness of a certain understanding of civil identity and personal freedom: the story, that is, of liberation as such, the ascent of the individual out of the shadows of hierarchy and subsidiary identity into the daylight of full recognition, dignity, and autonomy. This is the modern world's most powerful and attractive narrative about itself and its inmost principles, no matter how it is told: in Kantian or Hegelian or Romantic or Enlightenment terms—or even the tempered terms of a late democratic realism. Presumably, then, any postmodern theology worthy of the name will be one that, having fully absorbed this great narrative, nevertheless is willing to undertake at once both a critical appropriation and an appropriate critique of its plot: a theology, then, capable of assuming an ironic distance from any naive acceptance of that narrative in its own uninflected form and of situating it in a far larger critical and historical context, while not rejecting it out of dogmatic reflex. But then, if this definition be granted, much of what has come in recent years to be the "orthodox" form of postmodern theology signally fails to be truly *post*-modern at all.

At least, in the Anglophone world in recent years, among those generally designated as promoters of a postmodern theology—say, Richard Kearney or John Caputo—the title has come to imply a kind of recognizable composite of the more easily assimilated themes provided by an earlier generation of Continental thinkers: some Derridean poststructuralist bromides embraced within a broad Lyotardian claim to a suspicion of all "metanarratives" (except, naturally, the metanarrative of this postmetanarrative vantage on all metanarratives), somberly wrapped in a brooding atmosphere of mystically oblique, almost masochistically disinterested Levinasian ethical seriousness, framed within a Vattimo-esque salvific narrative of divine kenosis as the redemptive hermeneutical exhaustion of the transcendent in the immanent or (in more discursive terms) of every strong structure of being in the peacefulness of "weak thought," the whole concoction bedizened with touches of Foucaultian genealogy or Nancyan diagnoses of transcendental violence or Deleuzo-Guattarian talk of original rupture . . . or something like that. Generally the guiding pretense is of a theology that has shed the encumbrances of something called "metaphysics" and all its putative pathologies: inherently "violent" essentialisms, hostility or insensibility toward "alterity," and so forth; and what is supposed to emerge from this giddy confluence is a special piety—or, at any rate, ethos—that is tolerant of difference, peaceful and patient and unambitious and charitable.

I have to confess to something less than a tepid sympathy for this entire style of discourse. It may merely be fatigue on my part, but I have to say that to my mind the entire project of constructing a "postmetaphysical theology" is preposterous, rather on the order of producing "postatmospheric air," and that the notion that there is such a thing as the inherent "violence of metaphysics," rather than simply the relative violence or peacefulness of particular metaphysical regimes, is rather silly. More to the point, the claim to have escaped the metaphysical seems to me inevitably to reiterate (or maybe I should say "reinscribe") the most imperious of classic metaphysical gestures: that of the transcendental vantage that has, through some sublime moral and dialectical labor of spirit, achieved the privileged vantage of a transcendental surveillance of all stories other than one's own. To me, this is simply the repetition—albeit transcribed into a particular social and ideological key, and inflected with a particular sensibility—of the late modern story of an enlightened reason inhabiting no perspective at all and therefore entitled and able to dissolve all merely local narratives into provisional, mythical, tribal chatter.

II

In his preface to the *Philosophy of Right*, Hegel rather famously remarks that the owl of Minerva takes flight only as dusk is falling—which is to say that philosophy comes only at the end of an age, when it is far too late in the day to tell us how the world ought to be, and so can at most merely ponder what has already come to pass, and so begun to pass away. An epoch yields its guiding secrets to rational reflection only grudgingly, well

after its profoundest possibilities have already been exhausted in the actuality of history; "When philosophy paints its gray on gray, a form of life
has grown old, and cannot be rejuvenated . . . but only understood." It is
a winsomely tragic picture of philosophy, but not—as it pretends to be—a
humble one. It may seem to reduce philosophy to an essentially recon-
structive, rather than creative, labor, but in fact it is a picture that exquisitely captures philosophy's deep and perilous ambition to be recognized
not simply as an intellectual discipline but as wisdom itself; for true wisdom, as we know, belongs properly to the very old. It also suggests that
the greatest philosopher of all would be the one who could plausibly
claim to have come most belatedly of all, and so to have witnessed the
very last crepuscular gleam of the dying day and learned, as no one else
now can learn, how the story really ends. The highest aim of philosophy,
then, would be to achieve a kind of transcendental belatedness, an unsurpassable finality lying always further beyond all merely local or episodic philosophies. (Needless to say, Hegel entertained few doubts regarding just who that greatest philosopher might turn out to be.) And of
course Heidegger, with a very different, supposedly postmetaphysical and
therefore *truly* final finality, most vigorously took up the gauntlet Hegel
had implicitly thrown down—the challenge of devising a grand philosophical narrative that might enclose all other philosophical narratives
within its inescapable dialectical logic—by seeking to overcome the System, to escape the intricate capaciousness of its logic, and ultimately to
enclose it in a yet more ultimate and comprehensive story. And it is this
particular, very modern, and especially pompous form of metaphysical
ambition that I see in any philosophy that imagines it has achieved that
always more final station, there at the broad open mouth of the river of
historical dialectic, where all the currents of the metaphysical tradition
empty out into the infinite sea of difference.

Not that such a thing is really possible. To abandon any metaphysics
of a real analogical relation of dependency between the transcendent and
the immanent is, willy-nilly, simply to embrace a metaphysics of un-
mediable difference—or, as Deleuze so exquisitely phrases the matter, a
metaphysics of the univocity of being and the equivocity of beings. So, if
I might match the "alarmism" of postmetaphysical discourse with some
post-postmetaphysical alarmism of my own, it seems to me that this really is not a useful or particularly pacific approach to the pluralism and

"globalism" of our late modern condition. For one thing, it seems to me that to assert the absence of any transcendental structure of being, or at least one we can reason about, and so to assert by implication the consequent absence of any analogical grammar by which to negotiate the differences and likenesses—the particularities and universalities—that exist among beings, is to make the ultimate measure of difference, inevitably, strife. Or, at any rate, a transcendental condition of alienation, of each being from every other, which can be alleviated by, at most, whatever fluid and accidental alliances might prove convenient at any given moment. Quaintly, perhaps, I think it better to ask whether it is possible to articulate an ontology of transcendent—and therefore inexhaustible—peace that, by its transcendence, allows for the harmonization of innumerably many differences, endless analogical mediations and reconciliations and accords.

III

And this is why I think that this form of postmodern theology offers very little in the way of a model for dialogue with other faiths. A transcendental surveillance of all differences under a rule of absolutely indifferent difference can provide only very particular rules of engagement: dialogue can proceed only when all parties will consent in advance to a surrender of all claims to ultimate truth. These having thus been reduced to local or tribal artifacts of cultures now surpassed by both modern reason and postmodern suspicion, which are supposedly innocent of metaphysical ambitions, everyone can get along. This, I submit, is not very promising. Yes, traditions can talk to one another more fruitfully, honestly, and interestingly if they are willing to grant that approaches to truth are incalculable in their variety. But the representatives of those traditions are not really going to achieve much if they start from the assumption that truth as such has nothing to do with what they believe. In fact, to believe that truth as expressed in the finite possesses an incalculable number of aspects and inflections and forms is to believe also that there is such a thing as transcendent truth to begin with, which by its very absolution from the conditions of the finite allows for innumerable mediating forms of participation in its inexhaustible fullness. And it is to believe as well that the measure of that participation is one of analogical likeness in difference and difference in likeness, between distinct traditions whose *terminus ad quem* is one and the same transcendent horizon. To my mind, what we have come to think of as postmodern theology offers very little in the way of actual understanding across cultures; rather, it offers a way of reducing all cultures to a late modern Western narrative of the immanent rationality that starts from the assertion that there is no transcendent truth. There could scarcely be a greater impediment to intelligent and meaningful dialogue between religions.

Let me speak as someone who actually engages in interfaith dialogues at, I like to think, a fairly sophisticated level. All I can say is that I have found it wonderfully productive to engage in discussions with, say, practitioners of Vedanta and Bhakti in the unglamorously traditional form of comparative metaphysical and spiritual studies, repeatedly discovering remarkable conceptual and practical similarities and enlightening conceptual and practical differences, and proceeding all the while under the assumption that both those similarities and those differences indicate a horizon of transcendent truth that is approachable from the vantages of our several traditions but that, in its very transcendence, allows for a limitless variety of expressions: eternal truth, *sanatana dharma*. And, curiously enough, I have never encountered anyone among my Eastern interlocutors who (I believe) would really have felt I was honoring his or her tradition by claiming that it is every bit as irreducibly local and arbitrary and absolutely culturally contingent and historically exhausted as my own. Rarely have I met any serious religious thinker who would be content to grant that his or her tradition is best viewed as an exhibit in a museum. Nor do any of us have the right to expect as much. So it is worse than naive to imagine that we will have much success in talking to persons of other faiths if we insist on beginning from a set of critical commitments that are really simply the same old modern Western triumphalist narrative of history, merely transposed into a postmodern key. The always looming absurdity of the postmetaphysical vantage is that, under the pretense of a tender regard for difference, it in fact converts every particularity into just another instance of the same meaninglessness: a univocity of vanity and equivocity of vanities. This is not hospitality to the other; it is conquest, if of an especially dissembling kind.

IV

In the end, I have to say, my discontent with the "orthodox" form of post-modern theology is that, before all else, I find its professed fear of the "violence of metaphysics" to be both rhetorically hyperbolic and morally hysterical, while I take its complacency with regard to the postreligious rationalism of our age to be curiously oblivious to the extraordinary vi-olence that has always been part of the history and the logic of secular modernity: the oceans of blood spilled by the wars of the emergent nation-states, the nationalist and imperialist and colonialist adventures of early and late modernity, the racialist ideologies and totalitarian re-gimes incubated in the deep shadows cast by Enlightenment rationalism, the rise of early modern and industrial and late consumerist capitalism with all the evils—the rebirth of chattel slavery, the commodification of labor, the exploitation of impoverished labor markets, and so on—with which the whole history may justly be charged, the wars of terror we are willing to prosecute in the name of something called liberal democracy in order to protect the sacred space of that consumerist culture from any threat foreign or domestic, and so on. To my mind, no one has attempted with more generosity and geniality to create something that might genu-inely be thought of as a postmodern theology than has Gianni Vattimo, and I deeply admire the essential kindness that animates his lovely lyrical tale of the twilight of metaphysical ambition as a fulfillment of the Chris-tian proclamation of God's self-outpouring in Christ's historical hu-manity. And yet, even here, kindness can conceal a surprisingly sinister cultural imperialism. To follow Vattimo, one would almost have to imag-ine that secularism is of its very nature ontologically peaceful, and that it is only the persistence of metaphysical ambitions from earlier ages that sustains our prejudices, cruelties, aggressions, and ambitions. Vattimo's avowed intention for going on twenty years now has been to unite the history of the decline of every "strong thought of Being" to the history of the Christian proclamation of divine *kenosis*, and thus to show that the genealogy of philosophical nihilism belongs to the hermeneutical trans-mission of "salvation history." But the result is an understanding of sal-vation that seems to be quite incapable of any sort of prophetic critique of the course of Western history as a whole—which is to say, an under-standing of salvation that concerns not salvation from "this present evil world" of "principalities, powers, dominions, thrones," and so forth but what looks unsettlingly like resignation to its dialectical inevitability.

Let us recall that, traditionally speaking, the theology of Christ's *kenosis*—his relinquishment of the form of God for the form of a slave—is inseparable from an extraordinarily strong theology of the creature's *plerosis* in him. The language of abasement has always been wedded quite indissolubly to the language of exaltation; the language of messianic hiddenness to the language of transfiguration; the story of crucifixion to the story of resurrection. And any attempt to prize one pole of this language free of the other, or to convert their indissoluble simultaneity into a narrative of the supersession of the threateningly transcendent by the redemptively immanent, effectively erases the entire logic of the gospel as a story of salvation and turns it instead into a tragic fantasy about God's redemption from his divinity. I have to say, therefore, that as far as the prophetic or redemptive power of such a vision is concerned I suspect it has little of consequence to offer. To make any sense of the language of redemption, it has always proved necessary to speak meaningfully of God's transcendence. That is not to say, of course—and here I can be as postmodern as the next fellow at the bar—that we must speak in terms of the threatening vertical supremacy of the God of Being conceived as a hierarchy within totality, with the divine placed at the summit of its hierarchy, the founded and founding god of onto-theology, the speculative completion and surety of our world, which a *kenosis* would indeed exhaust; this is, after all, not really transcendence but merely the metaphysical ground of immanence. Neither, though, should we speak in terms of the vacuous negative transcendence of "God," conceived merely as the dialectically Wholly Other of something like the ethics of Levinas. Between the cataphatic and apophatic voices of transcendence there remains an open way of analogy: the discourse of a God who is most near in his otherness and most strange in his intimacy. In this open interval of the analogical, which never collapses into simple equivalence and so never reduces the action of God with us to the "fate" of God in us, God pours himself out in—without ever succumbing to—our history; and so there is, indeed, a history of *salvation*.

We obscure this *hermeneutical* truth when we choose to think of strength and weakness, or mercy and justice, or the form of the slave and the form of God, as merely the opposed terms of an antinomy; to speak only of weakness and say nothing of strength leaves us still within the logic of the immanent order of power—or the powers. After all, why does Vattimo imagine that a weakening of thought will always, even within the ambit of our Judaeo-Christian *Überlieferung*, simply weaken into charity? Does he imagine that charity is simply the ground into which all metaphysical ambitions must inevitably sink? In truth, the testimony of history tells us something quite different: that where philosophy grows weak and surrenders its transcendental longings the nihilisms of the will grow strong and become at times not only exuberant but boundlessly violent nihilisms. When philosophy evacuates its ivory towers and gorgeous palaces and enduring edifices of truth, cruelty and rapacity are often all too willing to take up tenancy in their vacant rooms. The decline of every strong structure of Being, as Vattimo (following Heidegger) is willing to grant, is a possibility of liberation within a condition of risk. But it is not clear to me that he or those who think like him have properly grasped how great that risk really is. What is it that the postmetaphysical order really invites us to become? Pure, punctiliar instances of acquisitive power and indeterminate appetite, gazing out upon a region of indifferent instances and occasions of the use of that power. History has delivered us, here at modernity's end, to the market, which has its own internal hierarchies and values, its own orders of the visible and the invisible. And within this new order so many things can be reduced to a new invisibility: that which we have been taught to see as formerly we could not—the "slave," the Third World laborer, the homeless person, the physically or mentally disabled, the destitute—can so easily be hidden again behind such visible and stable essences as the commodity of cheap labor, the economic burden of the unemployed, the irrelevance of those who lack the power of purchase. To equate the story of secularization with the history of salvation, or even to associate the two within a single hermeneutical transmission, all too easily allows one to forget the essentially apocalyptic element within the Christian proclamation, the summons to a Kingdom not of this world that, in its very transcendence, subjects every age of the world and every epoch of human ambition to judgment and (perhaps) healing. And so it is not mere metaphysical nostalgia to call always on that eschatological light—the particular history of God in Christ, seen from the vantage of Easter, a story of abasement and exaltation—continually to make the otherwise invisible irresistibly appear. One cannot do so, however, if one has surrendered a metaphysics of the difference between the transcendent and the immanent, the changeless and the mutable, the eternal and the fleeting.

V

Anyway, I am straying into the world of my own concerns, where it would be unkind to drag those who are present here today. Let me conclude simply by observing that it is of course quite a salubrious practice to attempt—again, critically and within a broader historical perspective—to free ourselves from the majestic mythology of the modern, to subject it to the judgment of the cross on all our triumphalist fantasies and ambitions, to allow ourselves the prophetic and ironic distance necessary both to appreciate what is truly liberating in the story of secular modernity, and even truly Christian, and also to deplore and deconstruct what is not. In this sense, all theology must now be "postmodern." My complaint, however, is that for the most part what we call postmodern theology is nothing but the fabulous mythology and ideology of modernity recapitulated. And so it probably makes better sense to set the entire category aside and to speak instead simply of something like a post-critical naïveté: an attempt, that is, to preserve the metaphysical frames of all our traditions but to do so from the vantage of those who have experienced and cannot forget the lessons of history. This means that we must certainly be willing (as the postmodern moralists among us insist) to approach our traditions anew with a sense of the plurality of human experience in a much larger world than our ancestors ever knew but to do so also with a serious attention to their metaphysical claims as indispensable and proper grammars of dialogue, reconciliation, and healing. And this means reclaiming those traditions from the vast ideological system of "mature" modernity and "liberating" secularity, as well as from the residual habits of thought that that ideology has bequeathed to what we hopefully but dubiously think of as *post*-modernity.

4

Martin and Gallaher
on Bulgakov

I

The time allotted is insufficient for any substantial treatment of a single fascinating book, let alone two, and insufficient even for just the material apposite to Sergei Bulgakov. I am ultimately going to say a bit more about Brandon Gallaher's volume than about Jennifer Newsome Martin's, and for the most melancholy of reasons: while I am more or less wholly persuaded by the latter's narrative, my disagreements with the former—as regards both its treatment of Bulgakov and the theological project it proposes—are fairly numerous. I believe Gallaher arraigns Bulgakov for several errors of which he is entirely innocent (almost miraculously so, in fact); and I am somewhat taken aback by Gallaher's unexpected reprise, if only obliquely, of certain of the more misguided responses to Bulgakov's Christology found in the "critiques" of Georges Florovsky and Vladimir Lossky (two honorable thinkers, who were nonetheless rather limited as philosophers and quite extravagantly out of their depths when attempting to come to terms with Bulgakov). So let me start by observing, before all else, that what impresses me most about Bulgakov, despite his undeserved reputation as an "unsystematic" systematician, is the astonishingly consistent rigor of his reasoning, and how comprehensively he anticipates and defeats objections to his positions. And, of our two authors here today, I believe that it is Martin who has taken greater care to recognize the shape of that reasoning and to grasp its logic.

II

Putatively a simple work of intellectual genealogy, delving down to a little explored subterranean tributary of that vast ocean that is Hans Urs von Balthasar's theological project, Jennifer Newsome Martin's *Hans Urs von Balthasar and the Critical Appropriation of Russian Religious Thought* is many other things beside: a reconstruction of the logic of some of the deepest themes in Balthasar's thought, an excellent introduction to the world of Russian "religious philosophy" in the nineteenth and twentieth centuries, an extended reflection on freedom and necessity in the relation of creation to God, an essay on Trinitarian metaphysics in modern systematic theology, and even something of a theological manifesto (though perhaps a sometimes inadvertent one—it can be so hard to tell with scholars of the sober and scrupulous sort). It is also a book that, as only rarely ever happens, makes substantial contributions to both Roman Catholic and Eastern Orthodox theological scholarship. Balthasar is such a titanic figure in modern Catholic thought not simply because he was so enormously prolific, or simply because he was so intimidatingly erudite, but mostly because he was inexhaustibly imaginative and daring as a thinker. And he lived at a particularly fortunate moment; he belonged to that first generation of theologians fully able to enjoy the intellectual liberty recovered for Catholic thinkers by the rise of the *ressourcement* movement and of what came to be called (at first opprobriously) *la nouvelle théologie*. And no theologian took more daring advantage of that freedom than did Balthasar. For him, the return to the patristic wellsprings of Christian thought was not a retreat to a body of static orthodoxies but a rediscovery of the speculative and spiritual vitality of the church's first great intellectual golden age. And, like the fathers, he believed that all the riches of human thought could be explored by, and claimed for, theology. His conceptual world was not only vast but wild as well; he was at once classical, Scholastic, Romantic, modern, and perhaps even a little postmodern. As such, he was better prepared than any other Catholic thinker of his time to appreciate and learn from the even more adventurous Russian "religious philosophers" and theologians of the late nineteenth and early twentieth centuries.

Martin's book addresses Balthasar's readings, criticisms, and appropriations of Vladimir Soloviev, Nikolai Berdyaev, and Sergei Bulgakov, and in doing so provides a surprisingly thorough treatment of many of the principal themes of the writings of each of these thinkers. She also makes it quite clear that, in a sense, Balthasar was resuming and qualifying the various attempts of the Russians to adopt what was best and to subdue what was worst in the brilliant, beguiling, and perilous thought of Schelling (in his middle and late periods), especially as regards questions of freedom and necessity within the life of the Trinity and in the relation between God and creation. In the process, she pursues her story through some of the deepest and most turbulent waters of modern Christian ontology and metaphysics, Trinitarian systematics and Christology, aesthetics and anthropology, without losing her way. Among the Russians in her story, Berdyaev comes off most poorly—and appropriately so—as repeating Schelling's most problematic, most incorrigibly mythological moments, without the compensating virtue of Schelling's immense speculative genius. For Balthasar, Berdyaev was more a spur than an inspiration. Soloviev, by contrast, with his far greater systematic and logical gifts, presented Balthasar with a model worthy of emulation, even if one also requiring some degree of diffidence. But, really, Balthasar's most consequential engagement with modern Russian theology lay in his encounter with Bulgakov. Martin's book lays out, probably for the first time, how deeply Bulgakov's work shaped or (at the very least) *provoked* Balthasar's thinking on such matters as the relation between freedom and determinacy in divine creation and, by extension, in human creativity, or the eternal basis of God's acts of creation and redemption in the Trinitarian *Ur-kenosis*, or the eternal hospitality of the divine nature to the drama of the *Triduum*, or the question of Christ's universality and the universal scope of salvation in relation to created freedom . . . Would, though, that Bulgakov's influence had been even deeper. This, at any rate, was my reaction to Martin's narrative. She does not say this, and she might well want to disagree, but it seemed obvious to me by the end that, for all his extraordinary learning and mercurial genius, Balthasar was still not Bulgakov's equal as a metaphysical or theological thinker. In a number of ways, Balthasar's thought on all these topics is more logically unfinished—even more impressionistic—than Bulgakov's and looks oddly deficient in comparison to the almost unnatural thoroughness of the latter's willingness to follow every argument and line of reflection to its uttermost end. But, again, that is only my view of the matter.

Perhaps the most exhilarating aspect of Martin's book is the vision of theology that it proposes. All the principal figures of whom it treats are controversial within their communions, precisely because they all refused to regard the history of Christian thought as a history of progressively discovered limits and newly erected barriers. For some—usually those who fancy themselves "traditionalists" because they imagine tradition to be something inert and finished, and as a rule usually finished just about a century ago—a doctrine is not a door that has been opened, inviting ever deeper explorations of the faith, but a door that has been closed and sealed against every trespass of the questioning mind. For them, tradition is not a living thing, animated by the Spirit, but a splendid and imposing ossuary, filled with brightly polished bones. Martin, by contrast, offers a picture of what she calls "Pneumatic theologizing," one in which every doctrinal determination widens, rather than contracts, the realm of pious speculation and reverent imagination.

As regards Bulgakov's thought in particular, moreover, Martin's book brings out especially well the many ways in which Bulgakov succeeded in describing a genuine and logically seamless consonance between the claims Christianity makes regarding, on the one hand, the immanent and infinitely sufficient divine life and, on the other, the contingency and gratuity of the economy of creation and salvation, all the while remaining completely cognizant of the metaphysical and theological difficulties this poses. I do not mean merely that Bulgakov understood that the *taxis* of the economic Trinity must be identical to the *taxis* of the immanent; I mean that he realized that any hint of arbitrariness in our understanding of the relation between God's transcendence and creation's contingency must have disastrous consequences for our understanding of both, because it will inevitably reduce our picture of God to one of some kind of finite agency whose actuality is surpassed by a larger realm of unrealized possibility, thus giving us, in place of the infinite God who is the source of all reality, a mere "ontic" god who depends upon a reality greater than himself. And such a god would not yet be God in any proper sense. If one follows Martin's excellent treatment of the rich metaphysical structure of Bulgakov's Sophiology, one sees how consistently Bulgakov conceived of creation as a free act falling entirely within the dynamism of the divine life, without (*pace* Gallaher) compromising divine freedom or creaturely autonomy. One sees this also in how beautifully he integrates the seeming divine rupture of the *Triduum* into his theology of the *Ur-kenosis* of the immanent Trinity: that infinite donation and surrender, that infinite receiving that is also the eternal constitution of the giver, that infinite outpouring in the other that is the eternal being of God. And one sees it yet again in the brilliance with which he unfolds the logic of divine humanization and human divinization in his treatment of the eternal Divine Humanity and in his magnificently subtle Christology. For me, Bulgakov, better than any other theologian of the last century, overcomes the danger of an extrinsic and arbitrary unity between God and creation, in a way that truly preserves the analogical interval separating them, and so avoids precipitating the story of creation and redemption into some form of Böhmean or Hegelian or Schellingian theogonic myth.

This is always a real peril, after all. The only way to avoid an incoherent reduction of our understanding of God to *a god*—a being who, in the language of Maximus the Confessor, possesses and is determined by a "gnomic" or deliberative will, and who is therefore some kind of *thing* that *happens*, and someone for whom creation constitutes a real relation and therefore a *pathos* that modifies his nature—is to insist, in good classical theistic fashion, that all of God's acts are *of* his nature in its eternal fullness. But in much modern systematic theology, following a logic dictated by the modern dominance of an essentially voluntaristic (and really quite incoherent) understanding of freedom, the tendency has been precisely the opposite: to begin from the assertion that creation and redemption are purely deliberative "choices" on God's part, manifesting his sovereignty or unmerited grace, and then to import this "gnomic" understanding of freedom back into the divine nature itself, to the point that God's life as Trinity comes to be understood as an eternal act of self-positing election. This is simply a nonsensical picture of God, at least if by "God" we mean the transcendent source and end of all Being; it would entail that God in himself as actuality is always still more originally *possibility*—that what he is in possibility exceeds what he is in actuality, and that therefore he "exists" as we do, as a *reduction* of potency to act. It becomes then not only possible but inevitable to imagine along with Schelling that logically prior to the Trinity lies the abyssal freedom of the divine *Urgrund*, which is necessarily a "freedom" consisting in *pure* spontaneity, undetermined by any rational relation to a final cause, but somehow positing an end for itself. But if God is most essentially will, without a final rationale, then his nature is "free" only in the sense of "absolutely arbitrary," rather like the collision of two objects randomly adrift in space. Thus God is nothing but a sheer, infinite, brute event. This is at once logically meaningless and theologically repugnant.

III

Once again, by virtue of all those dimensions of his thought I have already mentioned, as well as by virtue of the extreme clarity of his understanding of the *ontology* of divine transcendence and his grasp of the modal logic of the necessary and the contingent in relation to infinite being, Bulgakov never once falls into any of these traps. And here Gallaher and I are destined to disagree: I believe that he has inverted Bulgakov's reasoning and has himself failed to escape the very errors he attributes to Bulgakov. At least, Gallaher's own theological proposals, as laid out in his *Freedom and Necessity in Modern Trinitarian Theology*, often seem guilty of a defective (by which I mean, voluntarist) understanding of freedom, of an extremely problematic set of ontological assumptions, and of some conspicuous modal confusions.

For Gallaher, any affirmation of divine freedom in the economy of creation and redemption requires a dialectic of the equally valid assertions that it "could have been otherwise" and that it "could not have been otherwise" (38–39)—which is true in a general sense but entirely false in a number of specific senses; and, as Gallaher unfolds this simple principle, it eventuates in a theology that necessarily presumes a surfeit of possibility over actuality in God and so reduces God himself to a finite determination of Being rather than Being itself. Gallaher's way of negotiating his dialectic is to make God's "free dependence" on creatures— that is, the necessity of creation—consequent upon God's irrevocable *decision* to give himself to his creatures (38); for, once God thus gives himself, there can be no turning back (49); he has bound himself to the world in Christ. Ultimately, this involves the claim not only that God undergoes a voluntary "self-blinding," whereby he really waits upon the creature's response to his gift (242) and can really be "surprised" by salvation history (248) but also that even God's eternal self-determination in the Trinitarian life is, in some sense, open to being "otherwise" (246). I see such claims as logically very difficult to make sense of, despite Gallaher's many careful qualifications of such words as *election* and *decision*; nor do I consider his a proposal notably more appealing than the middle Schelling's theogonic mythology of a divine ground of abyssal freedom. And it seems to me also that Gallaher creates a great deal of difficulty for himself simply insofar as he is guilty of (in addition to his tacit voluntarism) a misapplication to God of a language of freedom and necessity that is logically appropriate (and then only with precise qualifications) to finite beings alone, for whom the fullness of reality is necessarily something lying beyond themselves, under the aspect of inexhaustible and indeterminate possibility.

Bulgakov seems to me the sounder theologian and metaphysician here. For one thing, he presumes a more classical and logically coherent model of freedom: as consisting essentially in the full realization of a nature in its own true end. True, for any finite rational being, inasmuch as its essence is not identical with its existence, any movement toward this realization is attended by the shadow of unrealized possibilities and entails deliberative liberty with regard to proximate ends. This, though, is a necessary condition not of freedom as such but only of finitude. Every decision of the finite will is a collapse of indeterminate possibility into determinate actuality; but the very realm of possibility exists only because there is an inexhaustible wellspring of transcendent actuality sustaining it. God, by contrast, simply *is* that actuality, in all its supereminent fullness—infinite Being, the source of every act of being. As such, he is infinitely free precisely because nothing can inhibit or limit the perfect realization of his nature, and so, as Maximus says, he possesses no gnomic will; for him, deliberative liberty—any "could have been otherwise," any decision among opposed possibilities—would be an impossible defect of his freedom. God does not require the indeterminacy of the possible in order to be free because he is not some particular determination of Being, some finite reduction of potency to act, but is instead that infinite actuality upon which ontic possibility depends. And in the calculus of the infinite—as Bulgakov so splendidly grasps—any tension between freedom and necessity simply disappears; there is no problem to be resolved because, in regard to the transcendent and infinite fullness of all Being, the distinction is meaningless. God is not a being choosing his nature from among a range of options; he simply is reality as such.

How precisely does Gallaher, then, understand the relation between God and Being? It often looks as if he sees it as something like a much larger version of our own creaturely relation to Being, which is of course one of contingency. One of the odder moments in his argument is his invocation of Heidegger's talk of the *Zwischen* or *Aus-trag*, the unifying difference of Being and beings, and his suggestion that such an idea be appropriated by theology as a model of the relation between God and world in Christ. This strikes me as surpassingly strange, inasmuch as, for Heidegger, the *Unterschied*—the differentiation—that allows for this *auseinander-zueinander-tragen* of Being and beings, and for their "joint" *Ereignis*, is entirely a function of "the finitude of Being." Really, as Lorenz Bruno Puntel and others have noted, for Heidegger both *Sein* and *Seiendes* are no more than the terms of an ontic economy, in which the indeterminacy of *Möglichkeit* is portioned out in the arising, "whiling," and disappearance of beings. In no sense is this an apt analogy for the relation between God and creation. Then again, neither should the relation between God and creation be understood as a reciprocally "real relation" between two discrete beings, each of which exists as a determinate reduction of possibility to act (which I also sometimes think is how Gallaher conceives it). Whatever the case, Bulgakov, with almost uncanny consistency, avoids all such mistakes.

IV

And so, finally, I simply have to demur from Gallaher's reading of Bulgakov, and most especially his criticisms. Where Gallaher claims that, for Bulgakov, God must create in order to be God (88), I would say that this gets Bulgakov's metaphysics completely backwards, and that for the latter—insofar as God is not a being defined by possibility and hence is infinitely free—creation inevitably follows from who he is. This in no way alters the truth that creation, in itself, "might not have been," so long as this claim is understood as a modal definition, a statement of ontological contingency, a recognition that creation receives its being from beyond itself and so has no intrinsic necessity. Where Gallaher claims, with some anxiety, that for Bulgakov creation and incarnation are prompted by God's "internal necessities" (89), I would again insist that such a worry makes no sense in regard to infinite Being (as Bulgakov clearly grasps). Where Gallaher asks how the divine Sophia can really encompass anything like an analogy of being between God and creation when, as in Bulgakov's thought, there is ultimately only divine Being (90–91), I would reply that this is in fact the very essence of any true *analogia entis*: that God alone has Being in himself, while creation receives its being wholly as imparted by God—divine being repeating itself differently, in the mode of the contingent. Does Gallaher mean to suggest that there is some realm of being that does not come from God? The interval of the ontological analogy lies within being itself, precisely because God is not *a* being, and because God and creation are not related to one another as two discrete instances of Being in the abstract. Where Gallaher accuses Bulgakov of having "fallen into the trap of Böhme, Schelling, Hegel, and Solov'ev" (93), my response is that this is a misreading of Bulgakov's very scrupulous ontology of the divine, and that in fact no significant modern theologian succeeded better at avoiding that trap. Where Gallaher argues that Bulgakov's metaphysics "undermines the giftedness" of creation (94), I would argue that the gratuity of a gift lies not in the possibility that it might not have been given but solely in the free intention of the giver; a wedding ring, for instance, is no less a gift because it is the *required* expression of the love that gives it, nor is my love for my child any less a free gift because I would of my nature be incapable of withholding it (in fact, that love makes me fully free by fulfilling my nature with its inevitability). By the same token, but on an immeasurably vaster scale, God's *infinite* intention of his own goodness in creatures is itself *infinite* gratuity. Where Gallaher complains that Bulgakov's thought is in danger of treating salvation history as the natural structure of creation (110), I would reply that this is among its chief glories, and the surest proof of its Christian orthodoxy. The purpose of creation *is* divinization. And in all those places where Gallaher complains that Bulgakov's thought obliges us to see creation as always already divine in its foundation, or that his theology of the Divine Humanity deprives the incarnation of God and the deification of humanity of their dramatic novelty (if that is the right term), I can only say that these are the very aspects of Bulgakov's thought that allow him to secure the rational cogency of the doctrines of creation, incarnation, and deification. Otherwise, it would all be a fabulous nonsense, full of magic transformations and monstrous hybrids. Nothing can become something wholly extrinsic to its nature; something can become only what it is, *sub specie aeternitatis*, even in becoming more than it *now* is; otherwise, its transformation would actually be only its annihilation and replacement by something else. The reason that the incarnation of the Son is the actual *redemption* rather than destruction of humanity is that all that makes us human is already wholly present in God, not only as the virtual eminence of all human "attributes," but as the very nature of the divine life of love; and, as Bulgakov grasped with peculiar genius, the reason that orthodox Christology makes sense—the reason that the Incarnate Logos is not a chimera composed of disparate natures but is instead at once wholly human and wholly divine, without conflict, separation, or diminishment—is that deification is the "natural" end of all we are, and therefore the eternal foundation of our nature. Thus, for Bulgakov, creation and salvation are one act: the way whereby the eternal divine Wisdom, "repeated" in the mode of the created, brings all things into being by drawing them to their divine source and end. For all of us, that whole story is the greatest of surprises—the awakening of everything from nothing, into the divine glory. For God, it is the perfect expression of who he is, in the absolute freedom of his infinite Being, which is infinite love. At describing this vision of things, and at fathoming its depths, and at following its logical intricacies to their necessary solutions, Bulgakov was the twentieth century's unsurpassed master.

5

Remarks to Bruce McCormack regarding the Relation between Trinitarian Theology and Christology

I

It is always a delight to enter into dialogue with Bruce Mc-Cormack, one of those rare North American teachers of systematic theology who is a distinguished practitioner of the art in his own right. He is certainly the most accomplished scholar of Barth in this country and is without question the pride of Princeton Theological Seminary, as his presentation today amply demonstrates. And I suspect that my role here today, apart from beginning our discussion with a few observations from the gallery, is to act as an advocate of the theology of Sergei Bulgakov, with whose thought Bruce's shares a great many themes and concerns. Actually, the points of convergence are quite extraordinary in number and subtlety. And, though the answers at which Bulgakov and McCormack respectively arrive are in many ways almost diametrically opposed to one another, in a sense they complement one another as well, as the two most internally consistent ways of resolving the dilemmas they address.

To begin with, however, I shall note, but not dwell upon, the presence of incidental phrases in this paper from which I naturally demur: there is, for one thing, the Reformed language of Jesus dying on the cross under the wrath and judgment of God, which I take to be a disastrous confusion of fragments of completely unrelated passages of scripture, as well as a rather blasphemous misrepresentation of the nature of God and of his action in Christ. Then there is the common but false claim that, in the New Testament and in scripture in general, the term *flesh* (σάρξ) refers to humanity as standing under the divine verdict and judgment; in fact, it absolutely never means that; it means quite simply *flesh*, in the sense of the perishable substance of our mortal bodies, and in Paul's thought simply means all the physical elements that belong to psychical rather than pneumatical bodies and that therefore cannot enter into the Kingdom of God. Then there is the general suggestion that the passion and death of Christ are somehow necessary moments in God's determination of himself in his eternal identity, to which I could not object more strenuously; the death of Christ on the cross is a contingent consequence of creation's fallenness, and its end is to fulfill a purpose that would have come to pass even in an unfallen world: the divinization of the creature through union with God. But all of these are probably obvious differences between us, which scarcely merit mentioning. So, I shall start in earnest from what I take to be an area of general agreement between McCormack and myself: the principle, that is, that the economy of creation and salvation is not something accidental or additional to the eternal *taxis* of the Trinity. Historically speaking—and one can confirm this from, say, Basil the Great's *De Spiritu Sancto* or Gregory Nazianzen's *Five Theological Orations*—the development of high Trinitarian doctrine and Christology traced a direct deductive course from the order of the economic Trinity to that of the immanent. Nor was this a mere supposition based on a suggestive analogy between the story of salvation and a set of metaphysical claims about the nature of God; it was, rather, the unfolding recognition of an essential identity. In fact, the whole of Trinitarian theology depends upon this principle, as we can have no knowledge of who God is in himself apart from the history of the Father joining us to himself in Christ through the power of the Spirit. That said, my understanding of what a coherent account of that identity necessarily entails would seem to differ from McCormack's quite radically. And among those differences none is more significant than that between McCormack's commitment to purging Trinitarian language of the principle of divine impassibility and my absolute conviction that only this principle makes Trinitarian language coherent. And I am not as reluctant as McCormack to rely on explicitly metaphysical considerations in forming my

judgments, for any number of reasons: I believe that God as Logos reveals himself to the rational intellect and will in all of creation, that the
gift of revelation must be received in modes appropriate to the creature
(including the capacity for metaphysical speculation), that in the creature's reception of revelation the *ordo cognoscendi* is the inverse of the *ordo
essendi* and therefore must start from the most natural movements of
human reason, and so on. So, confessedly, it is as much a philosophical
as a theological claim to say (as I want to do) that the terms *impassibility*
and *divine* are in fact logically convertible with one another. There can be
no other referent of the predicate *impassible* than the infinite God; there
can be no God who is not that one who is, as the fullness of all being, impassible. There is not out there, among the ensemble of beings, a single
discrete being who is God, who may or may not possess the attribute of
impassibility. Rather, like any number of other predicates—*infinity, eternity, simplicity, immutability*—the term *impassibility* is merely one of the
necessary entailments of the very concept of God as the transcendent
source of all reality. To me, therefore, the notion of divine passibility occupies the same logical space as the idea of a square circle or of a married
bachelor or of an intelligent and morally sane supporter of Donald
Trump. And far, indeed, from constituting some kind of paradox, the
statement that the God who became human in Christ is eternally impassible is a necessary affirmation of logic.

Of course, to make sense of that affirmation one must be absolutely
clear what the traditional language of impassibility means. It certainly
does not mean—as presumably we all know—that there is some capacity
or aptitude that God lacks, some kind of experience that is beyond his
ken; it is not a negative predicate, nor is it a statement about God's ability
to have knowledge of pain or pleasure or joy or sorrow. Of course God
knows all such things; he knows not only the suffering or joy of Christ
but my suffering and joy as well. He is omniscient. He knows our passions infinitely better than we know them ourselves. Nor is the truth that
God is impassible a claim regarding experience in any sense we might
normally imagine. It is simply a modal statement regarding how God
knows. In classical terms, the term *pathos* or *passio* is not necessarily allied to *experience* at all; it merely indicates the modification of one thing
by another and describes the relation between agent and patient forces
or substances within any instance of finite change. It certainly has little
or nothing to do with anything like the consciousness of phenomenal

qualia—such as the twinge of discomfort I may feel in my wrist when I hold it at an odd angle—inasmuch as consciousness as such was not even a topic of philosophical reflection in antiquity or the Middle Ages. A rock can be the subject of a *pathos*, because it is a finite and mutable reality and therefore possesses potentialities that can be actualized by adventitious agencies. It can be heated by the sun, for instance. And the heat of the sun in its turn, in being cooled by its absorption into that rock, undergoes a *pathos* of its own. The question is not what God knows (he knows everything) but the manner of that knowledge—whether, that is, he becomes acquainted with realities that are somehow beyond him and that therefore must communicate themselves to him by way of an extrinsic qualification of his "substance" that would actualize a hitherto unrealized potency. This would entail, after all, that God is a finite being among beings, in whom possibility exceeds actuality. It would also mean that he is not omniscient, for whatever he knows in the form of a passion he can know in only a limited way, because any knowledge gained from the subjective perspective of a patient substance can be known only under the aspect of the *pathos* it induces, as a subjective impression rather than a direct cognizance of the objective reality of the thing in itself. Impassibility is not a privation of the capacity for passions; rather, acquaintance through passion is a privation of the act of knowledge. But God has, as the Schoolmen would say, no real relations; he does not relate to things in the manner of one thing that can be qualified by other things but is the fullness of reality in whose perfection all finite things have their being. His is a *scientia matutina*, never a *scientia vespertina*. For him, the fullness of reality from whom everything receives both essence and existence, knowledge is entirely active. Even in becoming human, he did so through the creative act of assuming to himself—and thereby reducing himself to—a finite nature, and thus expressing the infinite treasures of his knowledge in the poverty of the experiences of flesh and blood. Nothing is thus added to the divine nature. The infinite does not admit of addition.

II

It is not my place, of course, to tell Bruce McCormack how to negotiate the theology of Barth on the relation between the economic Trinitarian

taxis and the immanent Trinitarian life, much less to tell him what ancient theological principles to honor or ignore. But, since he has recently
confessed to me his growing admiration for Sergei Bulgakov, and since
it seems to me that there are any number of tendencies in his thinking
that touch upon problems that Bulgakov addressed with such incomparable rigor, I like to think it would be a gracious gesture on my part to
recommend Bulgakov's manner of dealing with these matters as perhaps
more fruitful than the abandonment of a theological and rational principle that the vast majority of Christian thinkers down the centuries have
thought indispensable to a coherent theology. Not that I have time here
for an actual exposition of Bulgakov's "system" (if that is the right term).
I can only indicate those areas of his thought that seem to me most apposite to this discussion.

Before all else, I have to commend the sheer genius of Bulgakov's
attempt to unite, without the least logical caesura, what Christian tradition asserts regarding the immanent Trinity and what it says about the
pure gratuity of creation and salvation. I honestly believe that no other
theologian of the twentieth century addressed all the theological and
metaphysical difficulties posed by such a project with comparable clarity
or comprehensiveness. Certainly no other understood *better* the necessity
and difficulty of asserting simultaneously *both* that the *taxis* of the economic Trinity must be identical to that of the immanent *and also* that the
relation between the transcendent fullness of God's life and the gracious
contingency of creation and salvation cannot be an arbitrary one. On the
one hand, it cannot be the case that the identity of the immanent and
economic Trinity admits of no analogical interval, as then God's identity
would have to be something forged in the fires of created history, with all
the metaphysical and moral problems such a view entails. Conversely, if
the relation between them is imagined as merely an arbitrary determination of the divine will, which might just as well have expressed itself
otherwise in creation, then inevitably our picture of God must shrink to
one of some kind of finite agency making purely deliberative decisions,
which means an agent whose actuality is surpassed by a larger realm of
unrealized possibility; this then would give us, in place of the infinite
God who is the source of all reality, a contingent god who depends upon
a reality greater than himself. And it would be difficult to exaggerate how
consistently Bulgakov conceived of the free gratuity of creation as occurring entirely within the eternal dynamism of the divine life without

thereby losing a full appreciation both of God's freedom and of the creature's moral and ontological autonomy. Of course, much of this Bulgakov
accomplishes through the careful working out of his theology of a divine
Ur-kenosis, in which the eternal order of the divine Persons in the divine
life is seen as God's eternal self-outpouring in the other; this is at once
both the ontological foundation and also the wholly gracious gift of that
further outpouring that occurs in creation, the Incarnation, Christ's
death on the cross, and the perfection of creation by divinization. In that
infinite motion of donation and surrender that is the very life of God, that
infinite outpouring that is the constitution of the recipient of the gift, and
that infinite receiving that is also the eternal constitution of the giver,
every other motion of giving is wholly comprehended as the "free necessity" of the divine nature. And, of course, this picture is consummated
in—and absolutely requires—Bulgakov's treatment of the divine humanization and human divinization as eternally comprehended within
the eternal divine humanity, which is governed from first to last by his
subtle and exquisite Christology. Again, no other theologian of the last
century was as successful in overcoming the twin dangers of *either* an
extrinsic and arbitrary unity between God and creation *or* a dependency
of the divine nature on creation for its eternal determination; he was able
in his thought to preserve the analogical interval between God and creation without reducing that interval to a mere elective addition to the
divine identity and so avoided sacrificing the gratuity of creation and redemption to some form of theogonic myth, of the sort that was first perhaps ventured by Böhme, and that was ultimately perfected either by the
middle Schelling or by Hegel (depending on one's taste in such things).

It is hard to exaggerate, I think, how very important it is for a coherent Trinitarian theology to avoid this sort of mythic reduction of the
triune God to the personal history of *a god*; and it is equally hard to exaggerate how thoroughly this depends upon not allowing ourselves to think
of God as a discrete being who possesses (to employ, as I so often do, the
language of Maximus the Confessor) a "gnomic" or deliberative will, who
determines himself by the employment of that will, and who is therefore
some kind of *thing* that *happens*, and someone for whom creation constitutes a real relation and therefore a *pathos* that modifies his nature. This
means, however, that it is necessary to insist, in good classical theistic
fashion, that all of God's acts are *of* his nature in its eternal fullness. So

much of the systematic theology of the twentieth century, however, beholden as it was to an essentially modern voluntaristic understanding of rational freedom, took quite the opposite tack. Beginning from the assertion that creation and redemption were purely deliberative divine choices proceeding entirely from God's unpremised sovereignty and manifesting a grace that no created reality could ever merit, it then tended to import this gnomic understanding of God's freedom back into the very divine nature itself, ultimately arriving at the conclusion that even God's life as Trinity is a deliberative accomplishment of the sovereign will, an eternal act of self-positing election. This is a nonsensical picture of God, at least if we take the word *God* to mean the transcendent source and end of all things. Were this drama of divine self-determination true, it would entail again that God as actuality is always in himself still more originally possibility—which would be to say that what he is in possibility exceeds what he is in actuality, and that therefore he "exists" as we do, as a reduction of potency to act. At that point it is simply inevitable that the imagination will arrive where Schelling did and will conclude that logically prior to the Trinity lies the abyssal freedom of the divine *Urgrund*, and that this is necessarily a "freedom" consisting in *pure* spontaneity, undetermined by any rational relation to a final cause, but somehow positing an end for itself. But then, of course, if God is most essentially will, without a final rationale, his nature is "free" only in the most trivial sense, that of the "absolutely arbitrary," rather like a random natural event. God thus conceived is nothing but a sheer, infinite, brute event, which is a picture both rationally and theologically repellant. Quite apart from the necessary voluntarism of such a view, it constitutes a mistaken ascription to God of a language of freedom and necessity that logically applies (if at all) only to finite beings, for whom the fullness of reality is necessarily something lying outside their bounded substances and can be reached only under the aspect of inexhaustible and indeterminate possibility.

Bulgakov, however, never once fell into any of those traps, no matter how daringly close to their edges he was willing to roam. He was saved simply by the extreme clarity of his understanding of the ontology of divine transcendence, as well as by his obviously profound grasp of the modal logic of necessity and contingency in relation to infinite Being. In the end, he never abandoned the more classical and logically coherent model of freedom as consisting essentially in the full realization of a nature in its own true end. And he never forgot that, for *God*, this cannot depend upon choices among equally possible alternatives. Though it is the case for any finite rational nature, inasmuch as its essence is not identical with its existence, that any movement toward realization is attended by the shadow of unrealized possibilities and so must involve deliberative liberty with regard to proximate ends, this is only because the finite lacks the perfect freedom that God alone possesses. The deliberative will is a necessary condition not of freedom as such but only of finitude. Every decision of the finite will is a collapse of indeterminate possibility into determinate actuality; but the whole realm of possibility itself exists only as a contingent reality, proceeding from the inexhaustible wellspring of transcendent actuality. God, by contrast, simply *is* that actuality, in all its supereminent fullness; he is infinite Being as such, the source of every act of being. Hence, he is infinitely free precisely because nothing can inhibit or limit the perfect realization of his nature, and so, as Maximus says, he possesses no gnomic will; for him, deliberative liberty—any shadow of alternative possibilities, any collapse of opposed possibilities into one side or the other of the opposition—would be an impossible defect of his freedom. God does not require the indeterminacy of the possible in order to be free because he himself is not some particular determination of Being, some finite reduction of potency to act; he is instead that infinite actuality upon which ontic possibility depends. So it is that, in the logic of the infinite, any tension between freedom and necessity simply disappears; there is no problem to be resolved because, in regard to the transcendent and infinite fullness of all Being, the distinction is meaningless. God is not a being choosing his nature from among a range of options; he simply is reality as such. And Bulgakov never forgot this.

There is no clearer evidence of this than his theology of the divine humanity. It was here that he most perfectly realized the logical structure of the doctrines of creation and divine incarnation in relation to Trinitarian doctrine. In part, I want to say, this was because he was deeply aware of a principle upon which we should all be willing to agree (and a principle, in any event, that is quite irrefutable whether we wish to agree with it or not): to wit, nothing can become anything but what in some sense it already is, at least *in potentia*. Nothing can become something wholly extrinsic to its nature; something can become only what it is, as defined perhaps *sub specie aeternitatis*, but also as considered in itself as it *now* is. For, were it to become something wholly extrinsic to its own original nature, its transformation would actually be only its annihilation and replacement by something else. This is one of the many reasons why, for instance, the decadent manualist Thomist notion of the real possibility of a *natura pura*, and the concomitant claim that union with God is vouchsafed to the creature *wholly* as a gracious and extrinsic superaddition of a supernatural desire and supernatural object to a rational nature that could of itself rest content in a purely natural end, is such silly gibberish. The incarnation of the Son of God is the actual redemption rather than destruction of humanity precisely because all that makes us human is already wholly present in God—not only as the virtual eminence in the divine essence of all human "attributes" but as the very nature of the divine life of love—and because, conversely, all that will make us divine in Christ is already implicit in our nature's inmost essence. In all of us, and in all things, there sleeps the fallen god called by God to awaken and seek union with him as a natural end—to risk a formulation that will offend just about every Christian, but that merely expresses the inescapable conclusion of thinking the theology of divine incarnation and human glorification through to its logically inevitable terminus. As Bulgakov grasped with peculiar genius, the only reason that the doctrinal language of orthodox Christology makes any rational sense—the reason that we are not forced to think of the incarnate Logos as a kind of mythic demigod or horrid divine-human chimera composed of disparate natures but may instead see him as at once wholly human and wholly divine, without conflict, separation, or diminishment—is that deification is the "natural" end of all we are, and therefore the eternal foundation of our nature. No other understanding of Christian doctrine, I believe, is ultimately coherent; any other understanding, I would go so far as to say, must be no more than a fable about magical metamorphoses and splendid monstrosities and charming mirages. So it is that, for Bulgakov, creation and salvation are a single divine act: the way whereby the eternal divine Wisdom, "repeated" in the mode of the created, brings all things into being by drawing them to their divine source and end. For all of us, that whole story is the greatest of surprises. For us, at the far end of the *ordo essendi*, it is the awakening of everything out of pure nothingness, into the divine glory. For God, however, it is just the perfect expression of who he is in the absolute freedom of his infinite Being, which is infinite love.

III

Which brings me back to McCormack's proposal. He does not, happily, speak in terms of some sort of divine *Ur-entscheidung*, in which God somehow posits himself as Trinity as an act of will. Mind you, I have no idea whether he would be willing to use such language, even with what he would regard as the appropriate qualifications, but I certainly hope he would not. It is not merely the case that such language merely *seems* to make God sound like some eternal discrete, deliberating voluntarist agent whose individual will somehow enjoys a logical and executive priority over his nature. Rather, there is no consistent sense in which any attempt to account for God's eternal identity as Trinity in terms of a primordial "decision" can have any other logical result. It makes no difference if one asserts that this original decision has been taken from all eternity. The ontological structure of any "decision"—assuming we are using the word in at least an analogical continuity with our typical usage—is a specific relation between potency and act, the collapse of a realm of indeterminate possibility into a single specific trajectory of determinate actuality that thereby excludes all alternative possibilities. And, of necessity, the former is larger than (virtually more eminent, that is) and logically prior to (even if not temporally prior) the latter. The possible is always more original, while the actual is a posterior negation of every possibility that is not actualized in the moment of determination. And so, once again, in God potency would exceed act, and God would be only a contingent being. And this cannot be. The God who is is not one possible divine identity among others; he is the infinite actuality of all that ever is or could be, infinite reality as such, without unrealized potency in himself and prior to all potency in the realm of the contingent. But, whether he uses the language of decision or not, I cannot help but feel that McCormack invites into his theology many of the same distressing modal errors that bedevil the theogonic mythologies of German idealism or Böhmean mysticism when he speaks of the earthly life of Jesus as the *telos* of the eternal generation of the Son. Yes, indeed, the Trinitarian life of God must have an immanent *telos*, since God is not some kind of spontaneous natural event without rationale or form. And yes, too, the life of the incarnate Logos certainly must not be imagined as something merely incidental to who God is in his eternal nature. But to speak as McCormack does, it seems to me, leaves open only two avenues of interpretation. Either he means that the Son's generation is in some sense a kind of deliberative act of choice *for the purpose of* the economy of creation and salvation (in which case we merely have again the incoherent voluntarist picture of God, in whom potency is supreme over actuality) or he means that God's identity as Trinity is necessarily determined by way of history (in which case we have a picture of God as an ontologically contingent ontic process, in whom potency still precedes actuality). In either case, God is a mere being whose identity is forged out of a larger realm of possibility; and this larger realm must itself be dependent upon some more comprehensive actuality that is, therefore, higher than God. This cannot be made to hold together rationally. In the end, I think it remains necessary to say that the *telos* of the Son's eternal generation is the eternal Spirit of God, in whom all the fullness of the divine essence appears in the terminal mode of wholly accomplished love and knowledge. All of creation and all the history of salvation are necessarily eternally enfolded and unfolded within that order of divine relations, as the eternal expression in the realm of the contingent of that perfect and transcendent plenitude, whereby creation is truly united to God from the side of creation, but not as the temporal determination of the eternal divine life. I simply do not believe, for instance, that the brutal legal murder of an innocent man on a cross is a part of the eternal divine *identity*, or even simply that the sufferings of this life constitute a *necessary* dimension of God's eternity. Rather, the perfect faithfulness of the Son to the Father, even in circumstances that make it contingently inevitable that that faithfulness will lead to the cross, is the perfect expression of who God is in his eternal life of perfect love. Once again, it is simply a misunderstanding of the modal logic of divine transcendence to think that distinctions appropriate to finite beings—like that between necessity and freedom—can be applied intelligibly to the divine nature. The eternal divine humanity is neither a mere deliberative choice on the part of some mythical infinite psychological subject nor an unwilling accommodation with some force of necessity extrinsic to God's transcendent freedom. It is an eternal truth of the fullness of reality that God is. But only by preserving a strict conceptual demarcation between the notion of determination and that of expression—only by understanding that history can express but cannot determine God's eternity—can one preserve the rationality of the idea of divine transcendence. And this requires, without any possible alternative, the truth of divine impassibility.

6

The Devil's March

Creatio ex Nihilo, the Problem of Evil,
and a Few Dostoyevskian Meditations

I: Beginning and End

Within the bounds of our normal human experience of nature and history, no claim seems more evidently absurd than that creation is—in any but the most qualified, conditional, local, and inconstant sense—something good; and no piety seems more emptily saccharine than the one that exhorts us to regard our own existence as a blessing, or as grace, or as anything more than a sheer brute event (and a preponderantly rather horrid one at that). Yes, lilacs are lovely, puppies delightful, sexual intercourse (ideally) ecstatic, and every pleasure of the flesh and mind an invitation to the delirious dance of life. But all the things about the world that enchant us, viewed in proper proportion to the whole, are at best tiny flickers of light amid a limitless darkness. The calculus of our existence is quite pitilessly exact in the end. Children die of monstrous diseases, in torment; nature is steeped in the blood of the weak, but then also of the strong; the logic of history is a gay romp through an endless abattoir, a succession of meaningless epochs delineated only by wars, conquests, enslavements, spoliations, mass murders, and all the empires of the merciless. The few happy savages among us whose lives pass in an unbroken flow of idyllic contentment and end in a final peaceful sleep are so rare that their good fortune, posed against the majestic immensity of the rest of humanity's misery, looks like little more than one of fate's more morbid jests. Everything we love vanishes, and so do we; every attachment is merely the transient prelude to an enduring bereavement; every accidental happiness terminates in an essential sorrow. And, if the teachings of most religions are correct, even death offers most of us no respite from our misery, but only new dimensions and amplitudes and ages of suffering—ceaseless karmic cycles of transmigration, interminable torments in hell, and so on. The *conatus essendi* or *tanha* or whatever else it is that binds us to this world has plenty to feed upon, of course, as many good things are contained within the compass of the whole; but certainly the whole is nothing good. If, as Thomas and countless others say, nature instructs us that we owe God our utmost gratitude for the gift of being, then this is no obvious truth of reason but a truth more mysterious than almost any other—rather on the order of learning that one is one's own father or that the essence of love is a certain shade of blue. Purely natural knowledge instructs us principally not only that we owe God nothing at all but that really we should probably regard him with feelings situated somewhere along the continuum between resigned resentment and vehement hatred.

And yet Christians must, of course, believe in the goodness of all being, with a certitude that even the most sanguine Platonist could not match, because they are committed to the doctrine that all things are created from nothingness by a God of infinite power, wisdom, and benevolence. And so certain affirmations—metaphysical, moral, and narrative—prove inevitable for any coherent Christian reflection on the problem of evil, not only to answer the question of evil's origin, but also to defend the innocence of God against the evidences of finite experience. One of these affirmations is that evil possesses no proper substance or nature of its own, that it exists only as a *privatio boni*, that though it is real—exorbitantly and ubiquitously real—it is so only in the way that cancer is real: as a corruption and perversion of something that in its own proper nature is essentially good. Thus we may say that, in a purely metaphysical sense, God is implicated neither as substance nor as direct cause in the existence or effects of evil. Another equally indispensable claim is that evil possesses a history, one composed entirely of contingencies and comprising both a first and a last moment. Thus we may say that evil, in all its cosmic scope, is still only an episode, with no share in God's eternity. Another is that the proximate cause of sin lies in the mysterious difference between rational creatures' natural wills (which necessarily seek the one Good in which all things have their true beginning and end) and their deliberative wills (which, under the transcendental canopy of the Good, can nevertheless be diverted toward lesser goods and false ends). Thus we may say that evil is the creature of our choices, not of God's creative will. Yet another is that the moral apostasy of rational beings from the proper love of God is somehow the reason for the reign of death and suffering in the cosmos, that human beings—constituting what Maximus the Confessor called the priestly *methorios* (the boundary or frontier) between the physical and the spiritual realms—severed the bond between God's eternity and cosmic time when they fell. Thus we may say, as fantastic as it seems—and as fantastic as it truly is when reduced to fundamentalist literalism regarding the myth of Eden—that all suffering, sadness, and death, however deeply woven into the fabric of earthly existence, is the consequence of the depravities of rational creatures, not of God's intentions. Not that we can locate the time, the place, or the conditions of that event. That ours is a fallen world is not a truth demonstrable to those who do not believe; Christians can see it only within the story of Christ, in the light cast back from his saving action in history upon the whole of time. The fall of rational creation and the conquest of the cosmos by death is something that appears to us nowhere within the course of nature or history; it comes from before and beyond both. We cannot search it out within the closed totality of the damaged world because it belongs to another frame of time, another *kind* of time, one more real than the time of death—perhaps the divine or angelic *aeon* beyond the corruptible subsidereal world of *chronos*, or perhaps the Dreamtime or the supercelestial realm of the pure forms or the Origenist heaven of the primordial intelligences, or what have you.

In any event, this tale of a fallen cosmos (or something roughly like it) is the story that orthodox Christianity tells, and it can tell no other. From the outset, Christian doctrine denies that suffering, death, and evil in themselves have any ultimate value or spiritual meaning at all. They are cosmic contingencies, ontological shadows, intrinsically devoid of substance or purpose, however much God may, under the conditions of a fallen order, make them the occasions for accomplishing his good ends. It may seem a fabulous claim that we exist in the long grim aftermath of a primaeval catastrophe—that this is a broken and wounded world, that

cosmic time is a phantom of true time, that we live in an umbratile interval between creation in its fullness and the nothingness from which
it was called, and that the universe languishes in bondage to the "powers"
and "principalities" of this age, which never cease in their enmity toward
the Kingdom of God—but it is not a claim that Christians are free to surrender. There is a kind of "provisional" cosmic dualism within the New
Testament that simply cannot be evaded: not an ultimate dualism, of
course, between two equal principles, but certainly a conflict between, on
the one hand, a sphere of created autonomy that strives against God and,
on the other, the saving love of God in time. The explicit claim of Christian scripture is that God's will can be resisted by a real and (by his grace)
autonomous force of defiance, and that his purposes can be hidden from
us by the history of cosmic corruption, and that the final realization of
the good he intends in all things has the form—not simply as a dramatic
fiction, for our edification or his glory, or simply as a paedagogical device
on his part, but in truth—of a divine victory.

Very well, then. But once all of this has been established, curiously
enough, the question of the moral meaning of a created realm in which
evil is possible has not been answered but has in fact been made all the
more troublingly acute. For no picture of the autonomy of secondary
causes can *by itself* entirely exonerate an *omnipotent* and *omniscient* primary cause of the things that those secondary causes accomplish. Thus
the doctrine of creation still necessarily entails an assertion regarding
the eternal identity of God. Of course, chiefly it is an affirmation of God's
absolute dispositive liberty in all his acts: the absence of any external
restraint upon or necessity behind every decision of his will. And, while
one must avoid the pathetic anthropomorphism of imagining God's decision to create as an arbitrary choice made after deliberation among options, one must still affirm that it is *free*, that creation can add nothing to
God, that God's being is not dependent on the world's, and that the only
necessity in the divine act of creation is the impossibility of any hin-
drance upon God's expression of his goodness. Yet, paradoxically perhaps, this means that the moral destiny of creation and the moral nature
of God are absolutely inseparable. For, as the transcendent Good beyond
all beings, he is also the transcendental end of any action on the part of
any rational nature; and then, obviously, the end toward which God acts
must be his own goodness: he who is the beginning and end of all things.

And this eternal teleology, viewed from the vantage of history, is a cosmic eschatology. As an eternal act, creation's term is the divine nature; within the orientation of time, its term is a "final judgment." And so, no matter how great the autonomy one grants the realm of secondary causes, two things are certain. First, as God's act of creation is free, constrained by neither necessity nor ignorance, all contingent ends are intentionally enfolded within his decision. And, second, precisely because God in himself is absolute, "absolved" of every pathos of the contingent, his moral "venture" in creating is infinite. For all causes are logically reducible to their first cause. This is no more than a logical truism, and it does not matter whether one construes the relation between primary and secondary causality as one of total determinism or utter indeterminacy, for in either case all "consequents" are—either as actualities or merely as possibilities—contingent upon their primordial "antecedent," apart from which they could not exist. Moreover, the rationale—the definition—of a first cause is the final cause that prompts it; and, if that first cause is an infinitely free act emerging from an infinite wisdom, all those consequents are intentionally entailed—again, either as actualities or merely as possibilities—within that first act; and so the final end to which that act tends is its *whole* moral truth. The ontological definition of evil as a *privatio boni* is not merely a logically necessary metaphysical axiom about the transcendental structure of being but also an assertion that when we say "God is good" we are speaking of him not only relative to his creation, but (however apophatically) as he is in himself; for in every sense being *is* act, and God—in his simplicity and infinite freedom—*is* what he does. And for just this reason the final "solution" to the mystery of evil in a world created by a good, loving, and omnipotent God must be sought in eschatology; for everything depends not only on whether God will be victorious—we cannot doubt that he shall be—but also on what the nature and terms of that victory are.

Regarding this, however, actual history can tell us nothing. History, after all, being a mere succession of contingencies, cannot be redeemed by any *merely* historical event, as no event can ever constitute anything more than one relative and episodic good among all other events. Even the incarnation of the divine Son and the death and resurrection of Christ appear as saving truths only in the light of their ultimate meaning, as the invasion of history by the Kingdom that lies beyond history. But neither

can the totality of historical events be vindicated by some sort of higher
logic of the whole, which "redeems" the transitory evils of life by figuring
them into some ultimate sum that merely balances the accounts, absorbing evil within itself as a necessary part of the equation. Between the ontology of *creatio ex nihilo* and that of emanation, after all, there really is
no metaphysical difference—unless by the latter we mean a kind of gross
material efflux of the divine substance into lesser substances (but of
course no one, except perhaps John Milton, ever believed in such a thing).
In either case, all that exists comes from one divine source and subsists
by the grace of impartation and the labor of participation: an economy of
donation and dependency, supereminence and individuation, actuality
and potentiality. God goes forth in all beings and in all beings returns to
himself—as, moreover, an expression not of God's dialectical struggle
with some recalcitrant exteriority but of an inexhaustible power wholly
possessed by the divine in peaceful liberty. All the doctrine of creation
adds is an assurance that in this divine outpouring there is no element
of the "irrational": something purely spontaneous, or organic, or even
mechanical, beyond the power of God's rational freedom. But then it also
means that within the story of creation, viewed from its final cause, there
can be no residue of the pardonably tragic, no irrecuperable or irreconcilable remainder left at the end of the tale; for, if there were, this too
God would have done, as a price freely assumed in creating. This is
simply the logic of the truly absolute. Hegel, for instance, saw the great
slaughter-bench of history as a tragic inevitability of the Idea's odyssey
toward *Geist* through the far countries of finite negation; for him, the
merely particular—say, the isolated man whose death is, from the vantage of the all, no more consequential than the harvesting of a head of
cabbage—is simply the smoke that rises from the sacrifice. But the story
we tell, of creation as God's sovereign act of love, leaves no room for an
ultimate distinction between the universal truth of reason and the moral
meaning of the particular—nor, indeed, for a distinction between the
moral meaning of the particular and the moral nature of God. Precisely
because God does not determine himself in creation—precisely because
there is no dialectical necessity binding him to time or chaos, no need to
forge his identity in the fires of history—in creating he reveals himself
truly. Thus every evil that time comprises, natural or moral (a worthless
distinction in this context, really, since human nature is a natural phe-

nomenon) is an arraignment of God's goodness: every death of a child, every chance calamity, every act of malice; everything diseased, thwarted, pitiless, purposeless, or cruel; and, until the end of all things, no answer has been given. Precisely because creation is not a theogony, all of it is theophany. It would be impious, I suppose, to suggest that, in his final divine judgment of creatures, God will judge himself; but one *must* hold that by that judgment God truly will *disclose* himself (which, of course, is to say the same thing).

I learned this very early in my theological wanderings, I believe, from Gregory of Nyssa. At least, it was from him that I learned how very important it is for anyone who truly wishes to understand the Christian doctrine of creation not to mistake it for a merely cosmological or metaphysical claim but rather to recognize it as also an eschatological claim about the world's relation to God, and hence a moral claim about the nature of God in himself. In the end of all created things lies their beginning, and only from the perspective of the end can one know what all things are, why they have been made, and who the God is who has called them forth from nothingness. And in Gregory's thought, with an integrity found only also in Origen and Maximus, protology and eschatology are a single science, a single revelation disclosed in the God-man. There is no profounder meditation on the meaning of creation than Gregory's eschatological treatise *On the Soul and Resurrection*, and no more brilliantly realized eschatological vision than his *On the Making of Humanity*. For him, clearly, one can say that the cosmos has been truly created only when it reaches its consummation in "the union of all things with the first good," and that humanity has truly been created only when all human beings, united in the living body of Christ, become at last that "Godlike thing" that is "humankind according to the image." It is an unambiguously universalist vision of the story of creation and redemption, and one that I am certainly content to accept in its entirety without hesitation or qualification. In a sense, I think it the only plausible Christian vision of the whole. But I also know that, before I can embrace it with quite as unclouded a conscience as I should like, there is at least one obstacle that I have to clear away, or surmount, or circumvent. And it is an imposing obstacle. And no Christian thinker ever saw it with greater clarity than did Dostoyevsky, or described it more powerfully than he did, in the voice of Ivan Karamazov.

II: Vanya's Devils and Vanya's Devil

The first point probably worth making about *The Brothers Karamazov* is that nowhere in the novel does Dostoyevsky provide a full and convincing riposte to Ivan's arguments. Christian readers who want to believe that the book in the end provides the answers to the theological questions it raises almost inevitably fasten upon the figure of the Staretz Zosima and upon his mystical discourses; but they are wrong to do so, or at least wrong to imagine that Zosima offers anything more than a necessary but still altogether limited qualification merely of the way in which the question has been posed. He provides nothing remotely like a solution. Nor is there reason to think that Dostoyevsky intended Zosima's teachings as a sufficient counter to Ivan's arguments. Really, trying to identify anything like a final and comprehensive theological proposal amid the ceaseless flowing and halting, advances and retreats, of what Bakhtin called Dostoyevsky's "polyphonic poetics" is fruitless in the end. Rather, the principal contribution the novel makes to moral reflection on creation and evil lies in all the avenues of facile theodicy that it entirely cuts off—all the false, preposterous, ill-formed answers it precludes. Some of these, of course, the novel does not directly address at all. The "antinomian" answer provided by high Reformed tradition, for instance—which elevates a thoroughly modern and voluntaristic concept of divine "sovereignty" over any rationally consistent understanding of divine goodness and so dispels the quandary by effectively inventing a God beyond good and evil—appears nowhere in the book's pages. But this is a positive strength of the text: even if the Reformed position were not so curious a theological aberration, or were not so logically incoherent in itself (the way any voluntarist theology is), or were not dependent upon so huge a catalogue of exegetical ineptitudes, or were not so obviously morally repellant, it would still never have occurred to an Orthodox Christian like Dostoyevsky as a plausible variant of Christian faith. Rather, in the novel he starts from a genuinely Christian understanding of God as infinite love, willing only the salvation of all his creatures, and then forces himself (and his readers) to ask whether, even from that vantage, the claim that God is good can ever be reconciled with the terms apparently included in the decision to create the world we know. In fact, much of the singular power of the argument made by Vanya (Ivan) to Alyosha in the chapter entitled "Rebellion" lies in its rejection not merely of the worst and most morally repugnant versions of the Christian story—after all, any sane soul already knows that Calvinism is nonsense—but of what appears to be very nearly the most radiantly hopeful. Late nineteenth-century Russia was one of those places where a perennial Eastern Christian sympathy for universalist eschatologies had resurfaced among educated believers and in many quarters had become almost the standard view. Certainly it is as far as Ivan is concerned, though in his case it is also a view mingled with a quasi-Hegelian optimism regarding the rationality of history. He begins from the assumption that the true Christian story is that, in the end, "all shall be well, and all manner of thing shall be well," and that the Kingdom of God will be a reign of perfect harmony in which all souls will be reconciled with one another, and the greatest sinners will seek forgiveness from their victims and receive it, and all persons will together join in an everlasting hymn of praise to the God who made them, and none will doubt that all the evils of the former things have not only passed away but also made an indispensable contribution to that final heavenly music. At one point he briefly considers the possibility of an eternal hell for the reprobate but immediately dismisses it, correctly recognizing that simply "squaring accounts" with sin's victims through the superaddition of a yet greater and more abysmal quantity of suffering atop all the sufferings that time already comprises would in no way either recompense the innocent for their pains or achieve a true Kingdom of peace and harmony. And therein lies the peculiar subtlety and nearly irresistible force of Ivan's unrelenting, tortured, and haunting case for "rebellion" against "the will of God" in worldly suffering. For him, *even if* something like Gregory of Nyssa's vision of the last things should prove true, it will still be a happiness achieved as the residue of an inexcusable cruelty. Ivan allows himself no simple answers. He does not waste his time or ours by discriminating between the impersonal evils of nature and the personal evils of human malice, or by attempting to explain either away in terms of their immediate occasions or causes, or by struggling with the metaphysical puzzle of how evil arises within a good creation. Instead he concentrates all his attention upon the sufferings of the innocent, of children, and merely demands to know how, within any providential scheme whatsoever, those sufferings could ever really be an acceptable price to pay for the glory of creation.

Ivan, it must be noted, does not represent himself as an atheist; he refuses to take a firm position on whether God is the creator of humanity or humanity the creator of God, in part because the very idea of God would be so implausibly wise and holy an achievement for a vicious animal intellect like ours that he is loath to treat it as a trifle or mere fantasy. That said, he insists that God (if God there be) has supplied humanity with finite "Euclidean" minds, bound to the conditions of time and space, unable to grasp those transcendent designs by which God undoubtedly guides all things toward their final harmony with him and with one another. It is better not to worry, then, about ultimate things; our minds are conformed to the circumstances of this world, which are all that we can meaningfully judge. So, he says, he accepts that there is a God and even that there is an eternal plan that will, in its consummation, bring about a condition of perfect peace and beatitude for all creation; but it is creation, in fact, that Ivan rejects. This is the splendid perversity and genius of Ivan's argument, which makes it indeed the argument of a rebel rather than of a mere unbeliever: he willingly grants, he says, that all wounds will at the last be healed, all scars will disappear, all discord will vanish like a mirage or like the miserable invention of finite Euclidean minds, and that such will be the splendor of the finale of all things, when that universal harmony is established, that every heart will be satisfied, all anger soothed, the debt for every crime discharged, and everyone made capable of forgiving every offense and even of finding a justification for everything that has ever happened to mankind; and still he rejects the world that God has made, and that final harmony along with it. Ivan admits that he is not a sentimentalist, that indeed he finds it difficult to love his neighbor, but the terms of the final happiness God intends for his creatures are greater than his conscience can bear. To elucidate his complaint, he provides Alyosha with a grim, unremitting, remorseless recitation of stories about the torture and murder of (principally) children—true stories, as it happens, that Dostoyevsky had collected from the press and from other sources. He tells of Turks in Bulgaria tearing babies from their mothers' wombs with daggers, or flinging infants into the air to catch them on their bayonets before their mothers' eyes, or playing with babies held in their mothers' arms—making them laugh, enticing them with the bright metal of their pistols—only then to fire the pistols into the babies' faces. He tells a story of two parents regularly savagely flogging their seven-year-old daughter, only to be acquitted in court of any wrongdoing. He tells the story of a "cultured and respectable" couple who tortured their five-year-old daughter with constant beatings, and who—to punish her, allegedly, for fouling her bed—filled her mouth with excrement and locked her on freezing nights in an outhouse; and he invites Alyosha to imagine that child, in the bitter chill and darkness and stench of that place, striking her breast with her tiny fist, weeping her supplications to "sweet God," begging him to release her from her misery, and then to say whether anything—the knowledge of good and evil, for instance—could possibly be worth the bleak brutal absurdity of that little girl's torments. He relates the tale of an eight-year-old serf child who, in the days before emancipation, was bound to the land of a retired general and who accidentally injured the leg of his master's favorite hound by tossing a stone; as punishment, the child was locked in a guardroom through the night and in the morning brought out before his mother and all the other serfs, stripped naked, and forced to run before the entire pack of his master's hounds, which were promptly set upon him to tear him to pieces. What can a finite Euclidean mind make of such things? How, with anything like moral integrity, can it defer its outrage to some promised future where some other justice will be worked, in some radically different reality than the present? Ivan says that he does indeed want to see that final harmony, and to hear the explanation for why such horrors were necessary, but not so as to assent to either; for, while he can go some distance in granting the principle of human solidarity—in sin and retribution—he cannot figure the suffering of children into that final equation without remainder. What makes Ivan's argument so novel and disturbing is not that he simply accuses God of failing to save the innocent; in fact, he grants that in some sense God still will "save" them, in part by rescuing their suffering from sheer "absurdity" and showing what part it had in accomplishing the final beatitude of all creatures. Rather, Ivan rejects salvation itself, insofar as he understands it, and on moral grounds; he rejects anything that would involve such a rescue—anything that would make the suffering of children meaningful or necessary. He grants that one day that eternal harmony will be achieved, and we will discover how it necessitated the torments endured by children. Perhaps mothers will forgive the murderers of their children, and the serf child, his mother, and their master will all be reconciled with one another, and all will praise God's justice, and all evils will be accounted for; or perhaps the damnation of the wicked will somehow balance the score (though how then there can be that final harmony, when the suffering of the victims has already happened and the suffering of their persecutors will persist eternally, Ivan cannot guess). But, still, Ivan wants neither harmony nor the knowledge of ultimate truth at such a cost: "For love of man I reject it"; even ultimate truth "is not worth the tears of that one tortured child." Nor, indeed, does he want forgiveness: the mother of that murdered child must not forgive her child's murderer, even if the child himself can forgive. And so, not denying that there is a God or a divine design in all things, he simply chooses (respectfully) to return his ticket of entrance to God's Kingdom. After all, Ivan asks, if you could bring about a universal and final beatitude for all beings by torturing one small creature to death, would you think the price acceptable?

The chief reason that no Christian should ignore or seek to evade Ivan's argument is that, at base, it is so profoundly, even prophetically, Christian—though Ivan himself may have no awareness of this. His ability to imagine a genuinely moral revolt against God's creative and redemptive order has a kind of nocturnal grandeur about it, a Promethean or Romantic or gnostic audacity that dares to imagine some spark dwelling in the human soul that is higher and purer than the God who governs this world; but, in that very way, his argument also carries within itself an echo of the gospel's vertiginous annunciation of our freedom from the "elements" of the world and from the power of the law. And, if nothing else, Ivan's argument provides a kind of spiritual hygiene: a solvent of the semi-Hegelian theology of the liberal Protestantism of the late nineteenth century, which succeeded in confusing eschatological hope with progressive social and scientific optimism, and a solvent as well of the obdurate fatalism of the theistic determinist, and also of the confidence of rational theodicy, and—in general—of the habitual and unthinking retreat of most Christians to a kind of indeterminate deism. And this, again, marks it as a Christian argument, even if Christian *sub contrario*, because in disabusing Christians of facile certitude in the justness of all things, it forces them back toward the more complicated and subversive theology of the gospel, with its "provisional dualism" and its militant language of divine victory. Ivan's rage against explanation arises

from a Christian conscience, and so—even if he cannot acknowledge it—
its inner mystery is an empty tomb, which has shattered the heart of
nature and history alike (as we understand them) and fashioned them
anew. And yet, even so, even when all the bracken and weeds have been
cleared away—the seventeenth century's rational theodicies, with their
vacuous cant about cosmic balance and the best *possible* world, the eigh-
teenth century's vapid deist moralism, the nineteenth century's sub-
limely impersonal dialectical teleologies—Ivan's protest still remains
unanswered. For, even if the empty tomb of Christ is the secret "sedition"
hidden deep within Ivan's rebellion, one must still ask whether one can
reconcile that *divine* subversion of the present frame of *fallen* reality with
the story of God creating all things freely out of nothing and do so in such
a way as to reduce the "price" of that little girl's tears to nothing.

This is why I say, again, that it is a mistake to regard the discourses
of the Staretz Zosima as the novel's answer to Ivan's complaint. They
never even address the problems he raises. The old monk is a figure
of extraordinary imaginative gracefulness, a kind of idealized distillate
of everything most luminously beautiful in the Eastern Christian contemplative tradition, equal parts Macarius the Great, Isaac of Nineveh,
Serafim of Sarov, and Tikhon of Zadonsk. As such, he represents, not the
contrary position to Ivan's, but rather an entirely different orientation of
vision and moral intention. It is true that his posture is a necessary cor-
rective to Ivan's in various senses. Whereas Ivan claims that it is impossible to look from God's vantage upon the whole of creation, and that
therefore we can judge our experience of the world from only a finite and
Euclidean perspective, Zosima claims just the opposite: that by love we
can indeed see the world as God sees it; that, by looking with a burning
charity upon all our neighbors, despite their sins, and by looking with
that same charity upon all creatures whatsoever, we can in fact know the
glory and the truth of God's love in creating all things for himself. And
whereas Ivan's seemingly intensely personal rebellion is in fact essentially an abstract moral interrogation of the universal rationality of the
world, Zosima's seemingly cosmic vision of a creation utterly pervaded
by divine love is in fact an essentially intensely personal "suffering with"
all creatures that refuses to assume a detached universal perspective.
And very much at the heart of Zosima's vision is a radical acknowledgment of personal responsibility for the whole of reality, and of (however

mysterious this may be) a personal complicity in all creatures' sufferings. Before all else, he says, one must not presume to judge but must instead recognize oneself as the only proper object of judgment, whose own sin is somehow the ground of the sin and torment of all. Thus one must not only pour oneself out in love for all creatures but do so as a penitent, seeking the forgiveness not only of one's fellow human beings but of animals and plant life as well. This is splendid and is so in large part because it is sustained by a genuinely humble and ascetic refusal to look to the horizon of the absolute for answers or to seek out some total rationality of history that will make the pains and disaffections of the present moment tolerable. Yet, in another sense, not only does all of this fail to answer Ivan's argument; it in fact sharpens and refines it. For, while it tears away any possible presumption on the part of any human being that he may judge God from a position of moral superiority or purity, and so momentarily might seem to render Ivan's posture of defiance a little ridiculous, in truth it accomplishes quite the opposite: Zosima's teachings merely show that, though God is to be "judged" only against himself—"Who are you, O man . . . ?"—this nevertheless means that God and his works must therefore pass the judgment of a love capable of embracing all things without wrath or condemnation, and without indifference to any particular being. And so, still, the question remains: How can the tears of that little girl be an acceptable price for the drama of creation? After all, would Staretz Zosima himself—with his exquisite counsels on the necessity of loving children with the fullness of one's heart—create a world on such terms if he had the power to do so?

I do not know whether Dostoyevsky intended Zosima's final mystical discourse on hell to provide some sort of clarity on this point. In some sense, of course, it does, insofar as it expresses the dominant Eastern Christian mystical tradition of reflection on damnation, which tells us that the flames of hell are nothing more than the transfiguring glory of God experienced by someone who, having sealed himself within himself, "interprets" it as an exterior chastisement. Hell, Zosima insists, is not God's wrath visited upon sin but the self-condemnation of a soul that can no longer love, and that has therefore placed an impassable chasm between itself and all others. Nor can those who have subjected themselves to such torment be delivered from it, for it is all within themselves; even if dragged into paradise they would be more miserable there than in the heart of hell, for they could never reciprocate the love of the blessed. Their hatred for God and his creation is boundless, "and they shall everlastingly burn in the fires of their own hatred, and shall long for death and nonexistence; but death shall not be granted them." Thus hell is always and only the free choice of the damned, and it in no way detracts from or dilutes the infinite love of God. It is much the same picture provided in more colorful form by Grushenka's tale to Alyosha of the wicked crone whose guardian angel tried to rescue her from the lake of fire by pulling her out at the end of a spring onion she had once given a beggar (the only good deed she had ever performed), but who tried to kick away the other desperate souls clinging to her in hope of salvation and thereby cast herself back into the flames. If we are damned, it is because we damn ourselves and indeed wish to be damned rather than to submit to love. It is a powerful notion. It is also utter nonsense.

Not, that is to say, nonsense as a psychological truth: certainly whatever hell there may be is self-imposed, and in this life already we know that the rejection of love is a torment unlike any other, and we know also how easy it is for someone to cling obsessively to hate and resentment despite the misery they induce in him. What is nonsense is that such a condition is in any meaningful sense truly free, or that it could ever eventuate out of true freedom, or that it could be sustained "everlastingly" as a free act of the creature that would in no way inculpate God. Among more civilized apologists for the conventional concept of eternal damnation, the most popular defense has long been an appeal to creaturely freedom and to God's supposed respect for its dignity. But there could scarcely be a poorer argument; whether made crudely or elegantly, it invariably fails. It might not fail if one could construct a metaphysics or phenomenology of the will's liberty that was purely voluntarist, purely spontaneous; but that is impossible. For one thing, there is no real sense in which an absolutely libertarian act, obedient to no ultimate prior rationale whatsoever, would be distinguishable from sheer chance, or a mindless organic or mechanical impulse, and so any more "free" than an earthquake or embolism. On any cogent account, free will is a power inherently purposive, teleological, primordially oriented toward the good, and shaped by that transcendental appetite to the degree that a soul can recognize the good for what it is. The "intellectualist" understanding of the will is simply the only one that can bear scrutiny. Any act not directed toward its proximate object as "good," at least as "good for me," within a constant transcendental intentionality toward the Good as such, would be by definition teleologically irrational, and so not an act of the rational will at all. Thus no one can *freely* will the evil as evil; one can take the evil for the good, and even know that in doing so one is choosing what others condemn as evil, but for a rational spirit this cannot alter the prior transcendental orientation that makes all desire and action possible. Even God could not create a rational will directed to evil as evil; evil is not a substance, and reason is nothing but a teleological orientation toward the Good. To see the Good truly is to desire it insatiably; not to desire it is not to have known it and so never to have been free to choose it. Thus it makes no more sense to say that God allows creatures to damn themselves out of his love for them or out of his respect for their freedom than to say a father might reasonably allow his deranged child to thrust her face into a fire out of a tender respect for her moral autonomy. Freedom as a rational condition is nothing but the inability to mistake evil for, or prefer it to, the Good. And freedom as an irrational impulse, therefore, cannot exist. And the argument for hell as an eternal free choice of the creature becomes quite insufferable when one considers the personal conditions—ignorance, mortality, defectibility of intellect and will—under which each soul enters the world, and the circumstances—the suffering of all creatures, even the most innocent and delightful of them—with which that world confronts the soul.

We simply cannot in this way evade the shattering force of Vanya's question: If universal harmony and joy could be secured by the torture and murder of a single innocent child, would you accept that price? And once the question has been posed with such terrible clarity, we find its logic goes all the way down to the last lingering residue of unredeemed pain. Let us say that somehow, mysteriously—in, say, Zosima's sanctity, or Alyosha kissing his brother, or the tale of the callous old woman's onion—we could find an answer to the question that might make the transient torments of history justifiable in the light of God's everlasting Kingdom. Very well then, perhaps we might. But *eternal* torments, *final* dereliction? Here the price is raised beyond any calculus of relative goods, and into the realm of absolute—of infinite—expenditure. And the arithmetic is fairly inflexible. One need not imagine, in traditional fashion, that the legions of the damned will far outnumber the cozy company of the saved. Let us imagine instead that only one soul will perish eternally, and all others enter into the peace of the Kingdom. Nor need we think of that soul as guiltless, like Vanya's helpless child, or even as mildly sympathetic. Let it be someone utterly despicable—say, Hitler, or Donald Trump. Even then, no matter how we understand the fate of that single wretched soul in relation to God's intentions, no account of the divine decision to create out of nothingness can make its propriety morally intelligible, or whatever good it accomplishes anything other than relative and incomplete. This is obvious, of course, in predestinarian systems, since from their bleak perspective, manifestly, that poor, ridiculous, but tragically conscious puppet who has been consigned to the abyss exists for no other purpose than the ghastly spectacle of divine sovereignty. But, then, for the redeemed, each of whom might just as well have been denied efficacious grace had God so pleased, who is that wretch who endures God's final wrath, forever and ever, other than their surrogate, their redeemer, the one who suffers in their stead—their Christ? Compared to that unspeakable offering, that interminable and abominable oblation of infinite misery, what would the cross of Christ be? How would it be diminished for us? And to what? A bad afternoon? A temporary indisposition of the infinite? And what would the mystery of God becoming man in order to effect a merely partial rescue of created order be, as compared to the far deeper mystery of a worthless man becoming the suffering god upon whose perpetual holocaust the entire order of creation finally depends? But predestination need not be invoked here at all. Let us suppose instead that rational creatures possess real autonomy and that no one goes to hell save by his or her own industry and ingenuity: when we then look at God's decision to create from that angle, curiously enough, absolutely nothing changes. Let us imagine merely that God created *on the chance* that humanity might sin, and that a certain number of incorrigibly wicked souls might plunge themselves into Tartarus forever; this still means that, morally, he has purchased the revelation of his power in creation by the same horrendous price—even if, in the end, no one at all happens to be damned. The logic is irresistible: for what is hazarded has already been surrendered, entirely, no matter how the dice fall; the aleatory venture may be indeterminate in terms of God's intention, but the wager is itself an irrevocable intentional decision, wherein every possible cost has already been accepted; the irrecuperable expenditure has been offered even if, happily, it is never actually lost, and so the moral nature of the act is the same in either case. To venture the life of your child for some other end is, morally, already to have killed your child, even if at the last moment Artemis or Heracles or the Angel of the Lord should stay your hand. And so the revelation of God's glory in creatures would still always be dependent upon that sacrifice of misery, even if at the last no one were to perish. Creation could never then be called "good" in an unconditional sense, or God the "Good as such," no matter what conditional goods he might accomplish in creating. And, here too, the losing lot might just as well have fallen to the blessed, given the stochastic vagaries of existence: accidents of birth, congenital qualities of character, natural intellectual endowments, native moral aptitudes, material circumstances, personal powers of resolve, impersonal forces of chance, the grim encumbrances of sin and mortality . . . Once again, who would the damned be but the redeemers of the blessed, the price eternally paid by God for the sake of the Kingdom's felicity?

Hence, Zosima's qualification of Ivan's argument must itself be qualified if the terms entailed in God's act of creation are truly to be vindicated. And if, anywhere in the novel, a final answer (or hint of an answer) is given to the quandary, it is provided by the devil with whom the febrile Ivan converses on the night of his collapse. It is all too easy to fail to recognize this when reading the novel; perhaps its author did not see it either. Vanya's devil is one of Dostoyevsky's most inspired creations, one in which the combination of antic absurdity and deeply intelligent pathos is every bit as accomplished as in the figure of the Underground Man, but within a much more confined space. The conceits are all in such perfect balance—the devil's philosophical detachment, his world-weariness and amused nonchalance, his theatrical humility, his faded gentleman's attire, the appearance he wears of a penurious petty noble dependent on the hospitality of others, his rheumatism and bronchitis, his professed longing to be reincarnated as the obese wife of a merchant, his silly self-justifications ("I was marked out by some prehistoric decree that I have never understood to epitomize negation. . . . Man cannot live by Hosannas alone. . . . If everything earthly were governed by reason, nothing would ever happen.")—that they can render the scene's subtle undertones of moral gravity almost inaudible. Not that I intend to dilate on those here. I wish merely to call attention to the devil's admirable air of *fatigue*: with human and cosmic history, with the imponderable point-lessness of his own role of sending souls to perdition, with the self-importance of those who construct grand theories, and especially with the hilarious folly of the young radical philosopher who dreams of a fu-ture man-god beyond good and evil, beyond God. He seems to grasp that whatever truth this world might serve must lie altogether beyond the violence and imbecility of its immanent logic. He certainly would never be tempted to consider the problem of evil as a question regarding the universal rationality of history, as Ivan feels compelled to do. Nor cer-tainly would he be tempted to imagine that he could view the spectacle of cosmic suffering from outside, without involvement or responsibility— even if he cannot quite assume the penitential approach to creation of Zosima. He claims to believe that there is, no doubt, some great secret behind it all that he cannot divine; but he does not speculate on some final resolution of evil in which the Kingdom of God will emerge from the dialectic of history, or from the cosmic drama of a necessary suffer-ing. What he does do, however, is tell a delightfully silly story: that of the materialist philosopher who repudiated all law, conscience, and faith but who on dying found himself in the next world and was so indignant at this contradiction of his deepest convictions that he was promptly con-demned to a quadrillion-kilometer march through the void; at one point along the way, he even refused to continue walking and obstinately lay down for a thousand years, but in the end he was admitted through the gates of paradise and within two seconds declared it worth every step of his journey, and worth a journey of even a quadrillion quadrillion kilo-meters to the quadrillionth power, and joined in the heavenly chorus of praise. And then a little later, quite casually, the devil also remarks that he will himself someday have to surrender his post of negation, make his own quadrillion-kilometer march, and at last utter those Hosannas he has felt constrained by his role within the drama of history to withhold. Perhaps one can make too much of the tale, of course, and certainly one ought to be suspicious of the devil's sincerity. Even so, it is worth noting that the tale he tells is not one regarding a universal harmony somehow necessarily premised upon the unanswered tears of a little girl weeping in misery in the night. It is simply a story of a soul's pilgrimage out of the shadows and into the light, and of a forced rescue from a self-imposed ruin. It is not about a Kingdom achieved by way of time, through Spirit's diremption in the finite or the rational labor of history, but of a salvation graciously granted altogether beyond history. And it is a story that—at least, so it is obliquely suggested—leaves not even the devil out, not as a necessary force of dialectical negation, but as yet another rational spirit called to union with God.

Why is this interesting? Does it answer Ivan's argument for rebellion? No, not exactly. As even the devil's tale suggests, only the final vision of the Kingdom could possibly do that. Nevertheless, the problem Ivan poses is radically altered when the story of creation and redemption is told not as a narrative of the rational meaning of the whole, nor as a grand epic whose dénouement somehow depends upon a tragic drama of eternal loss, but rather as the tale of the rescue of all creatures from nonbeing, and then also from sin and ignorance, and finally even from themselves and their illusory "freedom," so that they may be drawn on to the God who will not abandon even those who abandon him. Seen from that vantage, the question of whether it was all "worth the price" is reduced from the status of a logically irrefutable arraignment of creation's goodness to that of a powerful intuitive moral anxiety. The time of sin and death, which we call history, cannot be—and this is the truth that Ivan sees so clearly—the foundation of God's Kingdom, as then it would be a final harmony sustained by an unredeemed injustice. Rather, it is the last residue of the darkness of nonbeing that God conquers in creation and salvation. That being so, the question of the price of that victory is not one of the rational calculation of relative goods, but one whose final answer is entirely the province of—and this is Zosima's truth—one who can see the whole of creation with the eyes of perfect love: that same little girl, though now lifted up into the eternity of the Kingdom, divinized, glorified, capable of a love like God's, which can forgive perfectly and thereby triumph over all evil. Yet even this forgiveness cannot bring the Kingdom to pass unless—and this is the truth to which the devil attests, even if only inadvertently—eternity reduce the price of evil to absolutely nothing. For if anything were to be eternally lost—the least little thing—then the goodness of creation could never be more in the end than a purely conditional goodness, a mere relative evaluation, rather than an essential truth. And then neither could God be the Good as such.

Again, the issue is the reducibility of all causes to their first cause, and the final determination of the first cause by the final. If Christians did not believe in a *creatio ex nihilo*—if they thought God a being limited by some external principle or internal imperfection, or if they were dualists, or dialectical idealists, or what have you—the question of evil would be only an aetiological query for them, not a terrible moral question. But, because they say God creates freely, they must believe that his final judgment shall reveal him for who he is. If God creates souls he knows to be destined for eternal misery, in himself he cannot be the good as such, and creation cannot possess any true moral essence: it is from one vantage an act of predilective love, but from another vantage, and one every bit as logically necessary, it is an act of prudential malevolence. And so it cannot be true. And this must be the final moral meaning of the doctrine of *creatio ex nihilo*, at least for those who truly believe that their language about God's goodness has any substance, and that the theological grammar to which that language belongs is not empty: that the God of eternal retribution and pure sovereignty proclaimed by so much of Christian tradition is not, and cannot possibly be, the God of self-outpouring love revealed in Christ. If God is the good creator of all, he is the savior of all, without fail, who brings to himself all he has made, including all rational wills, and only thus returns to himself in all that goes forth from him. Only thus can it be true that God made the world and saw that it was good; and only thus can we hope in the end to see that goodness, and also to see that he who made it is himself the Good as such.

7

Tradition and Authority
A Vaguely Gnostic Meditation

I

Along the uneven course of history's flow, there are those rare odd turns in the streambed at which—due to a very special set of conditions and an entirely chance confluence of forces—an obviously bad idea can seem like an extremely good one and, before reason or good taste can intervene, it is adopted. As time passes, other unpredictable conditions conspire to preserve that initial mistake, until what began as a mishap of circumstance is transformed by the relentless alchemies of habit into a fixed element of our world, and even sometimes into an institution invested with an immemorial authority, commanding not only our respect but our allegiance as well. Thus a foolish fortuity becomes an indispensable truth, an ungainly anomaly a golden standard; accident is converted into essence, contingency into necessity; the fly and the amber are one. No doubt certain examples have occurred to all of us here already: the designated hitter rule, the celibate priesthood . . . Holland . . . But we may not always appreciate how profound a challenge this sort of random metastasis of a momentary error into a revered tradition poses for many of our certainties regarding the meaning of the past and the continuities of culture. It should trouble us gravely to consider how easily any practice, just by persisting long enough, can be woven inextricably into the deepest fabric of shared memory and belief. It should, at the very least, make us question how confident we are in our ability to distinguish between genuinely enduring truths and mere tenacious conventions, or between healthy developments and signs of decadence. More fundamentally still, perhaps, it should make us wonder whether we can be absolutely certain that there really is such a thing as a *religious* tradition at all in any meaningful and logically cogent sense, in the sense that rational faith requires (that is, at once a source of irrefragable authority and a warrant for new interpretive discoveries), or whether instead the command that a religious tradition exercises over our minds has really been produced by nothing more than the mounting force of historical inertia.

Of course, we have to assume that such fears are baseless. And naturally our first line of defense against doubt on this score is the one we draw between true tradition and mere "traditionalism"—between, that is, the subtle discernment required by fidelity to the former (the scrupulous historical exactitudes, rigorous metaphysical interrogations, and tireless quest for spiritual wellsprings) and the brutish obduracy characteristic of devotion to the latter (the pathetic fascination with the extraneous and the arbitrary, the militant enthusiasm for the vulgar and the dainty alike, the concern for form rather than substance, the fastidious dread of gnats but insouciant tolerance for camels). In most cases, telling the difference seems effortless—as simple a thing as sorting out the living from the dead, tender affections from morbid obsessions, young love from necrophilia. Speaking merely for myself, for instance, I have become especially annoyed in recent years by certain kinds of Roman Catholic "traditionalists" whose numbers have been growing in this country over the past, say, decade and a half; and I find it seductively easy to satisfy myself that I can recognize the precise juncture at which their loyalty to sacred truth all at once degenerates into a perverted adherence to corrupt customs. And it causes me scarcely an instant's hesitation to admit that my judgments in the matter are prompted as much by personal taste as by sober analysis. More often than not, after all, the "traditional" Catholicism for which these benighted souls yearn is clearly not that of the ancient or mediaeval church (which was, after all, what the *ressourcement* movement and the "*nouvelle théologie*" were seeking to recover); rather, it is that of the Baroque era, which I happen to regard as the most decadent and repellant period of Catholic culture, both intellectually and aesthetically (in all things, that is, save music). A good number of them, in fact, at least among that tribe's theological cognoscenti, look

back fondly to what John O'Malley once called Catholicism's "long nineteenth century": that grim period when theological creativity had been
all but extinguished in the Roman church, and when the particularly
incoherent and debased system of "manualist" or "two-tier" Thomism
reigned triumphant. To me this is rather on the order of cherishing a desperate nostalgia for a debilitating case of jaundice that one vaguely recalls
from childhood.

And yet, even when I have made all due allowances for my own
biases and private predilections, my dismay at this sort of traditionalism
remains undiminished. I still cannot help but sense that among my "traditionalist" Catholic acquaintances there are far too many who love ritual
only when it is high and dry, many more who adore the stern guidance
of an unyieldingly firm ecclesial hand, and an altogether unsettling
number with an insatiable craving for taffeta, lace, and ermine—and yet
next to none who seem much interested in Christian charity or, for that
matter, in Christ. Almost all of them, in my experience, seem far too
ready to mistake nostalgia for piety, and intransigence for principle. And,
no sooner do I allow myself the thought that this may all be a very un-
charitable misperception on my part, than I receive some startling confirmation of my original prejudice. Some months ago, for example, in a
moment of weakness, just as I was drawing precariously close to mag-
nanimously excusing a student for citing Garrigou-Lagrange to me sympathetically, a column appeared in the magazine *First Things* that pulled
me back from the precipice by forcibly reminding me just how grotesque
this idolatry of the ornamental can be. Admittedly, the quality of that
journal has declined steeply since the days when my dog was regularly
writing for it; but this particular article, it seems to me, was indicative of
an extremely troubling spiritual pathology. Written by a young editor
named Matthew Schmitz, it was principally a celebration, at the expense
of Pope Francis, of the protagonist in the HBO television series *The Young
Pope*, as well as a particularly mawkish reverie about the grandeur that
was Rome in the days of unapologetic clericalism. The Young Pope of the
series is, it seems, a high ritualist, a severe formalist, a believer in structure and order, a Catholic triumphalist who wants the Vatican to purchase back the papal tiara. Schmitz, it seems, pines for such a pope, even
though—as he notes—the character he is praising also happens to be an
unbeliever. The program's great central irony, it turns out, is that its

protagonist is a champion of the institutional church but is not actually a Christian. This, though, did nothing to diminish our author's giddy enthusiasm. What does belief matter, after all, so long as the pontiff celebrates mass *ad orientem* in his magic ruby slippers? Of the series as a whole, he writes: "Reveling in supposedly old-fashioned garments like the papal red shoes and wide-brimmed *saturno*, it shows how attractive an unapologetically traditional Catholicism can be."

Not to me, I have to say. Quite the opposite, in fact. Then again, I never cared for Liberace's or Wayne Newton's wardrobes either (I even thought Carol Channing's a mite *de trop*). These days, of course—except in the occasional photograph of Cardinal Burke or on Bourbon Street during Mardi Gras—one scarcely ever sees anyone wrapped in the full pavonine panoply of Baroque ecclesial drag (shimmering satin *mozzetta*, billowing silk *ferraiolo*, gauzy gossamer *rochet*, gleaming *zucchetto* or pavilioning *saturno* or gaily tasseled *galero* . . .). But, on those rare occasions when I do catch a glimpse of some prelate of any rank swathed in the sumptuous clericals of bygone epochs, I have to confess that in the very next moment my mind conceives an image of him being hurled down a very long flight of granite stairs, violently striking every step along the descent, until he comes to rest at last on the rough paving stones of the plaza below, an incarnadined shard of broken and moaning flotsam amid a sea of exquisite fabrics. I find it a soothing image. If I then allow myself to dilate upon the fantasy a little, four or five pale youths with lank hair, clad in leather jackets and pointed Spanish boots, approach, exchange wicked smiles, toss away their cigarettes, and begin kicking him in the ribs, groin, and coccyx; when they tire of this, they strip him of his prettiest accoutrements and run away laughing to a nearby pawnshop whose most regular clientele are the "exotic" dancers from the adult cabaret next door. Soon thereafter the hyenas arrive . . .

Oh, but I ought not to wallow in this gorgeous idyll. I risk becoming malicious. Suffice it to say that I agree with the current pope that clericalism is a cancer in the body of any church. I believe that the days when Catholic priests dressed like petty royalty and demanded deference from the laity were among the darkest of Catholic culture. I laud Francis's jovially paternal mockery of young priests who like to preen about in the epicene frills and flounces and gewgaws of those times. I rejoiced, after his election, when he refused to have that ghastly matronly *mozzetta* draped over his shoulders. Not that I object to distinctive clerical garb, so long as it is properly shabby—worn cuffs, frayed collars, shoes mended with duct tape—but priests are servants to servants, slaves of slaves. They are God's janitorial service. They should dress as such. My own taste in clericals tends toward the austere black cassocks of the Eastern churches (which reserve more resplendent habiliments for liturgical uses alone). Rather than the Young Pope and his seventeenth-century sensibilities, my ideal would be Pope Celestine, who in AD 428 brusquely reproached certain bishops in Gaul for their elaborate finery: "We should be distinguished from common folk or others by our studiousness, not our attire; by our conduct, not our clothes; by purity of mind, not the care we lavish on our persons" (Discernendi a plebe vel caeteris sumus doctrina, non veste; conversatione, non habitu; mentis puritate, non cultu; *Epistola* 4.1.2, *Ad episcopos provinciae Vienensis et Narbonensis*, PL 50 431B). And, it usually seems clear to me, this is not *merely* a matter of taste. It seems obvious, broadly considered, why one should think Celestine a more faithful representative of a truly Christian understanding of ecclesial office than, say, a modern American cardinal in St. Louis who squanders a small fortune in diocesan funds on a ludicrous silk *cappa magna*, who luxuriates in exorbitantly opulent clerical garb, and who casually recrucifies Christ every time he slips his soft, sleek, suety little fingers into his velvet gloves. "What did you go out into the wilderness to gaze at? A reed being shaken by the wind? What rather did you go out to see? A man clothed in soft garments? Look: Those wearing splendid garments and living in luxury are in the houses of kings" (Luke 7:24–26; cf. Matt. 11:7–9). "He has pulled dynasts down from thrones and exalted the humble, he has filled the hungry with good things and sent the rich away empty" (Luke 1:52–53). "You lived on the earth in dainty luxury and self-indulgence. You have gorged your hearts on a day of slaughter" (James 5:5). It seems somehow important, at any rate, that the only splendid garments Christ ever wore were those cast about him by the soldiers of Herod before they returned him to Pilate (Luke 23:11), and the nearest thing to the regalia of high office a soldier's scarlet cloak, a reed scepter, and a crown of thorns. It hardly constitutes a violent leap of logic to conclude that it was Celestine who was the true disciple of the Man of Sorrows, inheriting and faithfully passing on a purer vision of the Christian life, while the aforementioned American cardinal is at most heir to a particularly obnoxious species of clerical pomp and to a meretricious sartorial fashion that in a pestilential season attached itself to the tradition like a toxic parasite.

And yet the issue is rarely quite that simple.

II

To begin with, the very concept of "tradition" is arguably incorrigibly equivocal. At least, it entails a certain necessary ambiguity regarding what kind of continuity it is meant to describe: in one sense, what is at issue is the continuity of unalterable practices and immutable beliefs, as preserved by the community to which they give shape; in another sense, however, it is the continuity of a dynamic process, one that accommodates ceaseless alteration without taking leave of the original impulse or truth that this process supposedly enucleates over time. And both senses are indispensable if the concept is to serve any very useful purpose at all: the word *tradition* must, that is, serve simultaneously as a justification for the retention of elements for which no intrinsic rationale can be adduced, or any rationale at all other than past practice, and also as a justification for the undeniable variety of historical configurations assumed and abandoned by what is supposedly a single enduring community or institution across generations. Any tradition that cannot be justified in both ways at once, at any given moment, is almost certainly one that is moribund. But this means also that the term *tradition* can very easily become a mystification of either stagnation or caprice (or, for that matter, of both at once): the former it can endow with the false grandeur of an ancient wisdom delivered once and for all, the latter with the modish allure of "doctrinal development." Of course, different faiths will tend to emphasize one side of the concept more than the other, as will different factions within each faith; some will be more jealous of the old forms, some more eager for the new. But in every case the same question hangs suspended above all talk of tradition: whether there can possibly be any account of that tradition capable of holding what is unalterable and what ceaselessly changes together in a single consistent and plausible unity, or whether instead we speak of "tradition" simply in order to distract ourselves from the fundamental arbitrariness of our beliefs.

The kind of distinction drawn above, moreover, between true tradition and decadent traditionalisms presumes that a tradition is capable of some kind of internal "originalist" critique of the forms through which it passes in the course of its history. But this presents something of a problem, inasmuch as the very concept of a living tradition entails a kind of double (or even circular) logic. In one sense, every tradition draws its authority from some sort of initiating moment of awakening or revelation or discovery (the call of Abraham, the Law at Sinai, the hearing of the Vedas, Easter, the Buddha's enlightenment, Lao-Tzu's oracles, the delivery of the Qur'an, Guru Nanak's awakening, and so on); and yet, no less essentially, the authority of that initial moment is validated only in and by the richness, capaciousness, and perdurability of the historical developments to which it can continually give rise (whether we attribute those developments to the working of the Holy Spirit or the wisdom of the ancestors or whatever else). Thus, to attempt to reduce the essence of a tradition to only a few simple indispensable inaugural principles, and so consign all the rest to the realm of the fortuitous or adiaphoral, is to forsake the idea of living tradition altogether and, in that very way, also to reduce the original source of the tradition to a punctiliar historical accident without any actual meaning or power. It can have no real consequences in time. Nothing then remains. A truly living tradition, therefore, must be capable of accommodating far more than what a strictly reductive originalism demands of its founding event, because these two poles—a tradition's original moment and its subsequent historical unfolding—legitimate one another reciprocally and inseparably. And, the moment this principle is admitted, the critical solvency of the originalist position begins to wane away. This is not a trivial matter. The examples I have given so far are positively garish in their obviousness. Only a tragically diseased sensibility could find the monstrous spectacle of a *cappa magna* morally or aesthetically palatable. Anyone who can look at a cardinal wearing a *galero* and not immediately think of a drunkard wearing an exceptionally hideous lampshade is simply a hopeless philistine. Most cases, though, demand a far keener power of discernment. And over *all* cases there looms the shadow of an ominous dilemma: *either* there is no real distinction between the essential and the inessential in a tradi-

tion, which would entail that the tradition as a whole is devoid of any coherent rationale, meaning, or critical power; *or* the distinction between
essential and inessential is immediately obvious, which would entail that
the larger tradition as a whole is mostly dispensable, being little more
than a chance coalescence of insignificant accidents wrapped haphaz-
ardly around what would otherwise be just an evident truth. Certainly the
witness of history does little to help us discriminate between the thing-
in-itself and its epiphenomena. There is not only far too much accumu-
lation and retention but also far too much attrition and forgetting; over
time, practices and forms continually attach themselves only to fall away
again unexpectedly, or else they persist for no discernible reason; the
seemingly fixed proves transient, the seemingly ephemeral permanent,
and no privileged vantage can be found from which one can tell the
dancer from the dance. This is why it is, perhaps, that the authority of
"tradition" can be invoked simultaneously in support of the most pitilessly reductive rigorism and also as a justification for an almost infinite
plasticity of practice and expression (even to the point of explaining away
seeming internal contradictions of principle or logic). And so, again, one
has to ask whether the very concept of "tradition" is a cogent one or is
instead essentially fanciful: a euphemism for whatever happens to happen, a mystification of sheer unguided eventuality; one damned thing
after another; local memory or (as is more often the case) false memory,
translated into habit and then preserved as irrational prejudice or sickly
nostalgia.

If this is not the case, however, then it seems to me that whatever it
is that is most vital to a tradition—whatever force or substance sustains
it as a continuity amid incessant change—must also be that which is
most inconspicuous, even invisible. If nothing else, if the source of a tradition's continuity were not in some sense essentially hidden, it could
never pass through, provoke, or survive so many successive conceptual
and practical configurations; if it were not something that silently abides
amid change, the constantly inexpressible within each transitory expression, it could neither tantalize the new into existence nor banish the old
to oblivion. How one knows this invisibility, however, is difficult to describe. What is known is not a phenomenon within religious experience
so much as the intentional horizon within which any religious phenomenon is able to appear, as at once a comprehensible form and an

inadequate symbol of a fullness of truth that has no final finite expression. It is the nimbus of the unseen that shines all around the seen, a boundless surfeit of meaning that lies beyond the scope of every formulation of the faith, an infinite distance that at once frustrates and continuously urges devotion and reflection toward a final rest. In a larger and perhaps ultimate sense, it is the horizon of a truly transcendental object of desire, the divine fullness that in its infinite simplicity is hospitable to limitless expressions but reducible to none. Faith itself, moreover, positively requires this hiddenness to live; the venture of fidelity is nothing other than a trust in the reality of some living truth that transcends the forms it animates. Otherwise every historical transition would constitute a defeat. So, the believer who abandons faith's preoccupation with the invisible and adopts instead the traditionalist's desperate adherence to the beguiling contingencies peculiar to some particular epoch or school has effectively forsaken tradition altogether and sought refuge in sheer wistfulness. It is its perennially hidden truth that endows any tradition with whatever internal power of critical discrimination it may possess; only that always more urgent yet always invisible impulse can free the faithful mind from the appeal of mere transient historical attachments and inspire it, however mysteriously, to correct aberrations and deformities within the tradition. Admittedly, faith's knowledge of that hiddenness is at most a kind of unspoken awareness of something that can never be exhaustively translated into simple concepts or words; it is, at best, what Newman called an "illative sense," or a special kind of what Polanyi called "tacit knowledge." Still, the proof that any tradition is a living one is precisely that it does not fiercely cling to every aspect of what it has inherited but instead exhibits an often astonishing ruthlessness in shedding the past, out of obedience to some still more original spiritual imperative. One might almost describe this as devotion to a secret history: so secret, in fact, that it can enter experience only indirectly, almost like a Lockean substance, wholly veiled by—and yet revealed only in—its accidents.

As for how we can know that this secret history is truly there to be told, when so much of the concrete history of a tradition consists in an unremitting sequence of accretions and dissolutions, we must in some sense rely on the evidence of that very process: its persistence, its obstinacy, its inexhaustibility. Still, obviously, every tradition must employ a set of hermeneutical tools to impose some kind of stability upon itself, and the nature of these tools varies radically from tradition to tradition. In the main, Christianity has placed enormous trust in the power of doctrinal definitions to elucidate its intrinsic rationality and to impose order upon its diverse expressions. But even these definitions—as the whole history of Christian theological factions and ecclesial confessions demonstrates—are invariably only a little less fluid in their acceptation than is the tradition as a whole in its cultural configurations. Certainly dogmas bring nothing to a simple conclusion, in part because they themselves rest their claims to validity upon that still hidden surfeit of truth prompting them, which always promises infinitely more than any specific proposition can ever express, and which therefore maintains its hiddenness even within its official expositions. Everything is proximate at best, suggestive at most. The history of doctrine tells us that every defined dogma is simultaneously a *terminus ad quem* and a *terminus a quo* and can be neither without also being the other; if this were not so, the very historical situatedness of any doctrine would render it incredible. Each dogma is a concrescence and summary of any number of prior forces but is also the inauguration of an entirely new series of interpretive departures, elaborations, conflicts, quandaries, and resolutions. It is anything but some pure distillate of belief, extracting the tradition's essence from its larger medium and concentrating it in a fixed form. Coherent dogma does not reduce but instead greatly enlarges the area of mystery within a creedal tradition and ultimately multiplies the questions that faith cannot yet answer. Dogmas establish certain boundaries but also invariably open up entire new vistas. And, again, they are credible precisely as consonant with that hiddenness that remains inexhaustibly more original (emanating from an irrecoverable initial moment in the past) and inexhaustibly more final (summoning us to a future in which at last we shall see no longer in a glass, darkly, but rather face to face).

III

We should pause, perhaps, to note that the very concept of doctrinal *definition* is also an invincibly ambiguous one. The history of dogma, dispassionately surveyed, is not the chronicle of a seamless process of long-held beliefs crystallizing from more inchoate into ever more precise formulations, as if the development of doctrine were little more than the process of the church finding the right words to express convictions present in the community of faith from the beginning. If we look back with unprejudiced eyes to, say, the ecumenical councils of the Christian past and the dogmatic promulgations they produced, we discover nothing like the continuous preservation of some settled *consensus fidelium* against the perverse novelties of heretical factions, much less an inexorable evolution of received religious truths toward increasingly exact creedal epitomes. What we find instead is the fitful generation of often willfully vague formulae describing genuinely unprecedented models of Christian confession. While every dogma draws upon the practices and language of the past, it also constitutes at once a synthesis and an innovation and may even so radically alter the meaning of past beliefs and claims that something entirely new is introduced into the tradition (albeit under the aspect of a *venerable* truth). This is inevitable. Dogmas arise when seemingly intrinsic contradictions appear within the evolution of a given tradition. And the conflicts produced by these internal stresses can, as a rule, be resolved only by the creation of new ways not only of expressing but also of understanding the past; and only in this way can the tradition get past what would otherwise be insurmountable impasses. Then, no less inevitably, in each case a certain degree of willful historical forgetfulness must be cultivated, so that a new version of the past can be invented, one purged of the very complexities and confusions that had demanded a new dogmatic definition in the first place. Where the essence of doctrine is concerned, it is often not enough to provide a satisfactory answer; it is necessary then to take the additional step of forgetting the question. What we call "orthodoxy" and "heresy" are retrospective and (to be honest) transparently ideological constructions—which is to say, *reconstructions* of what has been—meant to fortify every new doctrinal resolution by enfolding it in the misty mythology of some pure and exhaustive deposit of the faith wherein all later orthodoxies are always already present, like latent algorithms. Christians, of course, find it convenient to invoke the Holy Spirit's guidance whenever it becomes necessary to dispel doubts regarding the actual material history of doctrine—which, frankly, apart from this article of faith looks like little more than a unremitting succession of political compromises and rhetorical evasions.

And nowhere is the principle of inspired tradition more fully and more audaciously advanced than in Newman's splendid speculative fantasia, *Essay on the Development of Christian Doctrine* (that long, gallant attempt to extract a syllogism from a tautology). Even so, it is best to be honest here. Gore Vidal once remarked that everything changes except the avant-garde—and this is true: the attempt at originality for originality's sake tends with almost perfect regularity to eventuate in the trite and tediously predictable. But it is no less true that, as often as not, there is nothing so truly new as our "ancient" traditions. Just as the most "novel" ideas we venture are frequently mere recapitulations of old ideas, which have been largely forgotten precisely because they proved fruitless, so also the "timeless" verities we affirm are often wholly original and synthetic products of the special pressures of the present moment.

I do not mean to suggest, incidentally, that doctrinal definitions are not in any sense genuine developments of previous expressions of faith, or that they are just fanciful superimpositions upon a history from which they do not naturally emerge. I simply want to make clear that they are as much feats of creative reinterpretation and invention as they are deductions inexorably derived from the evidences of the past. Whatever they preserve they also revise. Hence the rather provisional shape of most dogmatic definitions, the minimalism and rather abstract formality of their phrasing. The conceptual contents of defined doctrines, when subjected to real scrutiny, invariably prove far more protean and mercurial and elusive than the hard propositional form of those doctrines would seem to suggest. In the end, the principal effect of a dogma is to close down a few unprofitable avenues of theological questioning precisely by opening up countless new, potentially more expansive avenues. And each doctrinal determination necessarily calls forth a ceaseless labor of interpretation and reinterpretation; but for this labor, that dogma would quickly become opaque, empty, and dead. One need merely consult the historical record to confirm this. Theological traditions remain vital only insofar as they are, in any age, in the process of being reconstructed. This means that every established doctrine requires restatement in formulations that preserve the received teaching precisely by subtly but continuously refashioning how it is to be understood. And these formulations must be feats of recollection, of critical imagination, and of inspired invention all at once—principled constructions poetically shaped in the present, from the testimony of the past, in the light of an indeterminate future. No tradition could long survive if it were really only the cumulative consequence of the cultural and intellectual forces of its own past; to continue to thrive and advance, it requires formal and final causes as much as material and efficient, shaping it and summoning it toward an end beyond the configurations it possesses at any given moment.

Take, for instance, the first and—at least, as the grand governing paradigm for all that followed in dogmatic history—most significant doctrinal definitions of Christian tradition: those of the first two councils, Nicaea and Constantinople. The "Arian controversy" constitutes, for all Christian memory, that crucial moment when the institutional orthodoxy of the politically enfranchised and publicly supported church for the first time (for want of a better word) *legislated* the proper form for faithful confession and in so doing demoted all seemingly incompatible forms of confession (however devout and intellectually sincere) to damnable expressions of faithlessness. Whenever Christians recite the Nicene-Constantinopolitan Symbol, and most especially when they confess (in whichever translation they use) that the eternal divine Son is *homoousios* with God the Father, they are putatively reciting a digest of the faith that has been recognized "everywhere, at all times, and by all peoples" as the one true orthodoxy. Moreover, it has been the fate of Arius to be remembered not merely as *a* heretic but as *the* heretic, the very archetype of all heretics—the man who, out of sheer perversity or malice, supposedly broke from the common belief of all good baptized Christians in what was still the faith's golden dawn, the wanton innovator who defied the word of scripture and the teachings of the apostles by rejecting what the church had always unequivocally taught regarding the Son's full Godhead and coequality of the Father. All of this is, of course, utter nonsense. In Arius's own time, it would have been absurd to regard him as either a traditionalist or a rebel (in part, because the testimony of neither scripture nor tradition was anywhere near so clear and homogeneous as later Christians were taught to believe). In point of fact, he was a profoundly conservative theologian and in the context of Alexandrian theology was without question a much more faithful representative of the oldest and most respectable school of Trinitarian speculation than were the partisans of the eventual Nicene settlement. Admittedly, his appears to have been an especially austere and unimaginative expression of the tradition in which he had been formed; but that is rather the point: if his teachings have been accurately reported (which cannot be assumed), it would seem that it was precisely because he was such a fierce traditionalist that he was unable to grasp the demands of tradition. Still, one can understand what motivated him. He was attempting to preserve a long-established and extremely plausible "subordinationist" metaphysics, one that seemed successfully to unite the divine and created realms in a continuous hierarchy of powers while still nevertheless affirming the absolute transcendence of God the Father. He even, as far as he was concerned, had scripture on his side. Even the first verse of John's Gospel seemed to honor the traditional distinction between God Most High—God as identified in Greek by the definite article: "*the* God," *ho theos*—and "God" (or "god") in a secondary, subordinate, and perhaps only honorific sense—*theos* sans article.

In much of the Eastern intellectual world of the empire during the first three centuries, in fact, and in Alexandria especially, something like a subordinationist metaphysics had long been the common property of pagans, Jews, and Christians. It was generally assumed that the highest divine principle, in its full transcendence, never came into direct contact with the world of finite and mutable things but rather had since the beginning expressed itself in some economically "reduced" form through which it created and governed the world. There had long been Platonists, like Plotinus and Porphyry, who had believed that the transcendent One was mediated to the lower world only through an order of progressively more derivative divine principles. There had been Jewish thinkers, such as Philo, who believed that God was mediated to his creation by a viceroy or "Son" or "Logos," a "secondary divinity" who had been the subject of all the divine theophanies of Hebrew scripture. Many Christians too had always shared this view. All parties to this vision had, with varying degrees of complexity or mythic richness, imagined the interval between God (or the One, or what have you) and this world to be populated by a hierarchy of greater and lesser powers. And all parties had also shared the conviction that the second "moment" of reality—the *Logos* or *nous* that most immediately proceeds from the supreme principle of all things—was a kind of economic limitation of its source, one that through itself directly, or through some yet more subordinate principle, constituted a kind of deferred contact between the highest divinity and the realm of discrete beings. And thus the whole of reality—terrestrial, celestial, and even divine—subsisted in a single continuum. It was a deeply attractive picture of things and in its Christian version seemed to make complete sense of the language of scripture. And the theology of Arius was a perfectly plausible, if stark, specimen of this metaphysics. For him, it was simply the purest Christian piety to insist that the Father was utterly hidden from and inaccessible to all beings, even the heavenly powers, and that it was only through his Logos that anything was known about him. Even the claim that the divine Son was in fact a creature, who at one time had not existed, was not an especially exotic supposition. That same piety dictated that only the Father could be understood as "unoriginate" in any meaningful sense. Many Christian thinkers of the second century, certainly, had believed that the Logos had been generated only a little while before the making of the world, so that he could effect the work of creation. Moreover, many Christians had long identified the Logos with the greatest angel of the celestial court, the Angel of Mighty Counsel, a kind of heavenly high priest who served the Father and who was his representative to all other beings, both there above and here below. As a traditional Alexandrian believer, then, Arius was clearly operating within the ambit of the faith as he had received it from a long Christian past. And, frankly, it is little more than a ridiculous accident of history that his rather ordinary theological career should have become the occasion for resolving a crisis. The crisis, after all, was not one of creed and confession, since Christianity had long accommodated a vast variety of beliefs regarding the nature of the divine Son. Rather, it was a crisis of imperial policy: the new Augustus, having adopted the faith, required a single visible structure of power and a single audible voice of doctrinal authority if the newly enfranchised institution of the church was to serve his ends and prove docile to his will. Arius was the victim in part of his own lack of imagination but in larger part of the new political circumstances of his age.

This is why it is that the settlement of Nicaea did not bring the controversy to an end, incidentally. There remained a great many very faithful Christians out there who thought the Nicene formula, and especially that daring and difficult word *homoousios*, had obscured a vital scriptural distinction—or, at least, a vital mystery that scripture had left open. And so, in the long aftermath of the council, any number of theologians proposed alternative solutions that they thought might restore a sense of that distinction. Among those who rejected the Nicene formula, as we all know, there were the "homoeans" who preferred to describe the Son as being "of similar substance (*homoiousios*)" with the Father, and there were the "anomoeans" who regarded the Son as being altogether "unlike" the Father; but what they shared was their fidelity to a Trinitarian language that they correctly regarded as being far more ancient than that of Nicaea, and that they plausibly judged to be more faithful to scripture. That the imperial church spent the better part of a century agonizing over the difference between words like *homoousios* and *homoiousios*—a difference on paper, after all, of only a single letter—has frequently been an object of mirth, caricatured as a silly contest between indistinguishable abstractions. But, for the Christians of the fourth century, the entire intelligibility of their faith was a stake. There were many issues, of course, informing the debate—scripture, liturgy, the common understanding of the faithful—but chief among them was the nature of salvation.

This was the crux of the matter, after all. It was an age in which salvation was still understood not, say, as some kind of forensic justification of the sinner before God, followed by admission into a happy hereafter, but rather as the real union of creatures with God himself. All parties to the doctrinal disputes of the time were committed to the belief that Christ had assumed human nature so as to free it from bondage to death and make it capable of a direct indwelling of the divine presence. For Athanasius or the Cappadocian fathers, for instance, the paramount question was how such union with the transcendent God was possible for finite creatures. If (to use the familiar formula) "God became man that man might become God," could it possibly be the case that the Son or the Spirit was a lesser expression of God or, even worse, merely a creature? Only God is capable of joining creatures to God; any inferior intermediary, especially one like the created Logos of Arius, will always be infinitely remote from God himself. The Cappadocian arguments against the Eunomians were numerous, complex, and subtle, but at their heart lay a single simple intuition: if it is the Son who joins us to the Father, and only God can join us to God, then the Son is God in a wholly consubstantial sense; and if, in the sacraments of the church and the life of sanctification, it is the Spirit who joins us to the Son, and only God can join us to God, then the Spirit too must be God in this wholly consubstantial sense. In Christ, they believed, God in his fullness really has come to dwell in our midst; and in the Holy Spirit, God in his fullness has really brought us to dwell in Christ. Thus, when we turn to the great exponents of Nicene theology in the fourth century, what we find in their texts is not merely a catechetical recitation of received wisdom but a patient practice of critical anamnesis, a discipline of recollection that is also a synthesis of the full testimony of the past. Perhaps the most perfect example of this is Basil of Caesarea's *On the Holy Spirit*, which argued as forcibly as possible—without overstepping the language of scripture or the Nicene Creed—for the full divinity of the Holy Spirit, against all doubters. Of course, the Spirit is nowhere clearly called either *ho theos* or *theos* in the New Testament; and Basil's treatise nowhere violates this rule of reticence (if that is what it is). It was left up to Gregory of Nazianzus, in his *Five Theological Orations*, to extend the boundaries of the received vocabulary and boldly to proclaim the full divinity of the Spirit. But Basil's text is fascinating for its sheer systematic comprehensiveness. It lays out a survey of the whole of scripture, as well as the most venerable liturgical usages of the church, and constructs a marvelously, even seemingly overwhelming case for the Godhead of the Spirit. And every step is governed by a single compelling question: What do Christians mean when they say that they have been saved in and by Christ, by the power of the Holy Spirit? By the end, Basil's case—and there simply is no more systematic treatment of the issue in patristic literature—powerfully suggests that only the full "homoousian" Trinitarian position makes it possible to view Christian belief as a coherent vision of God's action in Christ. And, indeed, by comparison to Basil's exposition of the faith, the Arian and Eunomian positions do seem to dissolve into fragmentary and contradictory mythologies. That may be only an appearance, admittedly—we know of the anti-Nicene party only through the reports of their adversaries—but Basil's accomplishment was an astonishing one in any event. On the one hand, his argument was in no sense procrustean or artificial—he truly drew on the language and beliefs and inherent logic of the Christian past—but, on the other, it was the result of a boldly creative interpretive labor. The tradition he described was arguably really already there in some sense, if one could piece it together in just the right way; but it required that piecing together, as well as a considerable degree of filtering out useless pieces, and when the picture was complete it still constituted something startling and new, and something that made the familiar strange. This same question of salvation, moreover, drove the Christological disputes of the following centuries and prompted the same kind of inspired syntheses. It could not have been otherwise. Any true and living tradition must be at once both the subject and the object of a constant and pious hermeneutical retrieval that, guided by an awareness of the history and logic of what has gone before, seeks to discover the tradition's dialectical unity and rationality ever anew. And thus openness to an unanticipated future is no less necessary than fidelity to the past. The Arians and Eunomians and their religious kith were, when all is said and done, the theological conservatives of their time and place; the members of the Nicene party were the daring innovators, willing to break with the past in order to preserve its spiritual force. The former were traditionalists, and for that reason their language ultimately proved sterile; the latter were theological and metaphysical radicals, and as a consequence their language gave the tradition new and enduring life.

IV

Surely there is for Christian consciousness a kind of ineradicable melancholy in all of this, and perhaps in the very fact of doctrinal definition as such. Doctrine is, in some sense—as much as it may be the poetic discovery of a shared language for speaking about God, and about God and humanity, and about the mystery of Christ—a language of disenchantment, a probationary discourse that tries at once to recuperate the force of a cosmic disruption in the form of institutional formulae and to create a stable center within history from which it may be tolerable to await a Kingdom that has been indefinitely deferred. Perhaps this is not to be lamented; one has to presume the workings of providence, to the degree that one thinks one can discern them in the midst of fallen time. Even so, Christianity entered human history, not as a new creed or sapiential path or system of religious observances, but as apocalypse: the sudden unveiling of a mystery hidden in God before the foundations of the world in a historical event without any possible precedent or any conceivable sequel; an overturning of all the orders and hierarchies of the age, here on earth and in the archon-thronged heavens above; the overthrow of all

the angelic and daemonic powers and principalities by a slave legally crucified at the behest of all the religious and political authorities of his time
but raised up by God as the one sole Lord over all the cosmos; the abolition of the partition of the Law between peoples; the proclamation of an
imminent arrival of the Kingdom and of a new age of creation; an urgent
call to all persons to come out from the shelters of social, cultic, and political association into a condition of perilous and unprotected exposure,
dwelling nowhere but in the singularity of this event—for the days are
short. It does not seem foolish to me to suspect that Christian dogma always has some quality of disappointment about it, some impulse to
anger, some sense that a creed is a strange substitute for the presence of
the Kingdom. And certainly, despite what I have said, part of the necessity of doctrinal orthodoxy in the age of the imperial church was not
simply political but truly "spiritual," for both good and ill. It was required
not just by the forces of imperial order but by the needs of an institution
that could survive the rise and dissolution of any political arrangement
as an enduring historical presence amid the flux of time. The Kingdom
did not come—not in the fashion we expected, at least, not in the time
allotted, not in the twinkling of an eye—and so the church became the
only visible, tangible form that Christian hope and expectation can now
take in this prolonged interval of indefinite delay. But then the church
must be one: what it is, what it believes, what words it speaks, what God
it invokes, what consummation it longs for—all of this must be radiantly
perspicuous if the church is really to chase away the shadows of doubt
and to provide believers with the strength to bear up under the burden
of a history of defeated expectation. This might even in some sense be
the deepest motivation prompting the notorious *odium theologicum* that
characterizes every age of Christian thought; perhaps the volatility of
theological culture has always been, at some level at least, a reflex of
fear: the dread that the truth of the gospel, exposed to the corrosive force
of ordinary time, will dissolve into the flux of an inconclusive history—
history without redemption.

It is only *by way of tradition*—as a passage through time, that is, as a
transmission, as the impartation of a gift that remains sealed, as a giving
always deferred toward a future not yet known—that the secret inner
presence *in tradition* can be made manifest at all, at least in a way that
does not immediately evaporate into the open sky of ordinary time. Only

in the ceaseless flow of its intertwining variations can the theme subtending the whole music be heard. And in part this is because whatever is imparted must be received in the mode of the recipient, with all his or her limitations and possibilities. In the end, after all, the historical and cultural contingencies of a tradition also constitute the vehicle of its passage through the ages. They are its flesh and blood in any given epoch, its necessary embodiment within the intelligible structures of concrete existence. Without those contingencies, the animating impulse of the tradition would be something less than a ghost. But, by the same token, once that vital force has moved on to assume new living configurations, the attempt unnaturally to preserve the earlier forms can produce nothing but a painted cadaver. Hence, true fidelity to whatever is most original and most final in a tradition requires a positive desire for moments of dissolution just as much as for passages of recapitulation and refrain. And the hermeneutical labor needed to understand any tradition requires disruption no less than stability, "progressive" ambition no less than "conservative" prudence, because it is only through the play of tension and resolution, stability and disintegration, that that which is most imperishable in a tradition can be fitfully perceived, or at least sensed. But, alas, there is no single formula for doing this well, or any simple method for avoiding misunderstanding. Such rules of interpretation as there are can never be more than general and rather fluid guidelines. They cannot even provide us, when we consult the witness of history, with a dependable scale of proportionality. It is quite possible (and on occasion it has happened) that even the most devout interpreter or community of interpreters, in looking back to the initial moments of the tradition and their immediate sequels and consequences, might reasonably conclude that the overwhelming preponderance of Christian history— its practices, presuppositions, civic orders, governing values, reigning pieties—has amounted to little more than a sustained apostasy from the apostolic exemplars of the church. That hidden source of the tradition's life remains a real and unyielding standard, not a majority consensus, and before its judgment even the most venerable of institutional inheritances may have to fall away. And yet, by the very same token, it remains hidden in the very act of judgment and thus can be the exclusive property of no individual or age. Anyone who arrogates to himself the power to say with absolute finality what the *one true* tradition is will invariably prove something of a fool, and usually something of a thug. But, again, to find the safe middle passage between the Scylla and Charybdis of a destructively pure originalism and a degenerate traditionalism, one must not rely on any particular method; one must instead simply attempt to practice a certain kind of hermeneutical piety. Tacit knowledge, faithful practice, humility before the testimony of the generations, prayerfulness, and any number of moral and intellectual virtues are required; but these can be cultivated only in being put into practice. In a very real sense, in fact, this is what "tradition" is when considered as a hermeneutical practice: an attitude of trusting skepticism, hesitant impetuosity; a certain critical hygiene of prudent reluctance, a certain devotion to the limitless fecundity of the tradition's initiating moment or original principle, a certain trusting surrender to a future that cannot alter what has been but that might nevertheless alter one's understanding of the past both radically and irrevocably. It is the conviction that one has truly heard a call from the realm of the transcendent, but a call that must be heard again before its meaning can be grasped or its summons obeyed; and the labor of interpretation is the diligent practice of waiting attentively in the interval, for fear otherwise of forgetting the tone and content of that first vocation.

In a sense, a tradition reveals its secrets only through moments of disruption precisely because it is itself, in its very essence, a disruption: it begins entirely as a *novum*, an unanticipated awakening to something hitherto unknown, and one that requires the entirety of history then to interpret. The wise believer cultivates hermeneutical patience before disruptions of practice or confession or self-understanding, not merely as a matter of tolerance or indulgence, but in order to be capable of a genuine attempt to recapture in the present something of the force of that initial displacement of normal expectations from which his or her tradition arose—that first event that set loose the "line of flight" to which the believer belongs. This is the only true faithfulness to the memory of an absolute beginning, without precedent: an empty tomb, say, or the voice of God heard in rolling thunder or inscribed on the wind in letters of fire. One might even say that a tradition exists only as a sustained apocalypse, a moment of pure awakening preserved as at once an ever dissolving recollection and an ever renewed surprise. And so any truly faithful hermeneutical return to the origin of a tradition is the renewal of a moment of revolution, and the very act of return is itself a kind of revolutionary venture that, ever and again, is willing to break with the conventional forms of the fleeting present in order to serve that deeper truth. What makes a tradition live is that holy thing within that can be neither seen nor touched, which dwells within a sanctuary into which the faithful cannot peer, but which demands their service nevertheless. To return to the source is to approach the veil of the Holy of Holies, to draw near once again to the presence upon the other side, even sometimes to enter in—though then only to find that the presence remains invisible, or hidden in a blaze of glory or an impenetrable cloud.

In this way, tradition sets us free. In a sense, every living tradition constitutes a sovereign apocalyptic exception to the reign of pure history, or (better) bare history: history, that is, understood as a chronicle of sheer consecutive causality, incessant eventuality as such, without term or final cause or import; the history whose only measure and meaning is death. History thus conceived, thus denuded of all the trappings of great epic or drama or dialectical process, without a secret to be disclosed or a rationale to be comprehended or a consummation to be awaited, is the ultimate prison of the rational spirit. And so—just as the reiterations and returns of ritual and liturgy displace the empty flow of time with a closed circle of "completed" time, timeless time, the living eternity of joyous repetition—so also living traditions gather up the moments for us altogether differently, rise above the ceaseless empty flow of bare history, shape all things toward a final truth, and thus displace the rule of bare history with the adventure of a coherent journey through the ages, from a remote beginning to a remote end. Tradition is in a sense the diachronic complement of ritual's periodic synchrony; it is history as always inflected by a force from outside time's continuum: history moving forward but with each of its moments bearing an oblique stress that pulls it toward something not confined to time. It is for this reason that no living tradition can be properly understood merely as a precious inheritance to be protected and curated. Even the act of reverently looking back through the past to a tradition's origin is also an act of critique, a judgment on the past that need not be a kind one, as well as an implicit act of submission to a future verdict that might be equally unkind with regard to the present, and even to a final verdict in whose light all the forms a tradition encompasses can be understood as at best provisional intimations of something ineffable and inconceivable. A tradition's life is this irrepressible apocalyptic ferment within, beckoning us simultaneously back to an immemorial past and forward to an unimaginable future. The proper moral and spiritual attitude to a tradition's formal expressions, then, is not a simple clinging to what has been received but also a relinquishing—even at times of things that had once seemed most precious: *Gelassenheit*, to use Eckhart's language, release. Only thus can one receive tradition as a liberating counterhistory, as the apocalyptic exception to bare history that promises us a higher truth than death: by remembering a first interruption, awaiting a last interruption, and attempting to sustain the theme uniting them in the interval. Only thus can one find the meaninglessness of bare history converted into a completed tale of vocation and judgment, of a call heard from far away that nevertheless summons one to a promised homeland. Perhaps, of course, the entire tale is an illusion at the end of the day, a fable we have told ourselves to carry us through the dark places of this world. Conversely, though, perhaps tradition comes to us instead as an entirely gracious invasion of history, shattering the walls of our prison: a gift awakening us (if we will listen) to the knowledge that the emptiness, the *kenoma*, of bare history is not our true home, and that our true story comes from—and must finally be told—elsewhere.

PART TWO

The Borderlands of Theology and Science

8

Where the Consonance Really Lies

I

When we ask, as some of us occasionally do, whether it is possible to discover or establish a true consonance between the modern sciences and theology, we are asking a question prompted first of all by nostalgia. We are casting a perhaps somewhat forlorn glance back, on the one hand, to a period four or five centuries ago, before any estrangement had begun to take shape between "natural philosophy" and theology, and before mechanistic models of the physical order had begun to evolve into a metaphysical naturalism; but also, on the other hand (and much more essentially), we are looking back to an almost timeless moment of innocence, at once immemorial and yet intimately known to each of us, when we were as yet unaware of any distinctions between different spheres of inquiry, let alone any dissonances among them. We all remember, without being able quite to recall it with any immediacy, the first dawn of wonder within us: that instant when the infinitely open question of everything posed itself to us all at once, but when it had not yet become a specific question about anything as such. Every attempt to know the truth of the world in later life—empirical, theoretical, hermeneutical, critical, speculative, spiritual—begins for all of us in an instant of naive surprise before the mystery of being, an unanticipated experience of the sheer fortuity and givenness of the world, a sudden fleeting moment of limpid awareness when one knows simultaneously the utter strangeness of everything familiar and the utter contingency of everything presumed.

This is that existential amazement that, as Plato and Aristotle both affirmed, first awakens us to the love of wisdom: an aboriginal summons to which, so long as we recall even the faintest shimmering trace of its uncanniness, we must remain faithful all our lives. And, at first, this primordial vocation is the same for everyone, as are the first stirrings of a response; no alienations are yet possible. But the initial moment passes, boundless possibility contracts into the actuality of a multitude of finite and divergent paths, habits of thought and decisions of the will make the luminous simplicity of the original experience ever more difficult to recollect, and at the last the mystery is lost somewhere amid the tangles of our methods and our prejudices. The day is long; the light of dawn soon fades from memory.

If we persist in asking the question long enough to allow that initial wistfulness to dissipate, however, and begin to pose it in more concrete terms, we all at once conjure up a host of ancillary questions, the most obvious of which is what precisely we think our words really mean. "Science," even more than "theology," is an abstraction, however disposed we may be today to imagine that it names a clearly defined realm of practices, comprising exact rules of method and comprehensive principles of evidence. Moreover, "modern science," in particular, is a distinct culture, with all the historical, linguistic, and conceptual conditionality that this entails; and every culture incubates within itself, even if only tacitly and tenuously, certain metaphysical presuppositions: what, for instance, constitutes reason; what the limits of knowledge are; what questions ought to be asked; which methods of inquiry should be presumed to reflect reality and which should be regarded only as useful fictions. And it is here, at the level of culture, that the truly irreconcilable conflicts between scientific and theological thinking are inevitably found; for in most circumstances it is not what we can prove but what we presuppose that determines what we think we know or imagine we have discovered. Before we can pose the question of the consonance between theology and the sciences, therefore, we must first make sure that we know what territories these cultures properly encompass, and whether there are still any to which both at once might be able to lay some legitimate claim. Otherwise we are likely to career across boundaries we do not even know exist.

For what it is worth, these days the most inept incursions and encroachments tend to come more often from the side of the sciences. Perhaps theologians have by now been sufficiently chastened by the memories of theology's past trespasses and so can see the lines of demarcation with greater clarity. At least, it would be a very poorly trained theologian indeed who produced anything as philosophically confused or as engorged with category errors as Lawrence Krauss's *A Universe from Nothing* (2013), or who exhibited a comparable ignorance of the difference between aetiological queries about our universe's origin from an antecedent physical state and modal queries about the possibility of physical existence as such—between, that is, cosmology and ontology. Nor can one imagine any serious theologian venturing interventions in the sciences as reckless as Richard Dawkins's maladroit attempts to master Thomas's *quinque viae* (at which one can only wince in pity and then look away). From whichever side the interlopers come, however, our first impulse when confronted by the conceptual disasters they perpetrate is, naturally enough, simply to reassert proper boundaries. To avoid the ghastly spectacle of Richard Dawkins attempting to philosophize, we are all too happy to adopt something like Stephen Gould's strict discrimination between two "non-overlapping magisteria," one concerned with facts, the other with values. But this achieves only the consonance of segregation—and at the cost of intolerably reductive accounts of both spheres. After all, the sciences invoke questions not only of physical origins, properties, and processes but also (even if only indirectly) of their intrinsic intelligibility, rational coherence, and even modal plausibility, which inevitably touch upon questions that classical theology asks as well. Yes, quite obviously, the physical sciences have nothing to say about *dogmatic* theology—say, Trinitarian doctrine or Chalcedonian Christology—which concern hermeneutical approaches to particular historical events, social practices, personal and communal experiences of salvation, or allegedly revealed truths. But there is also theology in the wider sense, as delineated by, say, Proclus or the Pseudo-Dionysius or Shankara or Nicholas of Cusa or Mulla Sadra, which embraces a set of logical and speculative claims about reality as a whole, and about an ultimate coincidence between its rational structure and its actual existence. And each of these claims entails still further deductive claims regarding the divine ground of all that is: that, when reduced to its deepest source or most irreducible ontological premise, nature proves to be contingent ultimately not on some material substrate or order but much more originally upon something analogous to mind, spirit, *Geist*—something, moreover, that is not simply yet another force among forces or being among beings but the infinite plenitude of both being and rational order, in which all finite things participate. And in regard to these deductions, curiously enough, the sciences are not irrelevant, even if they are in some sense only preliminary. (But I shall return to this below.)

Rather, then, than discrete magisteria absorbed in absolutely discontinuous regions of concern, it might seem better to adopt something closer to Thomas's distinction between theology and philosophy (including natural philosophy) and to say that we are concerned here with two autonomous practices of understanding, each of which encompasses vast areas of investigation concerning which the other has no competence, but which occasionally both converge upon the same area, albeit each according to its own idiom and constraints. Thus, for Thomas, both natural philosophy and theology may have a great deal to say about God (for instance), though the former might do so chiefly in terms of a Prime Mover or primary causality while the latter might do so chiefly in terms of the creator of heaven and earth or the Father of Christ. Even here, though, we risk making the issue of consonance too easy, if for no other reason than that a solution drawn from the high Middle Ages presumes a unified intellectual culture that, for better or worse, simply no longer exists. In a sense, the "scientistic" polemicist who stumbles across unseen disciplinary boundaries in an ultracrepidarian stupor is not always entirely in the wrong; there are now in fact contested territories where the dissonances are quite real. Certainly, before all else, there can be no accord reached between any theistic logic and the tacit mechanistic or physicalist or emergentist materialist metaphysics that so deeply informs much of the culture of the sciences today. And if we are seeking a consonance that consists in more than a few sporadic embassies between two otherwise alien realms, we have to interrogate precisely those cultural premises that now truly divide us. This is a rather delicate matter, naturally, because it involves a confrontation at a level that many in the sciences do not even acknowledge exists: that of their own metaphysical presuppositions. The first task, then, is to make the hidden metaphysical horizon of the modern sciences appear to view, and then perhaps to call it into question: not of course by simplistically conflating the cosmological and the ontological, as Krauss and Dawkins do, but rather by asking whether that essentially mechanistic picture of reality is adequate even to the realm of the physical. And I suspect that the best way to do this is to consider and reconsider the language of causality.

II

The extraordinary fruitfulness of modern scientific method was achieved, before all else, by a severe narrowing of investigative focus; and this involved the willful shedding of an older language of causality that possessed great richness but that also seemed to resist empirical investigation. The first principle of the new organon was a negative one: the exclusion of any consideration of formal and final causes, and even of any distinct principle of "life," in favor of an ideally inductive method purged of metaphysical prejudices, allowing all natural systems to be conceived as mere machine processes, all real causality as an exchange of energy through antecedent forces working upon material mass, and all real objectivity as the mathematical measurement of relative magnitudes. Everything physical became, in a sense, reducible to the mechanics of local motion; even complex organic order came to be understood as the emergent result of physical forces moving through time from past to future as if through Newtonian space, producing consequences that were all mathematically calculable, with all discrete physical causes ultimately reducible to the most basic level of material existence. And while, at first, many of the thinkers of early modernity were content to draw brackets around physical nature and to allow for the existence of realities beyond the physical—mind, soul, disembodied spirits, God—they necessarily imagined these latter as being essentially extrinsic to the purely mechanical order that they animated, inhabited, or created. Thus, in place of classical theism's metaphysics of participation in a God of infinite being and rationality, they granted room only for the adventitious and finite Cosmic Mechanic or Supreme Being of Deism or (as it is called today) intelligent design theory. But, of course, this ontological liberality was unsustainable. Reason abhors a dualism. Any ultimate ground of explanation must be one that unites all dimensions of being in a simpler, more conceptually parsimonious principle. Thus, inevitably, what began as method soon metastasized into a metaphysics, almost by inadvertence. For a truly scientific view of reality, it came to be believed, everything—even mind—must be reducible to one and the same mechanics of motion. Those methodological brackets that had been so helpfully drawn around the physical order now became the very shape of reality itself.

It was always something of a fantasy, of course. For one thing, even as a method, the mechanical model extends only so far. Pure induction is an impossible ideal. In the life sciences, for instance, organisms can only very rarely be investigated without any hypothetical appeals to purpose whatsoever, or without treating organic structures as intentional systems; and it is only a metaphysical prejudice that dictates that purposive language is no more than a useful and dispensable fiction. Moreover, before "higher causes" like form and finality could be excised from the grammar of the sciences, they had first to be radically misconstrued. Even such residual Aristotelian terminology as remained in the sciences had already, by the late sixteenth century, been mechanized, so to speak. One need only read Francis Bacon to confirm this. Form and finality had come to be seen as physical forces or influences extrinsic to a material substrate that in itself was not the pure potentiality of prime matter but merely a universal, subtle, ductile, unarticulated physical substance. The elements of nature were not imagined, as they had been in the classical and mediaeval synthesis, as having an intrinsic disposition toward order or vital integrity; they were seen simply as inert ingredients upon which formal determinations were adventitiously impressed, under the external guidance of final causes that operated merely as factitious designs. And so, seen thus, form and finality soon came to seem not only superfluous suppositions but little more than features of an inferior and obsolete mechanical model.

But, of course, one cannot really reject something one does not understand. Neither Aristotle's concept of an *aition* nor any Scholastic concept of a *causa* actually corresponds to what we—following our early modern predecessors—mean when we speak of a "cause." A better rendering of *aitia* or *causae*, in the ancient or mediaeval sense, might be "explanations," "rationales," "logical descriptions," or (still better) "rational relations." The older fourfold nexus of causality was not, that is to say, a defective attempt at modern physical science but instead chiefly a grammar of predication, describing the inherent logical structure of anything that exists insofar as it exists, and reflecting a world in which things and events are at once discretely identifiable and yet part of the larger dynamic continuum of the whole. It was a simple logical picture of a reality in which both stability and change can be recognized and described. And these *aitia* or *causae* were intrinsic and indiscerptibly integral relations, distinct dimensions of a single causal logic, not separated forces in only accidental alliance. A final cause, for instance, was an inherent natural end, not an extrinsically imposed design; and this was true even when teleology involved external uses rather than merely internal perfections (as in the case of human artifacts); it was at once a thing's intrinsic fullness and its external participation in the totality of nature. Thus, in the *Liber de causis* (that mysterious digest and theological synthesis of the metaphysics of Proclus that entered Western Scholasticism from the Islamic philosophical world), one of the principal "causes" of any isolated substance is the taxonomic category in which that thing subsists, the more "eminent" rational structure to which it belongs. In a sense, a causal *relation* in this scheme is less like a physical interaction or exchange of energy than it is like a mathematical equation, or like the syntax of a coherent sentence. Admittedly, this is a picture of reality that comes from ages in which it was assumed that the structure of the world was analogous to the structure of rational thought. But, then again, this was an eminently logical assumption—if only because there appears to be a more than illusory or accidental reciprocal openness between mind and world, and because the mind appears genuinely able to penetrate the physical order by way of irreducibly noetic practices like mathematics and logic.

In any event, perhaps it really was necessary to impose the discipline of this impoverished causal language upon the scientific intellect, if only to direct its attention to the finest and humblest of empirical details. But even so, as Hegel so brilliantly demonstrated, one can never really reason purely from the particular. Once the notion of causality has been reduced from an integral system of rationales to a single kind of local physical efficiency, it becomes a mere brute fact, something of a logical black box; description flourishes, but only because explanation has been left to wither. So it was that Hume, having seen the spectral causal agencies of the Schoolmen chased away, found causality itself now to be imponderable, logically reducible to nothing but an arbitrary sequence of regular phenomenal juxtapositions; even mathematical descriptions of events now became nothing more than reiterations of an episodic narrative without clear logical necessity. And this is indeed where we remain. Wherever induction fails to provide us with a clear physicalist narrative for especially complex or exceptional phenomena (like life or consciousness), we now must simply *presume* the existence and force of physico-mechanical laws sufficient to account for the emergence of such phenomena; and we must, moreover, do so no less casually and vaguely than those Schoolmen of old supposedly presumed "obscure" or "occult" formal and final causes. We are no less dogmatic than our ancestors; we merely have fewer clear reasons for the dogmas we embrace. The older physical logic was coherent, though speculative; the newer is incoherent, though empirical. When mechanistic method became a metaphysics, and the tinted filter through which it viewed nature was mistaken for an unveiling of nature's deepest principles, all explanations became tales of emergence, even in cases of realities—life, consciousness, even existence itself—where such tales seemed difficult to distinguish from stories of magic.

III

Nowhere is the essential arbitrariness of this picture of reality more obvious than in the alleged principle of the "causal closure of the physical," which is so often invoked as a scientifically established truth (on the rather thin basis of the fixed proportionality of matter and energy in the universe), but which is merely a metaphysical dogma, and one that even otherwise sophisticated theorists often translate into the crudest kind of physical determinism. I have known learned physicists who still talk as if—at least, once reality passes over the threshold of quantum decoherence—something like Laplace's fantasy holds true: a demon of superlative intelligence, knowing at a given instant the precise location and momentum of every atomic particle in existence, could both reconstruct the entire physical history of the universe and foresee its entire future. True, these physicists might all have granted that statistical thermodynamics probably dictates that this would not be literally possible; but still they spoke as if, in principle, all events at higher levels of physical organization must be reducible—without remainder—to lower, more particulate causal moments. Hence, if our demon could somehow account for irreversibility or quantum indeterminacies—maybe by a perfect grasp of maximum entropy thermodynamics or by an occult knowledge of quantum hidden variables—he could, from the dispositions of all the atoms and molecules composing me and my environment last Wednesday at noon, have infallibly predicted my presence here today, because everything we do is the inevitable macroscopic result of the ensemble of impersonal physical forces underlying our formal existence.

And yet we know this to be false. This is the special absurdity of allowing an artificial method appropriate to an isolated facet of reality—nature considered as a machine, which is to say nature considered as though devoid of anything analogous to purposive intellect—to hypertrophy into a universal judgment on all of reality, including those of its aspects—such as, obviously, those instances of purposive intellect that actually exist—to which such a method cannot possibly apply. To whatever degree I am a physical system, I am also an intentional "system" whose mental events take the forms of semeiotic (symbolic, interpretive) determinations, and whose actions are usually the consequences of intentions that are irreducibly teleological. As such, these intentions could appear nowhere within a reductive account of the discrete processes that constitute my actions as physical events; for final causes are not visible within any inventory of the impersonal antecedent physical events composing me. Simply said, I have reasons for being here, and reasons are qualitatively unlike mechanical forces, even when inseparably allied to them. Any good phenomenological description of my choice to be here would be one that could never be collapsed into a physical description of atomic, molecular, or even brain events. Yes, of course, at the level of the exchanges of matter and energy—or of their interchangeable mathematical values—the natural order may always have to even out into an inflexible equation. But the movement of those material and energetic forces is also directed by causal (or rational) relations of a different kind, which impose upon the flow of physical events formal and final determinations that are not merely the phenomenal residue of those events, and that are not visible to those aforementioned physical inventories. The obvious physicalist riposte to this, of course, is to claim that all intentionality is in some sense illusory, or reducible to complex electrochemical brain events, which are in turn reducible to molecular description, and then to atomic description, and so on. But that too is obviously false. Not that I have the time here to argue the point comprehensively (even if I thought it necessary). I will simply note that, over the past few years of my research in philosophy and science of mind, I have become more than convinced that every attempt to fit mental phenomena—qualitative consciousness, unity of apprehension, intentionality, reasoning, and so forth—into a physicalist narrative must prove a total failure. If nothing else, mental intentionality—in the full philosophical sense not only of determinations of the will but of every act of the mind in orienting itself toward specific ends, meanings, aspects of reality, and so on—is clearly a part of nature, and yet one whose irreducibly teleological structure is entirely contrary to the mechanical picture. This is why, among devout philosophical physicalists, such wild extremes as eliminativism and materialist panpsychism (with or without the supplement of the currently fashionable pseudoscience of "integrated information theory") are ever more in vogue. The mental, it turns out, is no more reconcilable to the modern picture of material nature than it was in Descartes's day.

Nor need we confine ourselves to the realm of the mental to call the mechanistic picture into question. It may well be that a conception of causality richer than what materialist orthodoxy can provide will ultimately prove just as necessary for molecular and evolutionary biology. At least, this is where a more diverse causal language seems constantly to be attempting to assert itself—top-down causation, circular causality, epigenetic information, symbiogenesis, teleonomy, convergent evolution, systems biology—even as traditional genetocentric neo-Darwinism strives to contain that language within its more linear narrative. And this is not simply on account of the failure of the human genome project to yield the master key to the entire mystery of life, from protein-folding to my love of Glenn Gould or Ella Fitzgerald. Life appears to be structurally hierarchical not only because evolution is a cumulative process, in which more complex levels are gradually superimposed upon lower, self-sufficient levels, but because every discrete organism possesses a causal architecture in which there can be no single privileged level of causation; each level depends on levels both above and below it, and none of these levels can be intelligibly isolated from the others as a kind of causal "base." At least, such is the contention of Denis Noble, perhaps the subtlest champion of systems biology or (as he also calls it) "biological relativity." Maybe there was a time when one could innocently think in terms of a master ground or center of life, with the DNA molecule as the primordial genetic repository of information (whatever that means). And perhaps it seemed to make sense to understand life in terms of a very simple dichotomy between replicators and vehicles (those clever selfish genes and the organic "robots" they program for their survival). Now though, argues Noble, we can scarcely even define a gene, let alone identify any genetic explanation of the entirety of living systems; nor can we ignore the degree to which DNA sequences are passive causes, variously informed and given expression as determined by the organism and its environment. And for Noble there is a special kind of beauty in the exquisite complexity of organic life; he positively delights in the interdependent simultaneity of all of life's functions, the way in which each level at once assembles the components of an immediately lower level while itself constituting a component of an immediately higher level: atoms, molecules, networks, organelles, cells, tissues, organs, holosomatic systems, complete organisms, populations, species, clades, the physical environment . . . He even, daringly enough, talks freely of natural teleology—in part because he understands that such teleology, properly understood, is an intrinsic rational determination within a complex system, not a factitious purpose extrinsically imposed by some detached designing intelligence, but in larger part because there clearly are levels of explanation at which purpose constitutes not just an illusory epiphenomenon of inherently purposeless material processes but a real causal power. An organ, no matter how stochastic its phylogenic history, exists within an organism *because* of the purpose it serves, apart from which it would not exist. And these levels are not reducible to one another but exist only as a totality. Within the hierarchy of relations, there may be discrete levels of organization but no independent causal functions. The entire structure is a profoundly logical and purposive whole.

Now, maybe this intentional structure somehow emerges— biochemically and phylogenically—from very primitive causes, which then become ingredients in a recursive system of interactions that were originally random or chaotic, and is therefore still reducible to a state prior to "purpose." But, unless we are using the word *emergence* as a synonym for *miracle* or *magic*, we are still obliged to assume that the formal determinations of organic complexity—or, as we now call it, their "information"—are already present in those causes in at least latent or virtual form, awaiting explication in developed phenotypes (and other "molar" forms); and so we are also obliged to assume that whatever rational relations may exist in organisms (including form and finality) are already present in those seemingly random states. That is to say, we need not assume that, prior to the complex unity of a living system, some extrinsic "design" existed within its material substrate like a kind of algorithm programmed by an intelligent designer; but we cannot doubt that everything that enters into the structure of a living system is already constituted by those rational causal relations that allow discrete purposive systems to arise. Even if we cannot say how life began, or how self-replicating organisms became available for natural selection, we can certainly doubt that those "higher" causal relations are accidental accretions upon some single isolated aspect of their relations. Irreducible emergence is a logical nonsense; whatever properties appear in an effect, unless imposed adventitiously, are already implicit in its "lower" causes, even if only in a kind of virtual state. Perhaps even matter, then, in its barest constitution, already has something of the character of mind.

Even Noble, I should note, does not appreciate quite how radical the consequences of a hierarchical view of life might prove. At one point in his book *Dance to the Music of Life*, he invokes the old experiment of placing, say, a dozen metronomes on a wooden table and setting each in motion independently; over time, the initially asynchronous oscillations of the metronomes will become perfectly synchronized, solely as the result of the chaotic interactions of the vibrations passing between them through the resonant material of the table. This, he argues, is a splendid example of an "initial disorder becoming highly ordered by interaction." But this is wrong. Actually, it is a case of an initial complexity, stochastically but intricately syncopated, reduced over time to uniformity—which is to say, maximal equilibrium achieved by subsidence to a minimal expenditure of energy. This is not the emergence of order, but a descent into an entropic state, which preserves only such order as it cannot entirely eliminate (though in time, if left undisturbed, even this order will vanish, as table and metronomes alike resolve into dust). To fit the picture that Noble's account of life adumbrates, the oscillations of the metronomes would have to arrive not at perfect synchrony but at something like the contrapuntal intricacies of a Buddy Rich cadenza or of Javanese and Balinese gamelan.

Then again, perhaps one need not look either to molecular and evolutionary biology or to the phenomena of mental life to see that the mechanical model of nature is defective. Really, perhaps, it is enough simply to consider the seemingly indivisible relation that exists between them in the very encounter between nature and mind: the intelligibility of the world and the power of thought to lay hold of it. Perhaps all we need consider is how it is that the inherently formal and intentional structure of rational thought seems to correspond so fruitfully to the rational structure of the world. This by itself invites us to reconsider something at least like causal language proposed in Aristotelian tradition, in which (again) nature's deepest rational relations are more like the syntax of a sentence or mathematical equations than like mere accidental concrescences of physical forces. Perhaps modern prejudice has the matter backwards; perhaps it is mechanism that should be regarded as the dispensable methodological fiction, while the purposive language we use to isolate specific organic functions is a true reflection of reality. Perhaps mechanistic models never were anything more than artificial constraints, by which discrete processes might be prescinded from a whole that, in itself, has something like the structure of intentional thought. After all, it is absurd to think that a model created by the willful exclusion of all mental properties from our picture of nature could then be used to account for the mental itself; and yet the mental is quite real, and quite at home within the natural order. If, then, one presumes a reductively physicalist model of all reality but is then confronted by *any aspect* of nature that, as in the case of consciousness or intentionality, proves utterly resistant to mechanical description, the only responsible course of action is to abandon or suspend the model in regard to the *whole* of nature. If the phenomenon cannot be eliminated, the model is false.

Nor can we stop there. Once again, a certain principle of logical parsimony asserts itself here and then invites or even obliges us completely to reverse our original supposition. Reason abhors a dualism, as I have said; ideally all phenomena should be reducible to a single, simpler, more capacious model of reality. Far from continuing to banish mind from our picture of nature, then, perhaps we should reconsider the ancient intuition that nature and mind are not alien to one another precisely because nature already possesses a rational structure analogous to thought. Perhaps the ground of the possibility of regular physical causation, in the energetic and mechanical sense, is a deeper logical coinherence of rational relations underlying all reality; and hence mind inhabits physical nature not as an anomaly but as a revelation of the deepest essence of everything that exists. The intentionality of mind then is neither a ghostly agency inexplicably haunting a machine nor an illusion reducible to nonintentional and impersonal forces but instead the most intense and luminous expression of those formal and teleological determinations that give actuality to all nature. What makes us believe we should—or, for that matter, can—think otherwise?

IV

What difference might all this make for the sciences, practically speaking? Little or none, really. The sciences need not aspire to total exhaustive explanation; they are often most powerful when they consist largely in local and narrow investigations, and then in theoretical interpretations of very particular discoveries. For the *culture* of the sciences, however, as well as for a true consonance (rather than a mere amicable segregation) between the sciences and theology, it could scarcely be more consequential. For one thing, it is always a salubrious hygiene to be reminded of the limits of our methods; and, for anyone committed to the search for truth, it is always wise to think about the universal frame of reality within which one's investigations take place. If one does this, one may approach a place where both the deepest aspirations of the sciences and the most essential affirmations of theology prove to be irresistibly apposite. When we think seriously about the complex rational structure of reality and the way in which it seems to be reflected in the structure of rational mind, we enter the realm of spirit, of intellect, of a formal and final logic in nature already analogous to mind or rational thought. Perhaps only for this reason can the veil of Isis be lifted and nature be revealed to mind, and perhaps it is also only for this reason that mind can inhabit nature. Here the physical sciences themselves urge us toward a certain metaphysical supposition. It may be that, pursued to its logical terminus, the very enterprise of scientific reasoning suggests or even secretly presumes that the being of the world—the ontological horizon within which it takes shape and exists—is something like an act of thought. Here the

questions of science and those of theology converge upon the same mysteries, not through some maladroit confusion of two incompatible kinds
of causal narrative (the cosmological and the ontological, say), but quite
naturally, because the very concept of causality still demands for itself the
full richness of all its possible logical acceptations. No physical science
can answer or explain away the mysteries that here come into view; neither can any theology; but both would do well to recognize the threshold
upon which they stand.

All the labors of the scientific intellect are undertaken within the
embrace of a structure of intelligibility that the sciences need not pretend
to understand, penetrate, or encompass but that nevertheless sustains
them in all their labors. That intelligibility is the transcendental horizon
toward which they necessarily strive, even when they hew faithfully to the
limits of their proper remit. It shows itself to be nothing other than that
original experience of the radiant mystery of being that first awakens the
desire for truth, but now translated into a fixed orientation of the rational
will. The sciences venture all their energies upon the reality of this ultimate rational intelligibility—upon the wager that the world's being and
its structure of rational order are one and the same event. Thus they undertake their perpetual journey toward an end that perhaps, in principle,
they cannot reach: to disclose a perfect reciprocal transparency between
mind and world, and hence an ultimate reality where existence and perfect intelligibility are convertible with one another because both subsist
in a single unrestricted act of spiritual intelligence. This, in theological
terms, is one of the paths of the mind's journey into God. And this is also,
at least in its ultimate intentions, a place where the consonance of scientific and theological reasoning is restored, on the far side of a provisional
separation that at times has become an alienation. Both pursuits set out
originally upon their different paths from the same innocent instant of
existential amazement, and both together end, after all their several pere-
grinations, at a place where description fails, but where that primordial
wonder finds its final consummation in wisdom: the threshold of that
mystery—the cause of causes, the explanation of explanations, the holy
of holies—toward which both are forever turned. And, however different
the paths by which they have reached this sanctuary, each approaches it
at the end ideally not as a stranger in a far country but as a pilgrim entering a long-sought holy land.

9

Should Science Think?

I

My purpose here today is not so much to advance an argument as to contemplate a situation—one historical moment within the evolution of science, along with one metaphysical question that seems inevitably to pose itself the more inexorably the sciences find themselves constrained rather than liberated by the mechanistic paradigm that, for centuries now, has reigned either as an explicit methodological remit or as an implicit metaphysical commitment in the culture of modern science. And, given the occasion of this conference, I have chosen for purely eponymous reasons to allow my reflections to take shape in relation to Jacques Maritain's understanding of the degrees of knowledge, as unfolded principally in three works: *Distinguer pour unir: Ou, les degrès du savoir* (1932), *Quatre essais sur l'esprit* (1939), and *Raison et raisons, essais détachés* (1948)—or, as it is known in English, *The Range of Reason*. This is not, however, an essay on Maritain as such; call it an instance of "thinking with" rather than "thinking about."

Moreover, the title of this talk is prompted by another and very different philosopher: Martin Heidegger. It was he who notoriously, in *Was Heißt Denken?*, proposed the somewhat impertinent and Orphic claim that "Die Wissenschaft denkt nicht"—science does not think—and who in his essay "Wissenschaft und Besinnung" drew an absolutely inviolable demarcation between the calculative and quantitative cogitations of science, on the one hand, and the properly philosophical or "thoughtful" activity of reflection or contemplation, on the other. Supposedly, Heidegger's is a claim that entails no opprobrium; it merely delineates discrete spheres of operation. In Heidegger's distinctive usage, you see, *Denken*—thinking—is understood specifically as the act of meditating upon the difference between Being and beings, and upon Being as such. The sciences are, of their nature, limited to quantitative investigations of the physical realm—scrupulously so—and so must not concern themselves with the *being* of the physical realm and must never imagine that they are competent to do so. Calculative thought is representational, so thoroughly so that it cannot even pause to reflect meaningfully upon the nature of representation as such. Even at their most theoretical, the sciences cannot pass beyond the bounds of a quantitative description of phenomena. "Physics as physics can make no assertion about physics," Heidegger tells us in "Wissenschaft und Besinnung," and the *Kluft*—the gulf—between calculation and genuinely contemplative thought is so vast that, from the vantage of the latter, the former scarcely qualifies as thinking at all. Again, no denigration of the sciences is intended, we are assured; but, of course, as is ever the case with Heidegger, the partitions he erects between philosophy and other spheres of inquiry tend to resist trespass from only one direction: the sciences cannot aspire to philosophy, he insists, but philosophy possesses—even if only by metaphysical inadvertence—a necessary power for determining the nature, problems, and limits of science. Modern science relies upon a certain metaphysical picture, he tells us, that of the *Ge-Stell*, of presentation and representation, which reduces the world to a collection of objects set before a subject, with no medium of ontological participation between them. Ours is the age of the world picture, and the sciences as we know them could not have come into existence, or accomplished such prodigies of discovery, invention, and destruction, apart from this essential set of metaphysical prejudices. None of this becomes a problem unless the sciences, not understanding how exiguous the scope of their speculative competency really is, attempt to expand their questioning into realms of thought to which they have no true access or attempt to exclude from their investigations the fuller dimensions of true thinking, which only philosophy can provide and apart from which all real *understanding* becomes impossible.

I should say up front that I am disposed to accept Heidegger's distinction almost entirely, but only out of spite. In part this is because it seems to accord so well with common experience. After all, everyone here could easily name several scientists who in recent years have attempted to enter into philosophical debate, chiefly on whether or not there is a God—Dawkins, Hawking, Stenger, Krauss, Coyne, and so on— and accomplished nothing more than to demonstrate that, whatever their varying degrees of proficiency in their particular fields might be, none of them could reason his way to the end of a simple syllogism without getting lost in the weeds by the side of the path. That one possesses the sort of calculative gifts necessary for scientific work clearly in no way entails that one possesses any gift for abstract logic. More charitably, however, I think that Heidegger's distinction does no more in the end than take science at its word, at least as it pledged its troth at the dawn of the modern scientific epoch. This, in fact, is arguably the foundational myth of modern science: that it is a chastely inductive discipline, which prescinds from all metaphysical commitments or presuppositions, and which especially refuses to consider the possibility of any kind of causal finality or purpose in nature, and instead presumes only a world of mechanically composed and mechanically interrelated objects of cognition. Modern science was born in a proud and defiant rejection of thinking.

II

Of course, as Maritain (for instance) understood with some acuity, the ideal is a quixotic one. Pure induction is a fantasy, an impossible task. And this for two reasons.

First, the methodological bracketing of finality and form has always been a custom more honored in the breach then in the observance. Even the simplest of investigations must begin within the context of an immense number of formal and purposive expectations. Forms, of course, prove indispensable: even the life sciences, when trying to dissolve organisms into particulate genetics and code, find themselves constrained by the hierarchical nature of organic life. As sedulously as they strive to establish a basis of life that is pure molecular chemistry, founded wholly upon physics, they find themselves thwarted by the seeming impossibility of reconstructing the formal complexity and reproductive power of life starting entirely from a molecular chemical basis. As yet there is no way of moving, for instance, from some supposed substrate of pure genetic information to the organic totality into which genetic materials are assumed. Gene expression is largely determined by organic systems and ecologies; it is not produced by a master code somehow spontaneously generated by chemical processes. To a happy vitalist like myself (or whatever it is that I am), this is no embarrassment; to a rapt devotee of the mechanical philosophy, it should be the greatest of scandals. And then, in addition to this consideration, there is the further consideration that teleology is methodologically inevitable. Biologists find more often than not that the best way to understand the objects of their scrutiny is to treat them as intentional systems. Inductive experiment is almost always already determined deductively by the question: What is this for? And it is as much a matter of dogma as of scientific scruple that the biologist then assumes that this is only a methodological convenience, a fiction that bears fruit more or less by accident.

Second, then, this assumption cannot logically be in any sense truly scientific; it is *only* metaphysical. It is—as Bacon and Leibniz both, with the charming naïveté of obtuse consciences, explicitly recognized—a necessary element within the project of transforming knowledge into power over nature. And the will to power, of its nature, is insatiable and demands absolute prerogatives for itself. Every form of reductive naturalism—which is to say, *all* true naturalism as such—is a sheerly metaphysical decision, whose relation to the practice of the sciences is arbitrary, suppositious, and ultimately ideological rather than probative.

III

Now, of course, naturalism might be a plausible metaphysical proposition, if only the universe did not actually exist. Unfortunately, it appears to be doing just that, which means that, before any other statement that might be made about the natural order, we are confronted with a truth that cannot be reduced to a natural explanation: the existence of nature. And, so long as there is a single fact that is *more than* or *other than* or *transcendent of* purely natural explanations, naturalism is false in its entirety. Moreover, naturalism is not even an intelligible position if it is not at some level convertible with the metaphysics of mechanism. This is a problem, however, since the mechanical philosophy never was anything more than a project for understanding nature *as if* it were a reality devoid of any mental dimension, and therefore a reality in which the products of consciousness—*qualia*, purpose, and so on—have no causal role to play. Yet naturalism, as a metaphysics, demands that finally nothing, not even consciousness, be excluded from the mechanical paradigm, even though there is no plausible means of accounting for consciousness within a vision of things from which consciousness has already been systematically eliminated as a matter of methodological principle. We see the consequences of this contradiction richly displayed in the current state of philosophy of mind. In the end, the naturalist project leads to absurdities like total materialist eliminativism, despite their logical incoherence, as a simple matter of logical inevitability. *Qualia*, intentionality, in short the whole orientation of the self toward the world and the whole transparency of the world to the self—by which alone the world is known to us, and by which alone we have a world—remains irreducible to physical causes. And so great is the qualitative difference between the subjective ground of consciousness and the objective realm of mechanical events (which is all a mechanistic method is capable of investigating) that no causal narrative seamlessly uniting the two could ever be produced. Moreover, of course, the world is known to consciousness only within the embrace of the transcendental ecstasies of the mind toward absolute ends: the good, the true, the beautiful (to name a few favorites); and this means that every act of the mind is not only teleological but teleologically contingent upon objects of intention entirely outside the physical order. Mind simply will not fit into the larger picture. And I could dilate upon these arguments at intolerable length if I wished. But all I want to say here is that naturalism is not so much a false view of reality as an utterly vacuous one; it is all but impossible to define what nature, as a self-sufficient reality, could possibly be. *Natura pura non invenitur.*

IV

Does any of that matter? Granted, it is a mistake for scientists to confuse their methodological commitments for a comprehensive metaphysical picture of reality; but, within the realm of genuine research, the method need not be questioned, surely. The sciences progress best when, in regard to the larger picture of reality that they have bracketed out, they remain chastely incurious. From Newton's ascetical *"Hypotheses non fingo"* and Laplace's brusquely and beautifully impious "We have no need of that hypothesis" to Niels Bohr's formulation of the standard Copenhagen interpretation of quantum mechanics, the true philosophical stance of the modern sciences has been that of a radical pragmatism. If one's inventories of physical objects and events, along with one's theoretical interpretation of those objects and events, together yield accurate predictions, then all that need be accomplished *is* accomplished. If we understand scientific knowledge to be the possession of a method that yields practical power, as is the Baconian tradition, then we need look no further than immediate results. Science must concern itself not with truth but with facts only, which is to say with what works. It need not be—in fact, it must not be—a Platonic contemplation of the hyperouranian splendors and divine ideals. Those are at best distractions from our experiments. So Heidegger is correct, it would seem: science should only calculate and compile; it ought not to *think* at all. This is, as it were, written into the very manifesto of the modern sciences as such.

Conversely, and confidentially, those of us who dabble in metaphysics then have no need to take much notice of the sciences; all we ask of the representatives of the science is that they remember what it is they are *not* doing. An inviolable partition may be erected between the two spheres of inquiry, both tribes may pursue their several gods, all will be bliss. Here, though, it seems to me worthwhile to ask a simple speculative question. I do not presume to know if it touches upon a likely contingency, though I strongly suspect it does. In fact, I suspect that I am asking it rather late in the day. And it is a practical question. Leaving the morality of the Baconian perspective entirely aside, what if it were the case that the method of sciences—pursued as it must be, unthinkingly—were to bring the scientist into confrontation with a conundrum that was entirely unanswerable, and even imponderable, apart from a revision of assumptions so basic, pervasive, and encompassing that they could only be considered metaphysical? Is it possible, within the paradigm of the sciences as we know them, that we can encounter contradictions that we cannot get past except through a radical reconfiguration of our expectations of reality itself? Or, more simply, what if the tacit mechanistic metaphysics to which the sciences, appropriately or not, are bound should become an impediment to the deeper knowledge that is adumbrated in our investigation by the discovery of such contradictions? This is how, according to Michael Polanyi and (more crudely) Thomas Kuhn, one scientific regime yields to another: A sufficient number of problems that the reigning paradigm cannot resolve accumulate, and at some inevitable point the paradigm shifts globally, comprehensively—perhaps metaphysically.

Now, let me emphasize again that this is something of a thought experiment. I am not presuming that the example I provide is a good one; what I am asking is whether or not the modern sciences, determined as they are by so unyielding a materialist metaphysics, would even be capable of recognizing the possibility of such a transition. If they had to, *could* they think? Does that remain a possibility for them? What if— again, this is purely speculative—the mechanistic assumption governing the life sciences—the presupposition that life is simply a fortuitous arrangement of intrinsically dead elements, functioning as a totality on account of a purely mechanical ordering of its parts—should continue to prove fruitless as an explanation of life, and especially of life capable of reproducing itself? What if life, as opposed to the mere physical components of the organic structure, cannot be reduced to inert chemical ingredients and then reconstructed again from those ingredients without invoking some other kind of causality to organize and animate them? I am not talking, incidentally, about something like intelligent design theory, which is merely the unwelcome recrudescence of an older version of the mechanistic philosophy; intelligent design theory consists in nothing more interesting than the claim that the machine is far more complex than we had previously understood, and that therefore a mechanic may have been involved in its construction. That need detain no one, because it does not alter the paradigm one whit; the materialist is challenged not to abandon his materialist presuppositions but merely to consider the possibility of an additional mechanical cause, one that will probably prove utterly dispensable in the long term. If a living organism really is nothing but a mechanistic arrangement of dead elements, then in the end it remains logically possible that any alleged mechanic will be explained away by some other physical cause or set of causes, and the scientist remains free to suspend judgment—forever. I am speaking of something far more fundamental: What if the essentially hierarchical nature of organic life is ultimate? What if the mechanistic paradigm is wrong from the beginning, and something suspiciously like a new vitalism or Aristotelianism or something equally "metaphysical" is required to understand the organizing principle of life capable of reproduction? What if there are no machines in nature, what if there is no such thing as dead matter, and what if life cannot be understood apart from the postulate of some sort of formal causality and some kind of directedness to an end? If indeed, as certain kinds of systems biology and certain schools of epigenetics already seem to suggest, the hierarchical nature of life is irreducible to a purely unilateral, purely ascending chemical mechanism, it may in the end prove impossible to avoid thinking of organisms also in terms of a certain causation "from above": perhaps, the "information" inscribed in genes (if that metaphor is still even useful) is not the residue of a mechanical process but is instead inseparable from life understood as a formal cause that assumes material causes into itself.

My question is not whether this is true but instead whether, if it were true, the sciences as currently constituted could think about it. The answer is "probably not": by virtue of the method that almost all the modern sciences presume, no medium, no scientific regime or protocol, exists by which the question could be investigated. At best, we might hope for a progressive confirmation of life's hierarchical structure, over which a pall of abysmal mystery would be left to hover forever; but no more than that. The mechanistic philosophy's renunciation of thinking, for the sake of induction, is a potentially infinite path of departure; it is no longer merely a matter of method but one of piety, and necessarily so: a vocation, a commitment of will and mind, a destiny. At the boundaries of the paradigm, the sciences reach a limit, both imaginative and empirical. Within those boundaries, they can continue to *accumulate* facts— that is to say, engage in a cumulative process, continuous but in some sense recursive—but they cannot interpret. Within the enclosure of those walls, they are at liberty; but beyond those walls lies the realm of the metaphysical, from which they have exiled themselves. They neither desire to pass beyond walls nor even know how it might be done if they should so desire.

At least, that is how it appears.

V

Perhaps this poses no practical problems. The question remains, how-ever, of whether the theoretical structure of the sciences really must re-main immovably fixed at that physical and epistemological rampart, and whether it should. Perhaps the question becomes more acute when one shifts one's attention from biology to physics. After all, for nearly nine decades now we have been roving the boundary regions between the clas-sical Newtonian universe and the surreal quantum universe without finding any place of repose. For those who have not heard the news, even after all this time, we know that the Newtonian and Einsteinian space-time that we all inhabit rests upon a foundation of purely potential physical functions, which may in fact never resolve themselves into the dimensions and regularities of classical space apart from the presence of consciousness. It often strikes me as strange that the champions of physicalism, at least in popular debate, show such passion for a mecha-nistic view of nature so long after the discovery that even the mechanical rules of locality, the unsurpassable constant speed of light, particulate identity, and mechanical separability have had to yield their authority to a picture of the universe that may make room for quantum superposi-tion, quantum entanglement, *spukhafte Fernwirkung*, and so on—or, no less mysterious, an infinite variety of parallel realities constantly distin-guishing themselves from one another in every instant. The conundrum, for instance, of the particle-wave duality (or, in Heisenberg's terms, the simultaneity of the corpuscular and undular models of matter) is one whose implications far exceed mere matters of detail within an other-wise plausible mechanistic narrative. Indeed, the vindication of Bell's theorem has demonstrated that quantum entanglement is not the illu-sory residue of hidden variables—separability may really not be there at the quantum level, and perhaps the reality of quantum objects is itself the illusion—and without separability mechanical causation cannot ex-plain the phenomena.

Let me pause for a small excursus here, for the sake of those who may not have heard: what the double-slit experiment established is that prior to any observation of the location of a particle it is possible to run an interference experiment. That is, a stream of, say, photons passing through two parallel slits will produce interference patterns on a photoreceptive surface; moreover, this happens even if the photons pass through the slits one at a time and therefore cannot interfere with one another, which means that the particles themselves, which leave their traces upon that photoreceptive surface, are also a wave function. This means that each particle at once must pass through both slits and neither, and through both one slit and the other. When, however, an observation is made of the photons before they pass through the slits, the interference disappears: because it is "watched," some think, the particle—for now it is entirely corpuscular in function as an observable object—passes through only one particular slit and leaves only a particulate impression. Stranger still, if observation is made between the slit and the photoreceptive surface, the wave function still seems to collapse, which means that the act of conscious observation appears retroactively to create the past history of the photon. And variations and elaborations of this experiment have been performed countless times. And, notoriously perhaps, with the determination of any particle comes the instantaneous determination of any other with which it has become entangled, even if the distance separating them is as great as the universe; what then of the laws of relativity?

Now, within the classic Copenhagen interpretation, it is simply accepted that the wave function collapses as the result of observation. The implication of this is that consciousness somehow stands outside the physical continuum of the potentiality wave, and that therefore it induces the collapse, which—if it is true—all at once does away with the postulate of a purely physical basis for consciousness, and with it the philosophical foundations of materialism. Eugene Wigner pointed this out with exemplary clarity long ago. And few if any of the many theoretical attempts to make sense of the phenomenon of the wave function's collapse have perfectly succeeded in removing consciousness, as an adventitious principle, from the picture. Most do not bother to try. Aage Bohr and Ole Ulfbeck have extended Copenhagen's rule of theoretical asceticism to the point of a benign ontological nihilism. For them, the quantum world of particles has no existence at all; there are, as far as the scientist is concerned, no such things as atoms moving in space, and it is a relic of Newtonian mechanics that we continue to rely upon such imagery. There are only the measurements themselves—the click of a

Geiger counter, say—and any additional supposition of particles causing the measurements is superfluous. The Ithaca interpretation, on the other hand—which says that there is a physical reality only to the correlations between entangled events or terms, and not to the things correlated—also leaves the seemingly sovereign role of consciousness in inducing the wave function collapse unchallenged. Successful theories of quantum decoherence may establish the thermodynamical boundary between the quantum and classical realms and may confirm that different parts of a single system go out of phase with one another as a result of an encounter with a macroscopic environment, but they still explain only the appearance of a collapse of the wave function; they do not account for the actual phenomenon of the instantaneous collapse induced by observation or dispose of the wave function itself, which till it collapses remains a superposition state of possible conscious observations.

As for many-worlds or many-minds models, which reject the collapse of the wave function altogether, and according to which the act of observation simply brings the observer into entanglement with the superposition state of the quantum system under observation (thus creating a plurality of parallel observations), they may do away with the paradox of entanglement producing instantaneous and so superluminal effects, but they too may not banish the question of consciousness: as W. H. Zurek has observed, since we do not perceive (any longer) a consistent superposition of alternatives but see only one determinate reality surrounded by numberless alternatives. So when, where, how is it determined what the observer records? A unified consciousness is at work, perceiving a unified result without a wave function, a corpuscular rather than undular result. And so somewhere, somehow, there is a unique perspective that is consciousness, wherein the world of experience exists and has its ontological ground. This may extend the boundaries of the wave function all the way to the realm of consciousness, but it does not explain consciousness away. If anything, it still may suggest that, apart from consciousness, the universe is nothing other than a haze of superposition.

VI

Now, again, a prudent pragmatism might recommend that the sciences abstain from any extravagant hypothesis here. If indeed our purpose is only to extend the realm of human power, which requires only ever more accurate models for prediction, then we may continue to advance in technological power without ever having to translate that power into a knowledge of the nature of consciousness or of reality as such. Perhaps, for instance, we may succeed in constructing quantum computers that rely upon that ultimate, most ghostly enigma of superposition, as well as upon quantum entanglement, and never need trouble ourselves with the metaphysical implications. But can we really preserve that boundary indefinitely?

Let me pause here and cast an eye in the direction of the putative topic of this conference, or at least of its eponym. I realize that we are all aware of Jacques Maritain's concept of the hierarchy of understanding, or the degrees of knowledge, but I will summarize quickly. According to Maritain, the sciences seek regularities, both hypothetically and experimentally; this is what he sees as the principal task of what he designates perinoetical thinking. It is only in a second moment of reflection, a slightly more ambitious adventure of reflection, that thinking passes through the phenomena and the regularities that can be ascribed to them, to arrive at various levels of abstraction. This he calls dianoetical thinking, whose first level is the perception of the essential natures of the things being examined, and whose second level is the discovery of physico-mathematical objects. When, however, thought ascends yet further, by an extension of analogy, to such metaphysical concepts as substances, transcendental terms, even God—then it is engaged in ananoetic thinking. Here it touches upon the highest objects of mental intention: those that are the most intelligible, universal, immaterial, and absolute. Two things should be obvious here: first, that Maritain's scheme describes a seamless continuity rising from empirical knowledge to the highest metaphysical contemplation; second, that it has the form chiefly of an ascent.

This calls attention to two correlated problems, it seems to me. In the first case, it is precisely that continuity that modern scientific method rejects, and that in fact runs contrary to the reigning prejudices of the modern experimental, inductive regime. Not only can the sciences not presume a metaphysical model of reality, but they are so entirely methodologically resistant to the metaphysical that they cannot lead to any conclusions that extend beyond the physical without thereby forfeiting their integrity as sciences. At least, this is the dogma of the age. In the second case, however, this model of successive degrees of knowledge, at least as Maritain describes it, fails adequately to represent the degree to which the perinoetic is never, under any circumstances, an autonomous realm of inquiry. This is not to say that Maritain was ignorant of the ways in which a metaphysical picture of reality can determine the course of scientific inquiry; it is only to say that the picture of a sort of Platonic ascent from the sensible to the transcendent does not always do justice to the extraordinary yet chronic dependency of our understanding of the sensible upon our prior apprehensions of the transcendent. In another sense, perhaps, the scheme is not quite Platonic enough: it fails to account for the ways in which our empirical knowledge is informed by a kind of anamnesis, and this in turn is a capacity either aided or hindered by the metaphysics to which we hold allegiance, conscious or not. The natural aspiration of the mind in science always presupposes a metaphysical frame of reference; all intelligibility at the perinoetic level always entails an act of interpretation, whose terms are provided by this frame of reference—this prior, metaphysical commitment, this ananoetic level of thought from which interpretation descends.

For roughly four centuries now, the reigning metaphysical commitment in the sciences has been that of mechanism—this despite the many discoveries in the sciences that have inexorably moved physics away from a purely mechanistic picture of reality. There was a perfectly plausible accommodation that could be struck between the physical and mental in this picture, however awkwardly, in the days when a casual dualism was still in vogue. Then it was possible and respectable to divide all of reality into two juxtaposed orders: a material order limited to mechanical law and constituted entirely by physical objects and events, and an immaterial order that is the domain of God and the soul, as well as of all the contents and movements of the mind: free choices, *qualia*, intentionality, abstractions . . . This accommodation becomes problematic, at least ideologically and conceptually, when intellectual fashions shift and it is no longer in vogue to accord the spiritual dimension of things any reality of its own. Logically, the physicalist hypothesis is incoherent; the attempt to absorb the mental into the physical narrative fails because the phenomena of consciousness prove utterly intractable to a materialist reduction. That, however, need pose no great dilemmas for the sciences, so long as they are clear in their purposes; some scientists may imagine that they are engaged in constructing a physical explanation of consciousness, when indeed they are doing nothing more than compiling a potentially endless inventory of correlations between mental phenomena and brain states; but that basic logical mistake does not necessarily have to inhibit their experimental work. A crisis may, however, be reached within the sciences themselves whenever the physical begins to appear to be—as a result of verifiable and repeatable experiments—somehow dependent upon consciousness, or at least begins to appear to be a reality from which the functions of consciousness, understood as a unique exception to the rule of mechanism, cannot be excluded. Or, then again, a crisis may arise when the rule of mechanism dissolves at the level of quantum events, and when therefore the regularities and solidities of classical physics must be rescued only by the interventions of some theory or another of consciousness as a principle in its own right. Not that I am saying this will happen. But it is not impossible that Eugene Wigner was right and that consciousness enjoys the power of determining the shape of reality precisely because it is qualitatively, ontologically distinct from the physical realm, and from the continuum of those superposition states that underlie everything, and hence a reality somehow logically prior to the classical realm of phenomenal reality.

What if, more simply, the epoch of unthinking science is one that is necessarily limited? What if the distinction between calculation and reflection, as Heidegger described it, is merely a temporary armistice, a period of probation? Then the entire period of the mechanistic consensus, the materialist metaphysics of the sciences, becomes itself merely a kind of immense thought experiment: let us proceed "as if" reality is mechanistic, as if consciousness can be either excluded from the regularities of physical nature or absorbed into them, until such time as we reach the explanatory limits of that "world picture." And what, then, would the paradigm shift away from mechanism look like? It may be that, for nearly four centuries, we have been enjoying the fruits of a mechanistic fantasy, which has remained our picture of reality as much as a result of inertia as of conceptual solvency. We have inherited a metaphysical picture, however, that is utterly unsuited to the metaphysics of mind; and for all we know we may have already arrived at a juncture at which that picture must begin to dissolve, because it has raised too many questions and discovered too many mysteries that cannot be answered or explained without a metaphysics of mind that is anything but materialist. It may turn out that life and consciousness are precisely what stand outside of, beyond, and above this picture of the world, and that this picture cannot remain coherent any longer as a result and will have to give way to a larger, more expansive, altogether unexpected picture that can accommodate at once both the material order and also all those wonders and mysteries and causal powers that the narrow mechanistic paradigm excludes. Perhaps this is a rather meager conclusion, especially inasmuch as it entails no prognostications of any kind about what that larger picture might look like; but it seems to me worth observing that we can now at least *imagine* a future in which theoretical science—especially if the sciences should aspire to a knowledge of truth, rather than merely to ever greater power over nature—may be obliged to start thinking again after all.

10

The Illusionist

On Daniel Dennett's *From Bacteria to Bach and Back: The Evolution of Minds*

I

It seems to me that we have come this way before. Some of the signposts are new, perhaps—"Bacteria," "Bach," and so on—but the scenery looks very familiar, if now somewhat overgrown, and it is hard not to feel that the path is the same one that Daniel Dennett has been treading for five decades. I suppose it would be foolish to expect anything else. As often as not, it is the questions we fail to ask—and so the presuppositions we leave intact—that determine the courses our arguments take; and Dennett has been studiously avoiding the same set of questions for most of his career. In a sense, the entire logic of *From Bacteria to Bach and Back* (though not, of course, all the repetitious details) could be predicted simply from Dennett's implicit admission on page 364 that no philosopher of mind before Descartes is of any consequence for his thinking. The whole premodern tradition of speculation on the matter—Aristotle, Plotinus, the Schoolmen, Ficino, and so on—scarcely qualifies as prologue. And this means that, no matter how many times he sets out, all his journeys can traverse only the same small stretch of intellectual territory. After all, Descartes was remarkable not because, as Dennett claims, his vision was especially "vivid and compelling" (in comparison to the subtleties of earlier theories, it was crude, bizarre, and banal) but simply because no one before him had attempted systematically to situate mental phenomena within a universe otherwise understood as a mind-less machine. It was only thus that the "problem" of the mental was born. The scientific *novum organum* (as Bacon called it) that achieved its first systematic expression in the seventeenth century, with its ambition to perfect a method of pure induction, proposed to the imagination the idea of a "real" physical world hidden behind the apparent one, an occult realm of pure material causation, utterly devoid of all the properties of mind, most especially intentional purposes. From at least the time of Galileo, a division was introduced between what Wilfrid Sellars called the "manifest image" and the "scientific image": between, that is, the phe-nomenal world we experience and that imperceptible order of purely material forces that composes its physical substrate. And, at least at first, the divorce was amicable, inasmuch as phenomenal qualities were still granted a certain legitimacy; they were simply surrendered to the custody of the immaterial soul. But mind was now conceived as an exception within the frame of nature. In the premodern vision of things, the cos-mos was seen as an inherently purposive structure of diverse but inte-grally inseparable rational relations—the Aristotelian *aitia* or *causae*, for instance, which are nothing like the uniform material "causes" of the mechanistic philosophy—and so the natural order was seen as a reality already akin to intellect. Hence the mind, rather than an anomalous tenant of an alien universe, was instead the most concentrated and lumi-nous expression of nature's deepest essence. This is why it could pass with such wanton liberty through the "veil of Isis" and ever deeper into nature's inner mysteries. The Cartesian picture, by contrast, was a chi-mera, an ungainly and extrinsic alliance of antinomies. And reason ab-hors a dualism. Moreover, the sciences in their modern form aspire to universal explanation, ideally by way of the most comprehensive and par-simonious principles possible. So, it was inevitable that what began as an imperfect method for studying concrete particulars would soon me-tastasize into a metaphysics of the whole of reality. The manifest image was soon demoted to sheer illusion, and the mind that perceived it to an emergent product of the *real* (which is to say, mindless) causal order. And so, it is just here, in this phantom space between the phenomenal and physical worlds, that the most interesting questions should probably be raised. But Dennett has no use for those. He is content with the stark choice with which the modern picture confronts us: to adopt either a Cartesian dualism or a thoroughgoing mechanistic monism. And this is rather a pity, since in fact both options are equally absurd.

Not that this is very surprising. After five decades, it would be astonishing if Dennett were to change direction now. But, by the same token, his project should over that time have acquired not only more complexity but greater sophistication. And yet it has not. For instance, he still thinks it a solvent critique of Cartesianism to say that interactions between bodies and souls would violate the laws of physics; but this, apart from involving a particularly doctrinaire view of the "causal closure of the physical" (the positively Laplacian fantasy that all physical events constitute an inviolable continuum of purely physical causes), clumsily assumes that such an interaction would constitute simply another *mechanical* exchange of energy in addition to material forces. Moreover, Dennett's approach has remained largely fixed through the years. Rather than a sequence of careful logical arguments, his method remains, as ever, essentially *fabulous*: that is, he constructs a grand speculative narrative, comprising a disturbing number of sheer assertions, and an even more disturbing number of missing transitions between episodes. It is often quite a beguiling tale, but its power of persuasion lies in its sprawling relentlessness rather than its cogency. Then again, to be fair, it is at least consistent in its aims. No less than the ancient Aristotelian model of reality, Dennett's picture is meant to be one in which nature and mind are perfectly congruent with one another and in which therefore the post-Cartesian dilemma need never rear its misshapen head. Rather, however, than attempt to explain nature in terms of a "mind-like" order of rational relations, as Aristotelian tradition did, Dennett seeks to do very nearly the opposite: to reduce mind and nature alike to a computational system emerging from "uncomprehending competences," as he calls them—small, particulate functions wholly unaware of the larger functions that, in the aggregate, they accomplish—of the sort whose principle was first fully understood by Alan Turing. And those functions, as retained, combined, and developed by the slow, diffident, mindless designing hand of natural selection, are—like the hugely intricate ensemble of discrete lines of code hiding behind the illusory simplicity of the icons on a computer's screen—the real engines of everything that happens, hiding behind the phenomenal simplicity of perceptible nature. In Dennett's telling, it is all very obvious: under certain chemical and environmental conditions, life will emerge in time and develop organisms with large brains, and these organisms will of necessity be social organisms. And social organisms require mental activity to survive and flourish. For Dennett, all evolutionary developments occur *because* they incorporate useful adaptations; he has no patience for talk of "spandrels" or fortuitous hypertrophies (such, say, as the sudden emergence of language) under the pressure of no evolutionary rationale at all. And, so sanguine is he in his certainty that necessity is sufficient explanation for *why* things happen that he often fails to consider whether the things that he claims have happened are, strictly speaking, possible. For him it seems evident that in the right circumstances, in time, natural selection will generate and preserve ever more competences without comprehension until, at some point of cumulative complexity, certain ensembles of those competences will *become* comprehension. Slowly, what we think of as self-awareness and reflective consciousness emerged from, and in fact remain wholly dependent upon, innumerable small, unconscious, discrete forces. Exactly how this happens, of course—how physical causality is wondrously inverted into phenomenal awareness—is never exactly clear; but for Dennett, once again, the distinction between the useful and the possible is a hazy one at best. And, in a sense, it hardly matters, since even the appearance of rational conscious agency, as something in addition to or formally distinguishable from those tiny competences underlying it, is for Dennett only a useful illusion; and, again, since usefulness explains all things—well, I shall return to this below.

In any event, something happened, and then there was language, which (once more) was very, very useful, and therefore naturally emerged, under the pressure of the social need to communicate, out of originally quite meaningless sounds and gestures. And once there were minds using language, culture evolved, and brains began shaping the reality they inhabited far more rapidly than the previous dynamisms of natural selection ever had. Even so, however, the process was more or less the same: an algorithmic distillation and recombination of "uncomprehending competences." Even the mental and cultural worlds were, it turns out, essentially emergent results of such competences rather than consciously designing or designed realities. They were the product of "memes," fragments of cultural usage that colonized and slowly reconfigured anthropoid brains and societies, and that perished or survived according to the mindless logic of natural selection. And that—though agonizingly protracted over several hundred pages—is the tale Dennett tells. Were it not for a half dozen or so of those missing transitions that I mentioned above, some of which are positively abyssal in size, it would no doubt amount to something more than just a ripping yarn. But, as it stands, it is nonsense.

Admittedly, part of the problem bedeviling Dennett's narrative is the difficulty of making a case that seems so hard to reconcile with quotidian experience; but that difficulty is only exacerbated by his fierce adherence to an early modern style of materialism, according to whose tenets there can be no aspect of nature not reducible to blind physical forces. For him, the mechanistic picture, or its late modern equivalent, is absolute; it is convertible with truth as such, and whatever appears to escape its logic can never be more than a monstrosity of the imagination. But then the conscious mind constitutes a special dilemma, since this modern picture was produced precisely by excluding all mental properties from physical nature. And so, in this case, physicalist reduction means trying to explain one particular phenomenon—uniquely among all the phenomena of nature—by realities that are, in qualitative terms, quite literally its opposite. Really, in this regard, we have progressed very little since Descartes's day. The classical problems that mental events pose for physicalism remain as numerous and seemingly insoluble as ever. Before all else, there is the enigma of consciousness itself, and of the *qualia* that inhabit it, since there is not—and probably can never be—any causal narrative capable of uniting the phenomenologically discontinuous regions of "third-person" electrochemical brain events and "first-person" experiences, or any imaginable science *logically* capable of crossing that absolute qualitative chasm. Then there is the irreducible unity of apprehension, without which there could be no coherent perception of anything at all, not even disjunctions within experience. As (for example) Kant realized, this is probably an insuperable difficulty for materialism; it is a unity that certainly cannot be reduced to some executive material faculty of the brain, as this would itself be a composite reality in need of unification by some still more original faculty, and so on forever, and whatever might lie at the "end" of that *regressus in infinitum* would already have to possess an inexplicable prior understanding of the diversity of experience that it organizes. For, even if we accept that the mind merely represents the world to itself under an assortment of convenient fictions, this would involve a semeiotic translation of sense data into specific perceptions and meanings; and translation requires a competence transcending the difference between the original "text" and its rendition. This problem, moreover, points toward the far more capacious and crucial problem of mental intentionality as such: the mind's pure directedness (such that all thoughts are always *about* things), its interpretation of sense experience under determinate aspects and meanings, its movement toward particular ends, its power to act according to rationales that would appear nowhere within any inventory of antecedent physical causes—all of which indicates an irreducibly teleological structure to thought incongruous with a closed physical order supposedly devoid of purposive causality. Similarly, there is the problem of the semantic and syntactic structure of rational thought, whose logically determined sequences seem impossible to reconcile with any supposed sufficiency of the continuous stream of physical causes occurring in the brain. And then there is the issue of abstraction, and its necessary *priority* over sense experience—the way, for instance, that primordial and irreducible concepts of causality and of discrete forms are required for any understanding of the world of events around us, or the way some concept of resemblance must already be in place before one is able to note likenesses and unlikenesses between things, or even the way in which the bare concepts of Euclidean geometry permit us to recognize their imperfect analogues in nature. And then, also, there are those more-than-abstract—in fact, *transcendental*—orientations of the mind, such as goodness or truth or being in the abstract, which appear to underlie every employment of thought and will, and yet correspond to no concrete objects within nature. And so on and so forth.

Traditionally, most philosophical approaches to these issues have merely restated the problems without any real advance in clarity (theories of supervenience, for example) or have tried awkwardly to evade them altogether (neutral monism, mysterianism). Sometimes a certain fatigue with the inconclusiveness of simple reductionism has prompted vogues in more exotic naturalisms (say, materialist panpsychism or quantum theories of consciousness), but these simply defer the question to an atomic or subatomic level without in any way diminishing the enigma. In a sense, perhaps, Dennett should be commended for his fidelity to the purer reductionisms of early modernity. In its austere emergentism, his position is very near to eliminativism: whatever cannot be reduced to the most basic physical explanations cannot really exist. But, alas, his story does not hold together. Some of the problems posed by mental phenomena he simply dismisses without adequate reason; others he ignores; most, however, he attempts to prove are mere "user-illusions" generated by evolutionary history, even though this sometimes involves claims so preposterous as to verge on the deranged. And, in every case, most of his argument consists in a small set of simple logical errors. The most conspicuous is one I think of as the "pleonastic fallacy": the attempt to explain away an absolute qualitative difference—such as that between third-person physical events and first-person consciousness—by positing an indefinite number of minute quantitative steps, genetic or structural, supposedly sufficient to span the interval. Somewhere in the depths of phylogenic history something happened, and somewhere in the depths of our neurological machinery something happens, and both those somethings have accomplished within us an inversion of brute, mindless, physical causality into, at the very least, the *appearance* of unified intentional consciousness. Then also there is Dennett's tendency to confuse questions about natural capacities for questions about their contents, as when he repeatedly mistakes the issue of intrinsic subjective qualitative consciousness for the issue of the extrinsic objective verifiability of the objects of consciousness, or as when he fails to distinguish between the mystery of rational thought as such and the simple aetiological question of how sophisticated practices of reasoning might have evolved. And then there is what one might call his "Narcissan fallacy": to wit, the tendency to mistake the reflection of human intentional agency in mindless objects, such as computers, for something analogous to a separate instance of mental agency. And then, also, there is his frequent failure to discern the difference between the literal and the metaphorical . . . But I am getting ahead of myself.

II

Dennett is an orthodox neo-Darwinian, in the most gradualist of the sects. This is a fair enough position, but the burden of any narrative of emergence framed in those terms is that the stochastic logic of the tale must be guarded with untiring vigilance against any intrusion by "higher causes." But, where consciousness is concerned, this may very well be an impossible task. The heart of Dennett's project is, as I have said, the idea of "uncomprehending competences," molded by natural selection into the intricate machinery of mental existence. As a model of the mind, however, the largest difficulty this poses is that of producing a credible catalogue of competences that are not ontologically dependent upon the very mental functions they supposedly compose. Certainly Dennett fails spectacularly in his treatment of the evolution of language. As a confirmed gradualist in all things, he takes violent exception to any notion of an irreducible innate grammar, like that proposed by Noam Chomsky, Robert Berwick, Richard Lewontin, and others. He objects even when those theories reduce the vital evolutionary saltation between prelinguistic and linguistic abilities to a single mutation, like the sudden appearance in evolutionary history of the elementary computational function now called "Merge" (which supposedly, among other things, all at once allowed for the syntactic combination of two distinct semantic elements, such as a noun and a verb). Fair enough. From Dennett's perspective, after all, it would be hard to reconcile this universal grammar—an ability that necessarily began as an internal faculty of thought, dependent upon fully formed and discrete mental concepts, and only thereafter expressing itself in vocal signs—with a truly naturalist picture of reality. So, for Dennett, language *must* have arisen out of social practices of communication, rooted in basic animal gestures and sounds in an initially accidental association with features of the environment. Only afterward could these elements have become words, spreading and interplicating and developing into complex structures of reference. There *must* then, he assumes, have been "proto-languages" that have since died away, liminal systems of communication filling up (pleonastically?) the interval between animal vocalizations and human semeiotic and syntactic capacities. Unfortunately, this simply cannot be. There is no trace in nature even of primitive languages, let alone "proto-languages"; all languages possess the full hierarchy of grammatical constraints and powers. And this is not merely an argument from absence, like the missing fossils of all those dragons or unicorns that *must* have once existed. It is logically impossible even to reverse-engineer anything that would qualify as a protolanguage. Every attempt to do so turns out secretly to rely on the syntactic and semeiotic functions of fully developed human language. At the same time, Dennett is probably quite right about how immense an evolutionary saltation the sudden emergence of language would be. Even the simple algorithm of "Merge" involves, for instance, a crucial disjunction between "structural proximity" and "linear proximity"—between, that is, a hypotactic or grammatical connection between parts of a sentence, regardless of their spatial and temporal proximity to one another, and the simple sequential ordering of signifiers in that sentence—without which nothing resembling linguistic practice is possible; yet that disjunction can itself exist nowhere except *in* fully developed language.

Dennett, however, writes as if language were simply the cumulative product of countless physical ingredients. It begins, he suggests, in mere phonology. A repeated sound with some kind of increasingly conventional connection to, say, some exterior physical situation somehow "embeds" itself in the brain and creates an "anchor" or "collection point" where syntactic and semantic meanings can then "develop around the sound." But what could this mean? Are semeiotic functions something like iron filings and phonemes something like magnets? What is the physical basis for these marvelous congelations in the brain? The only possible organizing principle for such meanings would be that very innate grammar that Dennett denies exists—and this would also seem to require distinct mental concepts. Not that Dennett appears to think the difference between phonemes and conceptual references an especially significant one. He does not hesitate, for instance, to describe the "synanthropic" aptitudes that certain organisms (bedbugs, mice, and so on) acquire in adapting themselves to human beings as "semantic information" that can be "mindlessly gleaned" from the "cycle of generations." But there is no such thing as mindless semantics. True, it is imaginable that the accidental development of arbitrary prelinguistic associations between, say, certain behaviors and certain aspects of a physical environment might be preserved by natural selection and become beneficial adaptations. But all semantic information consists in the interpretation of signs, conventions of meaning in which signs and references are formally separable, and in which semeiotic relations are susceptible of combination in other, larger contexts of meaning. Signs are intentional realities, dependent upon concepts, all the way down. And between mere accidental associations and intentional signs there is a discontinuity that no gradualist—no pleonastic—narrative can span. Similarly, when Dennett claims that words are "memes" that reproduce "virally," he is speaking pure gibberish. Words reproduce, within minds and between persons, by being intentionally adopted and employed.

Here, as it happens, lurks the most incorrigibly problematic aspect of Dennett's project. The very concept of "memes"—Richard Dawkins's irredeemably vague notion of cultural units of meaning or practice that invade brains and then, rather like genetic materials, thrive or perish through natural selection—is at once so vapid and yet so fantastic that it is scarcely tolerable as a metaphor. But a depressingly substantial part of Dennett's argument requires not only that memes be accorded the status of real objects but that they also be regarded as concrete causal forces in the neurology of the brain, whose power of ceaseless combination creates most of the mind's higher functions. And this is almost poignantly absurd. I suppose it is possible to think of intentional consciousness as having arisen from an improbable combination of purely physical ingredients (even if, as yet, the story of that seemingly miraculous metabolism of mechanism into meaning cannot be imagined); but it seems altogether bizarre to imagine intentionality as the product of forces that would themselves be, if they existed at all, nothing but acts of intentionality. What could memes be other than mental conventions, meanings subsisting in semeiotic practices? As such, their intricate interweaving would be not the source but rather the product of the mental faculties they inhabit; they could possess only such complexity as the already present intentional powers of the mind could impose upon them. And it is a fairly inflexible law of logic that no reality can be the emergent result of its own contingent effects.

This is why, also, it is difficult to make much sense of Dennett's claim that the brain is "a kind of computer," and mind merely an "interface" between the computer and its "user." Admittedly, the idea that the mind is a kind of software is a fairly popular delusion just at the moment, but that hardly excuses a putatively serious philosopher for perpetuating it—though, I admit, Dennett does so in a distinctive way. Usually, when one is confronted by the computational model of mind, it is enough to point out that what minds do is precisely everything that computers do not do, and that therein lies much of a computer's usefulness. Really, it would be no less apt to describe the mind as a kind of abacus. In the physical functions of a computer, there is neither a semantics nor a syntax of meaning. There is nothing resembling thought at all. There is no intentionality, or anything remotely analogous to intentionality or even to the illusion of intentionality. There is a binary system of notation that subserves a considerable number of intrinsically mindless functions. When computers are in operation, they are guided by the mental intentions of their programmers and users, and they provide an instrumentality by which one intending mind can transcribe meanings into electronic traces and another can translate those traces into meaning again. But the same is true of books when they are "in operation." And this is why I spoke above of a "Narcissan fallacy": computers are such wonderfully complicated and versatile abacuses that our own intentional activity, when reflected in their functions, seems at times to take on the haunting appearance of another autonomous rational intellect, just there on the other side of the screen. It is a bewitching illusion, but an illusion all the same. And, as I say, this would usually suffice as an objection to any given computational model of mind. But, curiously enough, in Dennett's case it does not, because to a very large degree he would freely grant that computers only *appear* to be conscious agents; the perversity of his argument, notoriously, is that he believes the same to be true of us.

III

For Dennett, the "scientific image" is the only one that corresponds to reality. The "manifest image," by contrast, is a collection of useful illusions, shaped by evolution to provide a kind of "interface" between our brains and the world, and thus to allow us to interact with our environments. The phenomenal qualities that compose our experience, the meanings and intentions that fill our thoughts, the whole world of perception and interpretation—these are merely how the machinery of our nervous systems and brains represents reality to us, for purely practical reasons. Just as the easily manipulated icons on a computer's screen conceal the innumerable "uncomprehending competences" by which programs run, even while enabling us to use those programs, so the virtual distillates of reality that constitute phenomenal experience permit us to master an unseen world of countless qualityless and purposeless physical forces. Very well. In a sense, this is simply the standard modern account of how the mind relates to the physical order. The extravagant assertion that Dennett adds to this account, however, is that consciousness itself, understood as a real dimension of wholly first-person phenomenal experience and intentional meaning, is itself only another "user-illusion." That vast qualitative abyss between objective physical events and subjective qualitative experience that I mentioned above does not exist; and, hence, that seemingly magical transition from the one to the other—whether genetic or structural—need not be explained, because it has never actually occurred. This whole notion that consciousness is an illusion is, of course, rather silly. Dennett has been making the argument for most of his career, and it is just abrasively counterintuitive enough to create the strong suspicion in many that it must be more philosophically cogent than it seems, because surely no one would say such a thing if there were not some subtle and penetrating truth hidden behind its apparent absurdity. But there is none. The simple truth of the matter is that Dennett is a fanatic: he believes so fiercely in the unique authority and absolutely comprehensive competency of the "third-person scientific perspective" that he is willing to deny not only the analytic authority but also the actual existence of the first-person vantage. At the very least, though, he is an intellectually consistent fanatic, inasmuch as he correctly grasps (as many other physical reductionists do not) that consciousness really is irreconcilable with a coherent metaphysical naturalism. Since, however, the position he champions is inherently ridiculous, the only way that he can argue on its behalf is by relentlessly, and in as many ways as possible, changing the subject whenever the obvious objections are raised.

For what it is worth, Dennett often exhibits considerable ingenuity in his evasions—so much ingenuity, in fact, that he sometimes seems to have succeeded in baffling even himself. For instance, at one point in this book he takes up the question of "zombies"—the possibility of apparently perfectly functioning human beings who nevertheless possess no interior affective world at all—but in doing so seems to have entirely forgotten what the whole question of consciousness actually is. He rejects the very notion that we "have 'privileged access' to the *causes* and *sources* of our convictions," as though knowledge of the *causes* of consciousness were somehow germane to the issue of knowledge of the *experience* of consciousness. And if you imagine you *know* that you are not a zombie "unwittingly" imagining that you have "real consciousness with real qualia," Dennett's reply is a curt "No, you don't"—because, you see, "Your only support for that conviction is the vehemence of the conviction itself" (363). It is hard to know how to answer this argument without mockery. It is quite amazing how thoroughly Dennett seems to have lost the thread here. For one thing, a zombie could not unwittingly imagine anything, since he would possess no consciousness at all, let alone reflective consciousness; that is the whole point of the imaginative exercise. And so, insofar as you are convinced of anything at all, whether vehemently or tepidly, and are aware of your conviction, you do in fact know with absolute certitude that you yourself are not a zombie. Nor does it matter whether you know where your convictions come from; it is the very state of having convictions as such that apprises you of your intrinsic intentionality and your irreducibly private conscious experience. Simply said, you cannot suffer the illusion that you are conscious, because illusions are possible only for conscious minds. This is so incandescently obvious that it is almost embarrassing to have to state it. But this confusion is entirely typical of Dennett's position. In this book, as he has done repeatedly in previous texts, he mistakes the question of the *existence* of subjective experience for the entirely irrelevant question of the objective *accuracy* of subjective perceptions and whether we need to appeal to third-person observers to confirm our impressions. But, of course, all that matters is that we have impressions at all. Moreover, and perhaps most bizarrely, he thinks that consciousness can be dismissed as an illusion—the fiction of an inner theater, residing in ourselves and in those around us—on the grounds that behind the appearance of conscious states there are an incalculable number of uncomprehending competences at work, in both the unseen machinery of our brains and the larger social contexts of others' brains. In other words, because there are many unknown physical concomitants to conscious states, those states do not exist. But, of course, this is the very problem at issue: that the limpid immediacy and incommunicable privacy of consciousness is utterly unlike the composite, objective, material sequences of physical causality and seems impossible to explain in terms of that causality—and yet exists nonetheless, and exists more surely than any presumed world "out there."

That, as it happens, may be the chief question Dennett neglects to ask: Why presume that the "scientific image" is true while the "manifest image" is an illusion when, after all, the scientific image is a supposition of reason dependent upon decisions regarding method, whereas the manifest image—the world as it exists in the conscious mind—presents itself directly to us as an indubitable, inescapable, and eminently coherent reality in every single moment of our lives? How could one possibly determine here what should qualify as reality as such? Dennett certainly provides small reason why anyone else should adopt the prejudices he cherishes. The point of *From Bacteria to Bach and Back* is to show that minds are only brains, and brains only aggregates of mindless elements and forces; but it shows nothing of the sort. The journey it promises to describe turns out to be the real illusion: rather than a continuous causal narrative, seamlessly and cumulatively progressing from the most primitive material causes up to the most complex mental results, it turns out to be a hopelessly recursive narrative, a long languid lemniscate of a tale, twisting back and forth between low and high—between the supposed basic ingredients underlying the mind's evolution and the fully realized mental phenomena upon which those ingredients turn out to be wholly dependent. It is nearly enough to make one suspect that Dennett must have the whole thing backward. Perhaps the scientific and manifest images are both real, but then again perhaps *only* the manifest image is. Perhaps the mind inhabits a real Platonic order of being, where ideal forms express themselves in phenomenal reflections, while the scientific image—a mechanistic regime devoid of purpose and composed of purely particulate causes, stirred only by blind, random impulses—is a fantasy, a pale abstraction decocted from the material residues of an immeasurably richer reality. Certainly, if Dennett's book encourages one to adopt any position at all, reason dictates that it should probably be something like the exact reverse of the one he defends. The attempt to reduce the phenomena of mental existence to a purely physical history has been attempted before and has so far always failed. But, after so many years of unremitting labor, and so many enormous books making wildly implausible claims, Dennett can at least be praised for having failed on an altogether majestic scale.

Consciousness and Grace

Thoughts on Bernard Lonergan

I

I hope I may be forgiven for speaking as much about a sequence of ideas inspired in me by the thought of Bernard Lonergan as
about his own distinctive projects and concerns—"on the edge" of Lonergan, so to speak—inasmuch as I do so principally as a tribute to the
power of his thought not only to explain but also to generate novel insights. For me, part of the peculiar significance of Lonergan's thought is
that it beautifully illuminates a usually obscure speculative territory (the
haunt of many exotic and as yet nameless fauna) where the theology of
grace and the philosophy of mind unexpectedly coincide—and coincide
so integrally, in fact, that the logical structure of each reveals something
essential to the structure of the other. Not that the connection between
the two spheres is always as obvious as it might be: there is definitely a
vital continuity across the distinct epochs of Lonergan's writings but not
always an explicit one, and certainly not on this issue. Still, that said, even
a casual reader of Lonergan (which generally means the reader who
knows only the nineteenth chapter of *Insight*) is likely to be aware of the
deductive liaison he draws between his epistemological theories and his
metaphysics of the divine. Here, at least, there is a clear movement from
what at first appears to be only a discourse on method—on the dynamism by which experience is unified and synthesized in understanding
and translated into active knowledge in judgment—to an ontological affirmation of the ultimate convertibility of the act of knowing with the act

of being itself, understood as an intelligible act of disclosure. In a sense, Lonergan proposed a new way of discerning that the inverse relation that obtains between the *ordo cognoscendi* and the *ordo essendi* is in fact a dynamic identity, the single order of reality in its fullness, which can be considered, respectively, either under the aspect of a limitlessly tireless act of comprehension or under the aspect of an infinitely inexhaustible act of revelation. And, from the perspective of finite intellect, this identity is progressively discovered not simply through the process of acquiring knowledge but even more crucially through that primordial and always restlessly open act of questioning that constitutes rational existence. This original questioning precedes and exceeds every particular field of investigation and interrogation and constantly opens each level of knowledge achieved to yet more expansive and indefatigable inquiries and yet higher levels of synthesis and unification. Or, as Lonergan phrased the matter, not only is the questioning *about* being; it *is* being, in being's movement of self-disclosure. For us, it proceeds from an insatiable desire to know, a desire that is, of course, transcendental in its essential structure: an unrestricted intention toward the true, good, and beautiful, the intelligible, rational, and simple, and therefore a constant and formally infinite movement of self-transcendence toward the horizon of being as a whole.

Moreover, we are all no doubt familiar with the way in which Lonergan translates his account of the finite conditions of the human search for truth into a necessary affirmation of the reality of God, understood as the one unrestricted act of understanding. Rational consciousness, in its restless yearning to bring all realities out of obscurity into the light of clear knowledge, persistently asks of every object and event why it is so and then asks the same of every answer reached, striving to understand each thing in itself, and then in relation to other things, and always abstracting those relations into ever more comprehensive frames of interpretation, advancing always toward an ideal universal intelligibility. In the very inexhaustibility of this process, and of reality's capacity to yield its secrets to rational reflection, the intellect implicitly recognizes that there is a single unconditioned reality in which both the knower and the known participate in their differing modes and discovers that this, the ontological premise of all partial acts of knowledge and of their openness to further understanding, is necessarily an intelligibility without limit or condition. And unrestricted intelligibility in itself—simple, unified, absolutely comprehensive ideal knowledge, purged of any surd of the empirical, occasional, or impenetrable—is simply pure infinite knowing as such, an unrestricted *act* of intelligence. Only thus, as a limitless approach to that infinite horizon where intelligibility and intelligence are indiscernible from one another, is the rational mind capable of its limitless range of questioning. And so, in its power to pose the question, the mind affirms God as the reality in which it lives and moves and has its being. Now, I admit, I am not always sure that a necessary presupposition is the same thing as a proof; but I am quite sure that it is something rationally undeniable. More to the point, I am quite sure that this relation between the rational mind and the transcendent fullness of self-disclosing being describes not merely the logical shape of a coherent epistemology but in fact every engagement between the knowing mind and the world as well.

Rational consciousness is never merely a reflection of reality conceived in a passive medium, as though the intellect were a kind of patient substance in a state of pure potentiality until it receives formation from a pathos, supplied by an extrinsic agent force; it is necessarily a dynamic movement of thought and will toward reality and becomes actual only as an intentionality toward either a particular or a general end, and toward the particular only within the embrace of its prior inclination toward the general. The mind knows by being actively disposed toward what lies outside itself and only thus is capable of interpreting experience as an experience of *this* or *that* reality. The world is intelligible to us only because we conceptually reach out toward it or reach beyond it, taking in the endless diversity of particulars by way of an indeterminate and abstract yearning for truth as such, and by way of an aboriginal inclination of the mind toward reality as a comprehensible whole, which permits the mind to receive the world precisely by composing it reflectively, discerning meaning in the objects of experience by interpreting them in the light of the whole. Every venture of thought toward an end, moreover, is prompted by an original desire of the mind, a "rational appetite": that is, a predisposition and predilection of the will toward beings, a natural longing for the ideal comprehensibility of all things, an implicit longing for that infinite horizon of intelligibility that is being itself. This, extravagant as it sounds, seems to me nothing more than obvious. The mind cannot help but organize experience into form and meaning and rational relations precisely because it is animated by a natural compulsion that exceeds all individual objects of knowledge. In fact, it is capable of disinterested, even uninterested acts of finite recognition and reflection only because it is always in action, driven by a prior and consuming interest in all of reality as such. Knowledge, even of the most mundane and occasional truths, would be impossible if not for this primordial desire, and for this unremitting adventure of the mind beyond itself and toward the infinite. And, inasmuch as desire is never merely a spontaneous and aimless ebullition of the will but is always moved towards an end, real or imagined, every rational act is intrinsically purposive, prompted by a final cause. And it exhibits the nature of that finality in the necessarily transcendental structure of its operation. All concretely limited aspirations of the will are sustained within formally limitless aspirations of the will. Thus all rational life involves an ecstasy of the mind out of itself and toward an end that by definition can reside nowhere within physical nature, or within nature in any sense. All rational experience and all knowledge is a kind of rapture, prompted by a longing that cannot be exhausted by any finite object. We can speak here of the transcendental notions that prompt the mind's adventure, but even these are unconditional objects of desire only as perfections of being, convertible with one another in the full reality of being itself: that one horizon toward which the mind is always turned and against which every finite object is set off, in clear and distinct outlines, in the great middle distance of the phenomenal world. This vocation of the mind to absolute ends, moreover, is no more a simple psychological state than the unity of consciousness is a simple condition of psychological integrity; in both cases, what is at issue is a transcendental condition of thought, which is in some sense logically prior to the finite identity and impulses of the ego. The vanishing point of the mind's inner coherence and simplicity is met by the vanishing point of the world's highest values; the gaze of the apperceptive "I" within is turned toward a transcendental "that" which lies forever beyond; and mental experience, of the self or of the world, takes shape in the relation between these two "extranatural" poles. The rational mind is able to know the world as a whole because it has always already, in its intentions, exceeded the world; and consciousness contains nature, as a complete and cogent reality, because it has always gone beyond nature and can understand and judge because it is obedient to absolute values that appear as concrete realities nowhere within the natural order. Even the empirical self, the psychological individual, is itself only part of nature as it takes shape in the interval between these poles.

A scrupulous phenomenology of what the mind does, then, and of the rational will's absolute preoccupation with being as a whole, discloses something rather astonishing: that the very structure of thought is an irreducible relation to God as its "natural" end. I would go so far as to say that teleologically the mind *is* God, insofar as it strives not only *toward* but necessarily *to become* infinite knowledge of infinite being. And I am enough of a classical metaphysician to insist that a final end is always a real rational relation intrinsic to what it affects (otherwise, what potential would it make actual in bringing an effect to pass?). To reduce rational life to both its origin and its end—all that precedes and exceeds the empirical, all that founds and elicits consciousness, the whole movement of thought in which the phenomenal world of things subsists—leads in both cases to the same place, the same simplicity—that which is most within and that which is most beyond, God knowing God—and all finite consciousness participates in being as a restricted instance of that unrestricted act. But then, just here, we find this phenomenology opening itself not only to metaphysics but to some of the most vital questions of theology. Specifically, it touches upon the most contentious theological debate of Catholic theology in the twentieth century, that of the "supernatural"—whether, that is, rational spirit could ever be anything other than an insatiable desire for God (as Henri de Lubac phrased the issue to Maurice Blondel). It raises the question of whether it is even logically coherent to imagine that a rational will could ever exist in a state of "pure nature" or rest content in a natural end. Or rather, indeed, it answers that question with a resounding "No." Such a concept is as much a contradiction of reason as is the concept of a square circle. Rational mind is nothing but the act of divine self-disclosure, considered from the vantage of the finite world's *ordo cognoscendi*. Even in the most ordinary employments of the rational mind, we are confronted by the truth that, no less than the orders of knowing and of being, the orders of nature and of grace are merely the two inverse expressions of the continuum of a single reality. And this is true not merely in regard to some superaddition of an extraordinary grace (how could it be?) but in regard to the essential natural structure of consciousness as such.

II

Perhaps, though, I am approaching this matter backwards, from an epistemological perspective that itself inverts the ontological order of causality—at least, inverts the order of things as regards Lonergan's own thought. In proceeding from questions of the dynamism of rational thought to those concerning the action of grace, I am perhaps reversing the course Lonergan's work actually took. Among his earliest substantial treatises, after all, were the four essays constituting his magisterial *Grace and Freedom: Operative Grace in the Thought of Thomas Aquinas*, which—no less solvently, perhaps, than Blondel's *L'Action* or de Lubac's *Surnaturel*—dealt a series of blows to that tragic Baroque synthesis that had produced the Thomism of the infamous "manuals." Already here perhaps, *in nuce*, lay the premises upon which a complete science of the act of knowledge might be built; and so perhaps, for Lonergan, it was actually the theology of grace that led the way toward a philosophy of mind, rather than the reverse. We should recall, at the very least, that the tacit metaphysics of modern mechanistic materialism, which in many ways remains the greatest obstacle to a cogent account of mental life, is in its own way a kind of "two-tier" system—even today, when reductive physicalism is ever at work attempting to conjure one of the tiers away altogether. Admittedly, it is a crudely dualistic system, but one whose logical defects oddly mimic those of early modern Thomism.

Anyone who has devoted any attention to the current state of philosophy of mind must be aware of the degree to which a certain model of what counts as real causality—that is, the impoverished picture of causes as always only mechanical exchanges of energy between distinct material forces—has, on the one hand, made it impossible to address some of the most elementary mysteries of mental life and has also, on the other, given rise to an interminable succession of ever more incredible attempts to evade the problems thus produced. Really, little of consequence has altered since the seventeenth century—which perhaps explains the curious reality that devout materialist philosophers of mind seem unable to imagine any alternative to their views other than the Cartesian. Nowhere is the impossibility of this situation more obvious than in the materialist's often invoked principle of the "causal closure of the physical," which is so obviously a mere metaphysical dogma masquerading as a scientific premise, and which even otherwise sophisticated theorists often translate into the crudest kind of physical determinism. I have known learned scientists who still talk as if—at least, once reality passes over the threshold of quantum decoherence into the realm of classical mechanics and Newtonian space, where you and I and (alas) the current president of the United States all exist—something like Laplace's fantasy holds true: a demon of superlative intelligence, knowing at a given instant the precise location and momentum of every atomic and subatomic particle in existence, could both reconstruct the entire physical history of the universe and foresee its entire future. True, they might all have granted that statistical thermodynamics probably dictates that this would not be literally possible; but still they spoke as if, in principle, all events at higher levels of physical organization must be reducible without remainder to lower, more particulate causal moments. Hence, if our demon could somehow account for irreversibility or quantum indeterminacies, by mastering maximum entropy thermodynamics or by acquiring an occult knowledge of quantum hidden variables through a judicious application of goetic magic, he could, from the dispositions of all the atoms and molecules composing me and my environment last Wednesday at noon, have infallibly predicted my presence here today, because everything we do is the inevitable macroscopic result of the ensemble of impersonal physical forces underlying our formal existence. And yet we know this to be false. To whatever degree I am a physical system, I am also an intentional agent whose mental events take the forms of semeiotic (symbolic, interpretive) determinations, and whose actions are usually the consequences of intentions. And all these determinations and intentions, being irreducibly teleological, could appear nowhere within a reductive account of the discrete processes composing me as a physical event; final causes are not visible within any inventory of the impersonal antecedent physical events composing me. I am here, not because of the blind physical force of destiny's winds at my back, but because at some point I conceived of and chose to act upon a set of reasons for being here, and reasons—functioning as they do as final causes—are qualitatively unlike mechanical forces, even when inseparably allied to them, and are visible nowhere among those mechanical forces. Any complete phenomenological description of my choice to be here would be one that could never be collapsed into a physical description of atomic, molecular, or even brain events. It is undeniably true that—at the causal level where exchanges of matter and energy occur, in obedience to an inviolable law of interchangeable mathematical values—the natural order may always have to even out in an inflexible equation. But the flow of those material and energetic forces, even as a mathematical constant, is also directed by causal (which is to say, rational) relations of a different kind—we may call them *aitia* or *causae*, so long as we distinguish these words from "causes" in the modern sense—which impose upon the flow of physical events formal and final determinations that are not merely the phenomenal residues of those events. The physicalist objection at this point is, of course, to claim that all intentionality is in a sense illusory, at least insofar as it is imagined to constitute a real rational orientation toward an effective final cause; rather, claims the physicalist, intentional states are reducible to complex electrochemical brain events, and those events are in turn reducible to molecular description, and that molecular description is reducible to atomic description, and so on. But that too is obviously false. Not that I have the time here to argue the point; but every attempt to fit mental phenomena—qualitative consciousness, unity of apprehension, intentionality, reasoning, and so forth—into a physicalist narrative has proved a total failure because it must do so. If nothing else, mental intentionality—in the full philosophical sense not only of determinations of the will but of every act of the mind in orienting itself toward specific ends, meanings, aspects of reality, and so on—is clearly a part of nature, and yet one whose structure is irreducibly teleological, and thus entirely contrary to the mechanical picture. The most obvious phenomenological contours of every mental act are precisely all those things that early modern method quite consciously banished from its view of nature in order to perfect a method of pure third-person inductive investigation. That being so, setting aside such exotic and ultimately unenlightening theories as materialist panpsychism or epiphenomenalism, the only plausible materialist approach to intrinsic mental events is to attempt to conjure them away as illusory; and yet they refuse to disappear.

Why, though, dwell upon this issue here? Because, as bizarre as it sounds, it is arguable that the first theoretically sophisticated modern attempt to describe acts of the rational will in physical terms, distinct if not divorced from intentional finality, was advanced by Domingo Bañez and other Baroque Thomists. They did this, I have to say, for the silliest and yet most unavoidable of reasons. As it happens, I have no sympathy for any party in the *de Auxiliis* controversy, for the simple reason that I regard the entire ensemble of issues driving it as a thicket of nonsense, based on a defective Western tradition of belief in predilective predestination, as well as of anxieties regarding an imagined tension between human and divine merit, or nature and grace, or natural and supernatural longing, or any number of other of those false oppositions by which Western theology contrived to mistake the continuity (under radically different modes) of the finite and the infinite, or the creaturely and the divine, for a dialectical tension between two opposed principles (in a vaguely single mode). But I can see how this tradition forced upon its inheritors a dilemma for which every solution was bad. It was the fate of the Bañezian party merely to propose the most repellant of them (an unpleasant job, but someone had to do it if the dialectic of intellectual history was to keep moving forward). The fear of any "synergism" between the divine and human, of the sort proposed by non-Thomist and therefore deluded theologians (like the Apostle Paul, who talked about it incessantly, the poor heretic), could be allayed only by a theory that at once asserted the absolute sovereignty of God as the sole power determining all things while also denying any divine complicity in moral evil (as it would be metaphysically abhorrent to imagine that God could intend evil as evil). Or, in Thomist terms, it was necessary to explain how God could directly create and determine the entity of a sinful act but not cause the sin as such. This is an impossible feat of dialectic, but a false dilemma is the mother of invention. The device by which the Bañezians proposed to rationalize the contradiction was that of the *praemotio physica*, which they eventually read back into Thomas (who had himself, to be fair, proposed nothing better, apparently because he preferred mystery to banality). The concept of physical premotion is intended, in principle, to safeguard a proper understanding of divine transcendence and omnipotence (though it does nothing of the sort). It is called "physical" in that it is not a moral premotion, of the kind that would act only as a final cause upon the rational will; it is instead a special application of real efficient agency on God's part. As a *pre*-motion, its priority is one not of time but only of causal order. As God is the primary cause of all causing, the argument goes, he must be the first efficient cause of all actions, even those that are sinful; and yet, as he operates in a mode radically transcendent of the creature's mode, he can do this without violating the creature's freedom to choose its own wicked ends. From eternity, you see, God has infallibly decreed which actions will occur in time, and he brings them to pass either by directly willing them or by directly permitting them. But divine permission cannot be indeterminate, such that God would have to "wait upon" the creature's decisions, for then God's power would be susceptible of a moral or epistemic pathos; rather, his eternal and irresistible "permissive decree" predetermines even the evil actions of creatures. Still, supposedly, God is not the cause of evil. After all, finite spirits cannot help but err if not upheld in the good by an extraordinary grace, and God is not obliged to supply the creature with any grace at all. But the Bañezians, alas, cannot stop at that point of comfortable ambiguity; for it would impugn God's sovereignty to suggest that he does not predetermine absolutely everything, including the act of sin, as if he were obliged to wait upon the creature's choice before being able to supply the "correct" physical motion of the will toward evil. To think he merely responds to his foreknowledge of a sin he himself has not set in motion by sovereign decree would be no better than Molinism; God does not *react* but instead efficaciously predetermines every sinful act as precisely *that* act and no other. This, though, he accomplishes by causing that act not morally— not, that is, by supplying a final end that would actively induce an intention toward evil—but entirely physically, solely by an irresistible and precise efficient movement of the will. As for human freedom, the argument continues, it is in no wise abrogated by the *praemotio*, because the proper definition of a free act is simply an act that is not *contingently* determined, logically entailed by its prior secondary causes; for an effect is deemed either necessary or contingent wholly in regard to its proximate cause. Since the premotion is a direct application to the will by the sovereign and irresistible efficiency of the divine, the sinful act it infallibly predetermines remains contingent as regards its antecedent secondary causes and so is by definition *logically* free. *Logically* the creature could act otherwise, though in fact this possibility will never, and can never, be realized; for though the creature's act is contingent in its own mode, it is necessary as eternally decreed by God. This is called a necessity of "supposition"; for it lies within God's omnipotence irresistibly to predetermine an effect *as* a contingent effect. In the case of the rational creature,

God infallibly causes him to act through his own intellect and will. Supposedly, then, God and the creature are not competing causes within the act, because their proper modes of causality are so radically distinct that each can be said *entirely* to cause the act, though as superior and inferior agents.

Now, I will not dwell upon all the bizarre metaphysical presuppositions underpinning this system, not even the unexamined assumption that creation *ex nihilo*—the immediate impartation of existence out of infinite being—is a kind of causality that, like a finite cause within nature, must determine a specific result (else God were somehow not the full source of all reality). One must know a great deal about the act of creation to know that; but, since we know of no "causality" in nature that can actually bring something into being out of nothingness, no one really can know such things. I will not even dwell upon the moral idiocy of a system that suggests that a naturally inevitable inclination toward sin that God can but does not correct is inherently culpable, or ponder the loathsome nature of a God who "permissively decrees" the self-damnation of rational souls. Neither is it worth talking much about the ludicrously specious reasoning that asserts that God can irresistibly cause the being and predetermine the willing of the act of sin, and do so *ante praevisa merita sive demerita*, and still not be the cause of the sin itself. This is just the sort of twaddle at which manualist Thomism has long excelled, and why it is so often more the parody than the practice of philosophy; and, again, the pathologies of Western tradition do not much concern me. Rather, I will simply point out that the very notion of a *physical* predetermination of *any* act of the rational will is a logical contradiction, an impossibility that even God would not have the power to bring to pass—any more than he would have the power to create a rational spirit capable of finding rest in a purely natural end. Lonergan recognized, first of all, that the very idea of a special *praemotio physica* in addition to one universal *motio physica* was an anachronism as far as the thought of Thomas was concerned. But, more crucially, he clearly recognized that any intrusion of physical causation upon the act of the rational will could be nothing more than an external compulsion of the body. The rational will is not an organ susceptible of physical efficiency. True, the *praemotio physica* is defined as an immediate exercise of God's power as efficient cause, not a general operation of material secondary causes in a mechanistic manner.

But that is of no consequence. It must still be understood as a determining cause wholly sufficient for its effect. But no merely physical cause can determine a moral result, any more than an antecedent sequence of material events could by themselves have made me choose to be here today. The rational will is *nothing but* an intentional movement toward a final cause, and one necessarily transcendentally oriented to the good as such, and thus can be determined only teleologically. The only way that God could predetermine its action would be by way of a moral cause, a direct communication to the intellect of a good end so perspicuous that the rational will could not resist its attraction. Or, to predetermine a sinful act, God would have to predetermine the sinful intention itself, by proposing an evil end to the rational will as a positive good; but then God would have to will the evil as such, which is impossible. Whatever, then, Thomas meant by speaking of the divine permission of evil, it could not mean what traditional manualist Thomism made of it—at least, not if Thomas was, as we have to hope, a better theologian and philosopher than his Bañezian interpreters. And here too, it turns out, the theology of grace and the philosophical phenomenology of mental acts qualify and clarify one another, in a way that neither could accomplish for itself on its own.

III

In any event, there is no need to pursue these issues further here. I cannot say with certainty that it was in light of his early studies in Thomas's theology of grace that Lonergan's understanding of the innate dynamisms of rational intellect took shape; or, conversely, that his developing ideas regarding the life of the mind made him especially acutely conscious of the deficiencies of the theology of grace in what had become the dominant neo-Scholastic tradition. But it is to me quite fascinating and enlightening that each of these two spheres of inquiry should so naturally and so forcibly imply, invoke, and enrich the other. I confess, I am not entirely sure what the title of this conference—"At the Level of Our Time: Lonergan between Today and Tomorrow"—means exactly. What is our time's "level," and what does it mean to be "at" it? But I can make a kind of sense of the subtitle, insofar as Lonergan seems indeed to offer remarkable resources for both the theology and the philosophy that lie for us "between today and tomorrow." Ours is a time when the old disputes over the theology of grace have been revived among certain traditionalist factions, and the old manualist synthesis has been disinterred from that shallow grave at the outskirts of town, near the striptease parlor, where we had so confidently left its cadaver—but not, alas, with a stake through its heart, garlic in its mouth, and its head severed from its trunk—and has been improbably and grotesquely resuscitated, so that it might spasmodically and grotesquely lurch and gibber its way through our theological institutions once again, spreading terror and havoc and bad metaphysics. At the same time, ours is also a period in which the philosophy of mind has both reached a point of logical crisis and become a surprisingly prominent item within the *agon* of current cultural ideology. And there are few, if any, other thinkers who offer more solvent or critically coherent ways past the impasses endemic to both realms, or who provide better evidence that those ways, when brought together, can fortify, clarify, and illuminate one another. Only now, perhaps, has Lonergan's time truly come.

PART THREE

Gospel and Culture

12

Concerning *By Man Shall His Blood Be Shed: A Catholic Defense of Capital Punishment,* by Edward Feser and Joseph M. Bessette

I

I would be lying if I claimed that my initial approach to this book was an unprejudiced one. I am firmly convinced—on the basis, I like to think, of a fairly sophisticated understanding of the theology of the New Testament and the early church—that no Christian who truly understands his or her faith can possibly defend the practice of capital punishment. But I was not unwilling to give the text a fair hearing. My convictions on the matter may be fixed, but they are not necessarily passionate. There have been various occasions over the years when I have found it possible to desire the deaths of some especially vicious criminals, including two who, as part of a robbery, casually murdered an exceptionally gentle friend of mine when I was an undergraduate. And I have never shed a tear over the Nazis executed by the Allies after the Second World War. I am quite able to be heartless toward the heartless. But this book would exhaust the ruthlessness of Torquemada. My expectations were low, but not nearly low enough.

I might have guessed that something was terribly amiss just from the book's title. There is nothing especially mysterious about it, admittedly. It is more or less inevitable that any substantial attempt at a Christian defense of capital punishment will repeat two tediously persistent exegetical errors—a misuse of Genesis 9:6 (hence the book's title) and a misreading of Romans 13:1–7. But it makes some difference which of the two is accorded priority. If the latter, then in all likelihood an argument is being made merely for the death penalty's theological liceity; if the former, an argument for its moral necessity. And so it is in this case: the claim Feser and Bessette advance is not simply that Catholics *may* approve of capital punishment but that they *must* and that it actually borders on heresy not to do so. Needless to say, an assertion that bold requires a formidable array of corroborating evidences; and this Feser and Bessette have singularly failed to provide. What they have produced instead is relentlessly ill-conceived: its arguments, philosophical and historical, are uniformly feeble; its treatment of biblical texts could scarcely be cruder; its patristic scholarship is careless to the point of slovenliness; it is theologically illiterate; and all too often it exhibits a moral insensibility that is genuinely repellant.

This last is true even if one makes an effort to ignore Feser and Bessette's transparent attempts to coerce their readers' emotions. Not that they admit that this is what they are doing; by their account, all they really want to do is "dissipate the fog of naïve sentimentality that too often prevails in contemporary discussions of capital punishment." They certainly do not intend, they say, to appeal to irrational passions. Yet they devote an entire long chapter to a revolting (if unsettlingly prurient) catalogue of particularly horrific "true crimes," just to remind their readers how evil real evil can be. I, for one, cannot imagine what else this could possibly be other than an appeal to passion. Everyone already knows, and would surely stipulate, that the world is rife with human atrocities and that their perpetrators certainly do not *merit* our mercy. There is certainly no need to resort to the pornography of cruelty to prove the point, except as a transparently cynical strategy for overwhelming rational debate with a different kind of sentimentality—to wit, that of raw fury. Whatever the case, however, the imputation is manifestly false: among principled opponents of the death penalty, very few could be accused of nurturing any tender illusions regarding the deeds or characters of violent criminals.

Really, whenever one party to a debate dismisses the ethical concerns of the other side as "sentimental," it is an all-but-infallible indication of the former's inferior moral imagination. And in the context of this discussion it is particularly revealing. To cultivate pity (or at least concern) for those who deserve no pity—even those justly condemned of monstrous evils—is not sentimentality but charity, the chief of all Christian virtues. It is a hard discipline, not mere spontaneous mawkishness, and is usually evidence of a genuinely diligent conscience. It is also an extremely valuable intellectual hygiene. Compassion is a philosophical virtue, one that makes it possible to grasp truths invisible to the morally obtuse; the limits of moral imagination, after all, are also the limits of the capacity to reason well. In truth, Feser and Bessette would have been wise to speculate upon no one's motives but their own.

II

The authors approach their topic from a variety of angles, which should be a strength of the book; unfortunately, their ambition far exceeds their expertise. They are obviously on familiar ground only when they frame the issue in terms of natural law. Here, at least, they can presume that most believing Catholics will accept the general principle on which their arguments rely: that there exists an essential consonance between the natural and moral orders, inasmuch as both proceed from and manifest a single divine source of rational truth. Even so, they take a great deal of time to say very little, and none of it very compelling. As is often the case when natural law reasoning is asked to bear more weight than it can, the arguments Feser and Bessette make are mostly blank assertions masquerading as deductions of logic; they are precisely as persuasive or unpersuasive as the reader wants them to be. This is inevitable. Nature and natural reason may quite plausibly indicate a certain set of rational prohibitions, and beyond that a smaller set of rational responsibilities; but at the tertiary level of moral reasoning, that of assigning penalties for the redress of misdeeds, nature provides no scale of calculation except "common sense," which is largely worthless. Thus Feser and Bessette try to argue for certain natural goods accomplished by the principle of punishment as such and then argue for the specific punishment of execution on the basis of a commonsensical principle of proportionality. It is all quite tidy and thoroughly unconvincing. But, to be honest, it scarcely matters whether it is persuasive or not. Even were their reasoning sound, it would be utterly irrelevant to a Christian view of reality.

Let us grant, for argument's sake, that the death penalty is indeed a just and proportionate response to, at the very least, willful murder. All right. So what? That has never been the issue of particular contention for Christians, for the simple reason that the gospel does not admit the authority of proportional justice, as either a private or a public good. The whole of the Sermon on the Mount, for instance, is a shocking subversion of the entire idea. And, throughout his ministry, the Christ of the gospels repeatedly and explicitly forbids the application of such punishment, even when (as in the case of the adulterous woman) this means contradicting the explicit commands of the Law of Moses regarding public order and divinely ordained retribution. According to Paul, moreover, all who sin stand justly under a sentence of death, but that sentence has been rescinded purely out of the unmerited grace of divine mercy; and this is because the *full* wrath of the Law has been exhausted by Christ's loving surrender to the cross. Again and again, the New Testament demands of Christians that they exercise limitless forgiveness, no matter how grievous the wrong, even in legal and public settings, and insists that for the Christian mercy always triumphs over judgment. In a very real sense, Christian morality is nothing but the conquest of proportional justice by the disproportion of divine love. So Feser and Bessette need to explain, before all else, why they imagine that Christians have any vested interest in the naturally just retribution for sin. Unfortunately, when they attempt to do this, they are defeated by their own lack of biblical and theological sophistication—which is vast. I do not mean, this is to say, that they are merely unacquainted with certain eccentric or recherché hermeneutical or dogmatic theories; I mean that they seem not even to be aware of the theology of the Apostle Paul. They literally do not know how fraught with difficulties and paradoxes the whole question of law, justice, penalty, and forgiveness is in the New Testament and early Christian thought. It is not even clear they have read the gospels with any particular care.

Perhaps if they had availed themselves of the work of biblical scholars, rather than incessantly quoting the opinions of commentators no more aware of the texts' ambiguities and language than they themselves are (such as, absurdly enough, J. Budziszewski), they might at least have tempered the reckless assurance with which they make their claims. If nothing else, they might have avoided overly buoyant claims for notoriously dangerous verses—such as Genesis 9:6: "Whoso sheds the blood of man, by man shall his blood be shed; for God made man in his own image" (RSV). This seems quite briskly precise, admittedly, but only if one neglects to quote the immediately preceding verses: "Every moving thing that lives shall be food for you. . . . Only you shall not eat flesh with its life, that is, its blood. For your lifeblood I will surely require a reckoning; of every beast I will require it and of man; of every man's brother I will require the life of man" (RSV). It might, after all, seem to undercut the universal and perennial authority of the literal reading of the Noachide laws to take note of the dietary restrictions that are so indiscerptible a part of the covenant (I suspect that neither Feser nor Bessette really believes that he imperils his soul by eating his roast beef au jus), or of the divine proprietary and cultic claims upon living blood that form so essential a part of its logic (which are not exactly "ethical" claims in the modern sense). Predictably, Feser and Bessette also call on Exodus 21 and Deuteronomy 19; but naturally they make no mention of, say, Leviticus 20, with its list of incredibly trivial capital crimes. Once again, however, who cares? None of this is of any actual consequence *for Christians.* Jewish tradition always enfolded the Noachide prescriptions into the Law, as that small portion thereof of which gentiles were capable; and it is the wrath of the Law as a whole that is, according to Paul, set aside—even conquered—by Christ. After all, as Paul says in Galatians, the Law is inherently defective, having always been communicated only by an angel, and then through a mere human intermediary.

It is when Feser and Bessette turn their eyes to the New Testament, however, that the argument goes disastrously awry. Their principal response to Christ's injunctions to unconditional forgiveness and against retaliation and judgment, for instance, is simply to argue that he is speaking only of private rather than public morality. But such a distinction would have been wholly unintelligible in the context of first-century Judaea; Christ's constant challenges were to the traditional applications of the Law, in which the personal, social, and jurisprudential were inseparable. As for the very clear rejection of proportional justice in the Sermon on the Mount, Feser and Bessette's only riposte is blandly to note that "Christ said in the very same sermon . . . that he had come 'not to abolish the law and the prophets . . . but to fulfill them.'" At this point, commentary seems otiose. Are they even making an effort here? Are they really unaware of the "redemptive irony" in Christ's legal pronouncements—how he repeatedly "fulfills" the Law precisely by negating the literal acceptation of its prohibitions and punishments? Are they truly that entirely unfamiliar with both the Law and the gospel? Apparently so.

And then, of course, there is Romans 13:1–7. (Here a barely suppressed sigh.) It is amazing how much is often made of these admittedly anomalous but still very mild verses. Even assuming that the whole passage is not a spurious interpolation (as a few scholars have unconvincingly but not irrationally opined over the years), it says very little and in the original Greek says far less than Feser and Bessette think. According to them, Paul's words have been "traditionally understood as a straightforward affirmation of the right of the state to execute criminals." This is false (despite the several misrepresentations of patristic sources they later produce). Even if it were true, however, it would constitute nothing more than an unfortunately prevalent error. The passage almost certainly says nothing about capital punishment at all. Again, Feser and Bessette really should have consulted a good New Testament scholar (or classicist) here. They assume that when Paul writes that "it [power, ἐξουσία] does not bear the sword in vain," he is speaking of something like the Roman *ius gladii*, a provincial governor's limited authority for pronouncing a death sentence. But, not to be too pedantic, the word usually translated as "sword" in this passage is μάχαιρα (*machaira*), which was the name for a large dagger or short sword generally carried at the waist in a μάχαιροδέτης (*machairodetēs*), a leather belt. Now, it is true that such a blade could be used to put someone to death; according to Acts 12, that was the means by which Herod had James the brother of Jesus killed. And Paul probably did use the word as a vague term for any sword. But, as a figure for the state's power to kill, one would properly speak of τὸ ξίφος (*to xiphos*)—"the sword"—wielded by an executioner. Thus, for example, Philostratus, when speaking of a magistrate empowered to pronounce the death sentence, describes him as "a judge bearing the sword," δικαστοῦ τὸ ξίφος ἔχοντος (*dikastou to xiphos echontos*) (*Vitae Sophistorum* 1.25.31); or, when the same author wants to indicate that Tigellinos was endowed by the emperor with the same remit, he writes, "Nero's sword was under his power": ὑφ᾽ ᾧ τὸ ξίφος ἦν τοῦ Νέρωνος (ʰyphʼ ʰō̤ to xiphos ēn tou Nerōnos) (*Vita Apollonii* 4.42). When, by contrast, Paul speaks of the power that τὴν μάχαιραν φορεῖ (*tēn machairan phorei*), the phrase almost certainly refers to a μάχαιροφόρος (*machairophoros*), a "carrier of a short sword," a word that usually meant a soldier but that could also refer to a military policeman, civil guard, or taxation enforcement officer (as we know from a number of Hellenistic papyri: *Amherst Papyri* 2.38; *Papyri Tebtunis* 35.13 and 391.20; *Bodleian Ostraca* 3.64; *Michigan Papyri* 577.78; etc.). This also explains the phrase "οὐ . . . εἰκῇ (*ou . . . eikē̤*)," "not in vain"—or, better, "not as a vanity." It is rather as if a modern writer were to say, "A policeman doesn't carry a gun just for show (so, if you create disorder, don't be surprised if he uses it)." Obviously, the force used by civil authority can be lethal; but that is something quite different from capital punishment. And, knowing as we do from Suetonius of the expulsion of Jews from Rome by Claudius in response to the "Chrestus" riots, and from Tacitus of the public disorder in Rome over taxes under Nero, it is not difficult to imagine the sort of recent events to which Paul was reacting. And yet *even that* does not matter much. Whatever Paul was referring to, this passage has *absolutely no* prescriptive content as regards how Christians should govern society (an eventuality that Paul never even conceived). So, yes, God may have providentially used the powers ceded to the pagan authorities of the ancient world to discourage sin; but that has no implications whatsoever for how Christians should conduct themselves in positions of authority. And no one in the early church imagined that it did.

Which brings me, reluctantly, to Feser and Bessette's treatment of the church fathers. It would be difficult to exaggerate how deplorable the scholarship is here. It is painfully obvious that neither Feser nor Bessette bothered to read the texts they cite; they merely went searching for anything that looked like a proof text, no matter how tenuous or fragmentary, without paying even cursory attention to what was actually being said, or in what context (I suspect they merely plundered some anthology of poorly translated quotations). They claim, for instance, that in the *Contra Celsum* Origen affirmed the right of the state to execute criminals, but when one consults the passage they cite one finds nothing more than a rueful acknowledgment of the *power* of the state to punish crime with force. The same is true of their citation from Gregory of Nazianzus. They also treat an elliptical turn of phrase in Athenagoras as a declaration of the validity of capital punishment rather than, as is actually the case, a mere impartial recognition of its reality. They absurdly read an unambiguous statement of the death penalty's propriety into John Chrysostom's praise of the Emperor Theodosius for refraining from a "justifiable slaughter" of Antiochene rebels. (Actually, to be precise, he praises the emperor for refraining from a δίκαιος φόνος [*dikaios phonos*], which might be rendered merely as a "lawful" or even "*customary* slaughter"; *dikaios* does not have anything like the simple moral connotation of our word *just*; but it seems never to have occurred to Feser and Bessette that the original texts were not written in English and that perhaps they ought to check—or get someone who could read the Greek for them to check—the original documents.) And so on and so on. Perhaps the greatest howler is a quotation they extract from Origen's fourteenth homily on Leviticus concerning the way in which certain sins might be absolved by penal death. They entirely fail to notice that Origen's tortured reflections on the literal reading of the seemingly bizarre list of capital crimes in Leviticus 20 is prompted by his certainty that capital punishment is absolutely forbidden by the law of Christ; nor do they notice that his conclusion is that such this-worldly punishments are figures of what awaits the impenitent in the world to come, extended to those who in the past were ignorant of the purifying torments of Gehenna. In fact, even when Feser and Bessette notice in passing that the fathers they mention all seem to advise against use of the death penalty, they fail to grasp that this is not merely a matter of personal predilection. Once again, the question of whether the death penalty is in some sense "just" is wholly irrelevant in the context of Christian belief. As far as the fathers were concerned, all of us *merit* death. This does not mean that they believed Christians are permitted to impose such a penalty.

Actually, an honest assessment of the early patristic consensus on capital punishment is really quite easily made. The general view was essentially that of Ambrose: the Sermon on the Mount's prohibitions of retaliation are absolutely binding on Christians, in both the private and the public spheres, for on the cross Christ at once perfected the refusal of violence and exhausted the Law's wrath. It is simply a fact of history that the more or less ubiquitous conviction of the earliest Christians—those whose communities most immediately arose from the church of the apostles—was that Christ's command not to judge others was more than a mere prohibition of private prejudice. Hence Christians were not supposed to serve as soldiers or magistrates. Gibbon quite accurately described the pagan view of this refusal of civic duties as an "indolent" and "even criminal" dereliction, which could be ascribed only to "pusillanimity" on their part (judgments that Gibbon plainly shared). According to the ancient document called the *Apostolic Tradition*, no one intending to become a soldier could be received into the church; and those who had been converted while already in the army were forbidden to carry out even a properly pronounced order of execution. Arnobius clearly stated that Christians were not allowed to impose the death penalty at all, even when it was perfectly just. Athenagoras stated that the killing even of those guilty of capital offenses must be repugnant to Christians, as they are obliged to view all killing of humans as a pollution of the soul. Cyprian too said that for Christians the innocent may never slay the guilty. Tertullian not only repeatedly asserted that Christians must not kill other humans for any reason but also claimed that when Christ disarmed Peter in Gethsemane he effectively stripped all soldiers of their arms, and numbered the office of executioner among occupations deserving of damnation. According to Lactantius, a Christian could neither kill a justly condemned criminal nor even arraign another person for a capital crime. Origen unequivocally stated that the law of Christ forbids all killing, legal no less than illegal, and opined that God providentially allowed the fall of the Jewish kingdom in order to end the practice of capital punishment among his people. True, in later centuries, under a Christian empire, the greatest of the church fathers acknowledged that the state had the *right* or *power* to sentence men to death; yet they repeatedly entreated the authorities to refrain from doing so, and lavishly praised them when they did so refrain, because they still believed the use of capital punishment to be wrong in principle for Christians.

III

Feser and Bessette are on firmer ground, naturally, when they shift their attention from the patristic epochs to the late Middle Ages; but this serves

more to weaken than to substantiate their case. For one thing, it is a necessarily abrupt shift, omitting mention of the roughly eight intervening
centuries precisely because these offer so little in the way of good evidence for their position. But they employ even the late mediaeval material quite indiscriminately. They are perfectly content to draw support
from arguments made in support of the execution of heretics (such as
those of Thomas Aquinas, who also affirmed the propriety of executing
thieves and counterfeiters). They even take Innocent III's decision to permit the execution of unregenerate Waldensians as proof that the legitimacy of capital punishment is *"a matter of Catholic orthodoxy"* (emphasis
theirs). The sheer non sequitur in such reasoning defies parody—as too
does the encouragement Feser and Bessette take from Leo X's declaration in *Exsurge Domine* in 1520 that the burning of heretics is in keeping
with the will of the Holy Spirit, or from the brutal penal practices of the
Papal States in the nineteenth century. Quite apart from their apparent
ignorance of how very little weight the Catholic magisterium accords
such precedents, it is amazing how much of their case rests upon the
legitimacy of the most barbaric evils perpetrated during what all morally
sane Catholics recognize as a period of profound and tragic institutional
decadence.

Perhaps, though, one needs to ask: Do Feser and Bessette believe it
theologically correct to burn heretics? Does that accord, in their minds,
with all their earlier talk of proportional justice? If not, then no sound
principle can be abstracted from arguments in defense of an inherently
wicked practice; all of it would be, to use a term common to philosophy
and law, fruit of the poisoned tree. If they do believe it morally correct to
kill heretics, however, then they have essentially excused themselves
from civilized Christian discourse. After all, the history of "holy murder"
within Christian culture is well established. In the earliest centuries of
the church, the killing of religious dissidents was regarded by Christians
as an abominable pagan practice. When a Roman emperor (or pretender)
executed the Spanish bishop Priscillian for heresy in 385, Christians as
eminent as St. Martin of Tours and St. Ambrose of Milan condemned it
as a return to heathen brutality. Throughout the so-called "Dark Ages,"
in fact, the approved penalty for obdurate heresy was simply excommu-
nication. True, in the twelfth and thirteenth centuries heresy again became a capital crime throughout Western Europe; but even then, it was

the state rather than the church that led the way. When the Holy Roman Emperor Henry III hanged a number of Cathars in 1051, he was reprimanded by the bishop in Liège. Admittedly, though, by the time that his later successor Frederick II (1194–1250) ordered the surrender of all convicted heretics to the secular arm to be burned, the institutional church contemptibly complied. And the Papal States, as Feser and Bessette gleefully note, were executing a wide variety of criminals well into the nineteenth century. All of which is quite a tragic betrayal of Christian principles, of course, as every pope in living memory has been happy to concede, and all of which Feser and Bessette seem to celebrate.

It is not clear why Feser and Bessette imagine that the past legal practices of the institution of the church or of its political adjuncts oblige modern Catholics to accept whatever principles or rationales, however loathsome, those practices might have embodied. None of those practices rested on dogmatic principles. And, anyway, if Newman was right (as believing Catholics had better hope he was, for the sake of the intelligibility of their faith), it is not only doctrine but also the church's understanding of its teachings that is clarified over time by the Spirit. There may be slight missteps, of course, but the general view of development tacitly taken by the magisterium is that there are no violent saltations, peripeties, or retreats from clearly stated new discoveries; there is only a relentless narrowing and intensification of focus. This suggests, among other things, that the teachings of the magisterium under the current pontificate are probably more trustworthy than those under the pontificate of, say, Leo X. And, grasp at ghosts though they may, Feser and Bessette are clearly struggling against the inexorable course that magisterial pronouncements on this matter have been taking for decades. But they twist and turn in every direction trying to evade or relativize the current teachings of the Catholic Church and to qualify the authority of those teachings however they can; and they do their damnedest to suggest that any seeming shift in the church's view of the liceity of the death penalty actually constitutes only a prudential judgment about its current applications. They also draw strangely pathetic comfort from Benedict XVI's anodyne statement that disagreements on the matter of capital punishment need cause no break in communion between Catholics. Very well. We can take it for granted that Feser and Bessette will not be excommunicated for having written this wretched book. That, however, is a far cry from some sort of papal blessing on their position. And in the end, as it happens, all their efforts are to no avail.

Admittedly, the Catholic Church has never committed itself doctrinally to the abolition of the death penalty, and it is true that magisterial interpretations of doctrine are somewhat fluid and of less-than-dogmatic authority. But it remains true that, in the eyes of the Catholic Church, the explicit teaching of the magisterium on matters of faith and morals is universally binding on the consciences of the faithful. And as regards this question that teaching is clearly stated in the catechism: the death penalty may be permissible solely—*solely*—"if this is the only possible way of effectively defending human lives against the unjust aggressor," though today, it goes on to observe, given the facilities available to the state for detaining criminals, such cases "are very rare, if not practically nonexistent" (2267). That is quite unambiguous, despite Feser and Bessette's labored and occasionally comical attempts to resist its obvious implications. The *only* time execution may be acceptable is when it is otherwise impossible to prevent a criminal from killing again. That means that *all* of the other arguments advanced by Feser and Bessette have already been decisively ruled out by the magisterium as morally insufficient; and this is not going to change. If any position, then, is to be regarded as contrary to Catholic orthodoxy, it is clearly theirs.

IV

All, therefore, that really remains intact among the wreckage left behind by this book's collision with the catechism is the one practical argument the magisterium still permits—that perhaps, but for the imposition of the death penalty in certain cases, innocent lives will be endangered. Alas, what Feser and Bessette cannot establish is that, even were that true, the number of the innocent imperiled by the abolition of the death penalty would be greater than the number imperiled by its exercise. Needless to say, they make all the standard arguments for how the death penalty discourages violent crime, and they offer the usual sorts of statistics and "commonsensical" arguments used to support this claim. Unfortunately, anyone who has followed debates on this issue over the years knows that there are statistics and commonsensical arguments for exactly the opposite position that are at least as convincing and plausible. It might help Feser and Bessette's case if, say, murder rates in Stockholm were to exceed those in Dallas; but as yet that has not happened, and none of the evidence they do have at their disposal is especially compelling. That leaves only the concern that violent criminals, if left alive, might escape confinement. This has occasionally happened, they argue, and so concern for public safety dictates that the dangerous murderers be put down. Since, however, it is endlessly possible to improve methods of incarceration and the transport of prisoners, a less sanguinary solution is always within reach.

The most disturbing aspect of this part of Feser and Bessette's argument, as it happens, is their response to the issue of false convictions. They acknowledge that mistaken verdicts will on occasion be handed down in capital cases but think the margin of error slight enough to be acceptable; after all, they reason, we drive motor cars and vaccinate our children, even though both practices inevitably claim a negligible quantity of innocent victims. Needless to say, these are ridiculous analogies, for any number of reasons—the vastly differing statistical orders of magnitude, for instance, or the variable element of human intentionality involved in each situation, or the practicability of available alternatives. Ideally, though, the reader will intuitively recoil from the simple brutality of Feser and Bessette's argument before ever having to take any of that into account. And then too there is the inconvenient proof amassed in recent years of just how high the rate of jurisprudential error tends to be. DNA testing has repeatedly proved that a great many cases in which the evidence had appeared irrefutable (some involving numerous eyewitness testimonies) have resulted in convictions of the innocent—which means that we may anticipate that in future, especially in cases where no DNA evidence is collected, there will continue to be miscarriages of justice in quantities far greater than the vanishingly small number of violent criminals who might escape confinement (especially as penal technology continues to evolve). Yet, once again, this scarcely matters. One can drag these debates out interminably, but all of them remain largely irrelevant to the essential question. Even if it would make the world a much safer place to kill off as many violent criminals as possible—and I think we can assume that it would—that still would not mean that it is something Christians are permitted to do. On the whole, the gospel is probably not a very good formula for protecting public safety. And, really, the question of what Christian commitment entails is not one that Feser and Bessette appear to be even minimally equipped to adjudicate.

In the end, the most appalling aspect of this book is not its shoddy reasoning, or its unsophisticated scriptural exegesis, or its theological ig-norance, or its inept scholarship, but just its plain moral coarseness. It is bad enough that Feser and Bessette are happy to support their case by drawing on arguments in favor of burning heretics, or that they are so phlegmatically willing to accept the occasional innocent person's execu-tion as (to their minds) a fair exchange for some vague and suppositious greater good whose reality they cannot even convincingly describe, let alone demonstrate. These are relatively mild examples of their deafness to the gospel. They make still grislier arguments than these. Twice, for example, they adduce the career of Giovanni Battista Bugatti—the offi-cial executioner of the Papal States who from 1796 to 1865 executed 516 convicted criminals by decapitating them with an axe or a guillotine, or by slitting their throats, or by crushing their heads with a mallet, or by having them drawn and quartered—as some sort of proof of the Catholic Church's commitment to the essential justice of the death penalty; and on neither occasion do they express the slightest alarm at, or disapproval of, either the number or the savagery of these killings. This is typical of the entire tone of the book; every page exudes an atmosphere of almost numbing callousness. Far be it from me to counsel hypocrisy, but the occasional faint touch of false tenderness would have been, if nothing else, decorous—just a small shiver of distaste, just the slightest melan-choly sigh.

It is all a very odd and unsettling picture of Christianity, really, rather like a familiar and beautiful painting monstrously distorted in a carnival mirror—the lovely rendered hideous, the exquisite grotesque. Perhaps this is simply the inescapable burden of Christian history's contradic-tions. We know how all this happened, after all. In the earliest days of the faith, in those communities in which the long echo of the voice of the apostolic church was still audible, and through it the longer echo of the voice of Christ, baptized Christians understood themselves as having been called to a form of life radically unlike that of the fallen cosmos. They belonged to a Kingdom not of this world and were absolutely for-bidden to take part in the orders of force—illegal and legal, wanton and "justifiable" alike—by which the powers and principalities exercise their sway; instead, they were required now to live by a law of charity so uncompromising that it might lead to their deaths and the deaths of many others. But that prolonged moment of apocalyptic liberty from the violence of history gradually faded; Christendom arose and ramified and assumed gigantic dimensions; and over the centuries the church and the fallen order from which it had initially offered an escape became inseparably intertwined, with consequences both good and ill. Then came Christendom's collapse, again for both good and ill. So, I suppose, it is inevitable that now there should be certain kinds of traditionalists who look back yearningly, not so much to the cultural prevalence of Christian faith, or even to the genuinely glorious achievements of Christian civilization, but rather to that grand and mighty institutional accommodation between Christ's and Caesar's realms, along with everything about it that was most inimical to the gospel. If nothing else, a book of this sort has the salutary effect of reminding us of just how pernicious that kind of nostalgia truly is. Happily—providentially—it too in time must fade. As the book of Hebrews says, the word of God is sharper than any sword, piercing enough to separate soul and spirit; and perhaps in the modern age it has been that word, operating secretly, that has so painfully but so redemptively separated faith in Christ once more from the institutions and instruments of worldly power. Would that the separation were already complete. It may be that the last vestiges of Christendom will have to vanish entirely from human hearts before the long echo of Christ's voice will become audible again in all its purity.

13

Further Reflections on Capital Punishment (and on Edward Feser)

I

According to Edward Feser, I seem "to think that the moral demands of the Gospel apply *in exactly the same way* to both the private sphere and the public sphere." And this, he goes on to say, "is not only not the Catholic position, it is not even the Eastern Orthodox position. It is merely David Bentley Hart's personal theological position, and he simply asserts it without argument." Ah. Except that I do nothing of the kind, and never have (though neither would I necessarily reject the proposition, since it seems a claim more dangerous to deny than to affirm; I would need to know precisely what "in exactly the same way" means in Feser's mind). I can see the cause of the confusion, however.

The issue is capital punishment, and Feser's angry expostulation comes near the end of his rancorous reply to two extremely bad reviews—one by me, one by Paul Griffiths—of the "Catholic Defense of Capital Punishment" that he and Joseph Bessette recently published under the title *By Man Shall His Blood Be Shed*. Now, in fact, nowhere in the course of my treatment of the book do I enunciate any general principle regarding the relation between public and private morality for Christians; I do, however, point out that the attempt made by Feser and Bessette to reconcile their enthusiasm for the death penalty with Christ's repeated prohibitions against retributive justice (the Sermon on the Mount, the woman taken in adultery, "seventy times seven," "you have heard it said, an eye for an eye, but I tell you . . . ," "judge not, lest . . ."—well, you no doubt know the relevant passages) by invoking such a distinction is a ridiculous anachronism. And indeed it is, as any good scholar of the New Testament or of late antiquity could tell him. Christ's moral teachings often concerned the interpretation and application of the Law—the preservation of its spirit but radical qualification of its letter—and in the context of first-century Judaism a partition between private and public observation of the Law simply did not exist. And, really, one does not even need to be a scholar of ancient Judaism to know this. Any attentive reader of the gospels will see that Christ explicitly applies his teachings to such matters as capital offenses (like adultery), lawsuits, theft of personal property, forced conscription of labor, and so forth.

In a larger sense, though, Feser's failure to follow what I actually said is only to be expected. After all, his book consists to a surprising degree in extremely careless readings, especially—though not exclusively—of the Bible and the church fathers. It is, to put the matter simply, an exorbitantly bad book, one that contains not a single compelling or solvent argument. Moreover, while its appeals to natural law are merely unpersuasive, its uses of scripture, theology, and the church fathers are almost fantastic in their awkwardness and crudity. It is obvious that neither author has even the most general grasp of any of these fields; and yet the conclusions they try to bring back from their maladroit ventures into the unknown are staggeringly ambitious. It is also a book whose moral coarseness borders at times on the surreal—as when Feser and Bessette casually write off instances of false conviction in capital cases as lamentable but acceptable statistical aberrations, like those occasional fatal reactions to vaccinations that have to be accepted as part of the price of public health. Hence the poor, or at least lukewarm, reviews the book has tended to receive. Feser, however, feels ill-used. And, in replying to his critics, he strives to give a meltingly moderate impression of his book's rhetoric and to make it sound as temperate and modest as possible; he claims that he and Bessette merely advocate that Christian society allow the death penalty as a legal option in cases of the most heinous evils, and nothing more. In actuality, however, they insist that Catholic orthodoxy positively requires support for the death penalty in principle, and they argue vigorously that the death penalty's application is a positive moral and social good to whose liceity Christian consciences are bound to assent by orthodox tradition. Admittedly, there are phrases in the book that, ripped from the context of the whole, sound more reasonable and diffident than the book in its entirety. But one need merely consult the text to see how disingenuous Feser's protests are.

Then again, in Feser's defense, I suppose it is possible that he and I (and Griffiths) simply have very different ears for tone. For instance, he faults me for objecting to the book's use (twice) of the career of Giovanni Battista Bugatti—the official executioner of the Papal States who from 1796 to 1865 executed 516 convicted criminals by decapitating them with an ax or a guillotine, or by slitting their throats, or by crushing their heads with a mallet, or by having them drawn and quartered—as some sort of proof of the Catholic Church's commitment to the essential justice of the death penalty. And he faults me in particular for professing astonishment at his and Bessette's failure to express sufficient dismay at the number or savagery of the executions. The book does not offer Bugatti as "proof" of any doctrinal point, he insists (not that I said anything about doctrine). And, as for dismay, he and Bessette did after all write: "We certainly would not defend the harsher methods of execution employed in the nineteenth century." And, who knows? Perhaps I should have been more deeply moved by those stirring words; and maybe my inability to discern in them a sufficiently seemly note of moral indignation is the result of my own excessive emotional fastidiousness. So then, let me rephrase the matter, for clarity's sake: it astonishes me that, from the number and savagery of the executions Bugatti carried out, Feser and Bessette should have concluded anything *other* than that Bugatti's career provides evidence of a deeply degenerate period of the papacy. I have a (perhaps superstitious) trust in the logical and legal principle that no good or sound principle can be extracted from "fruit of the poison tree"; and Bugatti's career was pure poison, from the point of view of either Christian doctrine or natural law. It might have occurred to Feser and Bessette that, quite apart from the cruelty of the methods used by Bugatti, and quite apart also from the laxity of the evidentiary standards adopted by the Papal States' legal apparatus, there might be issues of natural justice here so grave as to discredit the moral authority of the Papal States in that period entirely. After all, we have records of almost all these executions. Many were for murder, and perhaps in most of those cases the convictions were just. But many were for robbery or forgery or fraud. One person was put to death for lightly injuring a French officer in a fight. Another was killed for breaking shop windows. So really, on the whole, Feser and Bessette would have been better off not mentioning the matter at all.

Feser also arraigns me for dishonesty. I, however, plead mere unclarity. I did indeed write that Feser and Bessette "take Innocent III's decision to permit the execution of unregenerate Waldensians as proof that the legitimacy of capital punishment is '*a matter of Catholic orthodoxy*' (emphasis theirs)." Feser, however, is quick to point out that what he and Bessette actually wrote was this:

> In 1210, Pope Innocent III required adherents of the Waldensian heresy, as a condition for their reconciliation with the Church, to affirm a number of doctrinal points which included the following: "We declare that the secular power can without mortal sin impose a judgment of blood provided the punishment is carried out not in hatred but with good judgment, not inconsiderately but after mature deliberation." The significance of this passage is difficult to overstate. The context—again, a set of demands made to a *heretical* group as a condition for reconciliation—makes it clear that the pope held affirmation of the legitimacy in principle of capital punishment to be *a matter of Catholic orthodoxy*. (123–24)

So, Feser triumphantly notes, "What we actually and very clearly say is that the *doctrinal statement* that Pope Innocent required the Waldensians to agree to is what makes capital punishment a matter of orthodoxy. We don't say anything about the '*execution* of unregenerate Waldensians,' either here or anywhere else in the book." I see. Fair enough, I suppose. Even then, Feser is incorrect in saying that what the pope demanded from the Waldensians was assent to a "doctrinal" point (at least, if the *Enchiridion Symbolorum* is to be trusted); so his argument is false prima facie. But, as regards the point I was trying to make, the Waldensians in question were in fact under threat of death if they remained "unregenerate" and refused to accept the terms of reconciliation; and so, indeed, it is the pope's permission for the secular arm to kill those Waldensians that provides the *occasion* for the claim Feser and Bessette are advancing.

If, however, I failed to make myself clear, I am contrite and shall strive to do so now: I was again making an argument about "fruit of the poison tree" and doing so on the assumption (which I hope is correct) that Feser and Bessette would agree that the execution of heretics was an inherently unchristian practice.

What I do not understand, however, is Feser's complaint that I then misrepresented his book when I wrote this: "The claim Feser and Bessette advance is not simply that Catholics may approve of capital punishment, but that they must, and that it actually borders on heresy not to do so." All I can say is, read the book. Or rather, to save time, *vide supra* (note especially the sentence directly following the block quote overhead). *Orthodoxy, doctrine* . . . these are fairly unequivocal terms. Yet neither is actually appropriate. There is in fact not a single dogma of the Catholic Church that requires the liceity of the death penalty. The pope could tomorrow declare all capital punishment sinful and incompatible with Catholic teaching *ex cathedra*, and he would not be contradicting a single recognized *doctrine*. If you doubt this, *tolle, lege* any copy of Denzinger. And the current catechism of the church bears this out. (Feser complains that Griffiths and I do not deal with the fifty pages of arguments he and Bessette devote to their blustering and procrustean attempt to blunt the catechism's piercingly unambiguous statements on the matter. But that was a mercy on our parts. To refute those arguments it is enough to recite them.)

II

It may be that the greatest problem with Feser and Bessette's book is that their central argument is not so much false as irrelevant. They expend a great deal of energy on trying to prove that the death penalty is a *just* requital for certain crimes, and that both scripture and Catholic tradition acknowledge as much. But this is not the issue. Part of the confusion, I imagine, is that they have taken their disagreements with certain proponents of the "new natural law theory" (who do indeed argue that capital punishment is inherently unjust) as applying to the more specific question of whether Christians are allowed to impose or support capital punishment. But the question of justice has never been a matter of much contention. Most ancient authors, at least, Christian no less than pagan, were happy to grant the inherent justice of every form of the *lex talionis*, and the Christians were willing to go still further and assert that in a sense all of us stand under a just sentence of death. But a Christian is held to a higher standard than what merely conforms with justice. And it is Feser and Bessette's persistent failure to grasp quite what the issue is that partly accounts for, and even somewhat excuses, their misreadings of the church fathers. But only partly. What remains inexcusable is their habit of adducing passages wrenched out of context and then of violently misrepresenting their authors. I do not really care whether Feser and Bessette are so benighted as to think Christians can practice capital punishment; but how dare they attribute such a view to Origen, who explicitly believed that Christians are prohibited by Christ's law from ever imposing the death penalty? In his reply to his critics, just as he and Bessette did in their book, Feser quotes a passage from the *Contra Celsum* in which Origen acknowledges that (as Paul said) the (pagan) government of his time has the power to torture and kill those who resist it, and that it wields this power by God's permission, and attempts to show thereby that Origen is willy-nilly on the side of capital punishment. This is atrocious. Unfortunately, however, this is also the approach Feser and Bessette consistently take to *all* the patristic evidence in their book. One of the more glaring examples of their cavalier attitude toward the documents they raid for proof texts is one that I mention in my original review: a single phrase they pluck from a sermon of John Chrysostom's, praising the emperor Theodosius for refraining from a "justifiable slaughter" of Antiochene rebels, which they offer as an unambiguous statement of the death penalty's propriety. This is simply perverse. Even in English, of course, "justifiable" would be a rather vague way of expressing John's view of things; but, of course, John did not write in English. What in fact he commends the emperor for *not* undertaking is a δίκαιος φόνος (*dikaios phonos*), which might better be rendered as "lawful" or even "*customary* slaughter" (*dikaios* does not have anything like the simple moral connotation of our word *just*). But that is only a minor concern. As it happens, the sentence is taken from what is in fact one of the most earnest and impassioned attacks on capital punishment in the whole corpus of post-Constantinian patristic literature. Feser also, I might note, cites a passage (very inaccurately translated, incidentally) from a famous pair of letters by Ambrose, written well into the Christian period of the empire, addressing the issue of whether magistrates ought to be excluded from communion if they have handed down guilty verdicts for crimes that statutorily carry the death penalty. Replying to the widespread assumption that they *should* be excluded (which is quite significant in itself), Ambrose concludes that those magistrates who willingly exclude *themselves* from communion on such grounds are to be praised (which is even more significant) but then concludes that bishops are still not authorized to excommunicate magistrates for discharging their offices in good conscience. In this, it is worth noting, Ambrose was breaking with the practices of the pre-Constantinian Church—and even then only reluctantly. In those same letters he goes on to affirm at great length, and quite passionately, that Christians ought not to condemn even the guilty to death but should instead forgive them and then seek their salvation.

So it goes. I do not know whether it is ignorance or cynicism that makes Feser and Bessette appear so indifferent to the true convictions of the authors they cite, but I hope it is the former. Not that it matters very much. Even when Feser cites patristic texts that seem more congenial to his views, he still invests them with meanings they do not naturally bear. Yes, Augustine's eighty-seventh epistle affirms the right of civil authorities to use coercion and violence (probably including capital punishment). And in the *City of God* Augustine says that those lawfully deputed by a duly appointed authority to put a person to death are not guilty of murder. By that time, perhaps, this was becoming the accepted view; but it certainly had not been the view of the church of the first few centuries. And, more to the point, it was also a very weak claim, and one entirely devoid of prescriptive content. As it happens, Augustine not only disliked capital punishment but also believed that Christians, being called to a higher good than mere natural justice, should properly refrain from it (see Sermon 13 and Letters 100, 133, 134, 153, *inter alia*). Feser is right, I concede, on one detail in his treatment of late antique Christian pronouncements on the death penalty: Pope Innocent I did in fact once defend capital punishment, early in the fifth century. In the same document, however, he also defended torture, which I believe Feser would not do. And so we are back to that damned poison tree again.

In any event, it really is not very difficult to follow the story here. The very earliest Christian documents that address the question of the death penalty treat it as a practice wholly forbidden for Christians. This is not open to debate; the evidence is clear and overwhelming. Even the one church father from the first three centuries who professes to find some moral value in capital punishment in some extreme cases, Clement of Alexandria, does so in a text written for pagan readers, and not as a prescription for Christian practice (among second-century Alexandrian Christians it was generally held that the highest moral and spiritual truths could be grasped only by those advanced in the faith). Simply said, the communities founded by the apostles, for several generations, regarded the rejection of the death penalty as an essential truth of their faith; in consequence, they regarded it as improper for Christians to serve as magistrates or to act as executioners, or even for that matter to accuse others of capital offenses. After the conversion of Constantine, however, as Christianity became more and more intertwined with the ancient imperial order, ambiguities began to arise. Ambrose, for instance, was clearly disposed to regard the death penalty as contrary to Christian principles; he even believed that Christ on the cross had exhausted the wrath of the Law entirely. But his was a delicate situation, and he (unlike the Christians of previous centuries) had to negotiate the reality of a baptized pagan social order. Whether his solution was the correct one may be debated. But the point to take away from this is that, even when the later church fathers conceded that the civil authority *could* sometimes impose the death penalty without inviting the church's ultimate censure, they rarely if ever conceded that Christians *ought* to do so. What is certainly not the case is that there was a "patristic consensus" *in favor* of capital punishment. There was at most a tendency among the later church fathers to attempt to find some sort of reasonable balance between, on the one hand, the intrinsic incompatibility of capital punishment with Christian moral principles and, on the other, the reality of the progressive conflation between civil society as a whole and the community of the faith. I do not object to Feser and Bessette taking what comfort they may from that, such as it is. Ambiguity always provides an opportunity for those enterprising enough to exploit it. Feser and Bessette may see here a development of Christian self-understanding, just where I see the start of a slow drift away from the teachings of the apostolic communities. What to them may look like an emerging clarity may look to me like a deepening confusion. As one pleases. That said, I *do* object, and very strenuously, to their willingness to exaggerate and in many instances to dissemble the views of the authors they so confidently cite.

III

Anyway—one last excursus, since it leads naturally to my concluding ob-servations. Feser and Bessette take considerable comfort from Romans 13:1–7 (the bit about obeying authorities, fearing the power of "the sword," and so on). They have to do so, since the rest of the New Testament seems to reject all form of coercion, and these few feeble and vague verses are the only thing remotely resembling an approbation of lethal civil force. In my review of Feser and Bessette's book, however, I raised several points about these verses, the *least important* of which is the classicist's quibble that the original Greek of the passage gives almost no encourage-ment to the idea that Paul is talking there about capital punishment at all. To repeat: the word usually translated as "sword" in this passage is μάχαιρα (*machaira*), which was the name for a large dagger or short sword generally carried at the waist in a μάχαιροδέτης (*machairodetēs*), a leather belt. Now, Paul may have used this word for any sword what-soever, but the truth is that the sentence in which it appears—οὐ γὰρ εἰκῇ τὴν μάχαιραν φορεῖ (*ou gar eikē tēn machairan phorei*), "For it does not carry the sword in vain"—resembles no customary formulation for the power of capital punishment. For that, one would generally expect a reference not to a *machaira* but to τὸ ξίφος (*to xiphos*)—"the sword"—wielded by an executioner. And the problem is not just the noun but the verb as well. *Phorei* really does have the connotation of "carry around," not the grander connotation of "bear" in the sense of owning a special privilege or of wielding a special power. The verb that would make sense if Paul were in fact speaking of the power of capital punishment would be a straightforward ἔχει (*echei*): "has," "holds," "controls." (I offered some lines from Philostratus to illustrate the point.) Paul's Greek may have been lacking in elegance, but he certainly would have been able to make his meaning clear if he had had any special reference to the death penalty in mind. To a first-century reader, the phrase τὴν μάχαιραν φορεῖ (*tēn machairan phorei*) would certainly have summoned up the image of a μαχαιροφόρος (*machairophoros*), a "carrier of a short sword," which is to say a soldier, military policeman, civil guard, or taxation enforcement officer. Dangerous men, admittedly (especially if one caused a public disturbance), but not executioners.

Feser grants that I *may* be right in my interpretation of the passage but then cites a host of New Testament scholars (some of whom are indeed very fine scholars) who say otherwise and so dismisses my observations as debatable. In point of fact, they are not. Feser may be under the impression that all New Testament scholarship is of equal weight. Most of it, though, merely repeats conventional readings, however fallacious. He may also not know that many New Testament scholars are not classicists but instead got their Greek in seminary and so do not have much ear for antique Greek idioms. And in the sentence in question, again, both noun and verb are wrong idiomatically. Moreover, scholarship progresses, and we have learned a great deal in recent years about what a *machairophoros* was from a host of Hellenistic papyri (again, see *Amherst Papyri* 2.38; *Papyri Tebtunis* 35.13 and 391.20; *Bodleian Ostraca* 3.64; *Michigan Papyri* 577.78; etc.). There is literally *no* compelling reason for reading Paul's remarks as referring to capital punishment, and a host of very good reasons for not doing so. And, truth be told, given the overwhelming power of the New Testament's language forbidding Christians to exact retributive justice and proclaiming the overthrow of the wrath of the Law in Christ, Feser and Bessette desperately need this passage to say what they want it to say, with absolute clarity; they at the very least need it to say what they want it to say with at least some substantial degree of probability. It does not. But, again, this is the *least important* point to be made about these verses. The *most important* is that they concern only how Christians are to conduct themselves as subjects of a pagan empire. Paul never imagined that a Christian civil order might arise, or even that the world would be around long enough for Christianity to become socially respectable. This passage offers no prescription whatsoever for how Christians might conduct themselves in positions of power or how they might legislate and enforce civil order. There is nothing in these verses—absolutely nothing—that addresses what is required of Christians in regard to the prosecution of justice in the public or private sphere. For that, one must repair instead to the explicit moral teachings of the New Testament; and these, once again, uniformly forbid Christians any recourse to retribution.

Which brings me to my final observations.

IV

It is perhaps easier for me, writing from the perspective of Orthodox Christianity, than it is for a Catholic to dismiss Feser's arguments. In the East, the matter was never really debated, and no theological justifications for capital punishment ever really entered the tradition. On the whole, the Eastern Church more or less unanimously opposes the practice and has a long tradition of theological and spiritual teachers who have abominated it. All the major Orthodox jurisdictions have condemned the practice in recent years. But for Feser, the matter is not merely one of tradition but of logic; and that is where he ends his reply to Griffiths and me. He thinks, for instance, that I have ensnared myself in an impossible dialectical bind. And, to show this, he calls attention to certain lines from my review of his book:

> Let us grant, for argument's sake, that the death penalty is indeed a just and proportionate response to willful murder. So what? That has never been the issue for Christians, for the simple reason that the Gospel does not admit the authority of proportional justice, as either a private or a public good. The whole of the Sermon on the Mount, for instance, is a shocking subversion of the entire idea. Christ repeatedly and explicitly forbids the application of such punishment. . . . Again and again, the New Testament demands of Christians that they exercise limitless forgiveness, no matter how grievous the wrong, even in legal and public settings. And it insists that, for the Christian, mercy always triumphs over judgment.

Aha. "So," Feser triumphantly fulminates, "it's not just a matter of not *executing* murderers. We also have to refrain from punishing murderers *at all*, and from punishing rapists, bank robbers, kidnappers, embezzlers, et al. too. The jails should be emptied, and every cheek turned to every sadist who would slash it with a switchblade, let alone slap it. Let justice never be done, though the heavens fall." Here, Feser thinks, I have dropped my guard entirely, and he need only deliver the coup de grâce: "Now, either Hart would endorse such a policy or he would not. If he would, then he owes us an explanation of how such permissiveness is compatible with even the most rudimentary social order. If he would not, then he owes us an explanation of how he can rule out capital punishment, but not other punishments, consistent with the extreme principles to which he is committed. Until he resolves this dilemma, his objection is not a serious one, but just empty rhetoric."

Well . . . nonsense. Twaddle. Dare I say, Balderdash? Feser's silly hysterics aside, to say nothing of his spasmodic attempts at a logical argument, I do not need to explain a damned thing. I am merely reporting a fact about the New Testament's prohibition of retribution, one that even a cursory reading of the text will confirm; take the issue up with Our Lord. More important, though, there is no dilemma here to resolve. Forgiveness precludes the principle of *retribution*, but not every form of punishment or coercion. A mother may at once punish her child and also forgive him unreservedly. Not, however, if she kills him. Then the whole forgiveness thing is definitely off the table. Of course, as cheap rhetorical tricks go, the reductio ad absurdum is among the most redoubtable and always looks devastating for a few seconds, at least to the more pliant spectators. My point, however, is obvious, and Feser understands it perfectly well: he is arguing for the liceity of a Christian principle of retributive justice, whereas the New Testament consistently forbids Christians to adopt such a principle. Hence the modern Catholic Church's refusal to allow for any possible just application of capital punishment except in those vanishingly rare (or possibly nonexistent) cases when it is the only way to save the lives of others. No doubt the gospel's prohibitions on retribution require prudence where the law is concerned, which means discerning which sorts of punishments are essentially retributive and which instead allow for the reformation of the criminal. Since capital punishment leaves the criminal dead, it would seem to be the very definition of the former. A large fine, a period of confinement, a life sentence, even the force exerted against a criminal to prevent him from harming another person (even if that force should prove lethal)—all of these can be imposed without complicity in the logic of retribution, at least ideally. It is quite possible that there is such a thing as force that is purely nonretributive in intent, and such a thing as a punishment that is also an act of forgiveness, even of charity. The death penalty, however—or so both logic and the testimony of the earliest Christians tell us—cannot really fit either description.

That said, and perhaps somewhat shockingly, I am willing to grant that here Feser has at least raised an interesting point. The earliest Christians, as it happened, refrained not only from magistracy and from pursuing complaints regarding capital crimes; they apparently refrained from all prosecution. In many ways, the early church was so uncompromising and radical in its rejections of the old order that its ethos may very well have verged on a kind of anarchism. And indeed, in reading the New Testament, one finds very little encouragement for the idea that Christians as a whole have any responsibility for what Feser calls "rudimentary social order." I confess too that my understanding of Christianity (at least, that of the earliest centuries) is far more otherworldly and socially irresponsible than Feser's is. On the whole, he assumes that Christianity must be compatible with a well-functioning society, and that therefore Christianity in some larger neutral sense "works" as a way of promoting the social good. But perhaps Christianity, as presented in the New Testament, does not "work" very well at all or at least would not do so if it were consistently applied to life in this world. Of course, it has never really been tried, so it is hard to say with certainty. Still, it seems likely that a genuinely Christian social order—made up entirely of those committed to Christ, and governed entirely by the sort of "lawless law" described in the Sermon on the Mount or in Paul's depiction of the new life in Christ—might be impossible in practice, and therefore unimaginable in theory. I really do not know. I do not pretend to have any clear sense of whether a Christian social order could ever flourish this side of the Kingdom. I know only that Christians must live as if it could.

I know also that the story of the church's view of capital punishment is a great deal simpler than Feser makes it seem. I do not believe that anyone can possibly truly absorb the moral and spiritual teachings of the New Testament and conclude anything other than that there can be no genuinely Christian support for the death penalty. And the history of the early church bears luminous witness to this. In later centuries, admittedly, as Christendom progressively displaced the earlier, purer, and more perilous forms of Christian life, things did indeed become more confused. Loyalty to Christ and loyalty to the civil order were now no longer antithetical to one another, which meant that neither loyalty could remain uncompromised by the other. Hence, again, all the great spiritual achievements and all the tragic spiritual betrayals that constitute the history of Christian civilization. Now that that civilization has passed, though, with all the good and bad consequences that have followed from its decline, the movement of the ancient churches on this issue back toward the example of the early apostolic communities seems to have become inexorable. I think it appealing to take this to be a great work of the Holy Spirit, for what that is worth. Feser sees it in an altogether different light, just as he sees Christianity as something very different from what I take it to be. All I can say, once again, is that, weighing all the evidence in the balance—scripture, the history of the early church, the patristic evidence, the plain language of the gospel—his view seems impossible to support logically. And, frankly, the book he wrote with Bessette does immeasurably more to confirm that conclusion than to challenge it.

Orthodoxy in America

I

I am going to be somewhat vague and elliptical and willfully diffuse in the reflections to come; and this is because I have many questions but few answers, many intuitions but no certitudes, and many apprehensions and hopes but very little by way of foresight. So I beg your indulgence, even though I have no right to presume upon it. So—

As a rule, it is bad form to borrow someone else's personal anecdote, but sometimes a story is too perfectly apt not to repeat. So, the best I can do by way of decorum here is to acknowledge that this is something that happened not to me but to my eldest brother Addison, some years ago. He was in Constantinople, at the time—or Istanbul, if you are one of those pedantic sorts who feels it necessary to take account of the events of the last seven centuries—on a tour bus (which is a place one would rarely find him). Among his fellow travelers there was a recent American convert to Greek Orthodoxy, a middle-aged gentleman from some sultry quarter of the Deep South who, to judge just by his attire and his Scots-Irish physiognomy, could easily have been mistaken for your typical, genial, cheerful white-Naugahyde-encrusted arthropod happily scuttling along on his way toward a meeting of the Southern Baptist Convention. This in itself provided more than enough cognitive dissonance to endue the day's atmosphere with a touch of the surreal. But a moment of consummate absurdity arrived when, quite unbidden, this fellow lugubriously remarked—in a richly ruminant drawl soaked in tobacco and sarsaparilla—"Those Latins simply cannot understand what the sack of

Constantinople in 1204 still means to us." Now, my brother's appetite for the ludicrous is every bit as insatiable as my own, but this was just a little more than he could absorb with perfect equanimity. So, in as earnest a tone as he could affect, he mischievously opined that the Byzantines had had it coming, as redress for the 1182 atrocities against the metic Latins living in the city (massacre, countless women and children sold to Turkish slavers, and so on). Needless to say, the morose southern gentleman had no idea what my brother was talking about; but, then again, he had probably never heard of the sack of Constantinople either until maybe two months earlier. And so there was still something rather impressive in his ability to convert the latter into a shattering personal trauma throbbing like an open wound in his soul, the thought of which left him as inconsolably melancholy as the memory of the burning of Atlanta or the fall of Richmond. Somehow this kind of abrupt but total adoption of another cultural identity—even if it is little more than a fantasy version of that identity—is something of which Americans are uniquely capable. Perhaps this is because to be American is to be the deracinated child of some other land or people, or of several other lands and peoples. Our "proper" national identity is often little more than a bright, garish, fabulous surface spread thinly over forgotten depths; our national narrative is essentially an idea, never fully realized, of course, but serving to keep us borne aloft above the abyss of an immense historical oblivion. To be truly American, in the purest way, is to be a kind of empty Proteus, intrinsically nothing and so capable of becoming just about anything. All of which may amount to a special cultural genius for all I know; but it does raise questions regarding what must become of a tradition like Eastern Orthodoxy—or perhaps, I should say, the many traditions that constitute the Eastern Christian presence here—when immersed in that magical element of ceaseless dissolution and transformation that is American life. What, after all, does the fact of a man like the one my brother encountered on that bus really portend? As much as he had succeeded in transforming himself into a Byzantine tormented by the historical memories of all his Byzantine forebears, he had also succeeded in transforming the Byzantium of his imagination into something conformable to his own cultural sensibility and native capacity for immemorial resentments, regrets, desolate memories . . . And this is only to be expected. Every act of conversion involves a reciprocal transformation, a mutual act of appropriation. And this is why it seems fair to assume that, inevitably, Orthodoxy in America must in some sense become ever more America's special variant of the faith. And, so, what might that look like?

This might at first seem a trivial question. Orthodoxy has been here for quite some time, after all, and the effects of its transplantation to this soil are there for all to see. And, unlike its presence in its native lands, Orthodoxy exists here simultaneously in all its cultural expressions—despite which, it has proved a remarkably intransigent property, not only retaining much of its aboriginal culture but scarcely ever venturing across the lines of its own differing national jurisdictions. In that sense, the story of Orthodoxy in America has, for the most part, been just another version of the great American immigrant myth: peoples displaced from their ancient homelands by desperate need or buoyant hope (or both), beginning here anew while retaining a firm sense of their own cultures and ways and tongues. Persisting, prospering, remaining distinctive while still finding their place in the larger society. In each generation, some have married out of the faith, while others have married in, but the communities have remained fairly stable redoubts of ethnic and religious identity. In that sense, Orthodoxy in America has been a success in American terms, though perhaps for just that reason sometimes something of a failure in spiritual terms. After all, as significant as diverse Orthodox congregations have always been for the preservation of ethnic communities, this diversity of jurisdictions has also contributed to preserving the original sin of Orthodox culture: its all too frequent failure, that is, to detach the universal mission of the church from the local allegiances and worldly concerns of nations and ethnic groups. In a sense, although the Orthodox have come to America in the millions, Orthodoxy itself will probably never arrive here in its own right until the faith has shed—however painfully—the burden of preserving ethnic pride and identity, neither abandoning the past nor clinging to it too fiercely, and has finally achieved a single jurisdictional presence here. But I defer that issue for now.

To be honest, my interest is not in the ways that Orthodox communities have adapted themselves to the immigrant experience or the American way of life. I am much more deeply concerned with the ways in which America may refashion—reinvent, so to speak—Orthodoxy in its own image, alongside or within these transplanted communities, and then export the product abroad. And I am also concerned with the question of whether that synthesis, should it come about, would represent a new epoch in Orthodoxy, a genuinely American expression of the faith, ready to take its place alongside its more ancient expressions, or would instead turn out to constitute a profound challenge to the integrity of the tradition. Here there are both promises and perils. This is, after all, the chief danger America poses to all cultures. America is not merely a place, but also an ideology; it is not just a physical landscape, much less just an ensemble of shared memories and legends; it is a nation more constructed than cultivated, built around a political and social project always somewhat in flux but also more or less relentlessly oriented toward a future generated out of its own native ideals and values rather than out of any traditions it might have inherited from the lands its peoples left behind in coming here. Moreover, it intends that future not only for itself but also—distantly, dimly, but inevitably—for all peoples everywhere. And, in that sense, America is not only an ideology but something approaching a religion. It has its own sacred writ, its "founding fathers," its radiant eschatological visions, its hymns and prayers and benedictions. And it has its special national values, many of which—being essentially libertarian in form, in the American sense of "libertarian"—are largely irreconcilable with the gospel. It is also a stupendous and bewitching reality, exuberantly enormous and seductively grandiose and gloriously improbable. And so, when we try to think clearly about the destiny of the Eastern Church on these shores, we need perhaps first to ask whether Orthodoxy *in* America can indefinitely continue to resist incorporation into the native orthodoxies *of* America, while yet finding a way to be nourished by what this land provides.

II

To a very substantial degree, the future will be determined by how well Eastern Orthodox communities continue to adjust to the altogether singular situation in America with regard to conversions from other Christian communions, and most especially from various forms of Evangelical Protestantism. Conversions occur everywhere, of course, but usually in the form of individuals seeking a confessional refuge, to whose native forms they are all too willing to assimilate. In America since the 1970s, by contrast, the rate of conversion has increased to the point that, while the absolute number of converts may not be immense, the number relative to the Orthodox population is anything but negligible. More to the point, the community of converts in America is often sufficiently distinctive and sufficiently socially cohesive to constitute a kind of resident cultural presence within the larger Orthodox community. In fact, in the very special case of the Evangelical Orthodox Mission, we have a case of an entire ecclesial community being admitted, and yet not dissolved, into the church: a community with its own special history, longings, internal alliances, internal antagonisms, idiosyncrasies, and perhaps (alas) prejudices, left largely intact. True, in ages past entire tribes and nations were converted from paganism to Byzantine Christianity; but the situation in America today is not analogous to that. Rather, Orthodoxy has become a haven for a large if loosely affiliated community of Christians whose expectations of their faith have been formed as much by the traditions they have left behind as by the Orthodoxy they have embraced. They come into the church with many of their expectations regarding what Christianity truly is or should be thoroughly formed and unalterable. At times, this has had something of a refreshing and invigorating effect on local Orthodox parishes; but it has also at other times exercised a remarkably narrowing effect upon Orthodoxy as a presence within American society. For one thing, many of these converts—and again, perhaps unfairly, I would say especially converts from Evangelicalism—come from traditions that, being rather historically shallow manifestations of an extremely modern form of piety, have very little concept of licit theological latitude, or of theological complexity. Many of them are accustomed to think of Christian faith as simply a uniform set of explicit beliefs, almost a catalogue of propositions, susceptible of few interpretations. And, merely by an accident of history, most American converts have adopted the version of Orthodox self-understanding that became dominant in the latter half of the twentieth century: which is to say, the neo-Palamite synthesis, especially as promoted by those remarkable generations of Russian scholars whose writings opened the world of Eastern Christian thought to Western Christians. Now, I admit, this is an approach to Orthodoxy that I happen to think profound but also inadequate—to be specific, I think it frequently involves a remarkably violent and restrictive misreading of patristic tradition, and probably of Palamas himself, as well as a neglect of other dimensions of the tradition—but that is of small importance. Let a thousand flowers blossom, say I. I may be wrong, after all. What I think disastrous, however, is the inability of many American Orthodox converts to distinguish between that particular, rather synthetic school of Orthodoxy and the Orthodox faith as such. For them, nothing else in the rich tradition of Eastern Christian thought and devotion—say, the Byzantine scholastics, the Russian religious philosophers of the nineteenth century, and so on—let alone any movement within modern Orthodox theology that does not perfectly conform to the neo-Palamite system, counts as Orthodox Christianity at all. And it is these good souls, more than any other faction within the church, who tend to be the most obstreperous, rigorist, and self-confident guardians of what they regard as "pure" Orthodoxy, and the most eager to attack Orthodox scholarship and theological speculation that does not immediately correspond to the attenuated, abstracted, impoverished view of the tradition that they were taught. In place of the biblicist fundamentalism left behind, many tend toward a kind of neopatristic fundamentalism that is every bit as crude and pernicious.

Admittedly, every religious community has its share of purists and fundamentalists, and in the main they do little harm. And in the actual Orthodox *academic* world the Orthodox specimens are largely ignored. But in the particular case of the Orthodox Church in this country there is a moral peril that ought not to be overlooked. It is in the nature of conversion that it often involves not only a sincere affection for what one is converted *to* but also an earnest and sometimes resentful disaffection for what one has converted *from*. And this can bear a bitter fruit. Moreover, in the case of some former Evangelicals, conversion to Orthodoxy has often seemed an especially agreeable retreat to a more ancient Christianity precisely because it has allowed them to make their journey *ad fontes* without being forced to surrender something nearly as precious to them as Christianity itself: to wit, their hatred of Roman Catholicism. As a rule, Orthodox tradition has more than enough endemic suspicion of Western Christianity; and, of course, there are large and significant differences—doctrinal, theological, and ecclesial—between Eastern and Western Christian tradition. But, precisely because there are real differences that divide Christians, it is absolutely imperative that we not allow ourselves to deepen those divisions by exaggerating, misrepresenting, or (to put it bluntly) celebrating them. To be perfectly frank, the emerging American form of Orthodoxy—that is, an Orthodoxy shaped more by *converts to* than by *inheritors of* the church's traditions—has proved almost inexhaustibly fertile ground for any number of nonsensical claims regarding the differences between East and West; and some of these claims have had the extraordinary effect of distorting Orthodox understandings not only of Western Christianity but of Orthodoxy itself—indeed, by a kind of inversion of the logic of the anti-Catholic apologetics, of often reducing Orthodoxy to a parody of itself. Not to dwell on things too recherché, I cannot help but note that, in recent years, it has become something of a fashion among American Orthodox polemicists to claim that certain aspects of Catholic theology—the definition of God as *actus purus*, for instance, or affirmations of the absolute simplicity of the divine nature, or the metaphysics of divine transcendence that has come to be known by the formula *analogia entis*—are not only alien to Orthodoxy but irreconcilably inimical to it. What is curious about this is that all of these features of Catholic theology are in fact entirely identical with the traditional metaphysics of Orthodox tradition; in fact, as earlier generations of Orthodox scholars were well aware—from John Damascene to Sergei Bulgakov—they represent nothing other than the philosophical inheritance of the Greek fathers. And so now we find ourselves confronted with the absurd situation of Orthodox scholars claiming that certain essential elements of Orthodox tradition are in fact Latin perversions of the faith and sometimes offering in their stead varieties of theology drawn from Anglo-American analytic theistic philosophy (than which there is none more primitive in its ontological premises). This is rather tragic. After all, whether or not they have any particular interest in ecumenism, it would be a sad fate indeed if, in their eagerness to find new ways to differentiate their theology from that of Roman Catholics, Orthodox Christians in this country should succeed only in rejecting their own tradition.

III

And yet even this is not my principal interest. Over time, theological disputes either clarify themselves or subtly mutate into different issues altogether; and, on the whole, they have little effect on the daily lives of the faithful. Theologians are not really nearly as important as they imagine themselves, and the church as a whole would probably be better off if they were all periodically exterminated—say, every twenty years or so. I raise the matter only as illustrative of a larger set of concerns, regarding the slower alchemy of cultural transformations. As I have noted, America has a singular power for refashioning all things in its own image, and for doing so with an almost monstrously indomitable energy; for much of the world, this is both the appeal and the terror that America represents. And, as Orthodoxy here continues to develop in relation to this country's indigenous ideals, and as its ties to distant lands continue to become more strained and tenuous, and as its demographics become more diverse, there is every reason to suspect that it will become increasingly a reflection of the native temperaments and tacit ideals of America. And I do not mean simply that the Orthodox in this country will continue, as they have done for centuries, to accommodate themselves to the social realities of the nation, for both good and ill: say, America's admirable and wonderful ethnic diversity and pluralism, with its potentially benignly corrosive effect on Orthodoxy's often destructive confusion between preaching the gospel and preserving ethnic identity; or say, conversely, America's idolatrous adoration and sanctification of free-market economics in even its most perfidious forms, and the disgraceful dereliction of responsibility for social welfare that this perpetuates to the justifiable distaste of the rest of the developed world. I mean, rather, that Orthodoxy will continue to be shaped by an inevitably dialectical relation to America's distinctive spiritual ethos; and what this may produce may as yet be unimaginable. Orthodoxy is a tradition sunk in history, with deep roots of memory, and deep resistance to change. But, in a sense, the great dream or romance of America is the prospect of a people without history, a humanity that has, as none before it ever could, escaped the prison of memory.

Hence, though there is nothing like a distinctive American civilization, there definitely is a distinctly American Christianity. It is something fluid, scattered, fragmentary, and fissile, often either mildly or exorbitantly heretical, and sometimes only vestigially Christian; but it can nevertheless justly be called the American religion—and it is a powerful creed. It is, for one thing, a style of faith admittedly lacking in beautiful material forms or coherent institutional structures, not by accident but essentially. Its civic inexpressiveness is a consequence not simply of cultural privation, or of frontier simplicity, or of modern utilitarianism, or even of some lingering Puritan reserve toward ecclesial rank and architectural ostentation, but also of a profound and radical resistance to outward forms. It is, at its purest, a religion of the book or of private revelation, of oracular wisdom and emotional rapture, but not one of tradition, hierarchy, or public creeds. Even where it creates intricate institutions of its own and erects its own large temples, it tends to do so entirely on its own terms, in a void, in a cultural and (ideally) physical desert, at a fantastic remove from all traditional sources of authority, historical "validity," or even good taste (Mormonism is an expression of this tendency at its boldest, most original, and most effervescently uncouth). In one sense, this is not at all surprising. America was born in a flight from the Old World's thrones and altars, the corrupt accommodations between spiritual authority and earthly power, the old confusion of reverence for God with servility before princes—all of which Orthodox history contains in abundance. As a political project in its own right, the United States was the first Western nation explicitly founded on principles requiring no official alliance between religious confession and secular government. Ours was the first laicist nation. Even if this had not been so, the ever-greater religious heterogeneity of America over the course of its history would surely, sooner or later, have made such an alliance absurdly impractical. And so, in fact, America was established as the first truly modern nation, the first Western society consciously to dissociate its constitutional order from the political mythologies of a long-disintegrating Christendom, and the first predominantly Christian country to place itself under, at most, God's general providential supervision, but not under the command of any of his officially recognized lieutenants. The nation began, one could argue, from a place at which the other nations of the West had not yet arrived. And yet, when one considers the results of this odd apocalyptic liberty from history, it all seems rather astonishing. America may have arisen out of the end of Christendom, but it somehow avoided the religious and cultural fate of the rest of the modern West. Far from blazing a trail into the post-Christian future that awaited other nations, America went quite a different way, down paths that no other Western society would ever tread or even know how to find. Whereas European society—moving with varying speed but in a fairly uniform direction—experienced the end of Christendom simultaneously as the decline of faith, in America just the opposite happened. Here, the paucity of institutional and "civilizing" mediations between the transcendent and the immanent went hand in hand with a general, largely formless, and yet utterly irrepressible intensification of faith: rather than the exhaustion of religious longing, its revival; rather than a long nocturnal descent into disenchantment, a new dawning of early Christianity's elated expectation of the Kingdom.

Now, admittedly, I should avoid excessive generalization on this matter. Just about every living religion has found some kind of home here, bringing along whatever institutional supports it could fit into its luggage. Many such creeds have even managed to preserve the better part of their integrity. As I have said, this is certainly true of the Orthodoxy that arrived here in successive waves of immigration. Still, I would argue (maybe with a little temerity), such communities exist here as displaced fragments of other spiritual worlds, embassies from more homogeneous religious cultures, and it is from those cultures that they derive whatever cogency they possess. They are beneficiaries of the hospitable and capacious indeterminacy of American spirituality but not direct expressions of it. The form of Christianity most truly *indigenous* to America is one that is simultaneously peculiarly disembodied and unconquerably vigorous, and its unity is one of temperament rather than of confession. At its purest, in fact, it is free of almost all memory, and so of all anxiety: it strives toward a state of almost perfect timelessness, seeking a place set apart from the currents of human affairs, where God and the soul can meet and, so to speak, affirm one another. And Evangelicalism is the purest embodiment of this faith. It can lead to absolutely invincible faith. It can lead also to absolutely invincible intellectual narrowness. Moreover, American Evangelicalism often not only lacks any sense of tradition but is cordially adverse to tradition on principle: What is tradition, after all, other than manmade history, and what is history other than exile from paradise? What need does one have of tradition when one has the Bible, that eternal love letter from Jesus to the soul, inerrant, unambiguous, uncorrupted by the vicissitudes of human affairs? Despite the sometimes admirable virtues of this way of living, in its most natural, organic, and genuinely Christian expressions, and with the great generosity of soul that often accompanies it, in some of its most extreme, most emotive forms, it is a religion of total and unsullied reverie, the pure present of a beautifully childlike world, in which ingenuous outcries and happy gestures and urgent conjurations instantly bring forth succor and substance. And, at its most intensely fundamentalist, so precipitous is its flight from the gravity of history into Edenic and eschatological rapture that it reduces all of cosmic history to a few thousand years of terrestrial existence and the whole of the present to a collection of signs urgently pointing to the world's imminent ending.

IV

Why, though, I suppose one might ask, do I dwell on these things here? Obviously Eastern Orthodoxy in this country is in no danger of exchanging its basilicas for megachurches or abandoning the Divine Liturgy in favor of something like Joel Osteen's orgies of saccharine sentiment. Why, after all, should the prevalence of this native religious sensibility prove any greater challenge to Orthodox self-understanding than it has for, say, Roman Catholicism? Well, for one thing, Roman Catholicism in this country actually does often exhibit a number of odd social and cultural features that do, in fact, somewhat reflect the individualism, institutional insouciance, and ideological peculiarities of the American religious consciousness. But, more to the point, where Catholicism is strong, Orthodoxy is weak. The Roman Church is an immense presence here and is at least scaffolded by an elaborate and largely centralized institutional structure whose real source of stability is Rome and the larger communion of a church that circles the globe. Moreover, it has a remarkably vigorous and large intellectual tradition, incarnated in its innumerable great universities and colleges, which regularly produce scholars whose training in every sphere of theological, philosophical, and historical research is of the most exemplary quality and depth. None of this is true of the Orthodox Church. Admittedly, there are a number of fine Orthodox scholars out there; but they are not legion. This is only to be expected, given the histories of the lands where Orthodoxy resides. And, among the scattered jurisdictions that exist here, the resources for resistance to novel adventitious cultural forces are few and rather feeble. Now, this is not necessarily always a bad thing; for instance, Orthodoxy in this country, by very virtue of its institutional weakness, perhaps enjoys a moment of historical liberty from the worst aspect of Eastern Christian history—that is, the church's frequently servile relations to the state or to national identity. Like American Catholicism before it, American Orthodoxy has in many respects found itself freer to be the church. In generations to come, perhaps an Orthodoxy truly purged of these toxins might evolve in this land, if the hierarchies of our several communions can find some way of forging an institutionally unified church here (as, of course, is canonically proper in any event).

That said, even this will require a certain vigilance and spiritual intelligence regarding which aspects of American culture can nourish Orthodoxy on these shores, and which might instead transform it into just another variant of the American religious myth. What I have called the American religion here—fairly or not—is in fact the native form of spiritual life most likely to determine the shape that Orthodoxy continues to assume in this country, simply because the forms of Christianity it molds and animates are where the lion's share of conversions to Orthodoxy have been coming from for some decades now; and also because frequently it is these converts who are among the most dynamic and assured and vigorously proselytizing element in many congregations. For what it is worth—and conceding from the outset the difficulty of prognostication regarding large or local cultural developments—my belief is that we are indeed seeing a novel form of Orthodoxy taking form in this country, slowly but inexorably, that is at least as American as it is Orthodox. I suspect, moreover, that none of the existing Orthodox jurisdictions is quite prepared to recognize and respond to every dimension of this reality, or to understand it, or to know how to temper or guide its dynamisms as the need will arise. And such is the vigor of this new reality that it will inevitably begin to have an influence on Orthodox self-understanding in other lands. America, after all, is a tireless and uncontainable engine of cultural destruction and creation. This new American Orthodoxy will not, I think, supplant the more settled and ethnically restive communities here, but it will grow alongside and within them and will ever more overshadow them as a force within the larger culture. It will, I suspect, be an intellectually narrow expression of the faith, like the native forms of Christianity from which it borrows its energies, and will prove somewhat too hospitable to reactionary—and I do mean reactionary, rather than merely conservative—politics. And, I will be honest, I am apprehensive about it, even as I am hopeful that the wellsprings of Orthodox spiritual life and tradition will ultimately prove too deep and too inexhaustible to be overwhelmed by the formless and titanic power of American spirituality in its most exuberantly foolish and uncontrollable forms.

Frustratingly, perhaps, I have to end in ambiguity, posing questions I cannot answer. But to me it seems that there are two emerging possibilities within the Eastern Church here, and much will be determined by whether we possess the strength to control the one and the courage to embrace the other. The former is the appearance of this distinctive American Orthodoxy, which—as is so often the case with American religious movements—will be largely constituted by a fantasy history in place of real history, and a religious ideology in place of a living tradition. The latter, though, is the possible natural development here, as could happen nowhere else, of a self-aware Orthodoxy that has at long last severed its mission to speak the gospel from its institutional and cultural subordination to nations and governments and discrete peoples. Perhaps a day will then arrive when not a single Scots-Irish convert from the Deep South will feel in the least obliged to convince himself he is a Greek—for the Orthodox Church itself will remind him that in Christ there is neither Jew nor Greek nor South Carolinian, but all are one. This is to say, it seems to me—if there is a desire to pursue this end, and enough spiritual wisdom among us to persevere in that pursuit—that Orthodoxy in America may, by way of our anomalous national experience, discover a way of being not *American* but truly *universal* in its vision and form and thereby become ever more the church that it has always been called to be: the home of all humanity in the eternal body of Christ. If the Orthodox in America have a mission to perform special to them, a vocation to obey, a vision to seek, let it—pray God—be this one.

15

University and Magisterium

Remarks in Response to Reinhard Hütter

I

I have no great disagreements to report with Reinhard Hütter's presentation, at least none that I am qualified to advance, even
though I might confess some hesitations on my part in consenting to his
formulations. Moreover, as his remarks were admirably complete in
themselves, I feel able to offer little more than a few additional observations. To certain of his principal claims, moreover, it would be nearly impossible for any sort of believer to offer any serious objection. That truth,
as a transcendental condition of all inquiry and discovery and knowledge
and wisdom, is one, and that therefore all particular truths must be in
harmony with one another, seems to me a necessary conclusion not only
of metaphysical or theological conviction but simply of reason (both pure
and practical). And, inasmuch as I am more than willing to grant that
academic freedom is to be cherished, first and foremost, insofar as it allows for the realization of the *telos* of all education—universal knowledge,
that is—I agree also that freedom ought to mean more than the mere
negative freedom of liberty from interference (though it should mean at
least that much and often does not). Only thus can it constitute the freedom to realize the essence of the university. Moreover, Cardinal Newman
is surely correct that, as Hütter says, the university is free to the very
degree that it is philosophical, at least "philosophical" in the classical
(rather than analytic) sense: the rational aspiration of the will toward

truth in its diversity, integrity, and unity, which constitutes the transcendental horizon of the mind's striving toward knowledge as an intrinsic good. And I more than agree with Pieper on a principle whose prophetic urgency becomes ever more obvious each year as the beleaguered humanities are progressively reduced by administrators and benefactors to adjuncts of the business schools and to the polytechnical training programs that are taking over universities; there is no greater enemy to and corrosive agent of true academic freedom than the total instrumentalization of knowledge for pragmatic ends. To which observations one may add, with full approbation, Hütter's proposition that the catholicity of truth is served only by a curriculum that harmonizes all disciplines in their complementary but distinct integrities by emphasizing the philosophical dimension in each. I could go on.

Here, though, I prefer simply to add another observation regarding the problems with the reduction of all knowledge to *techne* in the modern university. Hütter properly calls attention to, and laments, the fragmentation of knowledge under a regime of mere negative freedom, and of the destructive instrumentalization of the disciplines. And he says enough, it seems to me, about the degree to which, under those conditions, any sense of the complementarity of all truths is either lost sight of or treated as a matter of indifference. He might have said more, however, about the way in which this approach to knowledge not only shatters the university into an irreparably atomized collection of specializations but—at the same time, perversely enough—works relentlessly toward the dissolution of many of those specializations themselves as genuinely distinctive fields of inquiry, each with its own native integrity and intrinsic substance. This is because, in relation to the humanities at least, the modern technical reduction of knowledge does not merely forsake the universality of knowledge as something diversely oriented to a single transcendental truth but substitutes for it the rather sordid universality of a remarkably sterile functionalism (either technical or, in its still deeper essence, economic). Thus we see university administrations arguing that the humanities ought to be understood not as intrinsic goods in themselves, whose fields of knowledge possess an inherent rationale and purpose in need of no further justification, but rather as vehicles for training the young in the application of various "general skills" (whatever the hell that means) to more important pursuits, such as building a business.

Thus the humanities need possess no particular content in themselves. The study of polyphony, painting, palaeography, or Proust (just to stick with a few of the P's for a moment) need not be about the mastery of any of those subjects as a good in itself, so long as that study can plausibly or vaguely be said to endue its students with the sort of tactical resources or mental agility that might aid them in the real business of life—which is to say, of course, life as business. The humanities are not in themselves the content of an education but only an occasion for the acquisition of something called, oh, "critical thinking." Proust, painting, polyphony— take your pick. It is the technique and not the thing itself that matters. And so, as much as it may seem urgent today that we should emphasize the complementarity of all truths, it is no less urgent that we should place every bit as great a stress upon the special integrity of each discrete discipline: how, that is, it mounts up toward the transcendental end of all knowledge only first in its own proper modality, through seeking and preserving its own intrinsic perfection, and thereby discovering how it provides one indispensably unique inflection of that "philosophical dimension" of learning of which Hütter speaks.

I suspect that, viewing these matters under their metaphysical aspect, I might be more radically uncompromising on some points than Hütter, judging from certain other disagreements we have had with one another in the past (friendly disagreements, that is). So I shall proceed with some delicacy here, at least as far as presuming that there is perfect agreement between us, just in case my language would not accord with his in every respect. So, I would phrase the matter thus: as the term of the unity of all knowledge in its "philosophical" dimension or "universal" range is teleological, and the end that gathers all these diverse modes of inquiry into an integral unity is necessarily transcendental, it seems to me that one can fully defend the unity, harmony, and diverse but concrete coherence of universal knowledge only by insisting that the sole intentional natural end for a rational nature is supernatural: nothing less than the divine simplicity itself. I mean to say, if I had any patience for the theologically indefensible but also logically and phenomenologically incoherent notion that rational spirit in its drive toward truth could ever rest satisfied in any natural end, or even that there is such a thing as pure nature comprising ends adequate to a rational appetite for truth— or if one imagines that the proper desire for the divine essence is only a

superadded *lumen gloriae* not necessarily fundamental to every employment of reason—well, then, why should I not accept the possibility that
the different disciplines possess immanent ends sufficient unto themselves, and that the harmony between different realms of knowledge
need function as nothing more than a formal and abstract license for a
perfect division of the sciences: a guarantee, that is, that their several
truths need never come into conflict with one another because their finite ends need never really converge at all? Again, my language may
prove more combative on this score than Hütter's; but I cannot forbear
to phrase it thus: the unity of the several truths peculiar to the disciplines
lies not in their compatibility or mere nonrepugnance one to another,
under the canopy of their formal agreement as natural reflections of a
transcendental unity of truth as such, but in the transcendent simplicity
of God's own being, to which they are necessarily oriented; and an ideal
curriculum would be one that consciously reflects the supernatural aspiration that is the most primordial impulse of all knowledge.

II

Now, on the matter of the special "glory" and "responsibility" of Roman
Catholic universities, to which Hütter adverts, I am constrained from
merely nodding in assent by two considerations. The first is confessional.
Writes Hütter in his third thesis: *"Authentic academic freedom in Catholic
theology is realized precisely in the fidelity to the testimonial propositionality
of revealed truth as conveyed by sacred Scripture and sacred Tradition, and as
specified by the Magisterium of the Church."* Here I cannot follow him, obviously, and have no real inclination to do so. When Hütter speaks of the
magisterium, he is speaking of a vehicle of the Holy Spirit whose special
vocation is to lead faithful minds toward Christian truth and to avert
error. When I speak of the magisterium, I mean just "some guys." So all
of that goes beyond my remit or my realm of intellectual sympathy. And
I must confess to finding the phrase *testimonial propositionality* somewhat
obscure (though that may be a purely pathological reaction, following
upon the trauma of having been reared in the Anglophone philosophical
world, with its positively constitutive inability to distinguish between
"propositions" and "thinking"). But, in principle, I understand what he
is saying.

My second consideration, however, is one of what I take to be a salutary dread of the "catechetical" approach to university education. And here I may, somewhat paradoxically, want to argue for the liberal freedom of even the Catholic university from too dogmatic a sense of mission. Not that I am accusing Hütter of this—but I want to make sure due weight is given to the thought that "negative freedom" in the scholarship of the university may conduce to a positive good, precisely because it does not allow us to mistake the theological or philosophical dimension of the curriculum as consisting in merely a body of *credenda* to be transmitted to the young, jealously guarded against innovation of every kind and preserved in the purity of perfect invariability. I have seen at a few Catholic institutions, and one in particular, the dire effects of a well-meaning Catholic faculty binding its educational labors to a single precise catechetical agenda. Among those effects I would include not only a failure to take adequately into account the challenges to the traditional language of faith and doctrine from modern thought and research but also a failure adequately to explore or convey the extraordinarily fertile diversity, richness, and even contradictory impulses of Catholic tradition. And this catechetical impulse also led in those cases to some remarkably silly deformations of teaching. I can think of one episode, in particular, in which a fiercely zealous Dominican lecturer of my acquaintance insisted on telling his undergraduate students that the seven great miracles recounted in John's Gospel are in fact directly representative allegories of the seven sacraments of the church. And, despite the ludicrous anachronism of such a notion, of which he was no doubt in some sense quite aware, he insisted in visiting this idea on his students, not as a spiritual exegesis of the texts (which might have been defensible, if a bit syrupy), but as an actual historical claim. And I could recount other instances in my experience of Catholic teachers, under the impulse of providing the young with edification and of assisting in the transmission of the doctrinal deposit, prosecuting their perceived missions by promoting historical illiteracy among their students.

Anecdotes aside, however, I am really talking about a more difficult and delicate problem: that of recognizing that theology (and hence the understanding of doctrine) is a living and synthetic and dynamic movement of thought (interpretive, creative, critical), some of whose expressions in the present may seem as troubling to traditionalists today as did the adoption of Aristotelianism in the thirteenth century to the traditionalists of that age. And many of these expressions—even though they be of the healthiest kind—can all too easily be misunderstood, suppressed, thwarted, and discouraged by too unimaginative, too authoritative, and too (dare I say?) *magisterial* a governance of the university. Doctrinal formulations are *termini*, admittedly, but *termini a quibus*, not merely *termini ad quos*, and knowing how to strike the right balance here between tradition and innovation is not necessarily going to figure high among the strengths of the magisterium, or of any other ecclesial power outside the university. In fact, it is simply a truth of Catholic intellectual history that university scholars have often proved better than those holding magisterial appanages at discerning what is or is not in keeping with tradition, and what areas of theology are truly fertile but as yet lie fallow.

For example, I am convinced that, just as Thomas was able to draw upon the recovery of Aristotelian models of thought in his day, there is a great deal that Christian theology has yet to learn and appropriate from certain schools of Hindu Vedanta and Cittamatra Buddhism (to take two examples out of many), and that Christian tradition possesses the dynamism and the intellectual and spiritual resources to do so. I have, however, seen honest, scrupulous, and doctrinally quite innocuous attempts at just this sort of synthesis met with positive hysteria by churchmen and collegians for whom anything other than recitations of the catechism or of *quod Thomas dixit* necessarily tends toward syncretic heterodoxy. It is hard to forget, for instance, the silliness, purblindness, and in fact deep cruelty with which Fr. Jacques Dupuis was treated for making assertions so theologically anodyne that they could give offense only to persons of willfully morbid sensibility. I have also seen Catholic teachers, again in one college in particular, refusing on principle, and with a positive pride in their intransigent stupidity, even to rethink what they took to be the proper traditional understanding of original sin (whether the language they repeated was merely that of Trent, that of Thomas, or that of Augustine, and even when it required an almost magical notion of the infusion of a rational soul in a nature otherwise merely subrational, and so on) in light of those evolutionary accounts of species parentage that emerge from sound genetic theory.

Again, I fear none of this from Hütter, and I am wandering far afield from the matter at hand perhaps. But to idealize the concrete institutional realities of the magisterium at any given moment would be as ill-advised as idealizing the Catholic university, and something more needs to be said about the difference between the universal knowledge of the university and the universality of dogmatic grammars. *Procuratio*—a scholarly virtue to which Hütter refers—is not *curatorship* but steward-ship of a living and thriving reality; it is a *cura horti*. If, as Hütter does, we wish to take the Mother of God as patroness and type of the highest pursuit of truth, then let us also do justice to the whole shape of that Mar-ian receptivity: incubation, nurture, but also surrender to the One who comes we know not whence and goes we know not whither: the One who asks, when it seems most shocking to do so, Who is my mother? Who are my brothers and sisters? Another way to say this is that, to my mind, the best model of the Catholic university would be essentially Christological, and this in the highest sense: a fully developed Logos-Christology. For the uniqueness of Christ can be understood in two ways. It can be seen as something ever more exclusive—even to the point of the dialectical extremism of the early Barth. But, alternatively, that uniqueness can be understood ever more comprehensively, as the singu-lar power of the incarnate Logos, God the Son, ever more fully to em-brace, transform, and illuminate all of nature and every natural aptitude in himself. This latter sense of Christ's uniqueness—the uniqueness of the Logos, the one who is the all, both human and divine, created and uncreated, creature and creator—surely is the vision proper to the Catholic genius (East and West, Orthodox and Roman). And it seems to me that for this vision to prosper in the modern Catholic university, and for it to suffuse and enliven the university as a diverse pursuit of a single transcendent good, it is necessary to affirm as far as possible the freedom of the Catholic university *for* the truth of God in Christ but to affirm also a very real and inviolable degree of autonomy *from* a purely "magisterial" mission. But, again, striking that delicate balance is not easy, and I do not pretend to know how to go about it. And, happily, I do not need to.

16

The Story of the Nameless
The Use and Abuse of History for Theology

I

Most of the history we read—and write—is a lie, though often enough a lie told in earnest. We fabricate the past as much as we recall it, if not more so, and almost invariably in ways that reflect an ideology that we either consciously seek to promote or unconsciously absorb from the society surrounding us. For the most part, this is nothing to lament, as long as we remember to think of written history primarily as a species of literature. In truth, the greater the historian, the vaster and more ingenious his or her misrepresentations are likely to be. And the greatest of all, those who are the most accomplished masters of detail and style need not distort a single fact in order to produce an entirely fantastic image of the past. We wince at the errors, simplifications, fancies, or vulgarities in the histories written by, say, H. G. Wells, Will Durant, Charles Freeman, or (God help us) Stephen Greenblatt. But before the grand, often factually impeccable, and yet somehow dazzlingly misleading inventions of Edward Gibbon, Theodor Mommsen, George Grote, or Thomas Babington Macaulay we should, if we have any good taste at all, pause in silent admiration, ravished with delight. We come away from *The Decline and Fall of the Roman Empire* with a vivid sense of the personality and prejudices of its author, and with the urbane, ironic echo of his voice lingering in our ears; but of the long tale of the waning of Rome, from the time of the Antonines to that of the Palaeologoi, our memory retains only a large gallery of brightly fleeting impressions, continuously coalescing and dissolving around the fixed center of the entrancing figure cut by Gibbon. (For what it is worth, it is among my favorite books.) Again, on finally closing Grote's *History of Greece* (another book I love), it is hard not to feel that the character it impresses most indelibly on the mind is not Peisistratus or Pericles but John Stuart Mill. Frankly, though, it is an expectation of only very recent vintage that written history should be viewed as a science, much less as a genre of philosophical or theological reflection. Admittedly, Thucydides was as much a philosopher and theologian (if the latter only by negation) as he was a chronicler of the past. And there have been other exceptional figures who have written history in a genuinely speculative vein; Ibn Khaldun certainly comes to mind. But, on the whole, Herodotus was the great exemplar of the guild, and his "method" defined the historian's mission: gather up as many good stories as possible, tell them well, and make as many hours as possible pass in pleasant distraction. And if, like Procopius, one is deft at a little lubricious gossip and a few ghastly anecdotes, one can make the whole confection a source of perfect gratification.

Moreover, we deceive ourselves if we imagine that there is such a thing as a specific and constant moral imperative that governs and animates the writing of history. Yes, on the one hand, we must *never* forget; but yes also, on the other, we *must* learn to forget. And it is rash to assume that either necessity outweighs the other. Historical memory can, ideally, make us aware of, and so responsible for, the sins of the past, the crimes of our countries and our forebears, all the wars and spoliations and enslavements that have marked the births and deaths of tribes and nations and empires. By the same token, however, it can also entrap us in a ceaseless cycle of impotent mourning whose emotional intoxications can relieve us of any real attention to the concrete moral demands of the present. At its most perfidious, historical recollection can become a support for and aggrandizement of our prejudices, a reinforcement of the myths of racial pedigree or national destiny or imperial grandeur, or can soothe us with sweet sickly nostalgias for past glories and lost honors. Howard Zinn (who may, by the way, provide the best model for theological historians to emulate) was in many respects a great American prophet simply because he was enough of a heretic to tell the truth about the past. But, conversely, Nietzsche also had an important point to make in reminding us that sometimes we thrive best by shrugging off the burden of the past and embracing a liberating oblivion. However one views the matter, though, this must not be forgotten: history as it has always been written, with only a few exceptions, has consisted in the narratives of those who have enduring names, most of whom were granted the special privilege of being remembered because in their own times they had enjoyed an immunity from the suffering and obscurity of the vast majority of humanity. Admittedly, this is an injustice that allows very little by way of redress, since the forgotten are for the most part forgotten altogether; now they really do have no names. Even so, if we can keep the fact in mind, we can at least apply ourselves to historical studies with enough ironic detachment to be capable of discerning where what we really know of the past (which is always far less than we think) can be distinguished from the fabulations and interpretations in which the record is always inevitably wrapped. Then, when we choose to write or rewrite the past responsibly—or simply, in reading, consider what we are reading with sufficient diffidence—we can recognize the ephemerality and cultural contingency of past interpretations. No doubt we are also in that very process imposing new, equally ephemeral and contingent interpretations on what we think we know, but that too we can learn to do with some degree of critical distance from our own prejudices. And we cannot really avoid the task. Because, despite all I have just said, historical thinking is not a choice for us but an irresistible call, a vocation as old as our consciousness of ourselves as human beings.

II

What is "history," after all? It is, before all else, the unique privilege and doom of our species. Other animals have "histories" only in an analogical sense, and only through us, insofar as we take the trouble to trace their genealogies, chronologies, phylogenies, and so forth. But they, blessedly, have no cultural consciousness and no language by which to abstract themselves from the perpetual present. At least, this seems to be the case and is surely the case for most species. For this very reason they exist in a kind of pristine harmony with each moment of natural existence. We have history precisely because we have been exiled—by both our natural capacities and our unnatural transgressions—from that one primordial moment that is every moment for the animal consciousness. History is the consequence of an original alienation, a departure from the natural order of repetition and return; and no reconciliation with the world we left behind is possible in this life. It is the state of "spirit" knowing itself now as posed over against the organic substrate of its being in the world, which has become something separate, objective, other. History is a schism placed within our very nature, within our very bodies, making even our material contingency always somehow other than our identities as participants in a story that moves forward from the present toward an open future. History is, before all else, the anguish of that exile and the delight of that liberty. We know ourselves—individually and as a species—not simply as a particular kind of thing, in the sense of an easily defined object of a deictic reference, but as a sequence of stories, all of which in their totality tell of our emergence and alienation from nature. And so we cannot help but reflect on this schism, under the forms provided by philosophy or art or natural religion, even though we are generally too immediately engaged *in* history—as an unavoidable and external problem to be solved—to allow much time for deep contemplation *of* history. The work of philosophical thinking—except among a certain group of analytic philosophers, who quaintly believe it is possible to think outside of historical, cultural, and linguistic contingencies, and who are oddly insensible to the reality that their own style of thinking is merely the effect of a certain historical and linguistic dispensation—must involve the attempt to recuperate into reflective knowledge what has objectively occurred in the endless encounter between human consciousness and the hard but not wholly intractable matter of nature, time, and culture. We really are historical beings, and what we are unfolds across generations, not merely across that meager span of decades that composes an isolated life. Philosophy must involve the conscious attempt to awaken from history as fate into history as wisdom. It was the genius of Hegel to have recognized this and to have understood that a complete philosophy deals both with what we freely create as a species and with the fate to which we are inescapably bound as individuals. It is the poetic labor of reconstituting our perpetual exile as rational freedom.

Now, if this all sounds a little too dangerously grandiose and German Idealist a characterization of historical thinking, all I can say is that I think the greater danger to be feared is that of a failure to grasp the full gravity and significance of attempting to remember wisely. And, it seems to me, there is a special calling of theological reflection with regard to historical memory, one that Christian thought has reliably betrayed throughout most of its existence. For one thing, the call to contemplate the meaning of history is not merely an invitation to engage with an archive of discrete facts in isolation but an imperative to attend to specific narratives, specific diegetic orderings of facts and memories. For another, every attempt to interpret the past is, either tacitly or explicitly, also an attempt to interpret the present and determine what is to come. In a sense, every significant historian is engaged in writing the future. And, in the case of Christian historians, this is a matter of extraordinary theological moment. Consider, for instance, Adolf von Harnack, who openly declared that the historian of dogma should seek not merely to understand what has been but also to shape what will be; every turn of phrase in his great *Dogmengeschichte* is subtly or brutally oriented toward purging Christian confession of all those elements that he—as a sane modern man, responsible German scholar, distinguished churchman, and loyal subject of the Kaiser—found most distasteful: its Judaism, its opulent Asiatic mythology of the slain and revived god, its Mediterranean extravagances, its mysticism, its pomps and rituals and preposterously labyrinthine dogmatic definitions and disputes. He graciously grants that all these obnoxious accretions were necessary vehicles by which the gospel was conveyed through unenlightened times and barbarous lands but also argues that now they are hindrances to rational belief and sober bourgeois values alike, and that the time has come once more to liberate the sweet simple "kernel" of the faith—"the Fatherhood of God and brotherhood of man"—from its rough and garish "husk." Well, beware of those who claim to know where the demarcations can be drawn between historical phenomena and their ahistorical essences. And yet Harnack's tendentiousness is a fairly minor lapse of probity in comparison to the more common and chronic derelictions of Christian historians. To me it remains a source of wonder that, with the obvious exception of intentionally hostile texts, most histories of Christianity remain little more than attempts to tell the story of the church in such a way as to defend or to advocate the reconstitution of this or that institutional practice, this or that style of confessional adherence, this or that doctrinal ideology—and little more. And it is surprising how often, even if inadvertently, these histories are nothing more than the same old tales of pedigree, further recitations of the narratives of those blessed with enduring names by virtue of their having occupied stations of social power. Rarely ever do they seem to emerge from a historical consciousness shaped by the radically different story told by the gospels, which should be retold in every age, regarding those nameless and disenfranchised souls whose world was invaded by the call of God in Christ, the crucified slave. This is a problem.

III

Of course, there is a certain ambiguity in the way the gospel story encourages us to think about history in the abstract, and so of history as an intellectual practice. We often try to discipline our metaphysical and religious imaginations by reminding ourselves that ours is a faith sunk deep in the soil of history, an eternal truth not only made manifest but actually accomplished by way of concrete historical events. Moreover, we try to recall that our spiritual participation in that event is mediated by our incorporation into a community that claims to embody a special transmission through time of that historical presence. All true. But, by the same token, we have to remember also that the peculiar form of the entrance of God's Kingdom into time was not an integration of God's story into ours but rather a shattering act of judgment, of damnation, and of resurrection in a spiritual body untouched by time and death. It is, in short, history as history's overthrow. Christianity first entered the world of late antiquity not as an institution or as a fully developed creed but first and foremost as an event that was without any known precedent and without any immediately obvious sequel. At its dawning, the gospel appeared within history as a proclamation regarding the sudden and irrevocable disruption *of* history, one that necessarily entailed— for those who believed that proclamation—a subversion or rejection of many of the most venerable cultic, social, and philosophical wisdoms of the ancient world. And the central event within the event that the gospel proclaimed was the resurrection of Christ. All at once—according to Paul, for instance—all the firm configurations and demarcations that gave shape to reality had been altered, or transgressed, or erased. All religious, social, racial, and national boundaries had been effaced, all of nature and history had been delivered over to the rule of Christ, all the spiritual and human agencies governing the cosmos—powers, principalities, thrones, dominions, the "god of this Age"—had been subdued by the crucified and risen Lord. The language of the book of Galatians is especially uncompromising with regard to the implications of this "interruption." There Paul states that the event of salvation in Christ was a complete liberation not only from the elemental powers (the *stoicheia*) to which all peoples had been subject but even from the power of the Law of Moses; for, holy though that Law was, it could not save and was itself rendered defective by having been delivered under the angelic dispensation of the present age, revealed first through a mere angel and then further through a mere human mediator, and operating therefore only as a kind of provisional "disciplinarian" (*paidagogos*). In Christ, however, a new age of liberty from all government but God's had arrived. In this sense, Christianity entered human consciousness not primarily as an alternative religious practice or creed but rather as an apocalyptic annunciation of the sudden invasion of historical and natural time alike by a Kingdom not of this cosmos. Within the spiritual world of Judaism, such a proclamation was intelligible, but even there principally as a prophetic announcement made out of season—"This day is the scripture fulfilled in your hearing"—which impetuously demanded immediate assent to what seemed a preposterous claim about the end of time having appeared *within* time. In the larger world of the empire, however, it was scarcely intelligible at all, except as a dissident and positively *irreligious* movement, defiant of the gods and daemons and sacred offices by which the empire was sustained and joined to the divine order. It was, above all, a profanation of sacred truths, the elevation of a crucified slave over all those duly appointed offices of religious and social order that had justly condemned him, and the blasphemous misconstrual of this criminal not merely as an innocent victim but as God's only Son. The pattern established in Christ—especially, for me, in the inexhaustibly suggestive story of Christ's confrontation with Pilate in John's Gospel—was one of martyrdom as victory, of power as the willingness to become powerless before the violence of the state and thereby to reveal the latter's arbitrariness, injustice, and spiritual falsehood. And how strange the gospel is here: for Pilate is precisely the sort of man about whom history is meant to be written; he has a name, has a face before the law, stands in a station given him by the sacred authority of the empire. Yet his story vanishes in the light of Easter. He is remembered today only insofar as he is written into the margins of the story of the slave and peasant God.

In its original form, then, the gospel issued a peremptory command to all who believed in it: that they come forth out of the old order altogether, abandon all the safe and stable economies of society and cult, and commit themselves irrevocably to the immediacy of that event—for the days are short. And, to be frank, such a command leaves little room for anything like "historical consciousness." The church was given birth in something like a state of crisis, of mingled joy and terror, in a moment out of time, as one age was passing and another coming into existence. The Kingdom was drawing near; the Kingdom had already arrived; indeed, the Kingdom was already within. Living thus in history's aftermath, and just on the threshold of eternity, the church could not at first have any expectation that it would soon be required to enter into history again. But it would have to do so eventually, and this meant that it would also have to become everything it thought it had left behind: an institution, a Law, a religion. What had begun as an eschatological irruption of eternity into temporal history would in the end—at the far side of a disenchantment so gradual that that initial hope of the imminent Kingdom, almost unnoticed, simply melted into thin air, leaving not a rack behind— have to become just another history: that of a particular creed and devotion and institutional heritage, oriented toward an eternity once again rendered unimaginable and inconceivably remote. Soon enough, the church would assume the religious configurations provided by its age, adjusted to accommodate a new set of spiritual aspirations. Jewish scripture provided a grammar for worship, while the common cultic forms of ancient society were easily adaptable to Christian use. A certain degree of natural "pseudomorphism" was inevitable: a crystallization of Christian corporate life (with all its novelty) within the religious space vacated by the pagan cults and mystery religions it displaced or outlasted. After all, a purely apocalyptic consciousness, subsisting entirely in a moment of absolute interruption, could persist for only so long. Still, it was an imperfect synthesis; the alloy of apocalyptic longing and historical continuity was never entirely stable. The Christian event proved to be far too refractory to be contained within institutions, even institutions of its own devising. At the very heart of its spiritual rationale there always remained an impulse to rebellion. Hence, down the centuries, Christianity has proved not only irrepressibly fissile (as all large religious traditions, to some degree, are) but ultimately self-destructive. Of all the religious cultures the world has ever known, only the Christian has naturally incubated within itself an impulse toward total and defiant faithlessness, militant unbelief, ultimate nihilism, not merely as occasional individual states of soul, but as large cultural movements. Even in its most redoubtable and enduring historical forms, Christianity is filled with an indomitable and subversive ferment, an inner force of dissolution that refuses to crystallize into something inert or stable but that instead insists upon dispersing itself into the future ever again, to destroy what confines it and to start anew, to begin again in the formless realm of spirit rather than of flesh, of spirit rather than of the letter. There is, simply said, a distinct element of the ungovernable and seditious within the gospel's power to persuade, one that we ignore only at the cost of fundamentally misunderstanding the character of the gospel. And this element, with its power to generate intrinsic stresses within even the humblest of Christian communities, could not help but produce a far greater and more chronic stress within the church as an enfranchised institution, supporting and supported by the instruments and establishments of human political authority. At times this was a fruitful tension, resulting in all those social and cultural goods that the Christian order succeeded at introducing into its world—all of which were inseparable in one way or another from the radical revision of the understanding of the human being and of nature that Christianity brought into human experience. Yet the moral failures were no less astonishing or numerous. And now we live in the time after Christendom, amid the rapidly vanishing fragments of its material culture, bound to it by only a few lingering habits of thought. Modernity is the post-Christian age, the reality of a culture that was shaped by the final failure of that accommodation. And we deceive ourselves if we imagine that that failure was not inevitable from the first.

It should be obvious to all of us that Christian culture could never have generated any political and social order that, insofar as it employed the mechanisms of state power, would not inevitably achieve its own dissolution. The translation of Christianity's original apocalyptic ferment into a cultural logic and social order produced a powerful but necessarily volatile reality. Whatever the good things were that it produced in the shaping of Western civilization, the process of accommodation also forced the faith to encumber itself with a weight of historical and cultural expectations wholly incompatible with the gospel it proclaimed. In becoming not only a pillar of culture but also a support of a human political and social order that necessarily sustains itself through the prudential use of violence, the church was attempting to close the spiritual abyss that had lain untraversably open between Christ and Pilate on the day of their confrontation, while requiring neither to depart from his native realm. This was impossible, even in some sense monstrous. And yet, at the same time, this impossible fusion created a cultural reality that for a time was animated—or, at the very least, haunted—by the language of the gospel: the often tacit but always substantial knowledge that all of human power's pretenses and delusions and deceits have been exposed for what they are and overthrown by God's incarnation as a man who was the victim of all the recognized religious, political, and social forces of his time and place. There was no way for such an alliance to avoid subverting itself. And so the concrescence of Christianity into Christendom necessarily led, over the course of centuries, to Christian culture's gradual mortification and attrition through internal stresses, until at last it was dissipated into the inconclusiveness of a human history that no longer lay open to the Kingdom. Christendom itself could not indefinitely survive the corrosive power of the revelation that Christianity itself had introduced into Western culture. Christian culture's often misunderstood but ultimately irrepressible consciousness of the judgment that was passed upon civil violence at Easter, by God, was always the secret antagonist of Christendom as a political order. Certainly, reflective intellectual historians have often enough noted the ironic continuity between the early modern rise of principled unbelief and the special "apocalyptic vocation" of Western culture; there is even some considerable truth in the observations of Ernst Bloch and many others that the Christian message contains always within itself the possibility of an atheistic terminus. Modern Western atheism is chiefly a Christian heresy and could not have arisen in a non-Christian setting. Ultimately, the historical force ultimately most destructive of the unity of the Christian culture in the West has never been some adventitious and hostile power arriving from elsewhere; all the forces of laicism—materialism, capitalism, collectivism, individualism, libertarianism, or what have you—are merely secondary and mostly reactionary effects of the activity of Christendom's most implacable enemy: Christianity. Though perhaps it would be better to say not "Christianity" but something essential to it that, as a result of the contradictions inherent in Christendom, has become alienated from its true rationality and ultimate meaning.

The question that confronts us now is whether we can properly recognize the cause of this dissolution of the old accords and thereby recover a proper sense of how Christian history diverges from the histories with which it has too often become entangled. If we cannot, then any theological questions we might wish to address to the Christian past become meaningless.

IV

What, really, is Christian history? Or, rather, what is the historical narrative that Christians should tell? Maybe now, at the end of Christendom, the question can be considered with a new clarity. When Christianity's initial moment of apocalyptic liberty from the affairs of nation and empire faded, and the church entered fully into worldly history again, its historical consciousness was subdued. Its memory was no longer obsessively preoccupied with that impossible invasion of time by eternity but began to become instead just another institutional and cultural repository of nostalgia, triumphalism, lamentation, resentment, and fantasy. Its history became, once again, the history of the great, of kingdoms and empires, of a church little distinguishable in structure and governance from kingdoms and empires, of tribes and peoples, of traditions somehow always already betrayed and in need of revival, or of offenses against the faith never entirely forgiven. And it also became again the narrative of the mighty, of those whose names endure because they had the power to move nations and kill enemies and destroy heretics. And, of course, it became mostly lies. Read Eusebius.

We in America should, I imagine, have an especially keen sense of the perennial corruption of Christian memory by the tales that we long to tell about ourselves. True, in one sense, the great dream or romance of America is the prospect of being a people without history, a people that has at last flown free of the cage of time and its fated economies. Of course, we escaped nothing—not class, race, nationality—but the original agitation and aspiration remain. America is still a great gnostic fantasy that reshapes material existence more rapidly, more alarmingly, more mercilessly, and more ebulliently than a people properly ballasted by historical consciousness would generally think possible or even desirable. And yet no nation, in the wake of Christendom's decline, has done more to confuse the story that Christians should tell with the kinds of stories sinful human beings long to tell. That very escape from history becomes, in the American imagination, the history of a chosen people fleeing the wickedness that is in the world, so as to become a holy nation set apart, called to recreate humankind in a new and Edenic condition. And somehow, then, with a buffoonish crudity almost unprecedented in terrestrial history—or, perhaps, an unfeigned naïveté positively touching in its earnestness, depending on how one looks at it—a good number of American Christians find it possible to believe that the proclamation of the gospel is of a piece with the defense of free-market economics, private property, libertarian democracy, gun rights, draconian penal laws, border walls, and the "War on Terror." Christian peoples of the past have often enough allied their confessional allegiances to the ambitions of the state. But where else, I wonder, have Christians so effortlessly and cretinously and yet so very relentlessly allied them to explicit ideologies that, taken in sum, constitute nothing other than the systematic negation of the gospel? Where else but here could the history of God in Christ have ever been told quite so falsely? And will Christianity ever really reach these shores?

In any event, Christians of every land, here on the far side of the divorce of throne and altar, and of the gradual disappearance of both, must reconsider what Christian memory truly is, what story the church truly tells. They must remember anew, entirely differently. Before all else, the center of memory must be displaced, away from chronicles of kings and councilors, but also away from institutional annals and servile concern for ecclesiastical authority. These things are part of the story, of course, but belong at the watery margins, and sometimes in the distant swamps of the epiphenomenal. Christians cannot tell the true story—and so cannot tell any story about the human past—unless they begin always from the memory of that apocalyptic interruption of human narratives that for us should reconstitute all memory and should in every instance of our understanding of the past unsettle our picture—reverse, so to speak, the order of meaning and truth, as John's Gospel does in describing the confrontation between Christ and Pilate. Told aright, the true story is first and foremost the story of those that human memory has accorded no names: the poor, the rejected, the despised, the enslaved (hence my suggestion above that Howard Zinn might serve as a model for the Christian historian). These abandoned persons, more or less exclusively, are the whole center of a proper Christian understanding of the past, and so of a proper Christian desire for the future. Though they have been deprived of their names, God has given them the name of Christ; though they have been forgotten, he has given them Christ's story as their own. Where they are, he is present; and, in human history, he is most truly present *nowhere* else. And so the Christian narrative should be a constant and subversive counternarrative, a ceaseless interruption and riposte. To know how to tell it, and to frame it theologically, is like learning to discern a picture cunningly concealed within another picture, a puzzle or hidden pattern, the true history of the Kingdom, which none can see except those who know to look for it. And, when it is told aright, God is there as well, among his people the poor; Christ is there, always risen and present, passing through the ages in the company of the forgotten and outcast.

This may not actually answer the question posed here today—that regarding the uses and abuses of history for theology—but in a sense it might help in the actual asking of the question. In a sense the whole of Christian history—from Creation to Judgment—is contained in the three days between cross and empty tomb and is fully unfolded in the life of Christ among the destitute, before those days and after. Before we can know what to make theologically of history, we first have to know what history we believe in, where its center lies, what its inner logic is. As Pilate asked, ingenuously for all we know, "What is truth?" There in the midst of the stories we generally desire to tell—amid the lies, that is, that compose most of our historical memory—is the one story that is perfectly true, and the one that we must learn to see, hidden within every epoch of the world, before theology can even begin to speak of what has been.

17

Beauty, Being, Kenosis

I

There is an old debate among Thomists about whether or not Thomas thought that beauty (*pulchritudo*) or the beautiful (*pulchrum*) possesses all the characteristics necessary for it to be designated a true transcendental. That is to say, is beauty an ontological perfection, one in which all existing things participate in some degree or other as a necessary condition of their very existence, and a property that in its infinite and absolute reality is convertible with all other transcendentals? Is it, properly speaking, one of the "divine names"? For myself, of course, the question of where Thomas actually stood on the matter is of only academic interest, and very little even of that. I am not a Thomist of any kind. I value Thomas greatly as a metaphysician of being, as the Western mediaeval thinker who best understood and reiterated and even occasionally synthesized the metaphysics of Ibn Sina, of late antique paganism, and of various Eastern Christian patristic figures; but I feel no attraction to Thomas the theologian (especially in his worst moments [*Summa th.* III, suppl., q. 94, as. 1–3; *Summa th.* I, q. 23, a. 83; etc.]). I mention the matter only as touching upon the larger question of beauty's status as a necessarily transcendental horizon of rational desire—which seems to me simply a phenomenological truism—and of its status as an ontological predicate. The traditional definition of the beautiful that Thomas repeated, at least in the condensed form that is most widely known, could scarcely be more elegantly or infuriatingly terse: "id quod visum placet" (that which, being seen, gives pleasure); and even in Thomas's actual words it is scarcely any more revealing: "Pulchra enim dicuntur quae visa placent" (*Summa th.* I, q. 39, a. 8: Those things, indeed, are said to be beautiful that, when seen, give pleasure). A rather bland and defective formulation, to be honest, and one that immediately raises the question of whether the beautiful—in the Platonic sense of τὸ καλόν, the intrinsically desirable as such—is even what is at issue. This is not simply because the formula obviously limits the word's acceptation to visual experience; by analogy, surely, it could be expanded to comprise the other senses, and perhaps certain supersensuous dimensions of experience (including imaginative or conceptual beauty: the loveliness of, say, the plot of a story, or even of an idea). Moreover, when given its maximum range of possible affective dimensions, the Thomistic definition contains at least one profound and indispensable insight: to wit, that the beautiful is something that pleases *simply* by virtue of being seen—or heard, or felt, or thought, or otherwise intuited—and for no reason other than that. The apprehension of beauty is characterized by simplicity and immediacy. By this, I do not mean that the beautiful is necessarily recognized by the instantaneity of the gratification it affords (some things require time to be appreciated fully) but only that, in any aesthetic experience, there is no other mediating concern that determines one's judgment of a thing's beauty or deformity. It is, simply stated, an experience of disinterested pleasure. Even when the occasion of the experience of beauty is at the same time an object of "interested" desire—one person's erotic fascination with another's physical loveliness, say—it is never impossible in principle to distinguish (even if it is often impossible in practice to separate) the recognition of beauty from the desire for what one admires. Of course, erotic desire is in a sense disinterested, in a way that, say, desire for money—which has no aesthetic basis—is not; but even an object desired for its monetary worth can incidentally also, in a distinct and immediate way, be desired also for the satisfaction it affords a purely rational appetite for beauty. Even the enterprising philistine who purchases a lovely canvas at auction as an investment might also, unexpectedly, find himself absorbed in the splendor of the thing itself.

What, though, does the Thomistic definition really tell us? Surely the essential question is not whether the beautiful pleases but why it pleases, and why in so distinctive a fashion. What is it that is intrinsically pleasing about it if the pleasure it provides cannot be reduced to profit, personal aggrandizement, or even purely sensual gratification? This is where, left to itself, a formulation like Thomas's begins to dissolve into banality. If anything, it is enlightening only because it is so manifestly inadequate. It indicates that Thomas, far from merely failing to describe the beautiful *sufficiently*, has in fact grandly failed to talk about it *at all*. In the same article in which he offers his definition of the beautiful, he goes on to enumerate the proper constituents of beautiful things with what—if we mistakenly think he is indeed talking about "beauty" in the fullest sense—looks uncomfortably like ponderous vulgarity, of the sort that irresistibly suggests a sensibility that could not be trusted to prefer a Van Gogh to a bullfighter painted on black velvet in luminescent pigments. The marks of the beautiful are, he says (with a wonderfully unironic and bland precision), three in number: integrity, right proportionality, and brilliancy. That is to say, first, that something is beautiful to the degree that it is complete: lacking in no essential feature and in no way disfigured by privation or distortion. A missing eye or damaged lip detracts from the beauty of a face, a crack deforms the surface of a lovely vase, an off-key note diminishes a bel canto aria. Second, all the parts of a beautiful object must be in pleasing proportion to one another, nothing should be either excessive or insufficient, all parts must be arranged harmoniously and in attractive balance. And, third, the beautiful thing must shine, must be radiant, in a quite concretely physical way; it must be clear, distinct, splendid, lustrous, brightly colored. In fact, one Thomist of my acquaintance often insists—with that fine and cavalier indifference to actual human experience at which Thomists so often heroically excel—that there is no such thing as a truly beautiful day without clear skies, golden sunlight, brilliant hues, and so forth (so if you think you have found gray days of silver rain and drifting mists beautiful, you are simply in error).

All of this is rather worthless, to be honest. Such language may suit whatever it was Thomas meant by *pulchritudo*, but certainly one could not meaningfully use it about "beauty," or about the "delicious perturbation" (as Plotinus phrases it) that true beauty excites in us. To do so would be to confuse the beautiful with the pretty, loveliness with flamboyance, the delightful with the merely obliging, enchantment with diversion. Yes, we take pleasure in color, integrity, harmony, radiance, and so on; and yet we also frequently find ourselves stirred and moved and delighted by objects whose sensible appearances or tones or other qualities violate all such aesthetic canons, and that somehow "shine" with a fuller beauty as a result. Conversely, many objects that possess all these ideal features often bore us, or even appall us, with their banality. At times, the obscure enchants us and the lucid leaves us untouched; plangent dissonances can awaken our imaginations far more delightfully than those simple harmonies that often seem insipid; a face almost wholly devoid of conventionally pleasing features can seem unutterably beautiful to us in its very disproportion, while the most exquisite profile can do no more than charm us. Rembrandt's brooding shadows are beautiful, while Thomas Kinkade's bizarre phosphorescences are repellant. Whatever the beautiful is, it is not simply harmony, or symmetry, or consonance, or ordonnance, or brightness, all of which can become anodyne or vacuous of themselves; the beautiful can be encountered—sometimes shatteringly—precisely where all of these things are deficient or largely absent. Beauty is something other than the visible or audible or conceptual agreement of parts, and the experience of beauty can never be intelligibly reduced, without a significant unexplained remainder, to any set of visible or audible material constituents. It is something mysterious, prodigal, often unanticipated, even capricious. We can find ourselves suddenly amazed by some strange and indefinable glory in a barren field, an urban ruin, the splendid disarray of a storm-wracked forest, and so on.

This is one reason, incidentally, for viewing accounts of beauty produced by evolutionary psychology with extreme suspicion. The best attempt at this—Denis Dutton's *The Art Instinct*—tries to ground the creation and enjoyment of art in sexual selection, which requires Dutton to ground the experience of beauty in the material conditions of affective pleasure. For instance, he begins his argument by pointing out that the most popular sorts of photographs in calendars are of landscapes that supposedly carry us back to our remote evolutionary beginnings in the sort of landscapes our phylogenic forebears would have sought out. And yet aesthetic experience is not *that*, surely. We may enjoy pictures of certain scenes that are agreeable to us at a purely physiological level, but what we find beautiful is, as a rule, almost entirely unrelated to material conditions of that kind. The form of a representation often fascinates us far more than the objects represented. A magnificent photograph of an uninhabitable desert can delight us in ways that a competent but uninspired photograph of a sapphire lake cradled amid emerald hills and ringed by flowering trees cannot. There is a kind of transfinite quality to the beautiful, a sort of gracious ubiquity, a generous absolution from the material conditions of its occasion.

II

I want to take a page here—and only a page—from Martin Heidegger: the closing lines of his essay "The Origin of the Work of Art," where he assimilates the *event* of beauty—the word is important—to the *event* of truth. And, for him, the event of truth is simply the coming to appearance, the manifestation, of that which *is*, made present in the purest immediacy of its being. He accepts the classical intuition that beauty is conceptually inseparable from such seemingly "static" concepts as form and image—*morphē* and *eidos*—but only insofar as he can reduce these terms, through one of his bravura feats of quasi-mystical philology, to ancient names for the advent of being within the world of finite causes. For him beauty is to be understood as a way in which the difference between being and beings is made manifest. This is one of those rare but precious moments in Heidegger's writings when the light momentarily breaks through the clouds and he not only asks the right question but comes close to giving the right answer.

I would go so far as to say that beauty, inseparable as it is from form, is not form. I would even say that beauty is not that which appears, and indeed does not itself appear as an object of reflection, but is instead the simple appearing of what appears. If that seems coyly or wantonly nebulous, I think it is a phenomenological truth that one can confirm for oneself from one's own experience. When we encounter the beautiful, what is it that compels us? What draws us in and awakens us to a splendor beyond our particular interests and desires and predilections in a canvas of Chardin or Corot, or a Bach violin partita? Not simply this or that aspect of its composition, certainly, or its neurological effect, or its clarity or vividness or suggestive associations, and so on, or even just the virtuosity of its execution. Rather, it is all these things experienced as sheer fortuity. I may be speaking of something elusive of exact definition, but it seems clear to me that the special delight experienced in the encounter with beauty necessarily involves an irreducible sense of the sheer, unnecessary thereness, so to speak, of a thing, the simple gratuity with which it shows itself, or (better) gives itself. It is an ontological fortuity to which our disinterested appreciation corresponds, and so we see it *here* as we would not elsewhere. Apart from this, even the most perfectly executed work of art would be only a display of artisanal proficiency, a display of pure *technique*. What transforms the merely accomplished into the revelatory is this invisible nimbus of utter gratuity. Rather than commanding our attention with the force of necessity, or oppressing us with the triteness of something inevitable, or recommending itself to us by its utility or its purposiveness, the beautiful presents itself to us as an entirely unwarranted, unnecessary, and yet marvelously fitting gift. Beauty—as opposed to mere strikingness, mere brilliancy—is an event, or even eventuality as such. It is the movement of a gratuitous disclosure of something otherwise hidden, which need not reveal itself or give itself. In the experience of the beautiful, and of its pure fortuity, we are granted our most acute, most lucid, and most splendid encounter with the difference of being from beings. The beautiful affords us our most perfect experience of that existential wonder—that *thaumazein*—that is the beginning of all speculative wisdom. This amazement perhaps lies always just below the surface of our quotidian consciousness; but beauty stirs us from our habitual forgetfulness of the wonder of being. It grants us a particularly privileged awakening from our "fallenness" in ordinary awareness, reminding us that the fullness of being, which far exceeds the moment of its disclosure, graciously condescends to show itself, again and again, in the finitude of an event: of a mere instance. In this experience, we are given a glimpse—again, with a feeling of wonder that restores us momentarily to something like the innocence of childhood—of being's *kenosis* in beings: that inexhaustible source that pours itself out in the gracious needlessness of creation. Beauty shines out in the midst of being as the sign and gift and ever-renewed revelation of what transcends discrete beings, exciting in us an eros for the source of all splendor and all delight. If, that is, we have eyes to see and ears to hear.

III

Clearly I am working within a classical discourse of the beautiful, even if I have misappropriated a page from Heidegger along the way. But the relation between the infinite and the finite, or the absolute and the contingent, or beauty in itself and the beautiful here below, can be construed in a great variety of ways. Typically it has, throughout the history of Western metaphysics, proved difficult to interpret the relation in a way that does not presume some initial moment of alienation, tragic loss, dialectical struggle between ideal forms and the intractability of the material substrate or the inviolable limits of finitude. This is true, at least, of practically every native idealism of Western philosophical history, from Plato onward. True, no idealism, properly speaking, thinks of the relation in a purely dualistic way; but even the classically "monistic" or "dialectical" idealisms always leave a tragic remainder behind in their account of the "there above" and the "here below": something finally unaccounted for and unredeemed. To show itself in the world of *doxa*, divine or ideal beauty must suffer some sort of negation, some sort of violence, a diminishment and distortion and dissimulation, a forced departure from its proper nature. Manifestation is always alienation in this world, even if it is also expression and revelation. The beautiful is a haunting reminder of something lost and a foretaste of what is to be found beyond the tragic limits of this world; and it points, always and only, up and away from the things of earth. All of which is true, but to all of which the Christian story necessarily adds another dimension—another inflection of grace.

This is why, in speaking of the event of the beautiful, I have used the Christological word *kenosis*. For the Christian story is one in which the tragedies of finitude belong to a history of alienation, yes, but not as the result of some sort of metaphysical necessity or inevitability. Rather, the infinite shows itself in the finite entirely in the form of a free and unforced gift, one that requires no estrangement of the divine from the divine nature, but that instead is a perfect and peaceful and gracious expression of that nature: for God always already is the infinite act of self-outpouring charity, the beauty that is also self-donating love. At least, this seems to me one of the obvious metaphysical implications of the way in which Nicene theology fundamentally altered the conceptual structure of the ancient world. The doctrinal definitions of the fourth century, along with all of their immediate theological sequels and ramifications, rendered many of the established metaphysical premises upon which many Christians (being good Hellenes) had long relied in order to understand the relation between God and the world increasingly untenable and at the same time suggested the need to conceive of that relation—perhaps for the first time in Western intellectual history—in a properly "ontological" way. At one time, it had seemed natural for many Christian thinkers to imagine God and the world as, somehow, part of a single ontic continuum, with the inaccessible Father mediated to the world below through the subalternate agencies of the Logos and the Spirit. In such a scheme, of course, the tragic interval of classical idealism—the impossible chasm between divine truth and its earthly shadow—remains in place. God in himself is the eternally inexpressive fullness of light, which puts forth only a derivative and reduced manifestation of its power in the divine Son, and then only a distant and defective representation of that power in creation. But with the definition of the Son, and then also of the Spirit, as coequal and coeternal with the Father, this entire metaphysical economy had implicitly been abandoned. These new theological usages and their necessary philosophical grammar demanded a revision of the older Logos metaphysics at the most radical of levels. For not only is the Logos of Nicaea *not* a lesser manifestation of a God who is beyond all manifestation; it is in fact the eternal reality whereby God is the God he is. God's eternal identity is fully convertible, without any reduction of degree, with his own manifestation of himself to himself; this convertibility is nothing less than that infinite act of self-knowledge and self-love that is God's transcendent life. His being, therefore, is an infinite revelation; his hiddenness—his transcendence—is always already manifestation; and it is this movement of infinite disclosure that is his being as God. God *is* Father, Son, and Spirit; and nothing in the Father "exceeds" the Son and Spirit; in that perfect life of infinite love, nothing remains unexpressed. The Son is the eternal and infinite icon of the Father, perfectly known and loved and illumined in the infinite glory of the Spirit. There is a perfect equality—without passage through negation or tragic alienation—of eternal beauty and its eternal expression.

It is within this understanding of the divine nature, then, that Christian theology must make sense of the second outpouring of God: the free, gracious, unnecessary, but eternally fitting act of creation. For the gift of creation occurs within the mystery of that infinite act of love and knowledge, as a further expression of its beauty, brought forth not from some limited and limiting medium but purely from nothingness, purely as grace, purely as a gift of the infinite within the finite. The beauty of God in creation is not simply impressed upon some external and unformed substrate that requires a reduction of the unseen transcendent beauty to the distorting constraints of the finite. That experience of the beautiful that awakens us, with such special force, to the difference between being and beings—that awakens us to the sheer fortuity of transcendent being's revelation in the things that are—is also a revelation of the originally and ultimately peaceful economy of being. It tells us that between infinite beauty and finite beauty there is no conflict, no dialectical tension, no betrayal of the divine. Rather, divine beauty is that transcendent truth of being in which creation graciously participates, and which creation discloses again and again as pure gratuity.

IV

It is this same interval of grace that is repeated—and reaches its consummation—in the incarnate Person of Christ. In him, one sees the difference between the divine and the human as an infinite *qualitative* distance, precisely because there is no conflict or rivalry between Christ's divinity and humanity; the latter participates in the former so naturally that the one person of the Son can be both fully divine and fully human at once. If the difference between God and humanity were a merely quantifiable difference between extrinsically related beings, the Incarnation would be a real change in one or both natures, an amalgamation or synthesis; but then Christ would be not the God-man but a monstrosity, a hybrid of natures that, in themselves, would remain opposed and unreconciled. Because, however, the difference between the divine and human really is an infinite qualitative difference, the hypostatic union involves no contradiction, alienation, or change in the divine Son. Because the difference between God and creation is the difference between Being and created beings, rather than a tension between two poles within a single ontological continuum (the "there above" and the "here below"), Christ is not an irresoluble paradox fixed within the heart of faith, or an economic accommodation between two distinct kinds of being. In his one person—both God and man—there is neither any diminishment of his divinity nor any violation of the integrity of his humanity. In Christ one glimpses at once both the perfect ontological interval of divine transcendence and also the perfect fittingness of the divine image to its archetype. For the perfect man is also God of God: not a fabulous demigod, but human in the fullest sense because divine in the fullest sense. The beauty of the historical Jesus of Nazareth perfectly reflects and discloses, within the fallenness of time, the true beauty of his Father; to see him is to have seen the Father; to see him with the eyes of faith is to see, within his very humanity, the true beauty of the infinite God.

This, then (to return to where I began), means that the Christian understanding of beauty enjoins us to see the beautiful in those very regions of reality from which a conventional scale of appreciation of the pleasurable would exclude it. The form of Christ inhabits at once a province of shadows and a realm of glorious light; he is at once nocturnally and diurnally beautiful; his is a way simultaneously of abasement and of exaltation. And these two ways are one: not two dialectically counterposed moments within an irresoluble paradox, not a before and after, but a venturing forth from and return to the Father that is one motion, one life, one dramatic action that overcomes the fallen world's defining horizon—death—not through reconciliation with the limits it marks, but through an infinite act of *kenosis* and glorification that transgresses it, passes it by as though it were nothing. All Trinitarian theology depends upon the belief that Christ's *kenosis* is not a moment of separation, a descent from some otherworldly *pleroma* into a condition of estrangement, but a manifestation of the one eternal act by which God is God. The relation between the *morphē theou* and the *morphē doulou*, it turns out, is not one of dissemblance but of an ever deeper revelation of the depths of the divine. The story of the Son's incarnation, life, death, and resurrection is not the story of a divine masquerade, of a king who goes forth in self-divestment simply to return to the estate he has abandoned, like the protagonist in *The Song of the Pearl,* losing himself in the far country and then finding his true self again only in his return to his distant demesne. The Son goes forth because going forth is always already who he is as God, because all wealth and all poverty are already encompassed in his eternal life of receiving and pouring out, his infinitely accomplished bliss and love: he is the God he is in his very divestment and in his glory, both at once, as the same thing, inseparably. In the Gospel of John, Christ's crucifixion is clearly presented as being also his glorification; it is in being lifted up upon the cross that he draws the world to himself. Even in Christ's dereliction, God's infinity is made manifest: in the agony of Gethsemane, in going into the region of death, which lies over against

God in enmity toward him and his creation, Christ shows that the divine infinity surpasses all separations, the divine beauty suffuses all distances; and the Resurrection shows that the Son traverses the infinite as the infinite gift, never ceasing to be the true form of God: the "excess" of his infinity remains beauty, even as it spills over and erases all boundaries. The greater the freedom of the Son's journey into this world, then, the more profound the difference spanned and the farther the distance traversed, the more surely is God God. God's power is manifest most profoundly in the Son's *kenosis* because God's power is the infinite peace of an eternal venture of love, the divine ecstasy whose fullness is the joy of an eternal self-outpouring. Thus the divine beauty has no proper "place," belongs to no hierarchy of conventional aesthetic values. A *purely* idealist metaphysics of the beautiful, at least as we often conceive of such a thing, can point in only one direction, away from the world toward the simple and transcendent source of all beauty; but Christian thought, with its Trinitarian premise, must also follow the path of beauty outward into the world, even into states of utter privation, and into states of deformity that still cannot conquer the radiant form of God. Christian thought does not simply ascend to the beautiful but finds the beautiful in the entire scope of the divine life, even as it proceeds downward into utter inanition: God ventures even into the godless, and still his beauty is there, undiminished by its consort with the finite, still—if we can see it—offered as gift, delight, and love.

V

This, I think, is the most radical and precious gift of Christian aesthetics: the eye of charity, which relentlessly but joyously insists on finding beauty even where we should not expect it, and even among the despised and rejected: the vision of love that invites and compels us to find the whole glory of being in the brokenness and humility of a crucified slave; this new depth of vision, this new apprehension of the inexhaustible scope of divine glory, this perfect unity of *kenosis* and *plerosis*, of consummate weakness and omnipotence. From a Christian perspective, the event of the beautiful is an experience, even if only fleetingly, of this love that is forever poured out in all and that leads back to the inexhaustible wellspring of love. This way of seeing things is finally possible only for the saint, who is the truest of true aesthetes, the truest connoisseur of eternal beauty in its infinite gratuity and inexhaustible generosity. He or she alone possesses an understanding of beauty, and is capable of a cultivation of vision, that transforms all of reality into icons of the transcendent, windows into the eternal. Most of us enjoy such vision only in fugitive glimpses. Our spiritual senses are neither so refined nor certainly so sensitive as they should be. We must rely on the vision of others, whether mediated to us in the arts or in the examples of saintly lives or by whatever means the beautiful condescends to give itself. Even so, insofar as we have eyes to see and ears to hear, in the event of Christ's presence in time we have been given—and are given ever anew—the knowledge of the beautiful in its eternal truth, which is infinite love.

18

A Sense of Style
Beauty and the Christian Moral Life

I

Any system of ideas can come, in time, to feel like a prison of the spirit—or at least of the imagination—if only because every system subsists as much in its disjunctions as in its connections. In order to guide reason along the paths it has laid out, theory requires rigid demarcations and stout partitions; if it is to frustrate those adventurous impulses that might prompt the minds it superintends to go in search of more inviting lands, it has to ensure that the garden maze's hedges are high and impenetrable, that the walls ringing the estate are impregnable, and that the ramparts are thronged with vigilant sentinels. But, for just this reason, no system can endure indefinitely (though practically any can enjoy periodic revivals): even the richest and most ingenious comes at last to seem not just trite but a kind of durance, a structure of arbitrary and barren conceptual conventions, long ago evacuated of any real intellectual vitality and now able only to incubate a morbid boredom. And those who manage to escape their confinement, invariably, do so in hope of finding a way backward or forward to something purer, more immediate, more original and innocent, something truer to the experience of the rational desire for the real. Of course, after a while, vagrancy can prove just as uncomfortable as captivity, and so the truant mind may very well begin building a system of its own, which will in turn become a prison that others will want to escape; but no doubt there is some kind of Hegelian or Heideggerean—some dialectical or epochal—necessity in that, so there is no cause for reproach.

It is bad form to begin with a digression, I suppose, so forgive me for dropping into my topic at such a perpendicular angle. And forgive me also for some broad general pronouncements in what follows. I want to make some rather comprehensive general observations regarding the place of beauty in Christian morality. But, before I can do that with sufficient confidence in my own motives, I feel I should first explain (or diagnose), without necessarily trying to justify, a deep unhappiness I have long felt in regard to what I take to be one of the drearier realities of modern Western philosophy, albeit a reality that expresses itself under a huge diversity of aspects: that is, the alienation of the ethical from the aesthetic. It seems to me I have to allow for the possibility that my state of mind on the matter may be attributable to nothing more significant than a kind of seasonal affective disorder, a special sort of melancholy induced by the fading light and warmth of a dying year—or dying philosophical epoch, as the case may be; perhaps it is all just natural restiveness. But I do not think this to be the case. I cannot help but feel that there is something genuinely amiss with most of the dominant tendencies in Western ethical thought over the past few centuries, a sort of fragmentary quality that renders any coherent picture of moral life all but impossible and that has reduced ethical reasoning to a state of incoherence rather like the one described by Alasdair MacIntyre in *After Virtue*. My unhappiness, I hasten to say, has nothing to do with some supposed decline of morality in the arts (as if there ever was such a thing)—some perceived failure on their part to instruct us in bracing moral truisms or to shape our characters in wholesome ways or to present us with edifying exemplars of purity and piety. I am an unapologetic petty aesthete of the most antinomian kind and as a matter of spiritual principle will always prefer a tastefully appointed opium den or an atmospheric low dive to a drab chapel or garish cathedral. I take it, moreover, to be an obvious truth, if a paradoxical one, that all "moral art" is inevitably bad, yet that all bad art is somehow deeply immoral. There is in a sense more holiness in an elegant blasphemy than in a clumsy pious platitude. I mean, rather, that I take it to be peculiarly distinctive of the modern conceptual temperament to believe that the ethical, at least in its innermost essence, is *of necessity* unqualified by the aesthetic—that pursuit of the Good, that is to say, is by definition something practically opposed to the pursuit of the Beautiful. And we tend to believe this even when we think we do not. Sybarites and sensualists we merely censure on moral grounds; eudaemonists we are likely to regard as frivolous or mad. It seems to me, however, that this prejudice condemns vast reaches of modern ethical reflection to a logically irresoluble aporia.

I suppose it was Kant—at least, he provides a convenient epitome here—whose thought first elevated this alienation to the full dignity, rigor, and symmetry of a true theoretical system; if nothing else, the large divisions of the Kantian critical project as a whole, and the speculative reticence imposed by the transcendental deduction determining them, foreshadow or embody or inaugurate (as one pleases) a very modern division of "transcendental" spheres. Certainly, Kant assures us that each of the distinct realms of pure reason, practical reason, and judgment requires its own order of intelligible laws, and that none of these realms relates properly to the other two except obliquely, by way of an occasional and purely proportional analogy. The apprehension of natural teleology, for instance, may also help to provide us with some kind of purely intuitive index of moral purpose; but we should never confuse the one for the other. For Kant, aesthetic judgments can never be anything more than reflective determinations of those "subjective universals" under which the experiences of beauty and sublimity might be subsumed. And the only rule for distinguishing one kind of experience from the other is scale—or, rather, the relative proportion or disproportion between our immediate sensory intuitions and the capacity of our cognitive powers to comprehend them. The beautiful, he believed, in its finite and finished specificity, can be wholly comprised by cognition and so can allow for a free play between understanding and imagination, providing us a pleasure that requires neither any prior determinate concept nor any posterior judgment (except that of the "form of finality"). The sublime, by contrast, exceeds comprehension in its arithmetical or dynamical magnitude and thereby obliges us to venture concepts that exceed the sensory; but, in this very way, the apparent experience of the sublime surpasses our powers of representation, provoking reason's abstract conceptual powers and awakening the mind to its own rational liberty from the limitations of sensible nature. Here alone, then, the Kantian critical project allows a glimpse within the aesthetic of, if nothing else, a moral capacity: that possibility of noumenal freedom that announces itself within the experience of a certain kind of cognitive surfeit. But that is all. At the threshold of practical reason, aesthetic judgment reaches its limit and can offer no guide to the content of the ethical; it can merely, at a distance, survey a promised land that it may never enter. It could scarcely be otherwise, of course, given the austere limits set by the transcendental deduction. For Kant, any metaphysical speculation beyond a scrupulously chastened "metaphysics of morals" must be thwarted by the limits of reason's apparatus of perception. Whereas an older metaphysics had allowed for an ultimate coincidence of the transcendental perfections—truth, goodness, beauty, to adopt one traditional inventory—in the simplicity of an ontological source beyond the finite, for Kant all the adventures of the speculative intellect must end at the wall of the antinomies, still as yet unresolved with one another. If there is such an ontological coincidence of the transcendentals, it lies, alas, on the other side and can be grasped by the philosophical mind as, at most, a useful supposition of reason.

It is an impasse peculiar to modern ethical thought, and so much of its pathos is an abiding sense of that wall's impregnability. The result, as I say, is a pervasive aporia or quandary that becomes all too conspicuous at certain embarrassing junctures within our ethical theories. Take, for example, John Rawls's theory of justice, which is so satisfyingly and comprehensively complete in itself once the moral agent has consented to make that small but crucial imaginative retreat to an "original position," but which cannot explain, except in the debile terms of a certain utilitarian calculus, what would prompt anyone to make that retreat and so ultimately fails to explain with any logical finality why anyone enjoying the advantages of an unjust social arrangement should desire justice for everyone in the first place. It is a finely designed system, of course; it simply lacks a visible point of entry. And, as I say, Kant's project in this regard—this dissolution of the transcendental moments of speculative reason into autonomous and incommiscible regions—adumbrates much of the larger situation of later Western philosophy. It even points the way obliquely toward analytic tradition's reduction of thought to its propositional simples, and ultimately to that tradition's ever asymptotic descent toward pure tautology, utterly purged of every last residue of synthetic deduction or speculation, and so of every analogical "confusion" of distinct domains of inquiry. Approached thus, of course, aesthetic thought achieves almost perfect impotence as a guide to moral or (God forbid) metaphysical speculation. In a broader sense, though, and taking in the

Continental tradition, it points toward a reduction of the language of the ethical to a tragic or paradoxical register, one always haunted by the categorical imperative's pitiless demand for perfect disinterest, the subtle but persistent requirement that one certify one's ethical deeds by invigilating them for any trace of "impure" motives. This is impossible, obviously. Kant himself felt the need to dispel the gloom of perfect deontology just a little by inviting the moral agent to enjoy a certain exhilaration in the knowledge of noumenal rational liberty vouchsafed by obedience to that imperative and even occasionally to entertain a certain consequentialist consideration of the ills that would, say, befall financial institutions and private economies if telling the truth were not a universal law. Apparently, at times, at the wall of the antinomies, even deontology's heroism fails it. Would that Kant had been more consistently inconsistent. And would that so much of modern ethical thought since his day were not so consumed with a really quite trifling concern for subjective disinterest in the moral life. The result has often been positively absurd. There is, for instance, something positively disturbing in the spectacle of an ethical philosophy as unremittingly and passionately religious as that of Levinas forced to express itself only in a language of incessant accusation, persecution, affective darkness, infinite obligation—lest any hint of joy corrupt the absolute purity of the moral will. And there is something poignant in how thoroughly the prejudice in favor of total disinterest condemns us to a language of the ethical devoid of any real concept of moral *character*. After all, in seeking to form souls in conformity with true virtue, should we not want to produce persons who by nature spontaneously *delight* in moral goodness?

Kant's larger divisions among the transcendental faculties of reason are, of course, altogether inadequate for any account of what the mind actually does in pursuing any of its transcendental ends, as many in the next generations of German idealist philosophers grasped (Schelling, perhaps, with special acuity). At least, it seems clear that—had Kant attended not merely to the formal conditions of reason but to rational consciousness as an act at once indissolubly unified and irreducibly intentional—he might not have rested content with a purely abstract cartography of the distinct regions of rational life. One really does not need even to assume a metaphysical position to see that there is, at the very least, an obvious phenomenological deficiency in the transcendental deduction.

Viewed directly as a single act rather than refracted through the prism of the critical project into a static delegation of discrete functions, thought as a force quite overwhelms reason as a structure. Not that I can offer such a comprehensive phenomenology here. All I can say, in summary of what I believe a close scrutiny of rational consciousness discloses, is that the mind is never merely a passive reflection of an adventitious reality, like a patient substance awaiting formation by an extrinsic agent force, or like a mirror in which external objects are merely reflected. How could it be? It is always an intentional action, a particular movement of thought and will toward a reality that must be pursued as either a particular or a general final end. And, in fact, mind has no actuality as a movement toward the particular except insofar as the particular is embraced within a more original rational volition toward the general—or, better, toward the transcendental. How else could the world be intelligible to us except as bearing a specific interpretation, governed by an act of evaluation? That is, how could anything be intelligible to us as an intentional terminus unless there were not a prior and abstract terminus—truth as such—toward which the mind is always already reaching out as its only place of rest? We know the world because, from the first, we exceed the world in our abstract longing for the true in itself; and we receive the world as a comprehensible totality only by way of this primordial intention that allows us to compose our experience of the whole by interpreting all proximate objects in light of that anticipated end. This is the unconditional rational appetite prompting the mind's every venture toward knowledge, this unremitting predisposition or natural compulsion of the rational will toward an infinite and simple horizon of intelligibility by which it organizes experience—which would otherwise be an undifferentiated storm of pure sense intuitions—into form and meaning and rational relations. And since desire by definition must be desire for something, and so can never be a purely spontaneous eruption of the will without rationale, every act of thought is purposive and (however subtly) must exhibit the nature of its final cause in the transcendental structure of its operation. All knowledge, every rational experience, is from the first a moment of rapture, of ecstasy, toward ends that must be understood as—because they must necessarily be desired as—nothing less than the perfections of being, ultimately convertible with one another in the fullness of reality's one source and end. These are grand claims, I know; and yet I think they can be verified in every instant of thought, if one seeks its origins with sufficient care. And, while this constant calling of the mind to absolute ends is not a personal psychological state, something of which we are aware at any given moment, it is nonetheless a necessary and logically prior condition of all thought. The world comes to us as the beautiful and glorious and hideous and terrible interval that lies between the mind's indivisible unity of apprehension and the irreducibly transcendental horizon of its intention, two poles that lie entirely outside the topography of the physical order or the psychological self, just as it appears within consciousness only as lying between the mind's telos and the first cause of its movement. The mind knows the world as a whole because it has always already, in its intentions, exceeded the world; and consciousness can understand and judge only because it is, in its primordial reality, obedient to those absolute orientations of the rational will.

A scrupulous phenomenology of what the mind does, then, and of the rational will's absolute preoccupation with being as a whole, discloses something rather astonishing: that the very structure of thought is an essential relation to God as its "natural" end. To desire to know is to desire that everything opaque in the world of experience—everything that defies thought's overtures and importunities and indiscretions—slowly disappear, because the ultimate ideal that the mind seeks is a point of perfect transparency, where the act of thought and the being of the world are indistinguishable one from the other. The mind longs from the first not only to reach but to become the divine mind, which is itself also the giving of being to all things in the very act of their being known. Teleologically, the mind is God; necessarily, that is to say, the end it seeks is that its knowledge should become the knowledge of all things in God. And here, it seems to me, one must grant that there is a logical inevitability in the assumption that a "final cause" is always somehow already a real rational relation within, and so constitutive of, whatever it affects. Otherwise, it would not be able to make the potential actual. Or, in slightly less Aristotelian terms, the mind can be moved only by what is in some sense possible for it, at the very least as a rational desire. If rational life is reduced to its deepest origin and its ultimate end—to what precedes and surpasses the empirical world, what founds and elicits the whole movement of thought in which the phenomenal world subsists—it turns out inevitably to be a finite participation in an infinite act of thought that is also the whole of being: the simplicity of God knowing God. Thus the basis of all knowledge and will is the natural desire of the creature for *theosis*, divinization. The source of ethical existence is a tacit anticipation within us of coming to enjoy the bliss of the gods, of becoming God in God. Whatever the purely formal structure of finite perception might be, whether as described by Kant or not, it must be understood phenomenologically as the last result and bare residue of the mind's persistent engagement with a transcendent realm beyond the limits of sensible nature, of which it already enjoys a tacit, proleptic, but genuinely primordial knowledge. Moreover, that transcendent terminus toward which the intentionality of consciousness is always turned discloses itself in the constant, if always incomplete, convergence of the mind's transcendental ecstasies in the life of the rational will as they ascend to their several ends: in the way, for instance, we occasionally find an act of moral goodness strangely and compellingly lovely, or in the way we experience the drive to establish a particular truth to be a morally compelling motive in itself, or in the way that we can experience a direct encounter with the numinous power of truly great art (as in Rilke's great sonnet "Archaïcher Torso Apollos") as a kind of moral judgment on our own deficiencies and derelictions (and so on). This is, if nothing else, as I say, an evident phenomenological fact. For Kant, the differing regions of critical reason stand apart from one another, irresolubly heterogeneous, inviolably distinct. But it is a certain classical view of the matter that in fact corresponds to our experience of reality: in the interweavings of our transcendental longings and intuitions here below, we have a foretaste of the ultimate revelation of their perfect coincidence in the divine nature there above. In the act of consciousness, as an intentional departure from its own unity of apperception toward the simplicity of its necessary transcendent end, desire, recognition, and moral surrender are inseparable. Any ultimate discrimination among these transcendental moments—in terms of distinct critical topologies or of distinct psychological faculties or of what have you—is a fiction of theory. And so the late antique "Neoplatonic deduction," so to speak, seems to enjoy an unassailable empirical credibility: what for us comes first in the order of knowing, each moment of finite objective experience among an incalculable diversity of finite experiences, comes in fact as the end product of the order of existence, a kind of final prismatic extract of the original unified light of being, and it remains the vocation of rational life to ascend to that still undifferentiated principle that grants the soul existence and to find the soul's temporal end in its eternal beginning.

I would also argue that beauty possesses a unique eminence in our experience of this ultimate coincidence. The good, the true, and the beautiful, being and unity—or however one might arrange their taxonomy—constitute the transcendental horizon of consciousness in its every rational movement. But, in a sense, for finite spirits the beautiful constitutes, as it were, the transcendental horizon of the transcendentals themselves. No other among them, from the vantage of this world, is so obviously an intrinsically desirable end. Beauty elicits only our delight, rather than our sense of ethical obligation or epistemic submission or animal needs, and does so before and apart from any further kind of imperative—utilitarian or selfish—in a way that, say, the good or the true need not if considered as an isolated terminus of volition or knowledge. These latter can all too easily be mistaken as desirable for purely consequentialist reasons. Of the beautiful this is not so. In a sense, beauty is the glory of transcendentality as such, morally pure precisely because it is never reducible to mere moral purpose, or to any purpose beyond itself; it is instead the very splendor of purpose, the fulfilment that makes the good the ultimate repose of the will and mind, in perfect concord. Thus, for instance, we know we have cultivated true virtues within ourselves (as opposed merely to a disinterested obedience to laws of behavior external to our own wills and desires) when we find ourselves able to delight spontaneously in the pursuit of goodness, or able to take a genuinely deep satisfaction—a genuinely intense aesthetic transport, I would even say—in the practice of charity. As a soul acquires the virtue needed to pursue all its transcendental ends with true ardor, it will find that they become ever more inseparable—even indistinguishable—from one another.

II

This, then, raises the rather delicate matter of taste, whether good or bad. For, if what I have said to this point has any truth to it, then the formation of virtue in any of us—the acquisition of the *habitus* of goodness—must necessarily consist to a great degree in a kind of sentimental education.

Ethics is in many respects a matter of cultivating good taste. And differences in ethical philosophy are, at some vital but usually unacknowledged level, differences of aesthetic disposition and predilection. Horace is correct, of course, as far as his admonition goes: *De gustibus non est disputandum.* But, to be honest, that is a pragmatic rather than an ethical rule. It is generally better not to debate these matters, in part because no one's powers of aesthetic discernment are infallible, but mostly because a philistine's defects of sensibility are usually incorrigible, and it seems pointless to argue with someone who prefers Norman Rockwell or Thomas Kinkade to Velasquez or Cezanne. In most cases, after all, it does not matter much. Even so, taste is not an unimportant thing. In any of us, it indicates how we are disposed to take reality in, how we are likely to recognize what is truly valuable or venerable and what is not, and how our desires are ordered or disordered. One's ability in any instant to recognize beauty or its privation, or to distinguish between the truly beautiful and the merely pleasant or meretricious, is as often as not an indication not simply of one's personal culture or formation but of one's moral aptitude for the splendor of the good. True, bad taste is often simply the consequence of bad education; but I tend to think that education is ultimately of little account here and that the beautiful has the power to recommend itself to any soul open to its advent and to evoke from that soul a spontaneous movement of love. Good taste is not always sophisticated; in fact, at its purest, it is remarkably innocent, guileless, even childlike. And, as often as not, extreme sophistication turns out to be nothing more than a laboriously cultivated vulgarity. Then, too, we all know that there are persons whose tastes in the arts are not particularly refined but who in the appreciation of real moral beauty are the rarest of cognoscenti, of the kind whose every judgment convicts the rest of us of our rude and barbaric ways. The beautiful knows its own, and they recognize its voice.

And so it is, also, that the experience of beauty is necessarily also the experience of judgment: not the judgment we pass on the beauty we encounter in the world but the judgment it passes on us. We see this, at least, fairly clearly laid out in the gospels. In much of John's, for instance, as has often been noted, eschatology becomes almost perfectly immanent. In those pages, Christ passes through history as a light that reveals all things for what they are; and it is our reaction to him—our ability or inability to recognize that light—that shows us to ourselves. To have seen him is to have seen the Father, and so to reject him is to claim the devil as one's father instead. Our hearts are laid bare, the deepest decisions of our secret selves are brought out into the open, and we are exposed for what we are—what we have made ourselves. And it is not only John's Gospel, really, that tells us this. The grand eschatological allegory of Matthew 25 says something very similar: "'Lord, when did we see you hungry or thirsty or a stranger or naked or ill or in prison, and did not attend to you?' . . . 'Amen, I tell you, inasmuch as you did not do it to one of the least of these my brothers, neither did you do it to me.'" In John's Gospel, one's failure to recognize Christ as the true face of the Father, the one who comes from above, is one's damnation, here and now. In Matthew's Gospel, one's failure to recognize the face of Christ—and therefore the face of God—in the abject and oppressed, the suffering and disenfranchised, is the revelation that one has chosen hell as one's home. And here, of course, is where the discriminating eye is invited by the gospels to find that deeper beauty, that divine light, where a poorer sensibility might find only an intolerable burden on one's sympathies.

This is, needless to say, the special difficulty of a truly Christian aesthetics: it requires us, whether we are inclined to do so or not, to seek the beautiful in regions of reality that a more conventional scale of appreciation would forbid us to consider. It demands of us a sensibility wholly governed by the form of Christ, as given to us in the gospels and in the whole of Christian memory; and this is a form that encompasses a perfect balance between the obscure and the lucid, the dark and the radiant, and one cannot separate the one side from the other without hopelessly losing sight of both. We cannot even with any real certainty draw clear demarcations within the story between Christ's abasement as the suffering servant and his exaltation as the risen Lord. It would be so much easier, naturally, if we could treat these as two distinct narrative moments, or perhaps three: the tale of a great king or prince who temporarily abandons his throne so that he may go out into his realm and walk incognito among his subjects but who then at the end of the tale returns home to his proper estate, to resume his true appearance and rank so that now he may dispense justice and mercy (as appropriate) to those souls among whom he briefly sojourned. But that would make a mockery of the story. More to the point, that is not how the tale has traditionally been told—in the gospels, in Paul's theology, in Christian recollection as a whole. The Son of God's venturing forth from the Father and the Son of Man's return to the Father are not two successive episodes, for then the former would be nothing more than an act of dissimulation and only the latter an act of divine revelation. The entire intelligibility of Christian belief rests upon the necessary belief that the tale in its entirety, in its every dimension—both the venturing forth and the return—is one act of God's self-disclosure, wherein there is no moment of alienation of God from his own nature: the Son's *kenosis* and *plerosis*, God's self-outpouring in the life of Jesus of Nazareth and humanity's fulfillment in Christ's unity with the Father, is one indivisible declaration within created time of who God is in his own eternity. This is, recall, the guiding premise of all traditional Trinitarian theology: that the eternal nature of God has been made really manifest in the economy of salvation. See, for instance, St Basil of Caesarea's *De Spiritu Sancto*, a text that makes explicit as perhaps no other ever has that every statement the tradition feels competent to make regarding the eternal *taxis* of the divine life depends upon the belief that Christ's incarnation and earthly career is not a moment of separation from his proper nature, a simple descent from his divinity into a condition of estrangement, but rather in its every dimension a manifestation of the one eternal act by which God is God. The appearance, then, of the one to whom the "form of God" properly belongs in the "form of a slave" is not a dissemblance of Christ's divine identity but rather the fullest possible revelation of its depths. Hence, in the Gospel of John, Christ's crucifixion is described as being also his glorification; it is when he is lifted up upon the cross that he drags the world to himself. The Son goes forth among us because the going forth of the Son is who God is from everlasting; the Son is raised up to the Father by the Spirit because that return of the Son to the Father in the glory of recognition and delight is the bliss of God's eternal life of infinite love. Christ's divestment of his glory and his putting on of his glory are one and the same divine act, seen from the vantage now of history, now of eternity. Christ's utter dereliction, even in the death of the cross, is also the indestructible beauty of that divine love revealing its fullness to us. The Resurrection shows that even the death of the Son was always already the victory of that love over everything that disfigures the beauty of God residing in all things. No matter how great the distance the Son journeys from the Father, he is always in that very motion drawing near to the Father in the beauty of the Spirit. This is the invincible divine ecstasy that simply is the life of God. Hence the divine beauty is, from our perspective, something quite subversive; revealed fully, it turns out to have no proper discrete place within any conventional hierarchy of aesthetic values. Rather, it somehow encompasses the whole of things in the mystery of its limitless graciousness. A purely idealist metaphysics of the beautiful can only ascend from the brokenness of this world toward the simple and transcendent source of all beauty (which is fair enough); but Christian thought, with its Trinitarian premise, must also follow the path of beauty outward into the world, even into states of utter privation, and find that that beauty is still present even there, even in "the least of these," if we can learn to see it.

This, though, is also the great moral and spiritual enlightenment—the enormous enlargement of sensibility and discernment—that a truly Christian aesthetics might bestow on those who seek to adopt it: the eye illumined by charity, the eye whose own light can make visible what otherwise would be forever hidden. To see the fullness of divine love, the greatness of the extremes that the shape of the divine life encompasses, in the very brokenness and desolation of a murdered slave is to have entered into an order of vision that can never simply take leave of the despised and rejected in its haste to find the loveliness and serenity and nobility of which they seem to have been utterly deprived. It is a way of seeing things powerful enough still to descry the glory of God amid that darkness, and still to rejoice in it. It can find the delight of love even among those who have been driven far from the light of this present world because it cannot now lose sight of the divine image that no extremity of ruin can extinguish. And, once we have been granted even the most fleeting moment of that sort of vision, we find that that deep, primordial, natural longing within us animating all rational desire—that longing to become gods, to be transformed into God in God—must henceforth be grasped by us under the form of a radical inversion: we must seek to become God only by being conformed to the self-emptying, self-humbling God who pours himself out into the most abject of conditions, solely out of love, and who thereby reveals the true shape of his eternal glory. Perhaps only the most saintly among us can really hope to enjoy such vision as a constant condition of the soul. It requires a cultivation of perception so capacious in its aesthetic sympathies that it can find within every concrete reality, however disfigured by sin and death, an icon of the transcendent beauty. But the Christian moral life, surely, consists in nothing if not the ceaseless aspiration to see as the saint sees.

So how, then, do we make this vision ours, as a kind of moral practice?

III

Obviously, there is no single answer. I can offer only my own somewhat perverse approach to the question itself and ask indulgence for the sheer simplemindedness that this entails. I confess, I do not know how to think in terms of "ethics," at least not if one takes the word as the name of some distinct field of inquiry; and I certainly do not believe in something called "Christian ethics," either as a discrete topic within theology or as a mere invariable canon of precise prescriptions and prohibitions. What I really believe in is, for want of a better term, a sense of style. What I put my trust in as a true guide to practical reason is the cultured ability to recognize, appreciate, imitate, develop, and vary certain forms of living in this world, certain seductive fashions. The formation of virtue within us, however any particular moral tradition might understand the shape that virtue should assume, must be a process of gaining mastery in the exhibition of a very particular personal manner: ideally, a manner that accords as beautifully as possible with all the transcendental ends that call us to themselves within the most primordial motives of the rational will, and so a manner that, in being mastered, naturally instills in one an ever deeper longing to arrive at the transcendent wellspring where all those ends are one; a manner that expresses something of the vast range of moral possibilities those ends provide and yet one whose fluid and lovely equipoise harmonizes them in a thoroughly plausible unity of character. For Christians, obviously, this cultivation of virtue consists in attempting to shape one's life in conformity with Christ's, precisely by trying to capture and adopt something of his unique style, and to preserve it as far as possible even in those situations when clear prescriptive clarity proves agonizingly elusive.

To see what I mean, consider for instance the story of the woman taken in adultery: it is a tale that in a sense refuses to leave us with any exact rule regarding any particular ethical situation, much less any single rule for all analogous situations; but it definitely provides us with a startlingly incisive exemplar of an extremely particular manner for conducting oneself, even in circumstances that might be fraught with moral ambiguity, or even with terror, and for negotiating those circumstances by way of pure bearing, pure balance. Christ's every gesture in the tale is resplendent with any number of delicately calibrated and richly attractive qualities: calm reserve, authority, ironic detachment, but also tenderness, a kind of cavalier gallantry, moral generosity, graciousness, but then also alacrity of wit, even a kind of sober levity ("Let him among you who is without sin . . ."). All of it has about it the grand character of the effortless beau geste, a nonchalant display of the special privilege belonging to those blessed few who can insouciantly, confidently violate any given convention simply because they know how to do it with consummate and ineffably accomplished artistry—aplomb, finesse, panache (and a whole host of other qualities for which only French seems to possess a sufficiently precise vocabulary). And there is as well something exquisitely and generously antinomian about Christ's actions here. It embodies the same distinctive personal idiom that is expressed in the more gloriously improbable, irresponsible, and expansive counsels of the Sermon on the Mount—that charter of God's Kingdom as a preserve for flâneurs and truants, defiantly sparing no thought for the morrow and emulous only of the lilies of the fields in all their prismatic indolence—and that is expressed also in everything about his ministry and teachings that, say, Nietzsche could interpret only as the decadence of a dreaming symbolist.

Admittedly, it is a difficult style to catch hold of, and not everyone cares to try. I was recently, for example, involved in public debates with some traditionalist Catholics who are advocates of capital punishment, as something not only permitted but actually enjoined by Christian belief. The claim is preposterous, of course, on any number of obvious grounds, and it required little effort to discover their errors in logic, theology, biblical hermeneutics, and historical scholarship. But I have to admit that what struck me most forcibly was none of that, but rather their sheer appalling bad taste. Clearly, those who think it possible to be faithful to the figure of Christ as he appears in the gospels and also to argue in favor of the death penalty are, before all else, philistines. Their sensibilities are manifestly too barbarous and obtuse to see and appreciate the style of Christ at all, because it is a style simply too refined, subtle, and elegant for them, and certainly too negligent of commonsensible ethical expectations and the regrettable necessities those sometimes entail; it is a style, rather, that expresses a form of life thoroughly absorbed in a far more essential and otherworldly loveliness. And yet, without a sense of this, what is Christ to any of us, considered as the form of God made manifest in the perfected form of the human being? Again, perhaps the story of the adulterous woman says it all. It enunciates no exact principles or laws, but it compellingly, inveiglingly invites us to adopt the style pervading Christ's actions as, so to speak, the most exquisite imaginable *dernier cri*. In dispersing the woman's accusers with a cool irony that leaves them haplessly silent, and in then granting her a forgiveness wholly unencumbered by any ponderous expressions of disapproving decency or piety, and without even any prescribed penance, Christ demonstrates how a single graceful gesture, performed with sufficient moral and aesthetic élan, can express all the dimensions of the beauty of charity. It may seem somewhat perverse, as I have noted, to suggest that the ethical should in this sense be ultimately reducible to the aesthetic; but it should be, even so, for the simple reason that what draws us to the good is that it is also eternal beauty. God himself is beauty, that is, and in the end, for Christians, we are joined to him in seeking the beautiful as he has taught us to recognize it in Christ, and in therefore seeking in every circumstance, however unanticipated, to express that beauty always anew, in ever more novel variations on that original "theme"—that unique and irresistibly attractive manner. At times, a sense of style really is everything.

PART FOUR

Literatures of Transcendence

19

The Shock of the Real

On *Journey to the Land of the Real*,
by Victor Segalen

I

The death of Victor Segalen (January 14, 1878–May 21, 1919) was perhaps an enviable one. This is not to say that it was not also tragic: he was still quite young, and his demise came unexpectedly for his family, and by an agonizingly trivial mischance. But I tend to be something of a fatalist in regard to the life spans of artists (the great ones, at least). Mozart was divinely destined to die young, an impossible prodigy appearing and vanishing in an instant like a flash of lightning crossing the heavens, while it was ordained from everlasting that Haydn should enjoy a serene longevity in which to unfold his genius; Keats grown old would have been a drastic error of taste on the part of providence, while it was absolutely necessary that Wordsworth begin as a "lyrical" radical but end up as a withered Tory sage penning sonorous banalities. And I suspect that Segalen, having reached early middle age, was already putting a severe strain on the short, bright length of thread Lachesis had allotted him. All the evidence suggests that his health was rapidly fading; one way or another, his days were coming to an end. And it was somehow fitting. For most of his life, he had been a living tempest of wildly diverse accomplishments, haunting inspirations, gnomic insights, and startlingly original ideas; but his was definitely a young man's genius, sustained by spiritual restlessness. With age, he might have succumbed to the temptation to elucidate, to dispel the enigmas and clarify the inchoate intuitions, to produce a system rather than give free expression to his natural creative ferment; and that would have been a great pity. It is everything unfinished, evocative, and frustratingly suggestive in his writings that makes them uniquely fascinating. And anyway, by the time of his death he had probably already achieved as much as he might reasonably have hoped: he had been a certified naval physician, an explorer, a poet, a novelist, an essayist, an ethnographer, a linguist, a sinologist, an aesthetic theorist, and a few other things beside. And he had produced a body of work of indelible novelty and brilliance. Borges, for instance, believed him a far more important figure in French letters than any of his more celebrated near contemporaries and credited him with having invented an entirely new approach to aesthetic experience, reconciling (without merging) the traditions of Asia and Europe. He had nothing left to do.

Frankly, moreover, even though Segalen would probably not have chosen to die at forty-one, he almost certainly would have delighted in the sheer mysteriousness of his death, and especially in the uncanny way in which it seemed to bind his life together in a closed circle. He died east of Brest, deep in the woodlands of Huelgoat, a place that had been a frequent retreat when he was a child and where his imagination had first begun to float free from its moorings in ordinary life. In his final days, he had been using opium in increasing quantities to alleviate a number of ailments and had been suffering from fainting spells for some months. Then one day he failed to come home from a long walk. His corpse was later discovered in the forest, resting against a tree as if he were sleeping, pale but apparently quite at peace. Flies had begun to gather at his eyes and the corners of his mouth. At his side was a complete edition of Shakespeare, bound in blue Moroccan leather, opened to a page of *Hamlet*. He had apparently bled to death from a deep laceration in one of his ankles, which he had probably gashed on a stone or root (though at least one old acquaintance suspected he might have made the incision himself). If I could add an apocryphal detail to the record here (as Segalen himself might have done), I would claim that his forefinger was resting on the lines "The undiscovered country, from whose bourn / No traveller returns . . ." A bit of an obvious conceit on my part, perhaps, but appropriate: in a sense, he had spent much of his life in search of an undiscovered country and had wandered the globe looking for it; and yet, if he ever truly found it, it was there that day, in the quiet of the woodlands he had known from childhood, near the place of his birth.

II

Segalen had always been fairly devoted to his native province. He had even amputated the acute accent from his surname—he had been born Victor Joseph Ambroise Désiré Ségalen—to make it more authentically Breton. Though almost everything concrete that formed him as an artist and "thinker" was acquired elsewhere, during his extended journeys around the earth, arguably the only true spiritual home he ever knew was the countryside outside Brest, where he had enjoyed an almost idyllic early childhood before being sent in 1888 to a nearby Jesuit school. But from an early age something else within him was urging him to venture out into the world of the unknown. After taking his baccalaureate in 1893, he had to leave the region in any event, in order to attend the naval medical academy in Bordeaux. There, in 1901, he wrote a thesis on the portrayal of neurosis in the literature of his day, part of which he published the next year as a treatise on synaesthesia in Symbolist writings. This soon brought him into contact with the editors of *Mercure de Paris* and with a literary set that included such figures as Max Nordau, Remy de Gourmant, and Joris-Karl Huysmans. The prospect of a literary career now opened before him. But it was not enough. And so his true "career" as a wanderer began the following year, when he decided to set sail for Tahiti—though it was no sooner begun than it was dangerously interrupted. Segalen contracted typhoid fever en route and was obliged to disembark in San Francisco, where he survived only by enduring a long, careful convalescence. It was a near brush with death, but a very fortunate one. It was there that he had his first revelation of China, in the displaced, distilled, concentrated, and fabulous form of Chinatown, and his sensibility began to acquire what would ultimately become its most vital element.

When at last he did reach Tahiti, Segalen became by default a kind of executor of the estate (such as it was) of Paul Gauguin, who had died just two months earlier. In the process he became deeply absorbed in the study of Gauguin's life and work. He even purchased one of Gauguin's final finished canvases, *Breton Village in the Snow*, for a mere seven francs (the auctioneer had displayed it upside down and offered it as a picture of Niagara Falls). For nearly three years he lived in Polynesia, where he witnessed and deplored the slow inexorable destruction of Maori culture before the advances of colonial "progress." Then, early in 1905, he made a brief visit to Djibouti, arriving not long after the death of Rimbaud, for whose legacy he soon assumed the same sort of accidental curatorship he had for Gauguin's. That February, he returned to France. He seemed ready now to assume the trappings of bourgeois life and to resume his fledgling literary career. He married and his first son was born. He struck up friendships with Jules de Gaultier and Claude Debussy and wrote a strange and lovely libretto for the latter—*Orphée-Roi*—which sadly was never set to music. He produced studies of Gauguin and Rimbaud, and even a treatise on cyclones in the Pacific regions. And in 1907 he published his first short story, in the pages of *Mercure*, and finished his first novel, *Les Immémoriaux*, which dealt principally with the plight of the Maoris under colonial rule. Again, however, the settled life proved impossible for him. That serendipitous delay in San Francisco had inspired his imagination with a yearning that the comforts of a life of letters in the French countryside could not satisfy. In 1908 he went to Paris to pursue serious studies of Chinese, written and spoken, and the following year he left for China and joined an expedition into that country's central territories.

Rather than return home at expedition's end, he stayed on, and in February of 1910 he summoned his family to join him. The three of them then traveled by way of Shanghai to Beijing, where Segalen somehow attached himself to the French delegation and was even, in his official capacity, granted an audience with the emperor. Then, in 1911, he managed to secure a position for himself at the Imperial Medical College in Tientsin, and there his daughter was born the following year. It was in these years that his greatest phase as an artist began. In 1912, he finished his lovely book *Odes* and then published (in Beidang) the first version of *Stèles*, a magnificent cycle of forty-eight poems written in the "genre" of imperial proclamations supposedly graven on stone steles on the empire's frontiers. Composed in Chinese and French, *Stèles* is a book without poetic precedent: mysterious, cold, at once both spare and gravely gorgeous; dispassionate, impersonal, remote, *monumental*, it somehow summons up, without describing, an entire fantastic world of deserts, mountains, palaces, and always more distant horizons. Segalen added sixteen more poems to the cycle in 1913, publishing them in *Mercure*, and then released the complete version of the book in the definitive edition of

1914. He also, during the same period, composed his brilliant novel *René Leys*, which would not be published in his lifetime: an altogether mesmerizing, often disorienting meditation on the shifting boundaries between reality and fantasy, built around a deceptively simple story about a Western visitor to Beijing seeking to learn the mysteries of the Forbidden City from an unreliable but magnetic "expert" in palace affairs.

By then, reluctantly, Segalen was back in France, having returned in 1913 in time for his second son to be born on Breton soil. He had no sooner arrived home, however, than he began raising money for another Chinese adventure, this time an archaeological expedition and topographical survey in the hinterlands between Beijing and the Tibetan border, which set out from the capital in February of 1914. It resulted in at least one significant discovery: on March 6 Segalen discovered and identified what remains the oldest specimen of statuary ever found in China, a decayed ancient sculpture of a warhorse trampling down a foreign invader. But the trip had scarcely begun before it was curtailed by the outbreak of the Great War, and Segalen was obliged to return to France to resume his duties as a military physician in a hospital in Brest. He was sent to the Belgian front for a brief period in 1915–16 but soon contracted some kind of debilitating ailment and was sent home again. This was probably the first sign of an infirmity that would wear upon him the rest of his life. Despite both war and illness, however, he managed to publish another book in June of 1916, *Peintures*, a series of glitteringly fragmented descriptions of fictional Chinese paintings. It is a remarkable work and, again, one without any literary precedent. Somehow it almost succeeds, as it flows along, in fashioning its own inner world of aesthetic experiences. And then in 1917, even before the war had ended, Segalen contrived to have himself sent on another Chinese expedition, this time ostensibly to recruit native labor for French munitions factories. This would be his last visit to China, and many of the changes he observed taking place there, such as the democratic reforms of Sun Yat-Sen, displeased him mightily; to him, these abrupt alterations of an immemorially ancient society seemed like nothing but further instances of the "colonial" and "capitalistic" homogenization of a world under the dominance of Western finance.

He did not have long to lament what he saw, however. He was recalled to Brest in March 1918, and, at that point, something—whether psychological or physiological is unclear—was broken in him. He was working away diligently at yet another long poem, *Thibet*, which even in unfinished form probably deserves to be ranked among his master-pieces. But he seemed to be reaching some limit within himself, just as the war was drawing to a close. His near-constant use of opium and his fainting spells began. In January 1919 he was hospitalized in a psychiatric ward and was then sent to Algeria to convalesce for two months with his wife as company. Whether this had any salutary effect is impossible to say, but it seems unlikely. In his journal he recorded that, though he was suffering from no illness that could be diagnosed, his body was failing him, and that he had abandoned any hope of remedies; "Je constate sim-plement que la vie s'éloigne de moi" (I note simply that life is moving away from me). Soon after his return home he was dead. Very little of his work had been published at that point; most of it had to wait decades to be discovered and issued in print in France. For a long time, he was for-gotten by all but a very discerning few.

III

One of those unpublished works, *Équipée: De Pékin aux marches thibé-taines* (Expedition: From Peking to the Tibetan frontier)—or *Journey to the Land of the Real*, in Natasha Lehrer's luminous new translation—is pu-tatively a short account of the abortive archaeological and topographical expedition of 1914. In reality, it is a combination of recollection and in-vention, as Segalen freely admits. It is a strange, oddly absorbing book in its own right, but one whose larger meaning is fairly obscure if it is not read in light of Segalen's aesthetics of "Difference" or "Diversity" or (to use his favored term) "*Exoticism.*" He was perhaps the first French cultural theorist to speak of cultural and aesthetic difference as an abso-lute value in itself, almost a kind of transcendental, dependent on nei-ther some more original unity of human experience nor some ultimate synthesis of distinct cultures in a higher "speculative" truth. He was not a champion, like certain later French theorists, of a kind of relativist or "perspectival" celebration of a merely abstract difference-as-such, since this effectively reduces all concrete cultural diversity to just so many di-verse instances of a single "truth." He did not pretend or aspire to occupy some vantage above or outside the play of cultural diversity, appreciating difference merely as a disembodied ideal. What he most prized in the encounter with cultural otherness was the brute shock of the impregnable, the mysterious surfeit of experience over expectation in those moments when one encounters the reality of a phenomenon that will not submit to dissolution into the familiar.

This made him something of a reactionary in respect to modern pieties about social progress. While he had no patience for race theory, for instance, he did believe in the inviolable uniqueness of distinct peoples, and of their separate imaginative atmospheres, and he was cordially hostile to anything that might dilute it—especially the homogenizing forces of Western imperialism, trade, and social democracy. This led to the rather curious situation that his anxiety to preserve traditional cultures against Western dominance was inseparable from a choleric distrust of any narrowing of class differences within those cultures, or of any broad social ameliorations at all. He did not like to see class divisions erased. Similarly, while he probably held women in general in somewhat higher esteem than he did men, he objected to any and every modern tendency that might lessen the distance or diminish the mystery separating the sexes. Women, he believed, should remain at once emotionally open but jealously enigmatic, spontaneously caring but cunningly selfish, forthrightly submissive but subtly indomitable, while men should remain essentially simple in their ruthlessness or their generosity, their impulse to command and their willingness to sacrifice themselves in perfect obedience to what they love or imagine. Each sex should remain unfathomable to the other; and no assault upon social and moral conventions must be allowed to endanger the precious iridescent veil of that mystery. For him, hierarchy was necessary as the only effective alternative to mediocrity.

Happily, Segalen's art transcends the more suspect features of his philosophy; and, in the end, his sympathy for other peoples and persons is more pronounced in his work than is his animosity to their social advancement. And, if nothing else, he was at least consistent in his convictions as far as his own natal station was concerned. He was as free of aristocratic pretensions as he was of any feigned solidarity with the peasantry; and, far from wishing to be Chinese, he was as anxious to preserve the impenetrable otherness of China against any personal impulse to "go native" as he was to preserve it against any sociological or political

attempt at cultural synthesis. For him, the animating principle of Exoticism was the appreciation of irreducible distinctions, over against the
mass global culture of capitalist vulgarity. And the heart of the Exoticist
sensibility is the recognition that, within a world of genuine differences,
the picture of reality that one particular people might cherish can never
be more than a set of arbitrary conventions, which should not be imposed on other peoples. Thus the Exoticist is ideally also a militant fan-
tasist, freely indulging in the exploration of other frames of reality, other
worlds even, and ultimately of that ineffable, intangible, but alluring
"Elsewhere" known only to dreamers and poets, which is a place lying
only in the past or the future or some other time altogether. Above all,
a true aesthetics of the diverse demands that we not resent that which
we find utterly incomprehensible in foreign culture but instead allow
ourselves to be drawn to the foreign by its very refusal to divulge its secrets. This is no sentimental romanticism of the charmingly unusual or
quaintly peculiar in other cultures. It is, rather, an austere and principled
rejection of the search for analogies by which to reduce other peoples to
amusingly defective shadows of ourselves, as well as a fierce and unrelenting willingness to expose the self to what it cannot surmount, and to
something by which it may even find itself shattered, so that in the salutary violence of that encounter the self might awaken to its own indefinable separateness and perilous fragility.

For Segalen, moreover, this enigmatic allure of unspoiled otherness
was positively erotic, in the most innocent and necessarily chaste of
senses: for him, it was the unattainability of the object of one's fascination that made the desire for it so exquisite. He adored the impenetra-
bility of cultural difference as a kind of invincible purity, something that
could only be lost the moment it was actually possessed, in the way a
Provençal troubadour ideally adored the unapproachable beauty and intact honor of the highborn lady of his *ballades*. And hence his insistence
upon the aesthetics of distance—of that interval of separation that cannot
be traversed without destroying what one does not understand. He was
convinced that, whenever we transform the strange into another version
of the familiar, we make the familiar itself vacuous and undifferentiated.
His dread of finding the whole world conformed to the image of the modern West was also a dread of the disappointment of an encounter with
"the Real" in which the self finds only itself once more; for this would

mean that the self is no more than a ghost, a banality, a cipher: just one more instance of an endlessly reiterated pleonasm. When, though, one has known the truly different in its irreducible otherness, even if only for a moment, one is transported out of oneself. This in fact was, for him, the true purpose of the expedition he undertook in 1914—this ineffable and always unique instant of surprise: "Before I began to think about the results, I experienced both shock and an immediate sense of beauty that is, for those who have known it, unassailable."

IV

It is within the embrace of this aesthetics of difference that *Journey to the Land of the Real* pursues its impossible object. For Segalen, we always approach the realm of the Real out of the realm of the imagination, not in order to take leave of the imagined, nor certainly to be disenchanted or "enlightened," but in order instead to discover that liminal place where the two realms meet and mingle, and where we find or forge a meaning greater than either. To him the Real can never be perfectly attained or decisively entered into, and yet the imagination can exist only in being called out of itself into that unconquerably concrete actuality that lies beyond it. And so we are always engaged in a conflict between two worlds: "between what one thinks and what one collides with, between what one dreams and what one does, between what one desires and what one obtains." In a very real sense, each of these worlds is revealed only by the other. Thus Segalen begins by announcing that he has no intention of scrupulously observing any clear distinction between the accurately recounted and the willfully fabulous. Thus also his narrative begins not with his expedition's departure from Beijing but rather with the way in which he first imagined the entire journey to the Tibetan frontier, in great detail, before ever setting out. For him, the impenetrable immensity of the Real initially takes the form of an ideal landscape, one that the Real itself alone can then either fulfill or fall short of or exceed. Only when the imagined Chinese wilderness has assumed its full dimensions for him does he make his (rather dreamlike) departure from his "porcelain room" and venture out into what lies beyond. And, again and again, he emphasizes both the concreteness and the fluidity of the experience of the

Real that follows. He praises, for example, the Chinese *li*, a unit for measuring the distance of a journey corresponding not to any constant fraction of the space traversed but rather to the varying conditions of the terrain and the gait of the walker. Perhaps his most valued companion on the journey is the "obligatory miniature god of travellers" that he takes with him, precisely because it is a figure resistant to all fixed meanings: "What a fine little pocket travel-god he is, an indispensable accessory for the vagabond I have become. Empty of dogma and so a lighter burden for my mules. I shall ascribe to him divine decisions that will pass like lightning from the Sinai of my head to his, which I will then retract with each new and successive Testament. And, because of the rich material from which he is hewn, I know that all this will be the colour of fuliginous gold, gilded smoky crystal, hot crystal, incomplete, and passionate beneath the icy glitter."

The book abounds, I should mention, in splendid set pieces, both descriptive and contemplative. There is a wonderful account of a desperate navigation of river rapids in a small boat, with Segalen himself obliged to man the *sao* when the captain is badly injured. There is a mesmerizing account of a European's coffined corpse recently carried out of Tibet, where the unnamed man had been killed twenty-two days earlier. There is an *almost* entirely incredible episode involving a village that somehow seems to exist outside the flow of history. There is a coldly sardonic meditation on the special art of the porters who quite literally bear the weight of the journey—though with an eerily sustained lightness of step—which ends in a ghastly fantasy of Segalen riding one of them like a horse. And so on. But each tableau serves in its distinct way to illustrate the jarring meeting, and the inconclusive struggle for dominance, between the imaginary and the Real. One of the homeliest and yet most brilliant of these illustrations is Segalen's reflection on the faint victory his topographical jottings allow him to achieve over the blank cartographic terra incognita whose spaces it is his business to fill in. As the unknown is gradually translated into the known, in however tenuous and symbolic a form, the indeterminacy of the possible is at once narrowed and intensified in the exactitude of the actual, and the imagination gradually surrenders more and more of its territory to reality; and yet the imagination finds itself not so much suppressed or displaced as deepened.

Even so, precisely how this relation between the provisionally imagined and the intractably Real is to be understood is rather elusive in Segalen's text. At one point, he describes the matter in Kantian terms: "*The phenomenal realm and the noumenal realm*—the world from which we come, and the one towards which we are heading." But several pages later he appears to contradict himself: "The Real here means nothing other than that which contradicts the pure game of thought; what can be touched, seen, smelled, measured or thought." In the end, his best treatments of the matter turn out to be those that are least analytic: "The Real has always seemed to me very womanly." He is at his most illuminating, in fact, when he imagines a woman "lying on the bed of the Real" and then—rather than reduce the image to some obvious allegory for some insipid concept—instead allows his mind to drift off into an entrancing meditation on the ineffable strangeness for Western men of the beauty of Chinese women, its enticing opacity, the way in which its allure and affect seem to escape the carnal calculations of a Western sensibility.

If, however, Segalen ultimately fails to provide a coherent definition of the Real (which would in any event, by his own account, be impossible), he comes close to providing a clear picture of difference, or at least of that experience of difference—that liberating shock of the impenetrable—that he so values. And it turns out to be an experience he knows not because it can be defined in itself but because it awakens him to his own essential otherness, his own difference from the familiar, his own inner core of the impenetrably Real. Perhaps the oddest episode in the book, and one written in a manner that stubbornly resists either a wholly literal or a merely metaphorical reading, comes near the end, where Segalen describes reaching the frontier of Tibet and meeting "the Other"—supposedly another European, dressed in faded beige, someone who should not be there, who responds to none of Segalen's queries, and whom Segalen suddenly and dizzyingly recognizes as himself, fifteen years or so younger, a "phantom part" of his own confused youth: "the pensive look, the adolescent expression, the startling charm of all the intuited hopes from that time, before harsh realisation stifles them one by one, selecting just a few to grow out of all proportion. So this is what I came all this way to find." And this is the end of the quest; nothing remains for the traveler but to turn back home. But Segalen pauses long enough to leave the reader with one final image, borrowed from traditional Chinese iconography: two beasts confronting one another over some indistinct object (perhaps a coin) lying on the ground between them. It is the best symbol he can find for the irresoluble confrontation between imagination and reality, and for that unutterable "between" over which neither can claim sovereignty but from which neither can achieve independence.

V

Taken in sum, Segalen's aesthetics of difference constitutes not so much a cogent theory as a comprehensively explored and charted sensibility. Followed to the end purely as a philosophy, Exoticism would probably yield only a familiar kind of incoherence, the sort of unsustainable imbalance produced whenever one extreme of a necessary polarity is emphasized to the exclusion of the other. It is easy, of course, to understand the pathos of Segalen's protest against his age. As a reaction to the homogenizing Western triumphalism of modernity, as well as an expression of a sincere solicitude for all those unique and irreplaceable things that modernity threatens to sweep away, it made perfect sense to elevate difference over identity as an absolute value and to assert that the event of "the Other" always precedes the rule of "the Same." And, after all, much of the history of philosophical systems consists in constant and predictable pendulations between contrary logical poles, thought "correcting" an excessive fixation on one by swinging away to an equally excessive fixation on the opposite. Still, by itself, Segalen's perspective is inadequate.

All knowledge, even knowledge of the limits of our knowledge, requires taking leave of extreme positions and learning to negotiate the analogical middles of things. Even to know in what sense and to what degree incommensurable things really are incommensurable requires some common proportion between them; a primordial difference, without any "equiprimordial" term of identity to differ from, would be beyond all thought, beyond even experience as such. Even the bare, brute "shock" of impenetrable otherness is recognizable as an affective intuition only through its measurable relation to the ordinary experience of "the same." If every true difference were just another utterly opaque instance of pure alterity, then all experience would be vacuously uniform; the different would itself be "the same," one empty cipher after another, always reiterated in the most depressingly unvaried fashion. The only way to preserve true novelty, true uniqueness, whether from dissolution into the merely familiar or from fragmentation into the trivially diversified, is to recognize a rule of analogy, an inseparable interplay of similitude and dissimilitude within everything that exists. This rule, precisely by transcending simple identity and simple difference alike, is able to hold them together in fruitful tension. This is the full dynamism of reality as it is actually available to experience. But to see this is, happily, to discover something amazingly unanticipated even in what we think perfectly familiar.

In a sense, Segalen's characterization of the first immediate encounter with true otherness is little more than an account of our first experience of any phenomenon whatsoever. Everything arrives for us initially as the "shock" of the Real, even when long familiarity so softens the blow that this shock remains below the threshold of conscious astonishment. That is because, in Scholastic terms, what is for us the first moment within the *ordo cognoscendi*, the order of understanding, is really the final moment within the *ordo essendi*, the order of being. We know everything first as an effect before we can know its causes. But then, in order to understand anything—in order even just to register it as some sort of discernible event—we have to attempt to move from the effect back toward the cause, in the hope of finding some common source of intelligibility that allows our consciousness and the object encountered to be joined in a concrete experience. We may not make it very far, of course, but we shall not even make it as far as the recognition of our failure to understand if we do not proceed according to an analogy with those things we do already know. Absolute difference is a nonsensical idea and should not be entertained even out of regard for the inviolability of "the Other." The only proper experience of otherness is simultaneously the joyous discovery that all real diversity gives expression to a genuine, if mysteriously inexhaustible, commonality. All cultural differences are, so to speak, variations upon the shared theme of the human, which it is equally destructive either to reduce to simple uniformity or to treat as incapable of harmonious accord. This shared human nature is a reality that we discover through its endlessly various but analogous manifestations in others and that we only thereby come to understand within ourselves. Cultural synthesis is not only possible but also, if it occurs naturally, an enrichment of our knowledge of our humanity and of the possibilities of experience. And the power of differing cultures truly to come to understand one another, precisely in their divergences from one another, is also the power of every soul to find the common human theme ever again, however strange and "exotic" the music in which it has been made audible. This, moreover, certainly points toward a shared ground of experience more original—and a shared end of experience more ultimate—than mere diversity as such.

Yet, all of this having been said, one must finally concede that Segalen's most fundamental insights regarding the relation between imagination and reality were correct. Most of us already, at some level, know as much. All of us, in every moment, are approaching the same frontier, the same as yet undiscovered country of the Real that lies just beyond the worldly horizon of the possible. This is the tragedy or irony or absurdity that encircles every life: as we strive forward toward an imagined future—enchanting, terrifying, perplexing—the implacable reality of the drearily or grimly inevitable is constantly approaching to meet us upon the same path. We know that the only full encounter with the Real is the encounter with death, because only then will all our questions be either answered or, at the very least, resolved. And the most that we can reasonably hope for is that, in the ever-diminishing interval between these two relentlessly advancing fronts, we might happen as often as possible upon objects and moments of true beauty. So, naturally, Segalen's journey to the Real reached its end only on that last day in the Breton woodland of his childhood, when the world for him returned to its beginning and then melted away altogether, and he encountered the final true commonality in which all difference either entirely vanishes away or wholly rises up into an ultimate harmony. For, at the last, the Real in its truest, barest essence is either nothing or everything, and the imagination can find its ultimate rest only in one or the other.

20

Empson in the East
On *The Face of the Buddha*

I

William Empson (1906–84) was not, as he is frequently said to have been, an "important critic," but only because there is no such thing. By the same token, neither was he a unicorn, a square circle, or a decent impulse in the heart of Donald Trump. What he was, however, was a thinker with an incisively original mind and a fine, lucid, and always lively prose style; and the exquisitely inconclusive analysis of great works of literature, at which he so excelled, provided him with endless occasions for displaying both. He was also a talented mathematician and a remarkable poet, though he largely abandoned mathematics after his undergraduate studies at Cambridge and stopped writing much poetry in his midthirties. He probably possessed most of the natural intellectual gifts of a good philosopher, if little of the temperament. His first and still most influential book, for instance, *Seven Types of Ambiguity*—which he wrote when he was twenty-one and published when he was twenty-four—exhibits a subtler and more penetrating understanding of language and its limits than does, say, Wittgenstein's *Tractatus Logico-Philosophicus*, published eight years before (not to worry, though: over the next several decades Wittgenstein would grope his way toward a level of sophistication comparable to Empson's).

By all rights, the publication of *Seven Types* should have secured Empson's future. It nearly did, in fact. While still in manuscript, it was enough to confirm the brilliance he had exhibited as a student and to win him a fellow's perch at his college, Magdalene, from which he could have looked forward to decades of long strolls along the Backs, long afternoons in the Pepys Library, long conversations in the upper combination room, and blessedly long *longueurs*. But all of it was, in fact, cut very *short* when a college porter discovered a package of condoms in his rooms. Today that would merely earn him plaudits for social conscientiousness, but Cambridge in 1929 was a very different world; the porter dutifully reported the abomination and Empson was expelled from his college and the university, his name literally expunged from its records. Any real employment, apart from some freelance cultural journalism, became all at once impossible for him in England. So, with the aid of his old tutor I. A. Richards, he departed for the Far East in 1931: first to a teachers' training college in Japan and then, after a brief return to England mid-decade, to China to take up an appointment at Peking University. This, however, became instead an absurdly austere teaching post in Kunming, among other refugee scholars, because the Japanese had rather rudely arrived in China at about the same time as Empson had. From 1939 to 1947 he was back in England, spending the war years working at the BBC alongside Louis MacNeice and George Orwell, and then was off again for another brief stint in China. By that time he had acquired a South African wife, Hetta, who was, like him, an unrepentantly salacious Bohemian, and with whom he had entered into a very "open" marriage. By the late 1940s, time and social change had scoured away the stain from his reputation, and he returned to higher education in the West: first at Kenyon College in Ohio, then at Gresham College in London, and finally, in 1953, at the University of Sheffield, where he remained till he retired in 1972. He was knighted in 1979.

However much of a professional calamity it may have been at the time, the episode that sent him scurrying eastward proved in many ways very fortunate for him. It exposed him to a whole new world of artistic sensibility that he otherwise might never have discovered but that naturally appealed to some of his deepest imaginative and aesthetic impulses. He had never been much drawn to most of the plastic high arts of Christendom; Renaissance sculpture for the most part left him cold. But in 1932, in the ancient city of Nara, he came upon some of the most famous of Japanese Buddhist statues and was awestruck—by their serenity and beauty, but chiefly by their deep humanity. Among the pieces

that awakened him to the more refined conventions of Buddhist statuary, and to their mysterious attraction, was the great seventh-century
Kudara Kannon at Nara's Hōryūji Temple; in the expression on the face
of the goddess bodhisattva, he thought he caught a glimpse not just of
her celebrated tenderness but of a range of subtle emotions, mysteriously
captured by the stylized abstractions and artistic tact of an extremely sophisticated iconographic tradition that he immediately adored but did
not yet understand. That same year, he began to write the first version of
The Face of the Buddha, which he would continue to redact and polish for
some seventeen years. Over the next several decades, moreover, his fascination with the history and significance of Buddhist sculpture grew and
deepened, along with a profound if diffident admiration for the religion
itself (at least as a cultural and moral force). In pursuit of his obsession
(which is not too strong a word), he made numerous journeys, often of
the most arduous kind, to famous devotional sites throughout Buddhist
East Asia, in the days when there were no air-conditioned railway car-
riages to bear him through the sweltering malarial latitudes of Korea,
French Indochina, Cambodia, Burma, China, Ceylon, and India. He absorbed everything he could, from Kungang in China to Theravadin Ang-
kor in Cambodia to India's Ajanta caves.

His studies led him to the conclusion that the Buddhist sensibility
excelled at striking a harmonious balance between contending impulses
of human will, thought, and emotion. He also came to believe that,
whereas the typical depictions of Buddhas and bodhisattvas in India
tended to emphasize only the detachment and divine remoteness of the
enlightened ones, the Chinese model had from very early on placed as
great an emphasis on their humanity; in fact, even that remoteness
had been elegantly transformed from the otherworldliness of the Indian
religious imagination to something more like the dignified patrician reserve of the Chinese gentry. Above all, he came to believe that at some
point, probably originally in Yungang, a set of sculptural conventions had
evolved—and had then become the governing standard for devotional
statuary throughout much of East Asia—which had achieved this humanization through an intentional practice of facial asymmetry. Here, it
seemed, Empson had again discovered a form of art whose most enchanting and powerful effects lay precisely in its ambiguity. Somehow,
by the subtlest of depictive gestures—a slight but clear variance, say, in

292 Empson in the East

the slant of the eyes, the arch of the eyebrows, the curve of the lips—the sculptors in this tradition had perfected a means of integrating two different expressions in a single visage, one of perfect imperturbable repose and one of active power exerted on behalf of the devotee, thus producing an image of the Buddha nature as at once both saved and saving, both detached and compassionate. They had done this, Empson believed, by making each side of the sculpture's face embody one of these aspects, while still not allowing the total effect to become jarring or incoherent. He began illustrating his manuscript with numerous photographic studies, and in some plates he created mirror images of the separate sides of certain sculptures, dividing each face vertically and juxtaposing each half with its own inversion. In two cases, the effect is quite striking and does seem to result in two almost contrary expressions; in others, however, the effect is scarcely visible at all.

To give his theory some sort of broader conceptual basis, moreover, Empson began flirting with ideas current in his day about a natural distinction between the human face's left and right sides, and with emerging discoveries about the different roles of the brain's two hemispheres. He became especially enamored of the psychologist Werner Wolff's notion that in every human face the left side expresses one's "wish-image" of oneself and the right the conventional visage one wants to show the world. In photographs of Churchill, for instance, Empson believed he could discern on the right side the demeanor of "the administrator" and on the left "the petulance, the rancour, the romanticism, the gloomy moral strength and the range of imaginative power." He also gave some consideration to the techniques of asymmetry used in carving Japanese Noh masks (where, in fact, he could have made a stronger case had he known more). Finally he came to suspect that the sculptural techniques he thought he had discovered had perhaps been inspired by an ancient style of fortune-telling that interpreted the two sides of the head separately. In the end, though, his true interest was not in the ways in which East Asian Buddhist sculptural tradition might have reflected some set of psychological or physiological constants about human beings but in its unique genius in embodying the contradictions of personality; and ultimately he came to the conclusion that the richness he saw in these images was to a great degree the effect of Buddhism itself.

If, he reasoned, one really could look at two different and historically removed images of Guanyin (or Kannon) and see in them the same subtle difference between a slanting right eye and a level left—the former expressing "the dignity of the aristocrat" and the latter "a gentle placid humanity"—and if again and again one could find the same pattern repeated and the same absorbing ambiguity embodied, perhaps this was on account of a particularly enchanting paradox. In Buddhism after all, he claimed, the principal religious impulse is the flight from personality, and the principal philosophical conviction personality's essential nonexistence: each of us is a confluence of multiple causal currents and elementary forces, without a substantial and stable identity; each self is only a perception, a momentary coalescence and dispersal of disparate streams of becoming, the phenomenal residue of a ceaseless process of change. For precisely this reason, however, it is perhaps a creed that allows for inordinate sensitivity to the complexity and (again) *ambiguity* of the self. "It would be an odd, but not an unreasonable, thing," writes Empson, "if the profoundest studies of character in all sculptures have proceeded from a painstaking application in detail of the doctrine there is no such thing as character at all." This, as it happens, is the text's most brilliantly provocative proposal.

In 1949, then, the text was for all intents and purposes ready for publication. And yet it is appearing only now for the first time.

II

The story of the fate of *The Face of the Buddha* is even more farcical than the Cambridge prophylactics episode and was certainly a source of deeper grief for Empson—though the full story was unknown for six decades. In the meantime, however, the book became a legend: the lost masterpiece by a revered writer, gone missing (so it was believed) in a London taxi. In reality, its disappearance was the result of a much more comical concatenation of mishaps. For some reason, when Empson went on one of his trips abroad in 1949, he gave the sole typed copy of the manuscript, along with all its photographic plates, to the more or less perpetually inebriated John Davenport. Davenport in turn, in a haze of chemical enthusiasm, staggered over to the offices of M. J. T. Tambimuttu, the wildly eccentric Tamil poet and editor who lived in a book-engorged apartment famed for its disorder and its copious vermin, and presented him with the manuscript as a work demanding immediate publication. When Davenport briefly emerged from his dipsomaniacal stupor the next day, he had lost all memory of the event. Shortly thereafter, Tambimuttu abruptly returned to Ceylon, entrusting Empson's book to his fellow editor Richard March, who then even more abruptly (and very inconsiderately) dropped dead. The manuscript at that point simply sank into the abyss of March's immense archive of personal papers, where no one knew to look for it. When Davenport had to account for the loss to Empson in 1952, the taxi story was either his best guess or the most plausible lie he could devise. And Empson knew he could never recreate the work he had so lovingly labored over all those years.

In 2003, however, March's papers were acquired by the British Museum, and two years later Empson's manuscript was discovered among them. Then, for no reason I can quite fathom, it took another eleven years for it to be published. Perhaps that is for the best, because this edition has been marvelously edited and introduced by Rupert Arrowsmith. And Oxford has abundantly illustrated the text with Empson's original photographs, as well as several lovely newer images of the statuary Empson discusses. Physically and as a work of critical reconstruction, it is a handsome and deeply satisfying volume. It also has all the graces one might expect of its author: the taut, disciplined, beguilingly limpid prose, the fine descriptive passages, the originality of perspective, the impatiently opinionated voice, the glittering aperçus. Empsonians should rejoice. It is not, however, a masterpiece. For one thing, Empson's theory of asymmetry is probably false; and I am not sure that one could not produce effects similar to his mirror-studies of bisected faces of the Buddha by doing the same thing to photographs of pieces by Donatello or Rodin. Symmetry is hard to achieve, and among thousands of sculptural exemplars similar instances of asymmetry will frequently be found. More important, the absence of any written record whatsoever of the technique, even in a culture as insatiably aestheticizing and precise as Japan's, is really quite devastating for the thesis. And, more important still, it is an inconvenient reality that, throughout Buddhist history, one of the distinguishing physical marks that indicate the Buddha's sublimity is his perfect bodily and facial symmetry; it seems unlikely that any iconographic school would have willfully violated this aspect of traditional devotion. All of which makes *The Face of the Buddha* a book of less theoretical consequence than Empson imagined—though perhaps, for that reason, one of greater literary charm. Like many works of art criticism, much of it is perhaps reducible to a catalogue of personal impressions; but Empson's descriptive gifts and the poignant uniqueness of his voice make that catalogue also one full of rare delights.

For me, I should note, perhaps the book's most revealing chapter is the last, entitled simply "Theology." As an account of Buddhism, it is too brief to be of any significance and in several places verges on guidebook banality. But it affords an excellent view of what fascinated Empson about Buddhism: its singular and counterintuitive ability to produce a compassionate, temperate, and contented form of life out of what looks very much like a system of metaphysical and religious despair; its cultivation of a moral grandeur uncontaminated by the tragic anxieties and morbidities he associated with much of Western religion; its remarkably civilizing influence on Eastern societies; and its serene skepticism regarding the grand metaphysical claims of the individual self. Above all, he admired all the ways in which it was unlike Christianity, which he utterly loathed. In later years, after all, he would write *Milton's God*, one of the most ferocious attacks on Christian beliefs written after Nietzsche. "The Christian God the Father," he wrote there, "the God of Tertullian, Augustine, and Aquinas, is the wickedest thing yet invented by the black heart of man." "Christianity has always had to be kept at bay by civilized consciences," for it is simply "a system of torture-worship," a degrading blood-steeped cult appealing to a Neolithic appetite for human sacrifice, inspiring craven adoration of an infinitely sadistic God, and in its early days embracing a "sex-horror" inimical to life. And so on. (For all his celebrated urbanity, Empson could occasionally slip away into adolescent tirades, and those pages in particular remind one of Havelock Ellis and Algernon Swinburne at their most bilious.) In Buddhism, however, despite its disenchantment with this world—which Empson also found troubling—he thought he had discovered an elevating and civilizing ethos unpolluted by such primitive fervors and cruelties.

It seems to me that one has to pause here if one wants to understand the peculiar passion that animated Empson's constant labor over this text. I sincerely doubt that Empson's guarded preference for the East over the West in so many areas of sensibility, intellectual and aesthetic, rested on quite the firm rational and moral basis that he imagined it did. At times, it looks suspiciously more like an emotional need than a calm personal appreciation. Empson was a materialist by conviction, though not on account of any particularly refined set of philosophical arguments. As a rule, his writing on issues of ultimate reality was curiously devoid of the searching subtlety he poured into his literary investigations. Too often, the rhetoric became hyperbolic and callow, intuitions overwhelmed observations, argument began to dissolve into denunciation, and fine distinctions disappeared altogether. In the end, it was certainly not a religious impulse that turned him eastward; he was as insensible to the religious grandeur of Buddhism as he was to any other form of spiritual devotion. Whatever he loved about it he loved at a quite uncrossable distance. To him, all religious belief was still just so much myth and masquerade when evening came, incorrigibly hostile to the senses and the flesh; and he himself continued to cling to a rather sullen and sometimes embarrassingly peevish faith in the priority of sensual life and individual desire and genital liberty as the only sources of real human happiness. He resented transcendence on principle. Admittedly, the Christianity he detested was often genuinely detestable—a creed of substitutionary atonement, of the Father pouring out his wrath on Christ on the cross, of original guilt, of a hell of eternal torments prepared by a pitiless judge, and so on—but I also think he made a conscious effort to know of no other. It is clear that he associated Christianity with all the forces that his nature rebelled against, and also I think with all the forces that had caused him disappointment and pain and repressed desire over the years (he was, for instance, exuberantly bisexual). In the serenity of Buddhism, he believed he had found something more forgiving, more tolerant, and altogether lacking in wrath. And by his lights he was quite right to do so. But, while he was not guilty of the worst kind of ingenuous Western romanticization of Buddhism, he was nevertheless not a Buddhist and could not have lived by its genuinely austere ethos if he had tried to do so. Ultimately, much of its appeal for him was possible, I suspect, because it made no demands upon him. And, for this reason, I am not sure he honored Buddhism any more by his admiration than he did Christianity by his enmity. He really understood Buddhism largely as a negation of something else and so probably understood it very little, if at all.

2I

David Jones

The Forgotten Modernist

I

I do not know if it is quite correct to say that public interest in the work of David Jones (1895–1974) is enjoying something of a revival just at the moment, since it was never very lively to begin with. In his own time, Jones was recognized by the discerning as an artist of remarkable originality and range, and by the most discerning as perhaps the finest British artist of the twentieth century. Certainly, he was the greatest "modernist" Britain ever produced, and among modern British *Catholic* poets and painters he was unequaled. He belonged to that very rare class of visionary artists who, like Blake, produced works that seemed to reach into other realms of being. He seemed to have discovered worlds of mythic, religious, and aesthetic meaning that had never before been revealed but that nevertheless felt as ancient and familiar as this world; and, also like Blake, he explored those other realms through both literature and the visual arts. And yet somehow his name never quite carried as far as the names of many of his contemporaries. Even the very literate are far more likely to have heard of the host of luminaries who knew him and praised his work than they are to have heard of him. Yeats, Eliot, and Auden thought him a genius—as did Stravinsky, Herbert Read, Christopher Dawson, Stephen Spender, Evelyn Waugh, Basil Bunting, R. S. Thomas, Geoffrey Hill, and many others. But still, to this day, his admirers are anything but legion; they constitute, at most, a coterie.

297

In part, this may be because Jones was not especially prolific, at least as a writer (as a painter, engraver, and illustrator, his works were reasonably copious). His literary fame rests chiefly on his two majestic epic poems: *In Parenthesis* from 1937 and *The Anathemata* from 1952. Other than these, his published writings consist in two collections of essays, a slender volume of poetic fragments, and a judiciously edited collation of some of his more interesting personal letters; and much of this material appeared posthumously. Moreover, his two major works offer few rewards to the casual reader. Both are at once deep and dense in allusions and evocations but diffuse in structure. The language is beautiful; its power to convey a sense of the sacred is often overwhelming, and its cadences and images are captivatingly mysterious; but it is also a broken—at times almost splintered—language, scattered across the page in shattered paragraphs, unfinished sentences, orphaned phrases and words, all borne along on a dreamlike flow of haunting figures and ghostly voices and distant echoes of the historical and legendary past. It is very much a modernist poetry, an attempt to gather up again the fragments of a ruined world, to recover a lost enchantment, to restore a sense of harmony amid an age of indomitable chaos. Ultimately it is irresistible. Once one has reached the wellsprings of Jones's singular lyricism, one can never tire of it. But, even so, one must make the effort to find those wellsprings.

Similarly, Jones's paintings and engravings belong to no school and obey no conventions, and so make no appeal to any established set of tastes or aesthetic prejudices. In every phase of the development of his style, there is a kind of timelessness; it is a visual idiom at once deeply rooted in premodern traditions of representation and symbolism, and yet wholly modern in its exuberance, its tantalizing but always unconsummated flirtations with abstraction, and its utter rejection of the opulences and sentimentalities of late Romanticism. As a poet, Jones was at least the equal of Blake (and certainly less prone to magnificent failures); as a visual artist, he was Blake's superior in every sense. Whereas Blake's best images are at most very arresting illustrations (often uncomfortably precursory of comic books), Jones's greatest paintings are endlessly absorbing products of an extravagantly rich and genuinely unique sensibility. His most rapturously beautiful aquarelles, for instance, are radiantly elusive things, almost intangible, and yet never merely ethereal or vague. Their hues are luminous, limpid, nacreous, iridescent, with an almost

otherworldly sheen about them. But the images themselves are impos-
ingly substantial, and practically rude in their quality of sheer irrepressible fertility. Many of his pictures are filled with dense tangles of vege-
tation, imponderably solid animal and human bodies, swirling fabrics,
star-crowded skies. Some are positively phantasmagoric, too full of form
to be taken in all at once; at times, figures emerge only gradually from
coils and undulations of lines and colors, like figures in a puzzle. As in
his poetry, in a great many of his pictures Jones was portraying not just
an affective atmosphere but depths within depths—layers of time, a European (and specifically British) landscape haunted by its pagan and
Christian past, and occasionally transparent to a still deeper realm *in illo
tempore* where memory and myth are one—while trying somehow to
make all those depths present at once. Again, one must make an effort.
To appreciate what one is seeing, one must discover for oneself what it
is in these images that makes them so fascinating. It is not, therefore, an
art that will ever be vastly popular.

Yet, all this having been said, this past year has seen not only the re-
printing by Jones's British publisher, Faber and Faber, of the four "minor"
volumes I mentioned above but also the release of a large, lavishly illu-
minated, and beautifully produced biography by Thomas Dilworth, perhaps Jones's most indefatigable champion today. None of this is likely
to inaugurate some great cultural recovery of Jones's contribution to
modern British poetry and painting. The days when long, difficult poems
were read by more than the tiniest and most eccentric minority, or when
strange and wonderful pictures could divert an appreciable number of
eyes from the popular media, are long past. But it is encouraging to see
Jones receiving even a small measure of the attention he deserves.

II

The principal attraction of Dilworth's biography, I should say upfront, is
purely physical. It is not only a handsomely designed volume; it is a trea-
sury of rare photographs and (most delightful of all) lovely reproductions
of an enormous number of Jones's paintings, engravings, and drawings.
For these alone, the volume is more than worth its price. It is also an exhaustive chronicle, and for those who want to follow the entire course of

Jones's life from cradle to grave it provides all the essential and incidental information one could reasonably crave. And it succeeds in conveying a fairly clear picture of Jones's personality, dispositions, and opinions. At the same time, it suffers from a few small but conspicuous defects.

For one thing, the prose is lucid but rarely engaging. It may be that Dilworth resolved on a self-effacing manner, confining himself to a spare, arid style so as not to distract attention from his subject. But there is such a thing as indecent modesty. Here, for instance, is the book's final paragraph: "A brilliant visual artist, the best modern native British poet, and the author of an original and convincing theory of culture, David Jones may be the foremost native British modernist. He created so much intelligent beauty during so many decades of psychological distress, that his creative life is probably the greatest existential achievement of international modernism." That would barely pass muster as the opening of a schoolboy's book report (at the very least, a good teacher would certainly deduct points for the repetition of the phrase "native British" in the first sentence); as a concluding summation of the achievements of an artist of Jones's magnitude, it is somehow simultaneously weightless and leaden. And, to be honest, there are a great number of passages in the book that read less like penetrating biographical portraiture than like official annals—or perhaps like dutiful recitations of the minutes of a conference or the contents of an appointment diary. Far too many times, Dilworth feels compelled to describe what Jones did that day, or the following Wednesday, or later that same month, or whenever, as well as what was discussed with x regarding y, without any obvious need to do so. And, for some reason more elusive than any other, Dilworth occasionally lapses into Freudian psychoanalysis. Admittedly, Jones was himself intermittently susceptible to the Freud superstitions of his time; he was also, in the judgment of his great friend Eric Gill, a "highly sexed" individual who maintained his chastity by the severest discipline of the will; and he was definitely given to depression and anxieties. But nothing is gained by Dilworth gratuitously interjecting the observation that, in regard to this or that aspect of Jones's life, "A Freudian might say . . ." That is a sentence that need never be completed (any more than one beginning "A carnival fortune-teller might say . . ."). And the effect is at times not merely obnoxious but ludicrous, as when Dilworth casually observes that a self-portrait painted by Jones (since it depicts only head and torso) might be taken as a form of "self-castration," or gravely opines that

Jones's frequent bouts of ill health might be explained by the Oedipus complex, since his sickliness as a child provided him an excuse to stay home with mother while his frailty as an adult allowed him to retire to bed and thus "return to the womb" (something that for Freud, Dilworth goes on to explain, serves as a substitute for copulation for those who suffer a fear of castration). At such moments, it is tempting to stop reading the text altogether and simply to immerse oneself in the pictures. But the temptation should be resisted.

If nothing else, Dilworth succeeds in placing Jones and his works in relation to the aesthetic innovations and reactions of his time and in disentangling Jones's sensibility and achievements from the thickets of any supposedly larger, more general "movement" of modernism in the arts. As it happens, the list of Jones's predecessors and contemporaries who might be said to have inspired his style is quite different from what many of the critics of his time imagined it was, or what we might now naturally assume. Many of the first readers of *In Parenthesis* or *The Anathemata* were certain they saw Joyce or Pound lurking in the background—both of whom Jones came to appreciate, but neither of whom actually exercised an influence on either work. Jones did acknowledge, for instance, the effect that St.-John Perse's *Anabase* (in T. S. Eliot's 1930 translation, *Anabasis*) had on him and on the development of *In Parenthesis*, but on the whole he was not an imitator of any vogues in the arts. By his own account, the fragmentary form of his poetry, the allusions, the symbolic heterogeneity were simply a consequence of the epoch of cultural and religious dissolution in which he lived. His "modernism," like that of his contemporaries, was not a school or aesthetic philosophy but simply the spirit of the age. So it is good of Dilworth to reconstruct the history of Jones's readings and special enthusiasms. It aids one in appreciating the distinctiveness of Jones's voice to know how deeply he drew on Sir Thomas Malory, Celtic Arthurian lore, Lewis Carroll's Alice books, *The Rime of the Ancient Mariner*, the verse of Gerard Manley Hopkins, and so on. It also sheds considerable light on a certain austere but curiously appealing impersonality in his art to learn how naturally he came by his very "modern" distaste for late Romantic sentimentality, affective excess, and self-expression—his spontaneous affection for Gregorian chant, say, or his dislike of Wagner, or his commendable inability to read *The Testament of Beauty* with interest, or his impatience with everything mannered, dainty, emotionally exhibitionist, and self-indulgent.

Dilworth also brings out well the connection in sensibility between Jones's art and his Catholicism. At least, one sees in his faith the same combination of a fascination with traditions from the deep past alongside a very modern fatigue with everything merely conventional or doctrinaire. He especially valued Catholicism's continuity with classical culture and its *sacramental* power to collapse the historical distance separating the present from Christian antiquity. For this reason, he lamented the abandonment of the Latin mass, which he saw as severing a precious tie to the ancient world. At the same time, however, he was nothing like the Catholic traditionalist of today who pines for the prissiness of the Baroque church and cherishes nauseous nostalgias for all that vanished satin and lace; his own taste in ecclesial fashions came from an earlier, sterner age. He regarded Trent, in fact, as a largely unfortunate event in the history of the church, one that had resulted in a deplorable intellectual and imaginative narrowing of Catholic culture. He loved the Scholastic period and spoke earnestly of the spiritual nourishment that Aquinas and Scotus had provided him. He also, however, was sympathetic to the figures of the previous century who had been abused as "modernists." And he regarded the formula *extra ecclesiam nulla salus* as abominable nonsense if taken in anything but the most expansively latitudinarian sense.

All of this is worth learning, and Dilworth's book provides a considerable service in bringing it into the light. In the end, though, one has to admit that his text—lacking any particular literary charm of its own—will be of interest only to those who have already fallen under Jones's spell. At its least exciting, it is only slightly more sparkling than a corporate employee's personnel file (with a few annoying annotations by the company psychiatrist); at its most exciting, it is still fairly tedious. Once again, the pictures are the book's most eloquent arguments for the importance of Jones's work. Still, while Dilworth has to be held accountable for the lifelessness of his prose, he cannot be blamed for not surmounting the one great obstacle that would inhibit any attempt to tell Jones's tale: to wit, that it is, objectively considered, extremely boring. Other than his service during the Great War, practically nothing ever actually happened to Jones. There were no great or especially heroic exploits. There was his one abortive engagement (to Eric Gill's daughter), and there were a number of hesitant, almost spectrally insubstantial infatuations with a variety of interesting women, all pursued with poignant ineptitude on his side, but there were no great or tragic romances. As is the case with many artists or thinkers, all his grandest adventures occurred within; all his great discoveries were of the spiritual variety; all his conquests were achieved over problems of technique or conceptual content or artistic form. His talent was monumental; his personal history was banal.

III

The whole narrative, in fact—once one subtracts all the teas and accidental conversations and train journeys and whatnot that Dilworth so punctiliously records—can be distilled into a few compact paragraphs without significant omission. Jones grew up in Brockley, on the east side of London, born to a father who was Welsh but who never taught his son the language (having himself been discouraged from mastering it by his family, for fear it would harm his social prospects), and to a mother whose "high church" taste for sacramental religion helped form the young Jones's general religious dispositions. His gifts as a visual artist appeared early (he drew quite a fine picture of a dancing bear when he was only seven), and his interest in Welsh myth and ancient poems (Old English and Latin chiefly) appeared soon thereafter. From 1900 to 1914, he studied at the Camberwell School of Art. Then came the war. From 1915 to 1918, he served as a private in the Royal Welsh Fusiliers, almost entirely at the front, in the trenches, watching a great many young men dying horribly; and the experience marked him, obviously, for life. In later years, the recurrent trauma of the war would cause Jones breakdowns and periods of creative paralysis; but it would also make its grim contributions to some of his most splendid artistic achievements.

After the war, he returned to his studies, now at the Westminster School of Art, where from 1919 to 1921 he worked under the tutelage of (among others) Walter Sickert. In the first year after the armistice, he also experienced his only recorded period of religious doubt, prompted in part by reading too much Jessie Weston and James Frazer; but it was extremely brief. In 1921, largely under the influence of Eric Gill, he converted to Roman Catholicism and apparently never looked back. He was especially drawn at that time to the books of Jacques Maritain, and in 1924 he became a tertiary Dominican. This was also the period, not at all coincidentally, of the first great flowering of his distinctive style as a painter, engraver, and illustrator. His faith now gave him a great over-arching theme under which to gather his diverse aesthetic intuitions and impulses. During more or less the whole of the 1920s, he belonged to the Guild of St. Joseph and St. Dominic, a society of Catholic artists in Sus-sex committed to the ideals of Distributism and devoted to aesthetic ex-perimentation, all under the watchful but generous eye of Gill. It was a time of extraordinarily rich accomplishment, and to all appearances Jones was destined for a distinguished career simply as one of the most original visual artists of his generation in Britain. All the while, however, he was also writing.

Books gestate more slowly than canvases do, of course. Even so, the first of Jones's two literary masterpieces would have probably been fin-ished sooner than it was had he not suffered a series of nervous collapses in the 1930s (an especially severe one in 1932), of the sort that would now be diagnosed as delayed post-traumatic reactions to his experiences in battle but that in those days were largely written off as evidence of neu-rotic frailty. Then again, but for those collapses, *In Parenthesis* would probably be neither as hypnotically lovely nor as starkly harrowing as it is, nor so perfect a union of the beautiful and the grim. One sees this even in simple episodes, such as a long, entrancing, simultaneously gnarled and lyrical description of soldiers slowly roused from sleep by the light of dawn to resume their journey:

> Fog refracted, losing articulation in the cloying damp, the word of command unmade in its passage, mischiefed of the opaque air, mu-tated, bereaved of content, become an incoherent uttering, a curious bent cry out of the smarting drift, lost altogether—yet making rise again the grey bundles where they lie. . . .
>
> . . . .
>
> As grievous invalids watch the returning light pale-bright the ruckled counterpane, see their uneased bodies only newly clear; fear-ful to know afresh their ill condition; yet made glad for that rising, yet strain ears to the earliest note—should some prevenient bird make his kindly cry.

Putatively the narrative of one Private John Ball and his regiment of mixed English and Welsh infantry—proceeding from their departure from England to their participation in the Battle of the Somme seven months later—it is an altogether mesmerizing mixture of realism and dreamlike dissociations, history and myth, the maintenance of rifles and the quest for the Grail. Take its description of men marching at night under the light of the moon:

> The rain stopped.
> She drives swift and immaculate out over, free of these obscuring
>   waters; frets their fringes splendid.
> A silver hurrying to silver this waste
> silver for bolt-shoulders
> silver for butt-heel irons
> silver beams search the interstices, play for breech-blocks under-
> neath the counterfeiting bower-sway; make-believe a silver scar with
> drenched tree-wound; silver-trace a festooned slack; faery-bright
> a filigree with gooseberries and picket irons—grace this mauled
> earth—
> transfigure our infirmity—
> shine on us.
> I want you to play with
> and the stars as well.

The journey the poem describes, in terms of ordinary time and space, passes through the English and French countrysides, over the Channel, under falling artillery shells and past rain-gorged trenches, over trip wires and revetments, through mud and mire, all the way up to the line, on its way to the violence of the front and, at the last, to the final, monstrous devastation of the Mametz Wood engagement (where, in fact, Jones received a bullet wound to the leg). In terms of mythic time and space, however—always just there on the other side of the thinnest of narrative partitions, and often breaking through to this side—the journey passes through Badon Hill and Camlann, the plains of Troy, the *Song of Roland*'s Roncesvaux, the shadowy lands of the *Preideu Annwn*, the *Mabinogion*, and *Y Gododdin*, the fields of (Shakespeare's) Agincourt, King Pellam's wasteland, even Wonderland; the literary and biblical allusions are legion, the religious imagery is all-encompassing. Earthily blunt depictions of men under arms mingle with fantastic revenants, like the figure of Dai Greatcoat, the deathless soldier who at one point boasts at length (like Taliessin before Maelgwn) of all the battles he has seen down the ages, war after war, legendary and historical alike:

> I was the spear in Balin's hand
>   that made waste King Pellam's land.
> I took the smooth stones of the brook,
> I was with Saul
> playing before him.
> I saw him armed like Derfel Gatheren.
> I the fox-run fire
>   consuming in the wheat-lands. . . .
> . . . .
>   I was in Michael's trench when bright Lucifer bulged his primal salient out.
> That caused it,
> that upset the joy-cart,
> and three parts waste. . . .

At the climax of the narrative, in the aftermath of the final battle, the *genius loci*—feminine, of course—walks among the dead, crowning them with garlands of blossoms:

> The secret princes between the leaning trees have diadems given them.
>   Life the leveller hugs her impudent equality—she may proceed at once to less discriminating zones.

> The Queen of the Woods has cut bright boughs of various flowering.
>   These knew her influential eyes. Her awarding hands can pluck for each their fragile prize.

Here, in the final section of the narrative, the language slowly melts into disconnected fragments of poetry and slowly fades away. Throughout the epic, the music of Jones's language remains fluent and captivating, while also remaining largely devoid of conventional ornamentation; and, for this reason, its final broken phrases are almost indescribably haunting in their lyricism and inconclusiveness.

The book won not only the praise of the brightest and the best readers and writers of the time but also the very prestigious Hawthornden Prize. Eliot was astonished at the depth of its genius. Yeats, on meeting Jones for the first time, very ceremoniously (if a little fatuously) bowed from the waist in tribute "to the author of *In Parenthesis*." It was not a popular success, of course, but was certainly a critical one; and, had Jones continued publishing at anything like a regular pace, he might have become more of a fixed star in the British literary firmament than he did. But his temperament, especially in its routinely shaken condition, was not well suited to courting public attention. He continued to produce paintings and illustrations with reasonable consistency and earned very good notices; but at his writing he labored slowly and irregularly, and it appeared for a time as if—having produced a single remarkable large poem—he would now devote himself exclusively to visual art. He continued to write, however, and if anything was becoming a more daring and innovative poet. Another particularly debilitating nervous breakdown in 1947 diverted him from his poetry (and from everything else) for a while, and he continued to struggle with bouts of depression and episodes of erotic frustration. At the last, however, he issued his second great work, *The Anathemata*, which some would argue was his supreme literary achievement. Auden, for instance, pronounced it the single greatest long poem written in English in the twentieth century (which, given the number of very long poems Auden himself had published, was anything but casual praise).

The Anathemata is a wilder, more dreamlike, more heterogeneous, and in many ways more sublime poem than *In Parenthesis*. Its exotic allusions are even more profuse, its language more incantatory, its form more magical. The imagery at times defies any single explanation but bears one along in its currents nonetheless.

> On rune-height by the garbaged rill
> > the scree-fall answers the cawed madrigals
> and there are great birds flying about.
> And (to sustain his kind)
> > the mated corbie
> with his neb
> > forcipate, incarnadined—
> prods at the dreaming *arbor*
> > ornated *regis purpura*

as his kind, should.
Each, after his kind, must somehow gain his kindly food:
ask of the mother thrush
                    what brinded Tib has said.
What does the Gilyak tell
                    to the gay-kerchiefed bear?

As a whole, the poem does not necessarily command the same kind of
emotional power as the earlier work, simply because it does not deal with
anywhere so tragic a theme; but it brings together the forces of historical
recollection, mythic imagination, and religious longing with greater freedom, inventiveness, and inspiration than any other work in the Anglophone modernist canon. It is almost a world unto itself—though a world
contained in fewer than ten seconds, at least according to the poem's plot
(if that is the right word). The poem supposedly, for all its enormous
length, recounts the succession of thoughts passing through the mind of
an English Catholic at mass during the course of roughly seven seconds.
But each thought, of course, has its layers and its depths—historical,
mythic, sacred—and the poem descends through them all. The poem's
larger theme (again, if that is the right word) is the presence of Christ's
sacrifice at the center of history and creation, and the countless ways in
which that centrality is foreshadowed and echoed in history, legend,
ritual, and religion, and in the full scope of, specifically, Britain's past.

Upon all fore-times.
                    From before time
his perpetual light
                    shines upon them.
                    Upon all at once
upon each one
whom he invites, bids, us to recall
when we make the recalling of him
                    daily, at the Stone.
When the offerant
            our *servos*, so theirs whose life is changed
not taken away
                    is directed to say

> *Memento etiam.*

After which it is allowed him then to say

> *Nobis quoque.*

In a sense, it is a long meditation on all the differing dimensions of Britain's particular *praeparatio evangelica,* and on the power of the mass to make all those dimensions present again in sacramental *anamnesis.*

> At the low entry
> stirs the sleeping dog?
> in Bedlam-byre once his bed.
> Here, in this high place
>   into both hands
> he takes the stemmed dish
>   as in many places
> by this poured and that held up
> wherever their directing glosses read:
>   Here he takes the victim.
> At the threshold-stone
>   lifts the agéd head?
> can toothless beast from stable come
>   discern the Child
> in the Bread?

Really, though, the imagery of the poem is far too rich and diverse to characterize; there is, however, a recurrent motif of ships at sea that bears much of the weight of the poem's continuity and that rises to a sort of symbolic climax at one point in the figure of the whole cosmos as a ship whose mainmast is the cross of Golgotha and whose keel is the divine Logos. On the whole, though, it is too vast and generously imaginative a book to reduce to summary; it is the nearest thing to a full unfolding of his inner world that Jones ever produced, and must be read to be understood, even in part.

It was also the last great literary labor that Jones would complete. The years that followed were largely uneventful. In the early 1960s, very belatedly, his two epics were published in the United States, and he was surprised not only by the critical enthusiasm they enjoyed here but by how very well many of the American critics understood them—better, indeed, than most of their British counterparts. (Though, to be honest, it should probably have occurred to him that the literary culture that produced Eliot, Pound, H.D., and others of their kind was one more than hospitable to long challenging poems brimming over with obscure allusions.) He continued patiently to write and to paint. In 1974, recognizing that his time was growing short, he published *The Sleeping Lord*, which contained various fragments of what had been intended as another long work, continuing the larger project of *The Anathemata*. That same year he suffered a stroke and died not long thereafter.

As I say, not a life that naturally lends itself to gripping narrative. But a life of incomparable richness nonetheless.

IV

It is a happy circumstance that the Faber and Faber reissues coincide so nicely with the appearance of Dilworth's book. They fill in the details of the story far more substantially than any biography can. *The Sleeping Lord*, if nothing else, affords the uninitiated a taste of Jones's lyrical voice and of his imaginative range. Admittedly, by themselves, the various poetic fragments are only suggestive traces of the far fuller vision expressed in Jones's large poems; but they are enough to convey something of his sensibility, and even something of his genius. On the other hand, *Dai Greatcoat* (originally published in 1980) provides a broad and invaluable entryway into some of the more interesting inner chambers of Jones's personality. It makes vivid much that Dilworth's book makes only sketchily visible. Jones emerges from these pages as an appealing but by no means ingratiating character. The reader is exposed to his wit and mental nimbleness but also to his disappointments, distastes, indignations, and doubts. He was most definitely an opinionated man, sometimes inflexibly so. But he was also a man of wide sympathies, with no capacity for sanctimony, and all of his most passionate convictions were clearly pervaded by his innate kindness. And, above all, these letters bear witness to a powerful intellect.

Part of that power lay in Jones's willingness to think long and hard about the very particular things that mattered to him. To pluck a passage almost at random, but one addressing a theme to which he returned relentlessly throughout his life when thinking about matters sacramental or artistic, and one perhaps central to the problem of "modernism" of every kind:

> The root trouble about a materialistic conception lies here—if things are thought of as simply utile—as for instance a radiator or a gas-fire or an electric bulb—then a kind of conflict arises in the mind of the artist with regard to them, and he tends to go to earlier forms of light and heat, as candle and wood-fire, when he is expressing the universal concepts of fire and light. This in turn creates a kind of loss of touch with the contemporary world—his world, after all—and a kind of invalidity pervades his symbols—it sets up a strain. However unconscious, it produces a neurosis. Previous ages did not know this tension.

On things, however, lying outside the immediate circle of his interests he squandered very little reflection indeed. He was not, for instance, especially perceptive or coherent regarding political matters; it is not even worthwhile speaking of left or right in regard to his views, such as they were. He could be beguiled by Spengler's rather too bloodied-and-soiled defense of *Kultur* against "civilization" or genuinely moved by the simplest egalitarian pieties; he was as suspicious of modern civil democracy as he was impatiently contemptuous of class privilege. At any given juncture, he could be reactionary, liberal-minded, conventional, seditious, credulous, or canny, and on the whole it is better to regard his political philosophy as a kind of general abstention from ideology. At the same time, his larger cultural insights were extremely acute and arose from long and intense contemplation of the place of the arts in society. On the whole, though he had no pronounced tendency toward any specific economic creed, he never departed far from the Distributist perspective he adopted during his days in the Guild of St. Joseph and St. Dominic. He was also deeply shaped by the aesthetic and moral thought of William Morris and John Ruskin. Above all, he was convinced that the consumerist ethos of modern capitalism is the most implacable enemy of a truly Christian social life, because it is the force most corrosive of a sacramental understanding of culture: it distorts the very nature of human beings as spiritual "makers," peculiarly open to creation and to the supernatural, because it alienates them from the work of their own hands and orients their desires toward false and immanent ends. The most important of Jones's essays is "Art and Sacrament," written in 1955 and included in *Epoch and Artist* (1959). It is here that he gives his fullest exposition of his beliefs regarding the inherent connection between artistic *poiesis* and sacramental worship, and between their respective powers of "re-presentation" in signs—of, that is, the "making present again" that which is past or far away "under other forms." For, in Jones's words: "Because the Church is committed to 'Sacraments' with a capital S, she cannot escape a committal to sacraments with a small s, unless the sacramentalism of the Church is to be regarded as a peculiar and isolated phenomenon. We know that such a view is not to be entertained and that the sacramentalism of the Church is a thing normal to man and that a sacramental quality is evidenced in the past works of man over the whole period of his existence so far known to us." It is an essay that should be read alongside two others, "Art in Relation to War and Our Present Situation" and "Use and Sign," both of which appear in *The Dying Gaul* (1978). Taken together, these pieces provide as complete an account of Jones's philosophy of the artistic act as he ever produced. His was a singular vision, to say the least, and one that was wholly internally consistent. More than that, it was also wholly consistent with Jones's art. It makes everything he created intelligible in a way that only adds to the power of his paintings and engravings and poems, and to their capacity to awaken the imagination to those other dimensions of time into which he seemed to be able to peer.

As I have said, it is unlikely that this current warm season of critical regard will do much to enlarge Jones's fame. And, after all, his high and distinctive place in the canon of the arts of the twentieth century is already assured among those who care about such things. Even so, it would be something of a blessing if—so long as his work is receiving new attention—the magnitude and rarity of his accomplishments could be impressed upon as many receptive souls as possible. He deserves that much. His is an art fully acquainted both with the tragedies of history and with the peculiar homelessness of modern humanity; but it is also an art that overwhelmingly argues that both can be escaped, and even redeemed, by the cultivation of a special kind of sacral memory, and also an art that grants us an immense variety of new and beautiful forms under which to try to recover it. It offers intimations of eternity precisely through its embrace of time's fullness. It seems to come to us from a deep past that all of us can almost—though not quite—recall, and from a radiant and restored future that all of us can almost—though, again, not quite—imagine; above all, it "reminds" us of a creation unmarked by the wounds of fallen time.

An Introduction
to Léon Bloy's
The Pilgrim of the Absolute

There are many angles from which to view Léon Bloy (1846–1917), but only a very few that present him in a particularly flattering light—at least, as regards his personality. Concerning his almost uncanny gifts as a master of French prose, or concerning the great variety of his achievements as a writer, no one can entertain any serious doubts. In the full swell and surge of his voice, his language shines, flows, shimmers, thunders, sings. And his fiction, even at its most disordered or intentionally rebarbative, possesses a power and energy that more than compensate for any formal defects of narrative structure. But, for the great majority of those who made his acquaintance, to know him was to dislike him (if not at first, certainly in fairly short order), and even a great many of those who know him solely from his writings find him frequently insufferable. He may have been a prophet, in the most biblical sense, but he was not a saint (or, at least, certainly not any kind of saint recognizable to ordinary perception). He was a man of extremes—rhetorical, conceptual, artistic, religious, emotional—who was quite incapable of the safe and comfortable middle where most of us have to live out our lives and forge our accommodations with the world around us. It is a waste of time to look for moments of moderation or vacillation, either in him or in his work; there is none to be found. On the one hand, he was an indefatigable engine of theatrical rage—torrents of indignation, vituperation, objurgation, bitterness, and spite—and he gave vent to his hostilities with an extravagance so remorseless as to verge on the psychotic. On the other hand, he was an inexhaustible wellspring of fervent and genuinely tender pity for the sufferings of the poor and forgotten, and there was an undeniable innocence in his implacable anger against the rich and powerful who left the destitute to their misery. But one does not have the luxury of choosing one side of his character over against the other. They were not merely inextricable from one another; they were inverse but equally essential expressions of a single indivisible temperament. He abounded in love and hate, and was capable of the one only to the degree that he was capable of the other. There was a single Bloy, and he was an angelic monster.

Though, on second thought, a better way of putting this might be to say that he was French. Exquisitely French, even. Hyperbolically French, in fact. Certainly no other people in Europe is as prone to wild oscillations between extreme poles—emotional, intellectual, spiritual, artistic, political—or better able to hide the violence of their contradictions behind an appearance of elegant equilibrium. For all the grandiose mythology of *les lumières*, the secret animating principle sustaining France's majestic cultural supremacy among the nations of the West is an almost total incapacity for sane moderation. Even the celebrated "rationalism" of the French Enlightenment was nothing more than a momentary fashion, an entirely *irrational* passion for a new vogue in desiccated abstractions (rather like an inexplicably insatiable taste for chiaroscuro etchings or charcoal brass rubbings). And this cultural habit of ceaseless polarity has often produced prodigies of glorious contradictoriness, of a sort that transcend mere paradox. Only the French, for instance, could have perfected a form of Christian literature consisting almost entirely in the negation of Christian piety. Call it a kind of Christian Tantra, or Aghori Catholicism, or Catholicism of the left-hand path. Baudelaire (1821–67) provides perhaps the prime example, having so brilliantly succeeded at concealing his deep if eccentric faith in his *journaux intimes* while presenting the public with a facade of dissipation, wantonness, blasphemy, and even Satanism, as if hoping to shock bourgeois society into acknowledging the reality of the diabolical and therefore (ineluctably) of the divine. Perhaps even Lautréamont (1846–70) was a specimen of the type, though he died before the unveiling of his promised "devotional" sequel to *Les Chants de Maldoror*. Certainly, Bloy's master Barbey d'Aurevilly (1808–89) was, as also was Bloy's (temporary) friend Joris-Karl Huysmans (1848–1907). And Bloy's own literary imagination roamed many of the same "negative" spaces. His *Sueur de sang* (1893) and *Histoires désobligeantes* (1894) brought the fashion in "horrid" tales—pioneered by Barbey in *Diaboliques* (1874) and Villiers de l'Isle-Adam (1838–89) in *Contes cruels* (1883)—to a kind of ghastly perfection. If anything, Bloy's stories were more brutal in their unadorned hideousness; they established an entirely new standard for sordid fictional material: bizarre depravities, battlefield butchery, putrescent corpses, insanity, mutilation, infanticide, incest, sickly erotic fantasy, even a prostitute's reanimated cadaver—all of it played over a basso continuo of morbidly repellant physical (and physiological) detail.

It was not, however, his taste for the macabre (which savored more of the moralist's bitterness than of the voyeur's relish) that caused Bloy's detractors to find him so obnoxious. It was the man himself, or at least the indelible impression he gave of himself in his writings. To be honest, a maliciously exhaustive catalogue of Bloy's moral faults would be all but indistinguishable from a simple dispassionate account of his personality. While he attempted to live the life of a holy renunciant, he excelled chiefly at subjecting his friends and acquaintances to unremitting financial importunities; and the sanctimony with which he demanded, rather than asked, for assistance earned him the title of "the Ingrate Beggar." True, as Bloy acutely observed more than once, Christians should give freely, without any expectation of gratitude (lest the left hand become aware of the right hand's largesse). Even so, he might have attempted the occasional decorous expression of thanks, just to appear gracious. Moreover, while his piety was undoubtedly deep and ardent, it frequently degenerated into delusion, and of the most self-aggrandizing kind. Not only did he imagine that this sinful world lay under the threat of some imminent moment of divine reckoning; he seemed convinced that he himself would have a prominent role to play in the final settling of all accounts. And his faith was often little more than militant credulity. He was especially susceptible to the deliverances of religious visionaries, so long as the revelations they proclaimed were sufficiently suffused by an air of divine wrath. It was typical of him that he should become a truculent champion of the Marian "apparition" reported at La Salette in 1846 by two peasant girls, according to whom the Blessed Virgin had not only confessed herself scarcely able any longer to restrain the impetuous rage of her Son against the people of France but also threatened to kill countless children by famine as heavenly retribution for the profanities regularly uttered by provincial cart drivers. To Bloy, the comic rusticity of the tale was rendered believable by the very vindictiveness of its message. By his own account he himself had a positive genius for hatred, and it seems never to have occurred to him to draw any kind of distinction between the sinner and the sin. Why then would God? It is genuinely chilling at times to observe the unalloyed glee with which Bloy contemplated the misfortunes, sufferings, and even deaths—the eternal damnation, in fact—of those he disliked, either personally or as a class. He was especially overjoyed by news of the deaths of the wealthy—wealthy women most of all. The sinking of the *Titanic* or of any other luxury liner, though a tragedy for the poor wretches making the crossing in steerage or laboring below decks, filled him with delight. He could not contain the ebullience of his mirth when a fire at the Opéra Comique in 1877 resulted in the "cremation of four hundred filthy bourgeois." Again, when a fire at the Charity Bazaar in May of 1896 (recounted in the pages of this volume) killed a great number of society ladies and their privileged daughters, he rejoiced at the thought of all those "chaste lilies" and "tender roses" being trampled to death under the feet of the panicked crowd, and of their charred remains being swept up into dustpans the following day. And, of course, he was a French chauvinist and bigot, even while despising the complacency and moral lethargy of his fellow countrymen. He adored Napoleon, oddly, with an almost idolatrous passion. He ventured out of France only once, for a brief sojourn in Denmark, concluded that the Danes were scarcely human and that their religion was a barbarous parody of Christianity, and returned home for good. The British he hated with a vehemence bordering on the genocidal. Russia he would have happily seen reduced to a sea of blood spreading around high mountains of corpses. He was bellicose and choleric, splenetic and vicious. His resentments were madly disproportionate to any wrongs he had ever suffered. His prejudices were impregnable to any assaults of charity. He was not merely irascible—he was cruel.

And yet . . .

This is the infuriating and baffling mystery of Bloy. All of this is true, and all of it truly deplorable—*and yet* Bloy was a man of extraordinarily sensitive and fierce conscience. His prophetic affectations were not, after all, completely delusory. Underneath the searing fevers of his prose—the gleaming floods of its lyricism, its vividly hallucinatory imagery, the chaotic opulence of its phrasing, the sheer delirium of its verbal beauty—and even underneath the unabated ferocity and malice to which it gave such overwhelming expression, lay a bottomless reservoir of sincere compassion and incorruptible integrity. When one encounters Bloy not in his role as a moralist but simply as a moral man, one has to conclude that even his rhetorical savagery was an overflow of a deeper and uncompromising spiritual purity. In those moments, it seems clear that his polemical voice came from another age—perhaps early antiquity, or even perhaps the days of the prophets of Israel—cursing in order to bless, calling down God's wrath in order to redeem. Even in its most extreme registers, there is an audible tone of desperate, apocalyptic urgency, an almost frantic desire to rouse Bloy's contemporaries from their contented slumbers. Certainly Bloy often seemed to speak out of a sense of God as the Lord who is wrapped in the cloud and fire of Sinai, who dwells among his people only in the impenetrable darkness of the tabernacle or of the sanctuary, or in the unapproachable and deadly holiness of the Ark of the Covenant. His, moreover, was the Johannine Christ, whose presence in history is already the final judgment, separating light from darkness, life from death. And he clearly felt a certain contempt for those of his readers who did not understand that Christian charity sometimes can—and occasionally must—express itself in gall, indignation, sarcasm, even enmity. Or rather, to put the matter somewhat differently, genuine love must often entail a concomitant hatred. One is unlikely quite to catch the music of Bloy's rages unless one knows what it would be like to stand among the poorest and most abused human beings, to see the neglect and heartlessness with which the great world passes them by, and while standing there, amid that needless and ignored human desolation, to imagine with satisfaction the rich of the earth made into carrion for crows, and yet to do so out of a heart overflowing with charity. It requires a very rare, delicate, and volatile temperament to be such a person; but that is who Bloy was.

Something of the man's measure can be taken from his vociferous detestation of the antisemitism of his time and place, especially the newly fashionable variety promoted by the political journalist and pamphleteer Édouard Drumont (1844–1917), but also the traditional, casually vicious French Catholic variety, of the kind one finds coursing through the work of that dreary fascist and ponderous mediocrity Reginald Garrigou-

Lagrange (1877–1964). Even when the Dreyfus affair strained his loyalties from every side (he sometimes seemed to resent Dreyfus for embarrassing his beloved France by his innocence), and even when his rhetoric lapsed into the sort of conventional supersessionism that his own more considered theological writings rejected, Bloy never ceased to defend the Jews against persistent calumnies and to insist upon God's special love for his people—indeed, for his kin. To Bloy's mind, it was not enough for him as a Christian merely to denounce lies about the wealth and usurious ways of international "Jewry"; it was necessary to proclaim ever and again "Le Salut par les Juifs" (to cite the title of his book of 1892) and to insist that every Jew, being a cousin of God incarnate, owned a divine dignity to which gentiles had no natural claim, and in regard to which the proper attitude of any gentile was one of grateful humility. In fact, there is no other Catholic thinker of the nineteenth or early twentieth century who better understood Paul's arguments about God's enduring covenants in Romans chapters 9 to 11, or who was more immune to the traditional Augustinian misreading of the text. For him, Christians are saved only by being grafted into a vine that is eternally the vine of Israel. To appreciate just how extraordinary all this was for a pious Catholic of Bloy's time, one need only compare his views to the noxious bigotries that pervade the writings of Catholic apologists of the time—even some still held in high esteem today (G. K. Chesterton leaps—or, rather, laboriously shambles—to mind).

No less extraordinary, however, was Bloy's profound and really rather magnificent mysticism of poverty. —Poverty, that is, as opposed to destitution: the former, he claimed, was the chief of Christian virtues, the most Christlike, the most beautifully in keeping with the Son of God's self-impoverishment in his incarnation among the nameless of the earth; the latter is an abomination in God's eyes, the inexcusable sin of the rich against the poor, the condition of the world's suffering servants to whom—and to whom alone—Christ came to bear glad tidings. There is no element in Bloy's thought more purely biblical than his conviction that true love for the poor must express itself as, among other things, an unyielding condemnation of the wealthy. Here he proved himself an heir not just to the prophets of Israel, with their ringing denunciations of the predatory rich, but to the evangelists and the apostles. Of course, Christian culture has spent the better part of two millennia studiously avoiding the plain meaning of the New Testament's numerous pronouncements on the spiritual state of the wealthy and refusing to acknowledge Christ's more or less exclusive concern for the *ptōchoi*, the abjectly destitute. (In our day, American Christians especially—with their bizarre inability to distinguish the worship of the Father from cheerful service to Mammon, and their ludicrous certainty that the gospel can be reconciled with capitalism, and their magical claims that the profits of the market are also a wealth in general that spontaneously communicates itself to the poorest members of society—tend to find it nearly impossible to imagine that God might not approve of their well-earned prosperity.) To Bloy, this willful forgetfulness was perhaps the greatest scandal of Christian history; and he adopted a rhetoric toward the rich that, for all its fierceness, is no more terrifying than the language of the New Testament: the Magnificat's prophecy of the condign downfall of the privileged (Luke 1:53), Christ's explicit prohibition upon storing up earthly treasure (Matt. 6:19–20), his command that his disciples divest themselves of all possessions (Luke 12:33), his assurance that no one who clings to his property can be his disciple (Luke 14:33), the deprivations that he promises will befall the rich in the age to come (Luke 6:24–25; cf. 16:25), James's fiery accusations of the rich as oppressors of the poor now facing the wrath of God (James 1:9–11; 2:5–7; 5:1–6), and so on. For Bloy, the rich man seeking admission into the Kingdom really did have only about as good a chance of gaining entry as the camel had of passing through the needle's eye; and more than once he limned hilarious psychological portraits of those decent prosperous Christians who are absolutely convinced that God truly adores the rich and that any apparent scriptural statements to the contrary have been misunderstood or distorted in transmission. One of the most brilliantly acid and yet oddly moving witticisms in this volume is his suggestion that the builders of the Tower of Babel were seeking to storm heaven not merely by rising to its threshold but chiefly by ascending high above "the naked angels" thronging the streets below. To Bloy's mind, the most witheringly contemptuous name he could assign to the devil was that of *Le Bourgeois*—the eternal Bourgeois, in fact, who is a murderer from the beginning. To be honest, his language at times verges on a kind of Manichean or gnostic dualism, with the rich cast in the roles of the archons of this aeon, under whose power the whole cosmos languishes in torment and darkness. To his mind, the disproportionate wealth of the fortunate few, having been extracted from labor and common resources, is not theirs by right, even if it is also the product of their industry and ingenuity; still worse, to the degree that it is withheld from the poor it is nothing less than theft and slaughter. This is a moral, not an economic, claim; Bloy did not speak as if the world's wealth were some sort of fixed quantity, or as if one man's surfeit is necessarily another's scarcity; he merely believed that those who are wealthy and who keep their wealth for themselves, even as the poor continue to suffer and perish, are in God's eyes the murderers of their brothers and sisters. It is in this sense only that he claimed that the joy of the rich is the suffering of the poor, and that—to cite one of his most famous images—the gold of the rich is the blood of the poor, flowing through the institutions and estates of the propertied few. Great wealth is the ultimate vampirism, the most ordinary of daily cannibalisms. And yet, says Bloy, from the diabolical vantage of this age it is poverty that is the greatest shame, the one truly immeasurable guilt; and so Christ in becoming a man assumed also the real material poverty of the forgotten and exploited and thereby assumed also the "guilt" of all men and women. In his reading of the parable of Dives and Lazarus, Lazarus is Christ himself, left to die in the dust, pitied only by the dogs. And this mysticism of poverty plumbs the deepest fathoms of Bloy's faith. More to the point, his picture of our social world as a Satanic economy of sacrifice, fed by the ceaselessly spilled blood of the destitute, monstrously transubstantiated into gold—as astonishing as it may be in its sheer uncompromising intensity—is an expression not only of his "genius for hatred" but also of his heroic capacity for love. And (for what this is worth) it also happens to be true.

In any event, there is no need to say more. Bloy is more than able to speak for himself, and in the pages of *The Pilgrim of the Absolute* he pours out the full range of his passions and rancors, loves and hates, prophetic inspirations and narcissistic delusions. It is a voice like no other, so eloquent and earnest that even its moments of pettiness can seem sublime. Above all else, it is the voice of a man who was hard to love but impossible to ignore precisely because he was apparently incapable of lying about his convictions, of temporizing in order to avoid causing dismay, or of seeking to evade the consequences of his beliefs. And such men, rare as they are, invariably offend. Happily, Bloy was able to delight as well.

PART FIVE

The New Testament

23

The First Radicals

I

It was in 1983 that I heard the distinguished Greek Orthodox historian Aristeides Papadakis, of the University of Maryland, blandly remark in an evening lecture that the very earliest Christians were "communists." In those days, of course, the Cold War was still casting its great glacial shadow across the cultural landscape, and so enough of a murmur of consternation rippled through the room that Papadakis—who always chose his words with severe precision—felt obliged to explain that he meant this in the barest technical sense: they lived together in a common life and voluntarily enjoyed a complete community of possessions (none of which characterized the "communism" of the Eastern bloc). The murmur subsided, though not necessarily the disquiet. Not that anyone should have been surprised. If the Christian communism of the apostolic age is a secret, it is as open a secret as one can imagine. If the word itself seems a mite too jarring, one can substitute something vaguer and more palatable, like *communalist* or *communitarian*, but the facts remain clear. The book of Acts tells us that in Jerusalem the first converts to the proclamation of Christ's resurrection, as the natural expression of their new faith, occupied a single dwelling, selling all their fixed holdings, redistributing their wealth "as each person needed," owning necessary goods communally, and claiming no private property for themselves. In this, moreover, they were simply obeying a pattern Jesus himself had established: "Each of you who does not give up all that he himself possesses is incapable of being my disciple" (Luke 14:33). It was not only to the rich young ruler seeking salvation but to all who wished to follow him that Jesus issued the command to sell all private possessions and give away the proceeds as alms (Luke 12:33).

This was always something of a scandal for the Christians of later ages, at least those who bothered to notice it. And today in America, with its bizarre piety of free enterprise and private wealth as intrinsic moral goods, it is almost unimaginable that anyone could adopt so seditious an attitude toward the inviolable sanctity of property. So, down the centuries, Christian culture has largely ignored the social provocation of the early church's organization or has siphoned off its lingering residues into small special communities (such as monasteries and convents). Even when that provocation has been acknowledged, it has typically been treated as something incidental to the gospel message (as defined by later tradition)—at most a brief accommodation with a particular set of historical circumstances, a prudent marshaling of resources against a hostile world for a brief season, but nothing essential to the faith, and certainly not a political philosophy. This is, at best, a very partial truth, and one of only the most trivial sort. Obviously the early church was not a political movement in the modern sense, since the very idea would have been meaningless. There were no political ideologies in the ancient world, no abstract programs for the reconstitution of society. Certainly, no one in the earlier church was advocating a "state" policy of seizure and redistribution. But, if not a political movement, the church *was* a kind of polity, and the form of life it assumed was not merely a practical concession to necessity or strategy for survival but rather the embodiment of its deepest spiritual ideals. And this communism was nowhere near so transitory an ideal as later Christians may have imagined. Neither was it a mere "incidental" of faith.

II

The early church's radicalism, if that is the right word, was impressed upon me repeatedly over the past few years as I worked on my own translation of the New Testament for Yale University Press. When my longtime editor initially proposed the project, I foolishly imagined it would be an easy task. Not that I thought the text a simple one. But over the years I had often "corrected" what I considered defective or inadequate versions of a great many of its passages, either for students or for myself, and I assumed that long familiarity with the Greek of the original had prepared me to turn it into English almost effortlessly. Moreover, I had long been annoyed by what I took to be the failure of previous translators to provide readers with a version that, rather than hiding the text's ambiguities and mysteries, left them in open view. So the prospect of producing a "subversively literal" translation was irresistible. Soon, though, I came to realize that, while I may have known a great many things about the text, I had yet to grasp many of them properly. I was well aware, for instance, that much of the conventional language of scriptural translation has the unfortunate effect of reducing complex and difficult words and concepts to vacuously simple or deceptively anachronistic terms (*eternal, hell, justification*, to give a few examples). But I had not adequately appreciated how violently those conventions impoverish the text or obscure crucial dimensions of its conceptual world. The books of the New Testament, I came to see, constitute an astonishing and often nearly impenetrable historical conundrum—not because they come from the remote world of late antiquity (a world I know well enough, sometimes better than my own) but rather because they often appear to make no sense even in that context. Then again, they may make just as little sense in relation to most later Christian history.

I found myself constantly in doubt, for example, regarding how to understand many constructions concerning things belonging to what is κοινόν (*koinon*), "common." Most particularly, I found myself wondering about the texts' frequently distinctive emphasis on κοινωνία (*koinōnia*), a word usually rendered, in fairly anodyne fashion, as "fellowship," or "sharing," or (a little better) "communion." But, in context, is that all it really implies? I came to think that, instead, it often refers to a precise set of practices within the early Christian communities, a special social arrangement that was considered integral to the new life in Christ—which is to say, the practices clearly described in Acts and alluded to in the New Testament epistles. How then should one read the exhortation in the letter to the Hebrews not to neglect *koinōnia*? Precisely what virtues and customs does it invoke? Or what does it mean when the first letter to Timothy tells believers to strive to become κοινωνικοί (*koinōnikoi*)—literally, "communal" or "communalist"? Certainly it is no mere recommendation of personal generosity. As best we can tell, after all, the local churches of the Roman world in the apostolic age were often something like attempts at small communes. And, when possible, those with more resources sent aid to those with fewer. This delicate web of communes constituted a kind of counterempire within the empire, one founded upon charity rather than force—or, better, a Kingdom not of this world but present within the world nonetheless as a kind of contrary and secret history, built around a radically different understanding of society and property.

More to the point, the New Testament's condemnations of private wealth are fairly unremitting and remarkably stark: Luke 6:24–25, for instance ("But alas for you who are rich, for you have your comfort"), or Matthew 6:19–20 ("Do not store up treasures for yourself on the earth"), or James 2:5–7 and (most terrifying of all) James 5:1–6 ("Come now, you who are rich, weep, howling out at the miseries that are coming for you"). The Apostle Paul consistently inveighs against πλεονεκτία (*pleonektia*), "acquisitiveness," while the Pastoral Epistles denounce αἰσχροκερδής (*aischrokerdēs*), "sordid desire for profit." And, while there will always be clergymen and theologians eager to assure us that the New Testament condemns not wealth but only its abuse, not a single verse (unless subjected to absurdly forced readings) confirms this claim.

III

It was all much easier, no doubt—this nonchalance toward private possessions—for those first generations of Christians. They tended to see themselves as transient tenants within a rapidly vanishing world, refugees passing lightly through a history not their own. Their attachments to the larger society were tenuous at best, and pervaded by an apocalyptic irony. But, as the initial elations and expectations of the gospel faded and the settled habits of life in this depressingly durable world emerged anew, the distinctive practices of the earliest Christians gave way to the common practices of the established order. Even then, the transition was nowhere near as abrupt as we might imagine. Near the end of the first century, the manual of Christian life known as the *Didache* instructed believers to share all things in common and to think of nothing as private property. The first Christians of the Syrian city of Edessa no sooner converted than they disposed of their belongings. Well into the second century, the pagan satirist Lucian of Samosata (ca. 125–ca. 181 CE) could report that Christians viewed possessions with contempt and owned all property communally. The Christian apologist Justin Martyr (ca. 100–165 CE) proclaimed that to be Christian was to seek wealth no longer but instead to make a common fund of all possessions, for redistribution to the needy. Even Clement of Alexandria (ca. 150–ca. 215 CE), who was the first significant theologian to assure a new rising class of propertied Christians that they could retain their possessions so long as they cultivated poverty of spirit, did so only grudgingly. He still called private property the fruit of wickedness and insisted that ideally all goods should be available for common use. Tertullian (ca. 155–ca. 240 CE) observed that Christians found a complete community of goods easy because they already shared a common soul and mind.

Even in the late fourth century, Basil the Great (330–79 CE) could bluntly state that there is no right to private property, that no one should have more than what is necessary, and that the rich seize what properly belongs to all equally and then claim it for their own simply because they got to it first. For him, private property was theft—bread stolen from the hungry, clothing stolen from the naked, money stolen from the destitute. Anyone, he said, possessing more than his neighbor has failed in duty to the poor and in Christian love. And he insisted that a Christian society must create a common public fund from which the needs of the destitute could be provided. His brother, Gregory of Nyssa (ca. 335–ca. 395), concurred. Ambrose of Milan (ca. 340–97 CE) refused even to grant that a rich man could make gifts to the poor; he could at most restore what already belonged to them. And sentiments no less uncompromising were voiced by Augustine (354–430 CE) and Cyril of Alexandria (ca. 376–444 CE). And then there was John Chrysostom (ca. 349–407 CE), some of whose pronouncements on wealth and poverty make Bakunin and Marx sound like timid conservatives. According to him, the chief cause of poverty is the dispersion of goods in private holdings, which produces both prodigality and parsimony. The rich are thieves, even if their property comes to them legally, through enterprise or inheritance, since everything belongs to all as part of the one common human estate. Those who keep any more of this shared patrimony for themselves than barest necessity dictates are brigands and apostates from the gospel. Those who think they work honestly by acquiring money, conducting business, and guarding their belongings are actually just corrupt idlers, recreants from the true work of charity. All we possess actually belongs to everyone, and no Christian should ever utter the words *yours* and *mine*. And he said much of this in sermons while he was archbishop of Constantinople.

That such language could still be heard in the heart of imperial Christendom, however, indicates that it had by that time lost much of its force. It could be tolerated to a degree, but only as a bracing hyperbole proper to a particular religious grammar—an idiom, that is, rather than an imperative. Christianity was ceasing to be the apocalyptic annunciation of something unprecedented and was becoming just the established devotional system of its culture, offering all the consolations and reassurances that one demands of religious institutions. As generations passed, the original provocation of the early church would subtly persist in isolated monastic communities and occasionally erupt in ephemeral "purist" movements—Spiritual Franciscans, Russian Non-Possessors, the Catholic Worker Movement—but, in general, Christian adherence had become chiefly just a religion, a support for life in this world rather than a radically different model of how to live. That was unavoidable, no doubt. Material conditions alter over time, but there are certain constants. No society as a whole will ever found itself upon the rejection of society's chief mechanism: property. And all great religions achieve historical success by gradually moderating their most extreme demands of believers. And so it is hard to extract a simple moral from the story of the early church's radicalism. But, for anyone for whom the New Testament is not merely a record of the past but a challenge to the present too, it is also hard not to conclude that the distance separating the Christianity of the apostolic age from the far more comfortable religious adherences of later Christian centuries—and those of the developed world today—is more than one merely of time and circumstance.

24

Paul's Theology Was Rather Different from What We Think

I

This past year, I burdened the English-speaking world with my very own translation of the New Testament—a project that I undertook at the behest of my editor at Yale University Press but that I agreed to almost in the instant that it was proposed. I had long contemplated attempting a "subversively literal" rendering of the text. Over the years, I had become somewhat peevishly displeased with almost all the standard translations available, and especially with modern versions produced by large committees of scholars, many of whom (I am convinced) have been predisposed by inherited doctrines and theological habits of thought to see things in the text that are not really there and to fail to notice other things that most definitely are. The conceptual world from which the New Testament emanates is one so remote from our own that it is almost never what we expect, and it requires an extraordinary effort of the imagination to think our way back into it. But committees are bland affairs and tend to reinforce rather than disrupt our complacencies. They also tend to leave inherited misconceptions firmly fixed in place.

Ask, for instance, the average American Christian—say some genial Presbyterian who attends church regularly and owns a New International Version of the Bible—what gospel the Apostle Paul preached. The reply will usually fall along predictable lines: human beings, bearing the *guilt* of original sin and destined for eternal hell, cannot save themselves through good deeds or make themselves acceptable to God; yet God, in his mercy, sent the eternal Son to offer himself up for our sins, and the righteousness of Christ has been graciously imputed or imparted to all who have faith. Some details might vary, but not the basic story. And, admittedly, much of the tale's language is reminiscent of terms used by Paul, at least as filtered through certain conventional translations; but it is a fantasy. For one thing, it presumes elements of later Christian belief that are absent from Paul's own writings. Some of these (like the idea that humans are born damnably guilty in God's eyes, or the notion that good deeds are not required for salvation) arise from a history of misleading translations. Others (like the concept of an eternal hell of conscious torment) are entirely imagined, attributed to Paul on the basis of some mistaken picture of what the New Testament as a whole teaches.

To me, at the far end of my labors, the picture looks very different. At least, if I were asked to summarize Paul's actual teachings, relying only on the Greek of his letters, I think I would tend to identify his *principal* point of emphasis not as original guilt and imputed righteousness (in neither of which he believed) but as the overthrow of bad angels. On the whole, furthermore, I would argue that a certain long history of misreadings of the Letter to the Romans—and especially chapters 9 to 11—has created an impression of his theological concerns so entirely alien to the conceptual world he inhabited that the real Paul occupies scarcely any place at all in Christian memory. It is true that Paul does address the issue of "righteousness" or "justice" and asserts that it is available to us only through a virtue he calls πίστις (*pistis*)—"faith" or "trust" or even "fidelity." But this virtue is for Paul explicitly one that largely consists in works of obedience to God and love of others, and the only ἔργα (*erga*), "works," that he is anxious to claim make no contribution to personal sanctity are certain "ritual observances" prescribed by the Law of Moses, such as circumcision or kosher dietary laws. Moreover, the chief importance of this for Paul is simply that the separation between Jews and gentiles has been annulled in Christ, opening salvation equally to all peoples, whether they are capable of the Law or not. For him, the whole issue is a matter of personal anxiety, a fear that God might seem unfaithful to his covenant with Israel and might seem to have abandoned one chosen people for another (which, he gratefully concludes, is not the case). And yet, all this said, this really is not his chief concern.

II

The essence of Paul's theology is something far stranger and is played out on an immeasurably vaster scale. For him, we are living in the final days of one world-age that is rapidly passing and awaiting the dawn of another that will differ from it radically in every dimension: heavenly and terrestrial, spiritual and physical. In the story of salvation, nothing less than the entire cosmos is at stake; and the great drama at the heart of that story is one of invasion, conquest, spoliation, and triumph. For Paul, the cosmos has been made subject to death, to whom we have been enslaved by our sin and by the malign governance of "angelic" or "daemonian" agencies, reigning over the earth from the heavens above and holding spirits in thrall below the earth. These agencies—these archons, these angelic beings whom Paul calls Thrones and Powers and Dominations and Spiritual Forces of Evil in the High Places—are the gods of the nations. Perhaps even the angel of the Lord who rules over Israel (so the Letter to the Galatians hints) is one of their number. They may be fallen in some sense, or mutinous, or merely deficient caretakers of the world; but, whatever the case, they stand intractably between us and God. Yet Christ has conquered them all.

In descending to the realm of the dead, Hades, and ascending again through the heavens, Christ has conquered all the powers below and above that separate us from the love of God and has borne them away captive in a kind of triumphal procession. All that remains to happen is the consummation of the present cosmic age: Christ will appear again, now in his full glory as universal conqueror, having subordinated all the cosmic powers to himself—literally, having properly "ordered" them "under" himself—and then, at the last, will hand over the whole of this reclaimed empire to the Father. Then the cosmos will be ruled no longer through wicked or incompetent spiritual intermediaries but directly by God. At times Paul speaks as if those who are not yet Christ's own will perish along with the age that is passing, and at other times as if all human beings will finally be saved; he never speaks of some eternal hell of torment for unregenerate souls. The new age that is coming, moreover—when creation will be transformed into the Kingdom of God and the frame of nature charged with divine glory—will be an age of "spirit" rather than "flesh." For Paul, these are two antithetical principles of creaturely existence, though most translations misrepresent the antithesis as a tension between God's "Spirit" and human perversity. But Paul is quite explicit: "Flesh and blood cannot inherit the Kingdom." Neither then can ψυχή (psychē), "soul," the life-principle or anima that gives life to perishable flesh. In the age to come, the "psychical body"—the "ensouled" or "animal" way of life—will be replaced by a "spiritual body," beyond the reach of death—though, again, conventional translations usually obscure this by speaking of the former, vaguely, as a "natural body."

I could go on, but there is no need. It is worth adding that Paul's voice is hardly an eccentric one in context. In John's Gospel, for instance, the story of salvation concerns the divine savior who comes quite literally "from above," descending from God's realm into the cosmos below, overthrowing its reigning archon, bringing the light of God into the darkness of our captivity, and "dragging" everyone to himself. And something similar, in varying registers, is true of most of the texts of the New Testament. As I say, it is a conceptual world very remote from our own. And yet it would be just another modern prejudice on our part to think that the truth or falsehood of the spiritual claims of the gospel can be judged on the basis of how plausible we find the cosmological picture that accompanies them. Quite apart from the possibility that their picture of reality might be in many significant respects more accurate than ours (at the spiritual level, at least), it would surely be a vulgar category error to assume that the story of God's overthrow of death and sin in Christ cannot be true in a way transcending the historical and cultural conditions in which it was first told. That said, the matter cannot be decided one way or another until one is certain what that story actually is. And this, it seems to me, will always involve attempting to recover the real tale from the very different tales that we have so frequently told in its place.

25

What It Says,
Not What It Means

I

I suppose I would describe the method I adopted in producing my recent translation of the New Testament as "Nabokovian." Not
that I was attempting to write like Nabokov, of course; I mean only that
I took something like the approach he took in his famous (or notorious)
Bollingen critical edition of *Eugene Onegin*. I decided at the very start that,
if there was to be any justification for a new translation at all, my first obligation was to attempt to communicate not what I believe the original
text *means* but simply what it *says*. In the patois of translation theory, that
puts my rendering firmly on the side of "formal equivalence" rather than
of "dynamic equivalence"—though, really, I prefer to avoid theory altogether and simply to think of the final product as "scrupulous to a fault"
(at least, when my impulse to self-flattery is at its strongest). I acknowledge, of course, that the translation of words on a page can never be free
of some interpretation of their contents; and this is especially true in the
case of documents that come to us from ages and cultures of which we
possess only very partial comprehension, and which therefore require a
constant effort of conceptual reconstruction. Even so, I am convinced
that it is precisely that historical and cultural remoteness that a translator
of an ancient document should first try to convey before attempting to
reduce the distance between text and reader; we can understand almost
nothing about any ancient work, it seems to me, if we fail to grasp how
much we do not understand about the world from which it came.

The translation was not originally my idea, I should note. It was proposed to me by my brilliant editor at Yale University Press, Jennifer Banks. But almost at once I grasped that there were "subversive" possibilities here, most of which I could accomplish just by resolving to be as literal as I could. For years, I had been frustrated by what I took to be the defects of almost all those standard modern translations of the Bible produced by large committees of scholars, all of which seem to me to be shaped not only by too many inherited habits of theological thought and usage but by the curious assumption that the distinctive idioms and conceptual vocabularies of Jewish, Christian, and pagan antiquity constitute nothing more than different ways of expressing intuitions and ideas that we today merely express in different (but "dynamically equivalent") ways. I tend to think that they actually express fundamentally different ways of seeing reality. To say, for instance, that someone is "full of days" is *not* simply to say the same thing that a modern person means in describing someone as "very old." But I had assumed too hastily that I could easily remedy things just by trying to render the text as "directly" as possible, without reference to later traditions or religious expectations. At times, this sufficed; but the New Testament abounds in words whose true significances are often painfully difficult to ascertain with confidence, and they are made all the more obscure by the history of misleading or vacuous terms we traditionally impose upon them: *justification*, for example, or *faith*, or *hell*, or *predestine*, or *ransom*, or *eternal* (and so forth). In regard to some terms, a real labor of philological and cultural archaeology is needed before one can guess what the "literal" meaning might be. For example, the New Testament words usually rendered as "ransom," and too often taken as indicating a penalty exacted from humanity by God the Father, almost certainly properly refer to the fee required for the legal manumission of a slave, and really only indicate the price God himself paid in Christ to liberate humanity from slavery in the household of death.

II

There are other words, however, that defy translation altogether because their ranges of connotation are simply too immense and varied to be captured in any available modern term. For example, the term *logos* as used in the prologue of the Gospel of John, typically rendered as "Word," should probably simply be left untranslated and then explained in a note or two (this, at least, was my solution). But then, more troublesome still, there are those few but extremely important words that can be neither simply translated nor simply left intact because they reflect a conceptual universe so remote from our own that we scarcely have even a feel for what they signify. Some of them, in fact, may originally have referred not so much to any stable object or property as to an otherwise nameless atmosphere of associations. For these, we lack not simply equivalent terms but the whole imaginative and speculative environment that once made sense of them; mysterious in their own time, they are all but ineffable in ours; and so we tend in each case to settle on something analogous to whichever of the term's possible nuances we have decided to take as its principal emphasis. Among such words I would include, perhaps surprisingly, the adjective αἰώνιος (aiōnios), which appears in the New Testament seventy-one times and which is typically translated as "eternal" in all but those rare instances where this would be absurd. This makes sense as far as it goes. Certainly, the reality to which the word refers often contains eternity among its attributes (though not necessarily in our common sense of a condition of endless duration). But I am unyieldingly convinced that this is not precisely what the word *means*. And, in fact, for some centuries after the time of the New Testament a number of significant writers (the Christian John Chrysostom, for instance, or the pagan Olympiodorus the Younger) used the word *aiōnios* to qualify something precisely so as to indicate that it was *not* eternal. *Aiōnios* is derived from the noun αἰών (aiōn), which is itself a fascinating word, and one often elusive of exact meaning, even though it began its life as a rather ordinary term for any fixed span of time. Originally, it was used to indicate a single person's lifetime; this is its typical meaning in Homer and the Attic dramatists. Over time, however, it acquired ever vaster dimensions and ever more numerous connotations. It came to mean, in many contexts, an epoch or an age, and even an entire age of the world. At some point, it had become so buoyant a term that it could float free of time altogether. Plato used it to indicate the supercelestial home of the changeless ideas, a world beyond the sway of sidereal time and the inconstancies of mutability, whose fullness is only fleetingly and fragmentarily reflected here below in the realm of χρόνος (chronos), the time of generation and decay.

In fact, Plato may have been the first writer to supply the noun *aiōn* with its adjectival form *aiōnios*.

In the Septuagint (which was for the most part the Bible of the early Christians), *aiōn* and *aiōnios* and a number of related terms came to serve as the Greek equivalent for various uses of the Hebrew word *ôlām*, whose history of meanings follows a course eerily similar to that of *aiōn*, and whose uses in Hebrew scripture span practically the whole range of references possible for either. Then, moreover, in the New Testament, it seems clear that there are numerous places where either the substantive or the adjective is employed, or where both are employed together (though this last is usually lost in translation), to refer, not to "eternity" in some abstract sense, but rather to the *ôlām ha-ba*, the "Age to come," the divine dispensation of the Kingdom, the restored order of creation that will succeed the *ôlām ha-zeh*, "this age," οὗτος αἰών (ʰoutos aiōn). Then again, however, in the Gospel of John (one could plausibly argue) the reference is not necessarily so much to an Age lying upon the horizon of history as to one abiding above history altogether, God's eternal realm beyond this cosmos. The Johannine meaning of *aiōnios* may then be closer to the Platonic than to any other. And, then also, there are other complications as well. And I dealt with all these ambiguities in my translation by . . . (well, that would be telling).

III

The moral of all of this is, perhaps, an unexpected one. At least, it was for me. As I say, when I began my translation I took it at as my primary task to restore some proper sense of the distance separating the world of the New Testament from ours—to make the text strange again, so to speak. At the very least, I succeeded in making it stranger to myself. And yet, curiously enough, it was precisely this desire to find that forgotten distance once more that allowed me to cross it, or rather allowed it to be crossed from the other side. As the historical backdrop of the texts drew further away, the players in the drama drew ever nearer. What emerged from my sometimes deeply frustrating struggles with everything alien and impenetrable about the early Christian conceptual world—especially as the veils of conventional phrasing and received ideas melted away—

were living personalities: the diverse voices of the scriptures' authors (many of whom were very ordinary men) became distinct for me, and progressively clearer, proclaiming something that to them was absolutely and consumingly urgent. And somehow I was hearing that urgency for the first time and being persuaded by it with a force wholly new to me. Precisely in making the texts strange—in trying to make them truly remote—I experienced them with an immediacy that I had never really known before. It was not what I expected. But, then again, *he* is never what we expect.

26

The Spirit of the Text

I

When I came to the task of producing my own translation of the New Testament, I knew that there are certain words and phrases in the text that present special difficulties and that no solution I chose would please everybody. In some cases, the difficulty lies in an inherent ambiguity in the word itself—an uncertainty regarding what concept or set of concepts it signifies or implies—but, in other cases, the difficulty lies precisely in the word's clarity, because any truly literal translation will fall afoul of dearly held theological or doctrinal conventions. After all, a very great deal of theological history consists in ingenious impositions of ideas upon texts to which they are, in fact, quite alien; and the history of scriptural translation has, as a rule, followed theology's lead. The result has been that successive versions of the Bible, obedient to the doctrinal expectations of their authors, have drifted ever further away from the world in which the original texts were written. At the end of the process, a perfectly pious consortium of translators can produce something like the New International Version, which is the Bible in much the same way that *West Side Story* "is" *Romeo and Juliet*.

To be fair, the real world of the New Testament is an unsettlingly strange one. So much of the great edifice of Christian theology, for instance, has been erected upon the writings of Paul; and yet, truth be told, what Paul actually believed and explicitly said would strike the ears of even most educated believers as bizarre. An obvious example (though perhaps not the most striking) would be his often stark opposition between the two principles of σάρξ (*sarx*), "flesh," and πνεῦμα (*pnevma*), "spirit"—with yet a third principle, ψυχή (*psychē*), "soul," weighing in decisively on the side of the former. Admittedly, in many passages in the New Testament, and especially in some of Paul's letters, it is impossible to tell whether the author is speaking of human "spirit" or of God's "Spirit." At certain crucial junctures, again in Paul's letters, the absence of a clear distinction seems almost intentional. Traditionally, though, translators have in moments of uncertainty chosen for the reader how she or he should understand the word, by either capitalizing the "s" or leaving it in the lower case; and far too often the letter is capitalized even when it clearly ought not to be. A particularly good example of this latter would be Galatians 5:17, where Paul (whose anthropology is considerably more "dualistic" than it is currently fashionable to admit) is clearly speaking of an opposition between the desires of "flesh" and those of "spirit" *within each human being*, but where most English translations quite presumptuously and unintelligibly describe an opposition between something definitely human (whether "flesh" or some unfortunate circumlocution) and "the [Holy] Spirit." Greek, though, is conveniently furnished with definite articles (as Latin is not), and where Paul is speaking specifically of God's "Spirit" he is generally able to indicate the fact: "*the* Spirit," "*the* Holy Spirit."

Theological tradition, however, especially in certain Protestant traditions, is loath to grant that Paul has any concept of opposed moral principles within our nature, and certainly loath to acknowledge that one of those principles—and the one in fact hostile to God's will—could be "flesh" in any but a metaphorical sense. The original editors of the aforementioned NIV were so confident upon this point that their version nonsensically rendered *sarx* as "sinful nature." And even many theological interpreters who would not consider visiting that kind of violence on the text persistently claim that Paul certainly never meant to suggest that our actual physical flesh is somehow implicated in our separation from God, much less in any division within us between an inclination to holiness and another toward sin. It has become something of a fashion over the last century for theologians to insist almost exclusively on the "worldliness" of Christianity, or on how exuberantly it affirms the material order—the material body especially—as the good creation of God, or on how radically the early Christian view of corporeality supposedly differed from that of more "Hellenistic" or "gnostic" or "idealist" schools of thought. But the truth is far more complicated.

II

There is nothing like an *absolute* dualism in the New Testament, of the sort that would suggest that the physical world is ultimately evil, or that the Age to come will not involve a redemption of the whole created order; but, even so, there is at least a very strong *provisional* dualism clearly present in much of the New Testament, and when the text speaks of "flesh" in opprobrious terms it is not employing a vague metaphor, for which some less upsetting abstraction may safely be substituted. As 1 Corinthians 15:40–54 makes quite clear—and as Matthew 22:30, Mark 12:25, Luke 20:36, and perhaps Acts 23:8 all powerfully suggest—many early Christians understood the difference between the mortal body and the resurrected body (whether Christ's or ours) as the difference between earthly flesh and a kind of life that has transcended the flesh. As Paul bluntly says, "Flesh and blood cannot inherit the Kingdom of God" (1 Cor. 15:50). At times, the early Christians, no less than their pagan or so-called "gnostic" contemporaries, had a somewhat jaundiced view of "this cosmos" or "this age," as well as of "this body of death," not merely as moral dispensations, but as physical realities. In fact, 1 Peter 3:18 and 4:6 even contrast (again, when accurately translated) Christ's death "in flesh" from his resurrection "in spirit." As strange as it may now seem to us, for Paul one absolutely essential element of the salvation achieved by Christ is, so to speak, physiological. For him, the Resurrection is a path to liberation from flesh and blood. Thus, for instance, when Paul distinguishes in 1 Corinthians 15:44–46 between the body human beings possess in this age and that which they will receive in the Age to come, he speaks of the former as a dissoluble and perishable composite of flesh and soul (*psychē*), a σῶμα ψυχικόν (*sōma psychikon*) but of the latter as an imperishable unity, a σῶμα πνευματικόν (*sōma pnevmatikon*): that is, an "animal" or "psychical body," on the one hand, and a "spiritual" or "pneumatic body," on the other.

In any event, in my translation I have refrained from changing every reference to "spirit" into an invocation of the Holy Spirit. I would regard doing so—however venerable the practice may be among doctrinally sensitive translators—not merely as a distortion of the text but as an act of deceit. After all, as small a difference as my rendering of "spirit" as "spirit" might seem to make in orthographic terms, in conceptual terms, and in regard to the light it sheds upon the intellectual environment in which the New Testament was formed, it makes all the difference in the world.

27

A Prayer for the Poor

I

David Graeber's *Debt: The First 5000 Years* (2011) is a strange, brilliant, frustrating, and perhaps indispensable book. It remains controversial among economists, of course, if only out of the resentment some of them feel at the very notion that an anthropologist might presume to intrude on their putative area of expertise, and to do so on so vast a historical scale. It continues, moreover, to strain the credulity of those who cannot imagine how anyone could genuinely entertain doubts regarding the practical inevitability of a monetary economic system or could seriously propose anarchism as a real alternative to the injustices of capitalism. And, of course, there are those who not unreasonably accuse Graeber of offering a grandly buoyant critique of the contradictions and cruelties of capitalist culture without the ballast of a few proposals for correcting the problems. But, exotic as Graeber's book was as an intervention in economic analysis, at its heart lay a rather ordinary observation, one that was made less grandly but more systematically a couple years later by Thomas Piketty in his magisterial treatise *Capital in the Twenty-First Century* (2013), and one in fact acknowledged by economic thinkers of every conceivable ideological persuasion, from Marx to Mises: that in many ways the difference between the poor and the rich is simply the difference between debtors and creditors, and that systems of credit are for the most part designed to preserve and exploit this difference.

The logic of this is not difficult to grasp. Once the principle of interest—especially compound interest—is recognized as a legitimate means of encouraging lending, it requires very little ingenuity indeed to create a system in which one person's poverty is another's source of wealth, and in which it is very much in the interest of creditors to see that the poor remain poor. Invariably, the destitute will often find themselves in desperate need of liquid capital; and, just as invariably, they will not have anything of sufficient value to convert into cash or to use as security on a sufficiently substantial loan. Hence, they will have no alternative but to consent to whatever rates and rules of interest their creditors see fit to impose. Especially predatory creditors, moreover—as any simple survey of the practices of credit card companies today will reveal—can arrange the terms of credit in such a way that the initial debt will be quickly magnified beyond any reasonable proportion, rendering the debtor perpetually incapable of discharging the financial burden under which he or she labors, and so able to do little more than make regular payments on the principal's interest (which, needless to say, grows more rapidly than the debtor can pay it off). Before long, the principal itself has effectively withdrawn from the visible world into a realm almost holy in its unapproachable exaltation, a mystery sealed within an inaccessible sanctuary, in the service of an unappeasable god. It really is an infallible formula. A few draconian penalties written into credit agreements (in extremely fine print), a few legal but unreasonably immense shifts in interest rates, a cynical liberality with regard to the amount of credit extended to persons too much in need to calculate the inevitable destructive consequences of accepting excessive credit, and all at once the penury of the unfortunate becomes an overflowing wellspring of revenues for the wealthy. Especially profitable for such creditors are the catastrophic medical emergencies that so frequently reduce the poor to virtual slavery, and that the American system especially—with a Darwinian prudence almost majestic in its stern, barbaric indifference to the appeals of pity or morality alike—refuses to alleviate. But, really, the legal apparatuses of almost all developed nations are more than accommodating enough to allow the credit markets to reap the fullest possible harvests from their lavishly seeded fields. No realm of economic activity is more casually and ineffectually regulated in most countries. In capitalist societies, the poor too—like everything else—can become a commodity; they are a natural resource that can be tirelessly exploited by the rapacious without ever being exhausted. The poor are with you always.

II

A recognition of the fundamental indecency of using interest to enslave the needy appears at least as early in human history as the Law of Moses. Hence its inflexible prohibitions upon all practices of usury within the community of the children of Israel (Exod. 22:25; Lev. 25: 36–37; Deut. 23:19–20), and hence the ancient Jewish condemnation of interest (Ps. 15:5; Ezek. 18:17). Hence also the care extended in the Law to ensure that neither Israelites *nor their neighbors* be reduced to a state of absolute impoverishment (Exod. 12:49; 22:21–22; Lev. 19:9–10; 23:22; 25:35–38; Deut. 15:1–11). Moreover, the Law not only prohibited interest on loans but mandated that every seventh year should be a Sabbatical, a *shmita*, a fallow year, during which debts between Israelites were to be remitted, and then went even further in imposing the Sabbath of Sabbath-Years, the Year of Jubilee, in which all debts were excused and all slaves granted their liberty, so that everyone might begin again, as it were, with a clear ledger. In this way, the difference between creditors and debtors could be (at least, for a time) erased, and a kind of equitable balance restored. At the same time, needless to say, the unremitting denunciation of those who exploit the poor or ignore their plight is a radiant leitmotif running through the proclamations of the prophets of Israel (Isa. 3:13–15; 5:8; 10:1–2; Jer. 5:27–28: Amos 4:1; etc.). So it should be unsurprising to find that a very great many of Christ's teachings concerned debtors and creditors, and the legal coercion of the former by the latter, and the need for debt relief; but somehow we do find it surprising—when, of course, we notice. As a rule, however, it is rare that we *do* notice, in part because we often fail to recognize the social and legal practices to which his parables and moral exhortations so often referred, and in part because our traditions have so successfully "spiritualized" the texts—both through translation and through habits of interpretation—that the economic and political provocations they contain are scarcely audible to us at all.

This is understandable, of course. But one does not need to be a scholar of Judaea and Galilee in late antiquity to notice how often Jesus speaks of trials, of officers dragging the insolvent to jail, of men bound by or imprisoned for undischarged debts, of unmerciful creditors, of suits brought before judges to secure a coat or cloak, of the unfortunate legally despoiled by the fortunate. In point of fact, the principal function

of the courts of the world in which Christ lived and preached was to settle claims made upon debtors by their creditors (almost always in favor
of the latter). And it was a world of exorbitant debt. The Galilaean peasantry to whom Christ first brought his good tidings had suffered for years
under the taxes exacted by Herod the Great; many whose taxes had fallen
into arrears had been reduced from freeholders to bound tenants by ex-
propriations of their already meager estates, or because they had been
forced to secure loans they could not repay with their lands and goods.
The tax collectors, the creditors, and the courts had long conspired to
make rural peoples and the disenfranchised of the towns and cities into
captives of their debts. And at times, of course, the only way those debts
could be resolved was by the sale of debtor families into slavery. Moreover, the restraint that the Sabbatical cycle had imposed on predatory
lending practices had been effectively nullified by the legal convention of
the *prosboul,* by which a creditor could place outstanding promissory
notes in escrow with the courts, along with an authorization for the
courts to collect payments (and retain fees), thus allowing that creditor
to evade the requirements of the Law. It was a practice that assured that
credit would continue to be available; but it was also one that made possible the sort of unrelieved exploitations of the indigent through permanent indebtedness that the Mosaic Code had sought with such extraordinary compassion to prevent.

One sees in the Epistle of James something of the resentment the
poor had come to feel toward those who subjected them to the constant
terror that they might at any moment be robbed of what little substance
they possessed by the suborned machinery of "justice": "Do not the rich
oppress you, and haul you into law courts as well? Do they not blaspheme
the good name that has been invoked upon you?" (James 2:6–7). And
Christ's words leave one in no doubt regarding his indignation at pitiless
creditors: in the parable of the unmerciful servant (Matt. 18:21–35); in his
furious denunciations of the hypocrites among the scribes and Pharisees
who, while making a show of piety, betrayed the mercy of the Law by "de-
vouring" the homes of widows whose husbands had died insolvent (Matt.
23:14; Mark 12:40); in the parable of the unrighteous steward, where the
exaggerated debts falsely accounted against the poor are called the "Mammon of injustice," and the unscrupulous steward who allows the debtors
to reduce those charges to their fair amounts is praised for his wisdom,
even though he acts from self-interest (Luke 16:1–13). In fact, Christ's

teachings on these matters could scarcely be more uncompromising in their hostility to the prudential concerns that had led to the creation of the *prosboul*, or more recklessly anarchic in their disregard of the economic consequences of ignoring those concerns. He tells his listeners not only to give freely to all who might ask—or, for that matter, might seize—anything from them (Luke 6:30) but also to lend to those in need without any desire for return (Luke 6:33–34). For those who seek the Kingdom of God, every year is the Sabbatical year, every year is the Jubilee. To the debtors of his time, on the other hand, Christ's advice was singularly and unspectacularly pragmatic: to try to settle suits out of court, even if one must do so on the way to judgment, on the road or in the street, before a judge can remand one to the court's officers for incarceration (Matt. 5:25–26; Luke 12:58). Do not refuse the plaintiff his plaint; in fact, give him more than he asks (Matt. 5:40).

III

Again, though, as I have said, we rarely notice how persistent a theme the issue of indebtedness is in Christ's teachings. And again, as I have also said, conventions of translation and habits of thought are chiefly to blame. In the actual text of the Sermon on the Mount, for instance, at least in the original Greek, an ominously archetypal figure, identified simply as "the wicked man" (ὁ πονηρός), makes a brief appearance. He is almost certainly meant to be understood as a depiction of the sort of avaricious, disingenuous, and rapacious man who routinely abuses, deceives, defrauds, and plunders the poor. It is he who ensnares men with false promises wrapped in a haze of preposterously extravagant oaths (Matt. 5:37), and he whom Christ forbids his followers to "oppose by force" (Matt. 5:39), and he from whom one should request deliverance whenever one comes before God in prayer (Matt. 5:13). And yet in most translations—and, more generally, in Christian consciousness—he is all but invisible. In the first instance, he is usually mistaken for the devil (quite illogically), while in the latter two he is altogether displaced by an abstraction, "evil," which has no real connection to the original Greek at all. This is a pity. And, really, it is somewhat absurd. Christian tradition has produced few developments more bizarre, for instance, than the transformation of the petitionary phrases of the Lord's Prayer in Christian thinking—and in Christian translations of scripture—into a series of supplications for absolution of sins, protection against spiritual temptation, and immunity from the threat of "evil." They are nothing of the kind. They are, quite explicitly, requests for—in order—adequate nourishment, debt relief, avoidance of arraignment before the courts, and rescue from the depredations of powerful but unprincipled men. The prayer as a whole is a prayer for the poor—and for the poor only. To see this, one need only look with unprejudiced eyes at the text as it appears in the gospel:

> Πάτερ ἡμῶν ὁ ἐν τοῖς οὐρανοῖς·
> ἁγιασθήτω τὸ ὄνομά σου·
> ἐλθέτω ἡ βασιλεία σου·
> γενηθήτω τὸ θέλημά σου, ὡς ἐν οὐρανῷ καὶ ἐπὶ γῆς·
> τὸν ἄρτον ἡμῶν τὸν ἐπιούσιον δὸς ἡμῖν σήμερον·
> καὶ ἄφες ἡμῖν τὰ ὀφειλήματα ἡμῶν, ὡς καὶ ἡμεῖς ἀφήκαμεν τοῖς
>   ὀφειλέταις ἡμῶν·
> καὶ μὴ εἰσενέγκῃς ἡμᾶς εἰς πειρασμόν, ἀλλὰ ῥῦσαι ἡμᾶς ἀπὸ τοῦ
>   πονηροῦ.

Most Christians who recite the Lord's Prayer in English—or what they take to be the Lord's Prayer—could be pardoned for failing to grasp what is at stake in these lines. The standard rendering, after all, quite successfully dissolves the hard, mundane, practical substance of those petitions into vague, ethereal, painless pieties. And, admittedly, the familiar translation of the prayer's first half is sound enough; Christ did instruct his listeners to address God as their Father in "the heavens," to hallow his name, to entreat the Kingdom's advent, and to wish for God's will to be accomplished here below as there above. But the second half it reduces to something less than a shadow of the original. "Daily bread," admittedly, is almost accurate enough, though the phrase would better be rendered "bread adequate for the day's needs"; but I doubt most of us quite hear the note of desperation in that phrase "τὸν ἄρτον ἡμῶν τὸν ἐπιούσιον δὸς ἡμῖν σήμερον"—the very real uncertainty, suffered *every* day, concerning whether *today* one will have enough food to survive. The next lines, moreover, the standard rendering comes nowhere near representing correctly. Simply said, ὀφειλήματα are not "transgressions" but "debts"; nor are they "debts" in a metaphorical sense—they are not sins that require some penance or recompense on our part—but are in fact quite literally the crushing burden of financial obligations under which the poor labor and suffer and die, to the advantage of the most merciless of their creditors. And the imperative ἄφες is a plea not for forgiveness in the moral sense but for remission of those obligations. As for the word πειρασμός, it certainly ought not to be read as "temptation" (as though it could be applied to a roving eye, a longing for chocolate, or an inclination toward embezzlement); it properly means "trial" and here almost certainly refers to literal trial in court under a suit brought by a creditor. And the closing petition's final invocation of "the evil man"—not "evil" in the abstract, or even the "evil one" in the sense of the devil—is almost certainly a reference to a creditor of an especially heartless and unscrupulous kind. Perhaps, then, a more faithful rendering of those petitions would be something along the lines of: "Give us our bread today, in a quantity sufficient for the whole of the day. And grant us relief from our debts, to the very degree that we grant relief to those who are indebted to us. And do not bring us to trial in court, but rather rescue us from the wicked man [who would sue us]."

It is easy to understand, obviously, how it is that over the centuries the Lord's Prayer should have come to be something else in the Christian imagination—something less specific, less concrete, more comprehensive, more unrelated to any specific economic conditions or any particular station in society. It could scarcely have served as the model of Christian supplication for all the baptized if its social provocations had remained too transparent or if it had remained too obviously an epitome of Christ's "preferential option" for the destitute and disenfranchised. After all, the tender feelings of the rich require protection too; their consciences should not be exposed to the pitiless light of moral absolutes. How else could the banker who has just foreclosed on a family home recite the Lord's Prayer in church without being made to feel uncomfortable? Even so, it was originally, and remains, a prayer for the poor, as I have said—a prayer, that is, for the poor alone to pray. Down the centuries, wealthy Christians have prayed it as well, of course, or at least have prayed a rough simulacrum of it. And God bless them for their sincerity. But, to tell the truth, it was never meant for them. Quite—one has to be honest here—the opposite.

28

Different Idioms, Different Worlds

Various Notes on Translating
the New Testament

I: The Mythology of the "Historical Present"

I should not take exception, I suppose, if critics occasionally question my choice to render all Greek present-tense verbs as English present-tense verbs in my recent translation of the New Testament. The same choice was made, as it happens, by Tyndale and by his successors on the committee of scholars who produced the King James Version, but most modern readers are so distracted by the older, nonsibilant form of third-person singular constructions that they generally fail to notice that when "Jesus saith" something or "goeth" somewhere he is doing so in a kind of temporally abstract narrative now. As far as I am concerned, this is the only way in which the texts should be rendered. Even so, while I am convinced that those who think otherwise are quite mistaken, I have to admit that they have at least come by their prejudice honestly, since they have been systematically misinformed on the issue all through the years of their theological education. For better than half a century, seminarians and divinity school students and teachers of the New Testament, all of whom typically began their study of Greek some time in their twenties (and then only the Greek of the New Testament texts, as filtered through defective traditions of translation and interpretation), have been indoctrinated with a remarkable quantity of nonsense regarding the use of tenses in Greek historical narratives from late antiquity. In particular, they have been taught to think that the constant but irregular use of present-tense verbs in the Gospels of Matthew, Mark, and John (it occurs very rarely in Luke) is in fact both regular and internally cogent and merely reflects a system of tenses different from that of modern European languages. They have been instructed as well to believe that, in context, these verbs would not have struck the ears of first-century auditors of the texts as shifts from past to present, incongruous or otherwise. They have also been told that this is a consequence of the way tenses originally developed in Indo-European tongues: that is, as indices not of the temporal *locations* of actions, so to speak, but rather of their temporal *quality* or "action types" (*Aktionsarten*). Thus, when reading the gospels, we will (or, in theory, should) find that the aorist is used strictly to indicate a punctiliar action, the perfect to indicate (obviously) an action in a perfected state, and the present to indicate an iterative or durative action. That means that the present tense, when used in a narrative of past events, supposedly sometimes has an imperfect force, sometimes is used of actions that continue into the real present, sometimes refers to repeated actions, sometimes describes a "gnomic" activity that is timelessly the case . . . . All of which sounds convincing so long as one does not actually attempt to apply this *Aktionsart* theory to the words on the page, where one will find nothing like a systematic employment of the present tense that fits the alleged pattern. "They crucify him" clearly describes neither a durative nor an iterative action (except, perhaps, in the mystical "Origenian" sense that Christ will be on the cross till the end of all things). In fact, the actual use of tenses in the gospel texts is so haphazard that one and the same action is often related in a confusion of tenses, the present alongside the aorist or the perfect. And so, as one last desperate attempt at rationalizing the indiscriminate, those same poor seminarians and divinity students and New Testament teachers have been taught that the historical present is in fact used to indicate *Aspekt*, temporal aspect, which is to say, the way an action appears from the point of view of the agents in the story (continuous or completed, principally). This, at least, has the advantage of being an unfalsifiable assertion, since of course all actions in a historical narrative are (or were) present events from the perspective of those who were there at the time. But, of course, that is why it is a meaningless claim. By that logic, everything and anything can be written in the present tense. Again, it is true that many very ancient tongues used tenses as indications of types or states of actions; but, also again, by the first century this was not the case in Greek and certainly does not explain the sudden spasmodic shifts to a present-tense verb in first-century Greek narratives about the past. Moreover, the texts of the New Testament prove every bit as resistant to this theory as to that of *Aktionsarten*, for the simple reason that, as I have just noted, the various tenses are typically combined utterly unsystematically in the narratives' various individual episodes, and even in one and the same sentence, clause, or phrase.

The truth is that all of these approaches are deeply misleading. They combine anachronism with bad reasoning, with the occasional banal truism tossed in. Especially hopeless is the *Aspekt* argument; one need only think about it for more than a brief moment to recognize its illogic. Yes, one can successfully apply it to certain verses (Matt. 20:30, for example: καὶ ἰδοὺ δύο τυφλοὶ καθήμενοι παρὰ τὴν ὁδὸν ἀκούσαντες ὅτι Ἰησοῦς παράγει, ἔκραξαν λέγοντες· ἐλέησον ἡμᾶς, [κύριε,] υἱὸς Δαυίδ), but of a great many more it makes no particular sense at all. Moreover, while gnomic uses of the present tense are fairly common to all languages—if I say, "I write for a living," I do not mean to suggest that I am writing in the very moment of the utterance—this has no bearing on the issue of how to render descriptions of past actions. It is intelligible for me to write a sentence like "He knew that I write for a living," but only because my present is still contained within the frame of what "he" knew about me *then*. I would not, however, write a sentence like "John Adams knew that Thomas Jefferson lives at Monticello" for the obvious reason that neither of the subjects in that sentence still belongs to a present to which I may meaningfully refer. And the *koinē* Greek of the New Testament possessed no greater "aspectual" temporal plasticity than our languages do today.

As for the invocation of *Aktionsart* theory, on the other hand, this merely betrays a surprisingly meager knowledge of Greek's various epochs. I am not perfectly certain about this, but I suspect that it was originally an influential article by Kurt von Fritz ("The So-Called Historical Present in Early Greek," *Word* 5 [1949]: 186–201) that alerted many New Testament teachers to the interesting truth that early Indo-European languages employed tenses as indices of the types rather than the times of actions and events. It must have seemed a blessed discovery. Ever eager to exculpate the evangelists as much as possible of any charge of literary infelicity or grammatical laxity, they saw at once a way of convincing themselves that the Gospels of Matthew, Mark, and John are not at all slapdash in their use of tenses but rather in fact unfold in rigorously precise accord with a method of historical exposition that was standard in the first century. Again, so long as one did not attempt to make the scheme fit the texts too closely, it seemed a good way of disentangling all those temporally heterogeneous sentences in the gospels. Sadly, what those hopeful Christian scholars were overlooking was that von Fritz was a philologist and was describing a Greek far older and grammatically far more complex than the simplified *koinē* of the first century. They should have noticed, at the very least, that von Fritz states in his article that the systematic use of tenses to indicate *Aktionsarten* in written Greek was already in decay before the time of Xenophon. By the time of the New Testament, Greek verbs were more or less invariably bound to temporal designations, as in modern European tongues. If anything remains of the older historical present in the New Testament, it is in the attenuated form of the occasional use of a present tense as something like a durative imperfect (such as Matt. 2:22: Ἀκούσας δὲ ὅτι Ἀρχέλαος βασιλεύει τῆς Ἰουδαίας ἀντὶ τοῦ πατρὸς αὐτοῦ Ἡρῴδου ἐφοβήθη ἐκεῖ ἀπελθεῖν), where we today would generally use a preterit or atemporal infinitive construction (at least, when writing). Even then, such verses are emblematic, not of any large and consistent narrative practice, or of some standard method for capturing the *Aspekt* position of some supposed agent in the tale, or of an *Aktionsart* function of tenses of the kind that obtained in the Indo-European dawn of the Greek tongue, but rather just of a few random idiomatic habits of speech and nothing more.

All these theories, to be honest, serve only to obscure the correct and much simpler explanation of the historical present as employed in late antique Greek literature—which is that it is an example of a perfectly ordinary practice in just about any language that possesses tenses at all, including ours. One of the odder critiques that floated my way in regard to my version of the New Testament was the curious suggestion of one indignant seminary teacher that I had rendered the "historical present" of the text into the English "literal present." *Literal*, forsooth. I am not sure what that could possibly mean, since I am quite certain that my translation does nothing to give the impression that the events of the gospel are occurring in the very moment that the texts are being read. In point of fact, I have merely rendered the *Greek* historical present as the *English* historical present. Here is what, for me, is the most bewildering aspect of the now standard claims made for and by seminarians and divinity students and teachers of the New Testament: the failure to notice that there is nothing at all in the texts' use of the historical present that is particularly alien to our own habits of historical narrative. In one notable respect, of course, the standard view is correct: in late antiquity, the effect of the use of the historical present on listeners to a text (and most persons received texts through the ear) would not have been jarring; but this is not because the shift in tense would have been grammatically inconspicuous. Rather, the present would have been heard *as* the present in the temporal sense but would nevertheless have seemed perfectly natural in the context of a tale told about the past. We today do the same thing; the difference is that we tend to limit the practice to spoken stories. "*I went to my girlfriend's house, because she wasn't answering her phone. When I got there, I see that her lights are on. Good. So I went to the door and knocked, just wanting to see if she's all right. I thought everything was fine between us. But suddenly the door opens like it's being blasted off its hinges and she's standing there staring at me furiously and holding a hammer in her hand. She doesn't say anything. She just gazes at me with a look of pure hatred in her eyes. And now I'm beginning to think something might be wrong. I attempt a cheerful smile and say, 'Can I come in?' Maybe that was the wrong way to start, because after several seconds had passed in silence . . .*" As we tell our tales, we move effortlessly and intuitively between temporal perspectives, wholly unsystematically but perfectly coherently, sensing—without needing any clear rule for doing so—when the action spontaneously invites a more immediate descriptive language and when the action should drift back into its more remote temporal frame. It is true that, in the late antique world, this fluidity of tense is characteristic of a great many *written* texts, as is not the case for us; but we should recall that, in that age, even a written text was also an oral text, both in the sense that it had been dictated by the author to an amanuensis and in the sense that it was heard by most of its "readers" as read aloud by a lector. So, the more colloquial the narration, and the less refined the author, the more the text reflects the cadences and qualities of natural speech. The reason that Luke almost never uses the historical present is that he is the most

educated and literarily accomplished of the evangelists and has undertaken not merely to tell a story but rather to indite a formally impeccable
and intellectually respectable treatise. The other three evangelists simply
lack his refinement as a writer or his ambition for his text, even if they
possess considerable natural gifts as storytellers. Their style might be denominated as "phrastic" and his as "syngrammatic." And, indeed, this is
what I should like, humbly, to submit to New Testament scholarship as
my contribution to its philological terminology—and, God knows, the
academy can never have enough obscure jargon. Rather than continuing
to propound an elaborate but empirically false account of the historical
past, in order to make the texts of the New Testament seem more polished than they are, we should learn simply to appreciate the difference
between phrastic and syngrammatic textual types. And, when translating
texts from the former category, we should render all the verbs in the
Greek originals into their true English equivalents—past as past, present
as present—because we recognize that this constant shifting of tenses is
an essential and even precious element of each text's rhythm, imaginative atmosphere, and narrative voice, the suppression of which is an incalculable impoverishment.

II: Idioms and Worlds

Admittedly, there are small differences between the ways the historical
present is used in the gospels and the ways we would use it in telling a
tale today. These are differences not of method, however, but only of tone,
of inflection, of discrete cultural modalities of memory and storytelling.
And it is precisely such differences, as it happens, that I am probably
most anxious should not be lost. Far worse, it seems to me, than failing
to see the ways in which ancient practices of narrative resemble our own
is failing to recognize and respect all the ways in which they are alien. As
I have said elsewhere, I do not believe that the difference between ancient
and modern idioms is simply a difference between distinct ways of saying the same things. Rather, it is a difference between distinct ways of
seeing reality, and therefore even the most seemingly impenetrable of
ancient idioms ought to be regarded as inviolable by the translator. One
should never transform an apparently obsolete metaphor or baffling

image into what one imagines to be its functional equivalent among the conventional expressions of the present. In fact, I would apply this principle even in cases of what might seem like mere differences of grammatical structure. It seems obvious, for instance, to write "the Father's beloved Son" as the reasonable English rendering of a Greek phrase that would more literally be rendered as "the Son of the Father's love"; and perhaps, in most circumstances, it would be wise to do so. But, when attempting to convey the text of scripture with as much immediacy as possible to those who know no Greek, I think it better to pause and reflect on whether, when comparing two such phrases, the difference in the very relations of words—which, for instance, are substantives or which are adjectives—might not grant us some small, maybe obscure access to another way of understanding a whole host of conceptual relations. Even, however, if one is not quite so fastidious as all that, one should absolutely never exchange the imagery of ancient turns of phrase for expressions proper to our time—especially where this would mean sacrificing the obscure grandeur and mystery of poetic tropes for the drearily prosaic phrases to which modern languages are more naturally prone. Where the original text gives the translator a concrete, delightfully naive metaphor like "apple of his eye," it is a crime against both good taste and hermeneutical discernment to write "his eyeball." Where the original text speaks of "many waters," the translator must not speak of, say, "a great quantity of water." Where the text tells us that "he was full of years," it is an inexcusable vulgarity to write "he was very old." Where the text speaks of "David's seed," it is not only an unseemly prudery to write "David's descendants" but also an act of crass indifference to a vast range of metaphorical associations: husbandry and harvests, fruition and fertility, roots and flowers, abundance and growth . . . Nor should we allow ourselves to imagine that the beauty and poetry of these deeply embedded metaphors and finely wrought turns of phrase are mere appearances, effects not of anything intrinsic to the language of the texts but only of their foreignness to us today. I have spoken elsewhere of the obstinately literal, "Nabokovian" philosophy I obeyed when making my translation of the New Testament, principally out of my desire to capture the distinct voices of the authors as well as I could (it seems to me, that is, that if the strange, obsessive, almost incantatory repetitiveness of John's Gospel, with its syntactically elementary but oddly sublime phrasing, does not read very differently from the precipitous, jagged, broken, and almost neurotically restless terseness of Mark's, something extremely important has been lost). But I should note as well that my approach was also dictated in great part by a view of the interrelation of the history of language and the history of perception somewhat similar to that of Owen Barfield. Poetry is more primordial to language than is prose, and poetic apprehension more original and natural than the more starkly calculative way of seeing things reflected in our "developed" tongues, and the world that inhabits and crystallizes within the language of one age is not the same as that which exists in another. Even physical qualities, it is arguable—color, perspective, sonorities, and so forth—are experienced differently in different epochs of the evolution of language and of the manner in which language constructs reality (at least, that is one way of understanding, say, the seemingly very strange color palette of Homeric Greek). All the subtle interweavings and disjunctions that compose the world's phenomenal and conceptual orders are established and sustained in grammar and semantics, metaphor and metonymy. Hence the poetry of ancient idioms must always be jealously guarded and preserved by the translator, so that the worlds they figure forth are never lost. To render the still living metaphors of ancient texts into the drab, denatured language and dead metaphors that shape and sustain our modern perspective is philistinism; to pursue "dynamic equivalence" is pure barbarism.

III: τεταγμένοι, χειμάρρος, ἀρσενοκοίτης, μαλακός, δεισιδαιμονέστερος, κόσμος

I would place most of the reviewers of my translation in four general classes: there are those whose principal interests are literary, and who base their judgments not on any special academic expertise or scholarly allegiances but only on their immediate reactions to a text; there are those who are—or regard themselves as—experts in New Testament studies; there are classicists; and there are those who have firm theological opinions that they expect to be confirmed by any respectable reading or rendering of scriptural texts. From the first class, the reviews have all been quite agreeable. From the second class, whether the reviewer is entirely enthusiastic or somewhat tepid about my work, there invariably comes the obligatory and staggeringly boring portion of the review where he or she lists the words or phrases that he or she would have translated differently (either for purely arbitrary reasons of taste or because he or she has published on those particular passages in the past and is rather disappointed not to have influenced the translation). From the third class, again, the reviews have all been pleasant to read from my perspective, but they too tend to include lists of alternative renderings (though generally, as classicists tend to know ancient Greek and ancient literature better than most New Testament scholars do, their lists are more interesting). From the fourth class, the observations are frequently doctrinaire and confused (one well-meaning young divinity school teacher, Wesley Hill, produced a review that, though fervently sincere, struck me as an almost perfect digest of every significant conceptual and hermeneutical error one can make in approaching the New Testament—not, I feel sure, because of any great intellectual limitations on Hill's part but because he has been taught to hold and cherish a great many false beliefs, scholarly and theological, of which he is yet to be disabused). At the end of the ordeal of submitting my translation to reviews (or near the end, since a few more keep trickling in), I have come away with no desire to amend my work, at least not as a result of anything the reviewers have said, but I have assembled a small list of words regarding which I suppose some further clarification might be in order. So:

1. τεταγμένοι. I have to admit that I know practically nothing about the scriptural arguments current among the various factions of Reformed tradition. In my translation, however, I inadvertently stumbled across one of the objects of contention littering the battlefield. It was just lying there unobtrusively in Acts 13:48: Ἀκούοντα δὲ τὰ ἔθνη ἔχαιρον καὶ ἐδόξαζον τὸν λόγον τοῦ κυρίου καὶ ἐπίστευσαν ὅσοι ἦσαν τεταγμένοι εἰς ζωὴν αἰώνιον. I rendered the verse thus: "And hearing this the gentiles were elated and gave glory to the Lord's word, and as many as were disposed to the life of the Age had faith." Apparently—at least, so I was informed by an earnest email sent to me by a Presbyterian minister—those of the Reformed tradition who insist upon a strict doctrine of predestination attach a great deal of significance to this verse and are absolutely convinced that the homely participle τεταγμένοι should be rendered at least as "ordained" and ideally as "predestined." My correspondent even accused me of intentionally enfeebling the verb for theological reasons. Actually, all I intentionally did was translate the word accurately; and, I have to say, one

must have a very small acquaintance with ancient Greek literature in general to imagine that τεταγμένοι could possibly bear the hermeneutical burden that this stream of Calvinist tradition apparently assigns it (but, then again, given that Luke's writings militate so thoroughly against the predestinarian line, I suppose old-fashioned Calvinists must grasp at whatever straws they can). True, the verb τάσσω does in fact mean "ordain," in the now nearly obsolete proper sense of "set in order," "arrange," "appoint," or "assign to a station"; in matters military, to which it has a common application, it means something along the lines of arranging soldiers in rank and file, or assigning them their stations on the battlements; principally, though, the emphasis in the verb is not upon the act of giving commands but only upon the work of setting things in appropriate order to prepare them for battle or unexpected aggression. In the passive or middle voice, therefore (and τεταγμένοι could be taken as either), its participial form has, at most, the force of "arranged," "ready for," "prepared for," "suited to," or (again) "disposed to." It would be absolutely misleading to render the participle as "predestined," as the verb has nothing to do with determining any fixed result. I soon learned that, among representatives of the Reformed factions, those of Arminian leanings expend a great deal of energy arguing that the participle should be read in the middle voice rather than the passive, and this is probably correct as far as it goes, both idiomatically and in the context of Acts. The tale, as one might recall, concerns the second of two sermons delivered by Paul on successive sabbaths at the synagogue in Pisidian Antioch: the first having made so great an impression on both the Jews and the gentile "God-fearers" of the congregation, Paul and Barnabas were invited to return the next week to continue their disquisition; but, on the second occasion, the Jewish congregants rejected Paul's message as heretical, having turned against it in the interim, while many of the gentiles were persuaded to accept it. It makes sense, then, to say that the latter group had "prepared themselves" or "disposed themselves" (as τεταγμένοι would mean if read as middle voice) to the life of the Age to come, since they had been ready since the previous week to be persuaded by Paul and Barnabas. Such a reading would also fit nicely with verse 46, where Paul tells the Jewish congregants, "You have passed judgment on yourselves"—or, better perhaps, "proved yourselves" (κρίνετε)—as unworthy of that life. One could, then, read the whole passage as saying that each of the two groups had disposed itself either for or against the gospel. But, really, it does not matter whether the participle is read as passive or middle; in either case, as any survey of the verb's use in the literature of antiquity would confirm, it has much the same force: "ready," "disposed to," "properly placed." To take it as a statement to the effect that God had irresistibly predestined a certain group of gentiles in Pisidian Antioch for eternal life *ante praevisa merita*, and to encumber the text with a doctrine of which it is wholly innocent, is both a philological and an exegetical catachresis (but, then again, in my confessionally bigoted soul, I tend to think that true of the Reformed theology of predestination as a whole).

2. χειμάρρος. A few readers, curiously enough, have expressed displeasure at my reading of John 18:1: Ταῦτα εἰπὼν Ἰησοῦς ἐξῆλθεν σὺν τοῖς μαθηταῖς αὐτοῦ πέραν τοῦ χειμάρρου τοῦ Κεδρὼν ὅπου ἦν κῆπος, εἰς ὃν εἰσῆλθεν αὐτὸς καὶ οἱ μαθηταὶ αὐτοῦ—which I render as "Having said these things, Jesus went forth with his disciples across the Kedron, which flows in the winter, to where there was a garden, which he and his disciples entered." The issue, quaintly enough, is the single word χείμαρρος (which was, more originally, χειμάρροος). This word, so the argument goes, did originally mean a "winter torrent" or "winterbourne" or "winter freshet," but by the first century it often had come to mean any torrent or stream; so why had I not merely written (as is common) "the brook Kedron?" One correspondent was even somewhat theatrically passionate on the matter. In point of fact, while the word could be used to indicate any torrent or flowing stream in the time of the New Testament, it could also be used with the more technical sense not only of a winter torrent in full flow but also of a streambed or ravine in which waters flow *only* during the winter months. And such is the case here. The Kedron or Kidron was (and still is) just such a ravine: a *nahal*, to use the Hebrew term, or a *wadi*, to use the Arabic. It lies to the east of Jerusalem, between the city and the Mount of Olives, and is dry for most of the year; it flows only during the winter's rainy season, when waters are carried down from higher elevations. Thus, precisely to indicate that it is just such a *nahal*, the Septuagint calls it χειμάρρους Κεδρών or χειμάρρους τῶν Κέδρων. Indeed, this very particular term is the standard translation of *nahal* throughout the Septuagint (strikingly, for instance, in Job 6:15, where it is used specifically to indicate a streambed that has run dry), and

so this should be presumed to be its function in all scriptural Greek. Nor is it mere attention to a technical detail, much less pointless pedantry, to insist on preserving this connotation in translating the passage from John. That the Kedron is specifically identified as a χείμαρρος or *naḥal* or *wadi* may be little more than an incidental feature of the text; but one dare not assume this to be the case. In John's Gospel most especially— consisting as it does in so intricate a web of symbolic associations—no image that appears in the text can safely be ignored, and most particularly not an image of water (flowing or not flowing, winter or summer, living or dead).

3. ἀρσενοκοίτης. I have no desire to rehearse the history of arguments surrounding Paul's apparent neologism in 1 Corinthians 6:9 (found also in the pseudo-Pauline 1 Tim. 1:10). Literally, it means "a man who beds males." It is popular among many conservative Christians, Evangelicals in particular, to take this as simply meaning "a homosexual" or "a gay man," for obvious reasons of social ideology. In my translation, however, I took the word as meaning a man who uses catamites. I do not believe that the ancient world had any clear concept of sexual orientation. There was an awareness of a variety of erotic tastes and of a fairly large spectrum of erotic behaviors, but not of enduring or innate homoerotic identities. The range of one's erotic activities was usually regarded as an index only of the exuberance of one's appetites and the latitude of one's inclinations. Romans 1:26–27 leaves no doubt which of those activities Paul especially condemned; but, in the culture in which Paul lived and wrote, the idea of deep and enduring romantic liaisons between adults of the same sex (most of whom would have been expected to be married and to have indulged in sexual congress outside of the marriage bed only as recreation, generally through concubines or prostitutes) scarcely had any existence at all (except, perhaps, among particularly sophisticated members of the patrician caste). The most common form of male homoerotic activity would have been a grown man's use of a young, even perhaps prepubescent male slave, one either in that man's possession or available at a price. Paul almost certainly coined the word (if it was his invention) from two verses in Leviticus as they appear in the Septuagint: Leviticus 18:22 (καὶ μετὰ ἄρσενος οὐ κοιμηθήσῃ κοίτην γυναικός· βδέλυγμα γάρ ἐστιν) and Leviticus 20:13 (καὶ ὃς ἂν κοιμηθῇ μετὰ ἄρσενος κοίτην

γυναικός, βδέλυγμα ἐποίησαν ἀμφότεροι· θανατούσθωσαν, ἔνοχοί εἰσιν). Two or three readers have suggested to me that this very fact proves that the word really ought to be rendered as "homosexual" after all. I am not sure why. In all likelihood, both of those verses also apply to the abuse of young male slaves by their masters or clients. I cannot begin to imagine what wildly anachronistic mental pictures of ancient Canaan or Israel those readers cherish.

4. μαλακός. 1 Corinthians 6:9 also mentions μαλακοί among those who are unfit for the Kingdom. The word μαλακός means "soft" and in antiquity could be used of fine fabrics, sweet tones played on a lyre, delicious breezes, and any number of other things agreeable to the senses. It had, moreover, a variety of connotations when applied to a man. Used in a good sense, it often meant gentle, delicate, mild, and congenial. Used in an opprobrious sense, it tended to mean self-indulgent, dainty, cowardly, luxuriant, morally or physically weak, lazy, and effeminate. Obviously Paul is employing it in the latter manner, as a term of denigration. In my translation, I rendered μαλακοί as "feckless sensualists," which provoked one or two objections. Again, a certain number of interpreters, for reasons of ideology (not to mention an obvious obsession with the issue), take μαλακός here as a word meaning something like "the passive partner in male homoerotic acts." There is no real warrant for this supposition, however; in fact, this definition is certainly wrong in any but a very particular context. For one thing, the textual evidence for such a reading, from any period of Greek antiquity, suggests a far less specific meaning. More to the point, though, persons who take the word in precisely that sense are basing their views on a distinctively modern set of psychological and moral presuppositions. It may be common today to associate effeminacy with homosexuality, but ancient persons generally did not do so. They saw no necessary connection between the two. In fact, a man was as likely to be called a μαλακός precisely because he was overly fond of the company of women and as a result spent an inordinate amount of time engaged in sexual relations with them. This, in fact, is one of the ways in which effeminacy was diagnosed in the *Physiognomonica*, an ancient physiognomic treatise traditionally but spuriously attributed to Aristotle. It was, for much of antiquity, early and late, considered a kind of unmanly daintiness to delight so much in women

that, once conjugal duty had been discharged or natural desire exhausted, one did not soon tire of feminine embraces and become anxious to return to the company of men. It was generally believed that only the weaker, more epicene sort of male, with something of a shamefully delicate and floriated personality, really cared to dally with Amaryllis in the shade. Think of Paris drowsily luxuriating in Helen's bed: the very type of the lazy and foppish sybarite. Thus it is that, in Plato's *Symposium*, Aristophanes notes, as if stating the obvious, that men who feel amorous toward other men are by far the most virile kind of lovers. Thus too Plutarch, in *Moralia* 7—the "Dialogue on Eros"—associates μαλακία with men who are romantically attracted to women, since such men must clearly be drawn toward things soft and yielding. And thus the Pseudo-Lucian, in his *Erotes*, treats lovers of women as the most effete lovers of all. True, within a homoerotic relationship, a male who occupied the "submissive" or "recipient" role was regarded as the μαλακός partner in the act of coition (and, given the ubiquitous misogyny of the age, this was seen as at once a "feminine" and a slightly shameful station); but the precise term for the one who occupied that role was κίναιδος, "catamite." Conversely, in a heterosexual relationship, the man was considered a μαλακός if he enjoyed the actual *company* of women, rather than just the use of their bodies. In many ancient texts, in fact, it is taken for granted that men who adopted effeminate manners, jewelry, perfumes, cosmetics, and sumptuous clothing did so precisely to make themselves irresistible to women, as it was assumed that women are most easily charmed by pretty, gracile youths, or by men capable of a certain feminine suavity. Chariton of Aphrodisias, in his novel *Callirhoe* (written, perhaps, about the same time as Paul's epistles or slightly later), provides a perfect portrait of such a lothario: a "prattling scrounger" (παράσιτος στωμύλος) whom a failed and envious suitor from Agracas has deputed to fortify malicious rumors impugning the honor of the beautiful Callirhoe by seducing her handmaid, thus allowing Callirhoe's young husband Chaereas to see him slipping into the house at night bedizened with all the common devices of the seducer's art: "gleaming hair and ringlets redolent with unctuous sweet perfumes, eyes daubed with paint, effeminate [*malakos*] habiliments, dainty little sandals . . . gaudily heavy rings glisten[ing]" (κόμην εἶχε λιπαρὰν καὶ βοστρύχους μύρων ἀποπνέοντας, ὀφθαλμοὺς ὑπογεγραμμένους, ἱμάτιον μαλακόν, ὑπόδημα λεπτόν.

δακτύλιοι βαρεῖς ὑπέστιλβον; *Callirhoe* 1.4). Plautus (ca. 254–184 BCE) refers to both the homosexual and the heterosexual specimens of the type transliteratively, calling the former a *cinaedus malacus* (*Miles gloriosus* 3.1.668) and the latter (in his role as a polished philanderer trying to inveigle married women into adultery) a *moechus malacus* (*Truculentus* 2.7.599). All this being so, we can assume that Paul's obloquies are aimed at a much wider and vaguer category of men: maybe something along the lines of idle voluptuaries addicted to soft clothing and fine foods and pretty music and perfumed unguents and copious wine and the caresses of either women or boys.

5. δεισιδαιμονέστερος. The verse in question is Acts 17:22: Σταθεὶς δὲ [ὁ] Παῦλος ἐν μέσῳ τοῦ Ἀρείου πάγου ἔφη· ἄνδρες Ἀθηναῖοι, κατὰ πάντα ὡς δεισιδαιμονεστέρους ὑμᾶς θεωρῶ. In my version, this appears as "And Paul stood in the middle of the Areopagus and said, 'Athenian men, I observe how exceedingly reverent you are toward the daemonian in everything.'" I feel a certain sympathy for those who recoiled from this rendering, but I would defend it, if not to the death, at least to the point of spoiling a dinner conversation. I have never liked either of the standard alternatives for δεισιδαιμονέστερος: in the benign sense of the word, "exceedingly religious"; in the malign, "excessively superstitious." The latter is inapposite to this verse in any event, despite its use in some translations. It is clear that Paul is not berating the Athenians for their superstitions but rather commending them for their natural piety, so that he can then appropriate their altar to the unknown god for his message. But, even in other contexts, the term *superstitious* seems wrong, if only because we use that word to denounce foolish beliefs regarding wholly fantastic things; in the ancient world, by contrast, to be δεισιδαίμων was to be excessively afraid of numinous forces that were believed to be very real but not as dangerous or malicious as certain foolish persons imagined. Again, however, Paul is using the word in the good sense. For that, as I say, "religious" strikes me as an inadequate rendering. For one thing, the word refers explicitly not to the God or gods above the heavens. Neither Paul nor Luke would have used the word to indicate the sort of devotion appropriate to faith in the one God Most High from whom all things come; neither would most pagans have done so. The word has to do, rather, with the whole sacred realm of powers pervading this cosmos

and mediating between it and the exalted, supercelestial realm of the truly divine, τὸ θεῖον. The secondary, more proximate divine orders of *daimones*—*genii, longaevi*, aerial sprites, the ethereal and spiritual forces pervading nature, the rulers of the planetary spheres, the angelic or daemonic governors of the nations, the entire glittering and multifarious host of spirits and angels and elemental powers—composed a whole unseen hierarchy of gentle and terrible and glorious and mysterious presences, uniting the realm of generation and decay here below with the eternity of the empyrean beyond the turning spheres above. What Paul is almost certainly not saying to the Athenians in the Areopagus sermon is that they are already aware of the true nature of God Most High; hence his claim that it is precisely the god they do not know that will prove to be the true God. I should note, moreover, that Paul himself certainly believed in the reality of the daemonian realm. It was a central tenet of his gospel that it is precisely these powers that Christ has subdued, not so as to destroy them or condemn them, but so as to place them in proper order under his feet—even (to use the pseudo-Pauline or Pauline language of Col. 1:19–20) to reconcile them to himself—in order then to hand over the entire spiritual and natural totality of the cosmos to the Father, that God might be all in all (1 Cor. 15:25–28). All this being so, it seems to me that no translation should allow the presence of the "daemonian" dimension in Paul's reported language to go unrepresented.

6. κόσμος. The venerable Luke Timothy Johnson has claimed that nothing is gained by my choice to transliterate this word as "cosmos" rather than as "world." He could not be more wrong. I have explained the decision in the postscript to my translation and in other articles written since, so I shall not dwell long upon the issue here. I will simply note once more that, for us, the "world" is *either* this planet we live on *or* the totality of human society. But in the New Testament the word κόσμος almost always refers to the entire universe of physical, spiritual, terrestrial, and celestial reality—angels and demons no less than human beings and animals, planetary and astral heavens no less than sea and land. When the Fourth Gospel's author describes Christ as the one who descends "from above" into this cosmos to overthrow both it and its "archon," or when Paul speaks of Christ's conquest of the cosmic rulers and powers on high, neither is speaking merely of what we mean by "world." By retain-

ing the term *cosmos*, absolutely *everything* is gained. And not to retain it is to obscure a very great deal about the *world* of the New Testament.

IV: The Vale of Abraham

I may be entirely mistaken here, I confess it; that is why, in my footnotes for the tale of the rich man and Lazarus in Luke 16, I freely state that mine is a speculative rendering. But, if I am wrong, it is not because my case is weak. The text of Luke 16:22–23 reads thus: ἐγένετο δὲ ἀποθανεῖν τὸν πτωχὸν καὶ ἀπενεχθῆναι αὐτὸν ὑπὸ τῶν ἀγγέλων εἰς τὸν κόλπον Ἀβραάμ· ἀπέθανεν δὲ καὶ ὁ πλούσιος καὶ ἐτάφη. καὶ ἐν τῷ ᾅδῃ ἐπάρας τοὺς ὀφθαλμοὺς αὐτοῦ, ὑπάρχων ἐν βασάνοις, ὁρᾷ Ἀβραὰμ ἀπὸ μακρόθεν καὶ Λάζαρον ἐν τοῖς κόλποις αὐτοῦ. My version of the passage reads thus: "And it happened that the poor man died and was carried off by the angels into the Vale of Abraham; but the rich man also died and was entombed. And lifting up his eyes in Hades, being in torment, he sees Abraham far off and Lazarus in his vales." The issue, obviously, is my eccentric choice to render κόλπος not as the conventional "bosom," but as the aggressively unconventional "vale." N. T. Wright, for instance, in an article in the *Christian Century*, complained that I had perversely chosen the metaphorical meaning of the word over the literal and in so doing had ignored the ancient Jewish idiom of "Abraham's bosom." Actually, neither meaning is either more literal or more metaphorical than the other, but it is true that "bosom" might have been the more *common* meaning in the first century; and, were Luke merely a common writer rather than quite an educated one, that would be an extremely significant consideration. As for the ancient Jewish idiom to which Wright so cavalierly alludes, it never existed as far as we know; it is entirely his invention. There is, it is true, a fragment of papyrus from Alexandria, probably from about the same general era as Acts, that mentions the κόλπος of the three patriarchs; but, of course, that does not tell us how the term or the image is to be understood there either. In what sense could three men share a single bosom, after all? Surely one should assume the phrase means "their midst," or "among them," or "their special place," or "their sheltering care," or even (to risk a wild conjecture) "their vale." Then, from some centuries after the time of Acts, there is a single

Mishnaic phrase that *might* refer to the same image, in the tractate *Kiddushin* (72b), where the third-century figure Adda bar Ahava is described as seated within "Abraham's bosom" (presumably *not* a metaphor). But this, it is generally believed, is a usage without deep roots in antiquity, perhaps borrowed from the Christians and entirely unilluminating as to what the *Greek* phrase used by Luke back in the first century really meant. It is possible, I happily grant, that κόλπος should be taken as simply equivalent to the Hebrew *cheyq*—the breast, or the fold in a man's garment located at the level of his chest—and understood literally. But Luke did not write in Hebrew or Aramaic, and he lived in a Hellenistic and Roman Mediterranean world, and he used its language, and he conceived of reality in the terms common to his time. This is all very important to keep in mind, because Wright has a still odder complaint to raise against my treatment of the parable: he objects truculently to my observation, in my footnote to the episode, that the rich man and Lazarus are depicted as occupying two distinct regions of the *one* realm of the dead (Hades or Sheol). Apparently, Wright is of the opinion that the story instead places the rich man in something like the hell of later Christian imagination, and Lazarus in something like its heaven. This is, as it happens, extravagantly anachronistic. In fact, there is nothing here to debate at all. All good scholars of late antique Judaism, Christianity, or paganism are aware that, in the first century, the common picture of the afterlife shared by practically everyone was of a region of the dead in which there are places both of torment and of beatitude. The κόλπος of Abraham—however one translates the phrase—is something like the Elysian fields of Greek myth, a place of repose for the good and the just, located in the postmortem realm of souls. This is, after all, very much the picture provided by 1 Enoch, which first-century Jews and Christians alike tended to regard as a truly prophetic work, and which exercised an immense influence over Christian belief in the first few generations of the church (but I shall come to that presently).

First, though, it is worth noting that one of the stranger features of Luke's story is that, whereas verse 22 speaks of Abraham's κόλπος (in the singular, that is), verse 23 speaks instead of his κόλποι (in the plural). For me, at least in terms of tone and consistency of imagery, this shift in number militates against any preference for a physiological rather than a topological understanding of the term. "Inward parts"? Perhaps, but that is not quite the same thing as the image of Lazarus resting his head upon the chest and within the embrace of father Abraham. And here one has to understand that the word κόλπος really did have an enormous range of uses, almost none of which were metaphorical, strictly speaking, but some of which were nonetheless situated at the more poetical end of the rhetorical spectrum. A κόλπος was originally something folded or enclosed, and as a physiological designation could be used for just about everything from breast to viscera to uterus to female genitalia. It could also mean a purse or a fold in fabric; and as a word for the pectoral fold in a man's garment, in which he might carry money or papers, it acquired its association with the chest or bosom on which a head might tenderly be laid. Then again, it could also mean a lap, so perhaps we should think of Lazarus sitting in the lap of Abraham, or (for that matter) of the divine Son sitting in the lap of the Father (John 1:18). In either case, the image is a fetchingly sweet one, I suppose. But the word also meant other kinds of enclosed spaces, like bays or gulfs or valleys, especially when employed for evocative effect. Luke was clearly a man of refined literary tastes and education, surely with some training in rhetoric, and there would have been nothing outlandish in his giving his narrative a touch of—well, whatever the first-century equivalent of "Tennysonian" would be . . . Theocritan, perhaps—color by using the somewhat more ornate phrase. He is relating a fable about the lands of the dead, after all. Certainly, for the educated the word had a long literary pedigree. One thinks of Pindar, for instance, speaking of the victory that came "to Epharmostos in the Valley of Nemea": Νεμέας Ἐφαρμοστῷ κατὰ κόλπον (*Olympian Odes* 9.87). Or of Thucydides: καὶ ἔτι καὶ νῦν Πιερικὸς κόλπος καλεῖται, "and even now it is still called the Pierian Valley" (*Peloponnesian War* 2.99). In particular, the plural form used in verse 23 is reminiscent of Sophocles speaking of "the Valleys of Eleusinian Demeter, common to all," παγκοίνοις Ἐλευσινίας Δηοῦς ἐν κόλποις (*Antigone* 1121). Still, truth be told, none of this would have prompted my choice of translation if not also for my belief that I recognize the source of Luke's imagery.

Which brings me back to 1 Enoch. It is difficult to exaggerate how influential the intertestamental "Noachic" literature was for the Jews and then Christians of the first century. On the whole, too many New Testament scholars over the years have neglected properly to assess not only the three centuries of Hellenistic culture in which Jewish culture had been steeping by the time of Christ and the apostolic church but also the profound importance for the early church (quite explicit at numerous places in the New Testament) of the angelology, demonology, cosmology, and eschatology of texts like 1 Enoch and Jubilees. Too often in the past, the first-century Judaism of pious New Testament and early church studies has been a fantastic abstraction, decocted from equal parts the biblical prophets and later rabbinic Judaism, while the pervasive Greek and Persian and apocalyptic and other influences of that remarkably and gloriously culturally promiscuous age have been ignored or treated as extraneous minor features of late antique Judaism, as well as (of course) *corruptions*. I would, in fact, put N. T. Wright in this category of scholars. Whether or not that is wholly fair, though, this much I can say with confidence: no one who knows how intermixed the cultures of the Hellenistic world really were should be surprised by the suggestion that Luke's picture of the realm of the dead looks very much like the one that was, by his time, common to just about every Mediterranean and Near Eastern culture. Much less, however, should it surprise anyone to learn that Luke's imagery resembles that of the book of Enoch (from which, I think it likely, it was at least partially drawn). To see this, one must consult what remains of the original Greek text, since the complete Ge'ez translation preserved in the Ethiopian Bible contains a number of errors that obscure the picture (most consequentially, the Ethiopian translator regularly confused the adjective κοῖλος with the adjective κάλος). But in chapter 22 of the Greek text of the book's first section, "The Book of the Watchers," we are granted a vision of the realm of the dead. It is depicted as a region set among a chain of mountains and comprising four "hollows" or "vales" (τόποι κοῖλοι, κοιλώματα) that have been entirely separated (ἐχωρίσθησαν) from one another; one of these vales is full of light and flowing water, while the other three are dry, deep, and dark. Here the dead await the judgment, the righteous in the place of light with its refreshing springs of water, the various classes of the unrighteous in the various places of suffering and darkness. Here too, I believe, or in some topography of Hades very similar to it, Luke has placed Lazarus and the rich man: the one in the Vale or Vales of Abraham, the other in a dark, dry, fiery valley of suffering. This does not prove my translation correct; but it does prove it sufficiently plausible, and perhaps more plausible than most alternatives.

V: Spirit, Soul, Flesh

In the introduction to his book *The Corinthian Body*, Dale B. Martin
wisely observes that the Judaism of the first century, not only in Greek
and Roman cities, but also in Palestine, was a Graeco-Roman religion,
indelibly affected by a dominant Hellenistic culture, as well as by the culture of Rome. For him, first-century Judaism was "an ethnic subculture"
within the Mediterranean Hellenistic world. So, writes Martin, "any firm
distinction between 'Greco-Roman' and 'Jewish' in this period is therefore historically misleading, even if, for some people, it is theologically
important." How very true, and how very unfortunate that those theological prejudices persist despite their untenability. I have to say, I wel-
come Martin's words—to which no sound scholar of the Roman world
could possibly take exception—as a kind of salutary admonition but also
as an encouragement. This is because I intend to take N. T. Wright as an
antagonist here, not out of spite, but rather because I see much of his
work as emblematic of a larger historical tendency in New Testament
scholarship. I can think of no other popular writer on the early church
these days whose picture of Judaism in the Roman Hellenistic world
seems better to exemplify what I regard as a dangerous triumph of theological predispositions over historical fact in biblical studies—one that
occasionally so distorts the picture of the intellectual and spiritual environment of the apostolic church as effectively to create an entirely fictional early Christianity. Naturally, this also entails the simultaneous
creation of an equally fictional late antique Judaism, of the sort that once
dominated Protestant biblical scholarship: a fantastic "pure" Judaism
situated outside cultural history, purged of every Hellenistic and Persian
"alloy," stripped of those shining hierarchies of spirits and powers and
morally ambiguous angels and demi-angelic *nefilim* that had been incubated in the intertestamental literature, largely ignorant even of those
Septuagintal books that were omitted from the Masoretic text of the Jewish Bible, and precociously conformed to later rabbinic orthodoxy—and,
even then, this last turns out to be a fantasy rabbinic orthodoxy, one
robbed of its native genius and variety, and imperiously reduced to a kind
of Protestantism without Jesus.

No such Judaism ever existed, either in the days of Christ and the
apostles or in any other period; but it has enjoyed a long and vigorous life

in Protestant dogmatics and biblical criticism. And I was recently reminded of this by Wright himself when he publicly objected to a footnote in my own recent translation of the New Testament. In that note, I mentioned more or less in passing that Paul seems to have thought that some of the narratives of the Jewish Bible not only were apt for allegorical readings but might also have originally been written *as* allegories. For Wright, this was tantamount to a suggestion that Paul did not believe in the reality of God's covenants with Israel. Now, needless to say, nothing of the sort follows logically from my observation; more to the point, my footnote did nothing more than call attention to Paul's own words. (And, really, how often does Paul *not* employ allegory in reading scripture?) But Wright's anxiety is quite in keeping with a certain traditional Protestant picture of the pagan and Jewish worlds of late antiquity, one that involves an impermeable cultural partition between them—between, that is, the "philosophy" of the Greeks and the "pure" covenantal piety of the Jews. And, as I say, the results are sometimes comic. Unfortunately, they are at other times positively disastrous. Nowhere is this more strikingly the case—and nowhere does Wright's work in particular present a more troubling specimen of pious exegetical violence to scripture—than in regard to the New Testament's use of the words πνεῦμα (spirit), ψυχή (soul), and σάρξ (flesh), as well as to the theologies of resurrection that attach to them.

We are, of course, far removed from the world of the first century, and so it is natural for us, when we encounter these words and others like them in the New Testament, to see them as having only very vague imports, apposite to mistily ill-defined concepts or spectrally impalpable objects. We almost invariably etherealize or moralize their meanings in ways that entirely obscure the picture of reality they originally reflected. The earth on which we live, for example, is not divided from the several heavenly spheres by the lunary sphere, nor is the aerial realm of generation and decay here below separated by that sphere from the imperishable ethereal realm of spiritual forces there above. Thus, for us today, even such words as *heavenly* (ἐπουράνιος) and *earthly* (χοϊκός) convey practically nothing of the exquisite cosmology—at once concretely physical and vibrantly spiritual—in which the authors of the New Testament lived. And inevitably, when we read of "spirit," "soul," and "flesh" in the New Testament, the specter of Descartes (even if unnoticed by us) imposes itself between us and the conceptual world those terms reflect; we have next to no sense of the implications, physical and metaphysical, that such words had in the age of the early church. Even "flesh" becomes an almost perfect cipher for us, not only because we lack the perspective of ancient persons, but also because of the drastic oversimplifications of Christian tradition with which we have been burdened; we think we know—just know in our bones—that the early Christians unambiguously affirmed the inherent goodness of the material body, and that surely, then, Christian scripture could never have meant to employ the word *flesh* with its literal acceptation in order to designate something bad. Thus, as we read along, *either* we convince ourselves not to notice that almost every use of the word is openly opprobrious, and that the very few that are not are still for the most part merely neutral in intonation, *or* we acknowledge this fact but nevertheless still insist to ourselves that the word is being used metaphorically or as a lexical synecdoche for some larger conceptual construct like "the mortal life in the flesh, stained with sin and lying under divine judgment." In the world of Protestant scriptural scholarship, this latter strategy reached a kind of cartoonish climax in the early editions of the New International Version of the Bible, where the word *flesh* was in many cases rendered as something like "sinful nature" (I would check the exact wording, but that would involve picking up a copy of the NIV). This is utter twaddle. In the New Testament, *flesh* does not mean "sinful nature" or "humanity under judgment" or even "fallen flesh." It just means "flesh," in the bluntly physical sense, and it often has a negative connotation because flesh is essentially a bad condition to be in; belonging to the realm of mutability and mortality, it can form only a body of death. Hence, according to Paul, the body of the Resurrection is not one of flesh and blood animated by "soul" but is rather a new reality altogether, an entirely spiritual body beyond composition or dissolution. And this is how his language would have been understood by his contemporaries.

To grasp this fully today, however, one really has to take leave of the Cartesian picture of things. One must cease to think that only the material body possesses extension in any sense; one must learn not to treat words like *soul, spirit,* and *mind* as interchangeable terms for one and the same thing; and one must most emphatically not think of soul or spirit or mind as necessarily incorporeal in the absolute sense of lacking all extension or consistency. None of this resembles the ancient view of things. And one must be especially conscious that the words πνεῦμα and ψυχή were not nebulous terms in the religious or speculative vocabulary of the Hellenized world; neither in most cases were they likely to be confused with one another, as *spirit* and *soul* can be in modern English, because they were usually used as precise names for two distinct principles that were not only already resident in the created cosmos; in some systems of thought, in fact, they named principles practically antithetical to one another in their metaphysical and religious meanings. In different eras, places, and schools, admittedly, each of these words carried somewhat different, if never entirely unrelated, connotations; but each word always had a clear significance. And Paul used both terms in ways that were very much part of the philosophical and scientific lingua franca of his age. In the broader system of ideas in which his picture of things subsisted, "soul"—ψυχή or *anima*—was chiefly the life-principle proper to the realm of generation and decay, the "psychical" or "animal" substance that endows sublunary organisms with the power of self-movement and growth, though only for a short time. And the bodily life produced by this "animating" principle was understood as strictly limited to the aerial and terrestrial sphere. It could exist nowhere else, and most certainly not in the heavenly places. It was too frail, too ephemeral, too much bound to mutability and transience.

"Spirit," by contrast—πνεῦμα or *spiritus*—was something quite different, a kind of life not bound to death or to the irrational faculties of brute nature, inherently indestructible and incorruptible, and not confined to any single cosmic sphere. It could survive anywhere and could move with complete liberty among all the spiritual realms, as well as in the material world here below. Spirit was something subtler but also stronger, more vital, more glorious than the worldly elements of a coarse corruptible body compounded of earthly soul and material flesh. Thus too the word *spirits* was common parlance in late antiquity for all those rational personal agencies and entities who populated the cosmos but who were not bound to vegetal or animal bodies and so were immune to death: lesser celestial gods, daemons, angels, *nefilim*, devils, or what have you (what one called the various classes of spirits was a matter of religious vocabulary, not necessarily the basic conceptual shape of their natures). These beings enjoyed a life not limited by the conditions of the lower elements (the στοιχεῖα) or of any of the intrinsically dissoluble combinations thereof.

Even so, none of these beings was typically considered to be incorporeal in the full sense, at least in the way we would use that word today. The common belief of most educated persons of the time was that, if any reality was bodiless in the absolute sense, it could be only God or the highest divine principle. Everything else, even spirits, had *some* kind of body, because all of them were irreducibly local realities. The bodies of spirits may have been at once both more invincible and more mercurial than those with an animal constitution, but they were also, if in a peculiarly exalted sense, still physical. Many thought them to be composed from, say, the aether or the "quintessence" above, the "spiritual" substance that constitutes the celestial regions beyond the moon. Many also identified that substance with the πνεῦμα—the "wind" or "breath"—that stirs all things, a universal quickening force subtler even than the air it moves. It was generally believed, moreover, that many of these ethereal or spiritual beings were not only embodied but visible. The stars overhead were thought to be divine or angelic intelligences (as we see reflected in James 1:17 and 2 Pet. 2:10–11). And it was a conviction common to a good many pagans and Jews alike that the ultimate destiny of great or especially righteous souls was to be elevated into the heavens to shine as stars (as we see in Dan. 12:3 and Wisd. 3:7, and as may be hinted at in 1 Cor. 15:30–41). The "blissful abode" of the righteous was something visible to the naked eye at night, up there in the shining aether far beyond the region of air below the moon (see, for example, *Orphic Hymn* 37, or even *Aeneid* 6.743–51). In the Jewish and Christian belief of the age, in fact, there really appears to have been nothing similar to the fully incorporeal angels of later Scholastic tradition—certainly nothing like the angels of Thomism, for example, who are pure form devoid of prime matter and therefore each its own unique species. In fact, it was a central tenet of the most influential angelology of the age, derived as it was from the Noachic books of the intertestamental period, that angels had actually sired children—the monstrous *nefilim*—on human women.

It is even arguable that no school of pagan thought, early or late, perhaps not even Platonism, really had a perfectly clear concept of *any* substance without extension. For Plotinus, for instance, "soul" was "incorporeal," but not in the way we might assume; while the soul in

376 Different Idioms, Different Worlds

Plotinus's system was not susceptible of "material" magnitude, and hence could contain all forms without spatial extension (*Enneads* 2.4.11), it was still "incorporeal" only in the sense that it possessed so subtle a nature that it could wholly permeate material bodies without displacing their discrete material constituents (*Enneads* 4.7.8²). Neither "spirit" nor "soul" was anything quite like a Cartesian "mental substance." Each, no less than "flesh and blood," was thought of as a kind of element. "Spirit," for instance, in certain antique schools of natural philosophy and medicine, could be defined as that subtle influence or ichor that pervades the veins and passages of a living body and, among other things, endows it with sense perception—by filling, for instance, the nerves or porous passages between eye and brain. For many persons, in fact, this vital influence was literally "physically" continuous with the "wind" that fills the world and the "breath" that swells our chests. This is almost unimaginable for us, of course. When today, for instance, we try to make sense of John 3:8, we are frustrated by the absence in English of any word adequate to all the meanings present in the original's use of πνεῦμα. The Greek reads: τὸ πνεῦμα ὅπου θέλει πνεῖ καὶ τὴν φωνὴν αὐτοῦ ἀκούεις, ἀλλ᾽ οὐκ οἶδας πόθεν ἔρχεται καὶ ποῦ ὑπάγει· οὕτως ἐστὶν πᾶς ὁ γεγεννημένος ἐκ τοῦ πνεύματος. My attempt at a rendering in my translation, whose inadequacy I sheepishly acknowledge in my footnote thereto, is this: "The spirit respires where it will, and you hear its sound but you do not know where it comes from or where it goes; such is everyone born of the Spirit." I could, however, in each instance have written not "spirit" for πνεῦμα, but "wind" or "breath"; instead of "respires" for πνεῖ, I could have written "blows." Perhaps, then, this: "The wind blows where it will . . . such is everyone born from the wind." Or, perhaps, "The breath breathes where it will . . . such is everyone born from the breath." Happily, no translators have yet visited anything like that on us. But, still, all the various possible meanings would have been audibly present in the text for its author and for those who heard it read aloud in the earliest Christian communities. Even if we are aware of this, however, we are still likely to read the verse as a kind of play on words—at most, an illustrative simile. And, needless to say, our fully formed theological concept of the Holy Spirit disposes us, on grounds of piety alone, to see it as such. But it probably should not really be taken as wordplay at all. If we could hear the language of πνεῦμα with late antique, Graeco-Roman ears, our sense of the text's meaning would not be that of two utterly distinct concepts—one "physical" and one "mystical"—only metaphorically entangled with one another by dint of a verbal equivocity; rather, we would almost surely hear only a single concept expressed univocally through a single word, a concept in which the physical and the mystical would remain undifferentiated. To be born of spirit (or Spirit), to be born of the wind of life, to be born of the divine and cosmic breath vivifying and uniting all things—it would all make perfectly simple, straightforward, "physical" sense to us. Whatever the case, though, this much is certain: it was widely believed in late antiquity that, in human beings, flesh and soul and spirit were all present in some degree; "spirit" was merely the element that was imperishable by nature and constitution.

This is why it is that those traditional translations of 1 Corinthians 15:35–54 that render Paul's distinction between the σῶμα ψυχικόν (psychical body) and the σῶμα πνευματικόν (spiritual body) as a distinction between "natural" and "spiritual" bodies are so terribly misleading. The very category of the "natural" is otiose here, as would be any opposition between natural and supernatural modes of life; that is a conceptual division that belongs to other, much later ages. For Paul, both psychical and spiritual bodies were in the proper sense *natural* objects, and both in fact are found in nature as it now exists. He distinguished, therefore, not between "*natural*" and "spiritual" bodies, but only between σώματα ἐπίγεια, "terrestrial bodies," and σώματα ἐπουράνια, "celestial bodies." And this, again, is a distinction not between natural and supernatural life, but merely between incommiscible "natural" states: ἀφθαρσία, "incorruptibility," and φθορά, "decay"; δόξα, "glory," and ἀτιμία, "dishonor"; δυνάμις, "power," and ἀσθένεια, "weakness." In speaking of the body of the resurrection as a "spiritual" rather than "psychical" body, Paul is saying that, in the Age to come, when the whole cosmos will be transfigured into a reality appropriate to spirit, beyond birth and death, the terrestrial bodies of those raised to new life will be transfigured into the sort of celestial bodies that now belong to the angels: incorruptible, immortal, purged of every element of flesh and blood and (perhaps) soul. For, as Paul quite clearly states, "Flesh and blood cannot inherit the Kingdom of God; neither does perishability inherit imperishability": σὰρξ καὶ αἷμα βασιλείαν θεοῦ κληρονομῆσαι οὐ δύναται οὐδὲ ἡ φθορὰ τὴν ἀφθαρσίαν κληρονομεῖ. And, of course, he also says that those who are in Christ have been made capable of this transformation precisely because, in the body of the risen Christ, the life of the Age to come has already appeared in glory: οὕτως καὶ γέγραπται· ἐγένετο ὁ πρῶτος ἄνθρωπος Ἀδὰμ εἰς ψυχὴν ζῶσαν, ὁ ἔσχατος Ἀδὰμ εἰς πνεῦμα ζωοποιοῦν. . . . ὁ πρῶτος ἄνθρωπος ἐκ γῆς χοϊκός, ὁ δεύτερος ἄνθρωπος ἐξ οὐρανοῦ. οἷος ὁ χοϊκός, τοιοῦτοι καὶ οἱ χοϊκοί, καὶ οἷος ὁ ἐπουράνιος, τοιοῦτοι καὶ οἱ ἐπουράνιοι· καὶ καθὼς ἐφορέσαμεν τὴν εἰκόνα τοῦ χοϊκοῦ, φορέσομεν καὶ τὴν εἰκόνα τοῦ ἐπουρανίου, "So it has also been written, 'The first man Adam came to be a living soul,' and the last Adam a life-making spirit. . . . The first man out of the earth, earthly; the second man out of heaven. As the earthly man, so also those who are earthly; and, as the heavenly, so also those who are heavenly; and, just as we have borne the image of the earthly man, we shall also bear the image of the heavenly man." This is for Paul nothing less than the transformation of the psychical composite into the spiritual simplex—the metamorphosis of the mortal fleshly body that belongs to soul into the immortal fleshless body that belongs to spirit: ἡμεῖς ἀλλαγησόμεθα. Δεῖ γὰρ τὸ φθαρτὸν τοῦτο ἐνδύσασθαι ἀφθαρσίαν καὶ τὸ θνητὸν τοῦτο ἐνδύσασθαι ἀθανασίαν, "We shall be changed. For this perishable thing must clothe itself in imperishability, and this mortal thing must clothe itself in immortality."

It is not so much Christian dogma as indurated habits of thought and imagination that make Paul's language in 1 Corinthians 15, or, for that matter, Romans 8, so impenetrable to modern Christians. No matter how clear Paul's pronouncements are, the plain meaning of his words still seems so terribly "pagan" or "Platonic" or "semignostic" to modern Christian ears, and of course all of those things are usually regarded as being very bad. Thus the picture persists of resurrection, even in Paul's thought, as something along the lines of a reconstruction and reanimation of the earthly body. N. T. Wright, in the very odd and misleading translation of 1 Corinthians 15 that appears in his very odd and misleading *The Kingdom New Testament*, at one juncture turns σῶμα ψυχικόν and σῶμα πνευματικόν into, respectively, "embodiment of ordinary nature" and "embodiment of the spirit," which is bad enough; but then the translation devolves further into a distinction between "the nature-animated body" and "the spirit-animated body," which is simply atrocious. For one thing, the very word *animated* is deeply problematic, since it is arguably already a synonym for ψυχικόν, and since it is extremely unlikely—in fact, historically speaking, probably impossible—that Paul thought of the spiritual body as a kind of articulated organism, consisting in an extrinsic liaison between something animated and something animating. He almost certainly thought of "spirit" as being itself the substance that will compose the risen body, rather than an extrinsic life-principle that will come to reside in a revived and improved material body. Wright, however, seems to imagine something like two different phases of some variety of Cartesian dualism, one mortal and the other immortal, but in either case involving the combination in a single composite of an animated material body and an animating immaterial force. This is the purest anachronism. Worse still, Wright follows a deeply misguided tradition of translation in imposing an opposition between "natural" and (one must suppose) "supernatural" on the text; that too, as I have said, is anachronistic. Worst of all, in his translation the central opposition between the two distinct principles of soul and spirit—which runs through the entire New Testament and which is crucial to its anthropology, theology, and metaphysics—has been entirely lost. But Wright has his own understanding of resurrection, one more or less consonant with the casually presumed picture today, even if it is one entirely alien to the world of first-century Judaism and Christianity. His categories are not those of Paul—or, for that matter, of the rest of the authors of the New Testament.

There is, admittedly, no single consistent account of resurrection—either Christ's or ours—in the New Testament; but there is most definitely a prevailing tendency to view resurrection in terms quite similar to Paul's. Only one verse, Luke 24:39, seems to advance a contrary picture; there, more or less reversing Paul's terms, the risen Christ proves that he is not spirit precisely by demonstrating that he possesses "flesh and bone." Here, needless to say, the word *spirit* is being employed with its most debased and vulgar meaning, "ghost." And even Luke, over the course of his two books, seems somewhat inconsistent on the terminology appropriate to resurrection (I suspect because he was drawing on diverse earlier sources). There is, at the very least, ample scriptural evidence suggesting that Paul's language in 1 Corinthians 15 may be little more than a précis of a theology and metaphysics of resurrection not at all uncommon in many of the Jewish circles of his time. Certainly, his may have been one of the standard Pharisaic views of the matter. We almost unquestionably see evidence of this in Acts 23:8: Σαδδουκαῖοι μὲν γὰρ λέγουσιν μὴ εἶναι ἀνάστασιν μήτε ἄγγελον μήτε πνεῦμα, Φαρισαῖοι δὲ ὁμολογοῦσιν τὰ ἀμφότερα, "For the Sadducees say there is no resurrection—neither as angel nor as spirit—while the Pharisees profess both." It seems quite clear from that phrase "μήτε ἄγγελον μήτε πνεῦμα" that the concept of resurrection described here is, like Paul's, that of an exchange of the "animated" or "psychical" body of this life for the sort of bodily existence proper to a "spirit" or an "angel." Admittedly, some older translations rendered this passage incorrectly, as saying that the Sadducees believed neither in the resurrection, nor in spirits, nor in angels, but that is obviously not what the Greek means. Neither, however, does it say what Wright's translation quite inexcusably gives us: "The Sadducees deny that there is any resurrection, or any intermediate state of 'angel' or 'spirit.'" That is about as flagrant an act of eisegetical presumptuousness as one is likely to come across in any translation; clearly this is not at all what the original says, or anything it could possibly be taken as implying. Nor am I convinced that Wright really in his heart of hearts believes that this is what Luke's language means, or that he is unaware that he is willfully impressing an alien concept upon the text in order to make it better align with the "reanimation" model of resurrection that he has invented for the first century. The passage plainly has nothing whatever to do with any idea of some intermediate state between death and resurrection; it is the resurrection itself that is described as the assumption of an angelic or spiritual condition. (Really, if one is so frightened of that mythical monster "Hellenization" that one needs to go to such dubious lengths, I think it would be wiser to give up on the New Testament altogether; because, the more one reads it in light of the wider spiritual and philosophical beliefs of its age, the more it seems to disclose a world in which—at least, as regards which of the Graeco-Roman world's shared visions of reality a person or people was likely to adopt—there really was neither Jew nor Greek, but all were one.)

Consider also Mark 12:25, Matthew 22:30, and Luke 20:35–36, all of which tell us that, for those who share in the Resurrection, there is neither marrying nor being married—after all, there will no longer be either birth or (so notes Luke) death—because those who are raised will be "as the angels in heaven," or "in the heavens," and will in fact be "the angel's equals" or "equivalent to angels" (ἰσάγγελοι). It is difficult not to think that here Jesus may be telling the Sadducees that the theology of resurrection that he shares with the Pharisees entails no notion of a revived animated material body; it asserts, rather, that the raised will live forever in an angelic manner, an angelic frame.

Nowhere in scripture, of course, is this fundamental opposition between flesh and spirit given fuller theological (and mystical) treatment than in John's Gospel; and nowhere else is the promise that the saved will escape from a carnal into a spiritual condition more explicitly or repeatedly issued. The Logos of John's Gospel does, of course, "become flesh" and "tabernacle" among his creatures, but this involves no particular affirmation of the goodness of fleshly life; the Logos descends to us that we might ascend with him, and in so doing, presumably, shed the flesh. This is the entire soteriological morphology of the gospel, after all: the tale of the descent from above of the Father's only Son—the Son who has come down from heaven and who can, therefore, go up to heaven again (3:13)—so that those who are born from above, of water and spirit, can see the Kingdom of God (3:3-5); τὸ γεγεννημένον ἐκ τῆς σαρκὸς σάρξ ἐστιν, καὶ τὸ γεγεννημένον ἐκ τοῦ πνεύματος πνεῦμά ἐστιν, "That which is born of flesh is flesh, and that which born of the spirit is spirit" (3:6). At the same time, of course, no other gospel places greater emphasis upon the physical substantiality of the body of the risen Christ—Thomas invited to place his hands in Christ's wounds, the disciples invited to share a breakfast of fish with him beside the Sea of Tiberias—but even this is perfectly compatible with Paul's language.

It is, as I say, extraordinarily difficult for modern persons to free their imaginations from the essentially Cartesian prejudice that material bodies must by definition be more substantial, more concrete, more capable of generating physical effects than anything that might be denominated as "soul" or "spirit" or "intellect" could be. Again, however, for the peoples of late Graeco-Roman antiquity, it made perfect sense to think of spiritual reality as more substantial, powerful, and resourceful than any animal body could ever be. Nothing of which a mortal, corruptible, "psychical" body is capable would have been thought to lie beyond the powers of an immortal, incorruptible, wholly spiritual being. It was this evanescent life, lived in a frail and perishable animal frame, that was regarded as the poorer, feebler, more ghostly of the two conditions; spiritual existence was something immeasurably mightier, more robust, more joyous, more plentifully alive. And this definitely seems to be the picture provided by the gospels in general. The risen Christ, possessed of a spiritual body, could eat and drink, could be felt, could break bread between his hands; but he could also appear and disappear at will, unimpeded by walls or locked doors, or could become unrecognizable to those who had known him before his death, or could even ascend from the earth and pass through the incorruptible heavens where only spiritual beings may venture.

And then there is 1 Peter 3:18–19: ὅτι καὶ Χριστὸς ἅπαξ περὶ ἁμαρτιῶν ἔπαθεν, δίκαιος ὑπὲρ ἀδίκων, ἵνα ὑμᾶς προσαγάγῃ τῷ θεῷ θανατωθεὶς μὲν σαρκί, ζωοποιηθεὶς δὲ πνεύματι· ἐν ᾧ καὶ τοῖς ἐν φυλακῇ πνεύμασιν πορευθεὶς ἐκήρυξεν, "For the Anointed also suffered, once and for all, a just man on behalf of the unjust, so that he might lead you to God, being put to death in flesh and yet being made alive in spirit, whereby he also journeyed and made a proclamation to the spirits in prison." This verse is extremely easy to overlook, or at least to misunderstand. It is usually read as relating the same story found in 1 Peter 4:6, which seems to tell of Christ evangelizing the dead in Hades so that, though they had been judged "in flesh" according to human beings, they might live "in spirit" (not "in *the* Spirit") according to God. While that verse too is germane to my remarks here, the verses from chapter 3 do not refer to the same episode. For one thing, whether or not the evangelization of Hades was understood as having occurred during the interval between Christ's death and his resurrection, the tale cited in chapter 3 is explicitly about something Christ accomplished *after* his resurrection. The parallel construction "θανατωθεὶς μὲν σαρκί, ζωοποιη-θεὶς δὲ πνεύματι" employs two modal datives—*in* or *by* or *as* flesh, *in* or *by* or *as* spirit—to indicate the manner or condition, first, of Christ's death and, second, of his being made alive again, while the conjunctive formula ἐν ᾧ seems to make it clear that, by being raised "*as* spirit," Christ was made capable of entering into spiritual realms, and so of traveling to the "spirits in prison." Again, the word *spirits* was a common way of designating rational creatures who by their nature do not possess psychical bodies of perishable flesh. And the specific reference in this verse is not to the "souls" of human beings who have died but to those wicked spirits—those angels or daemonic beings—imprisoned in Tartarus until the Day of Judgment (mentioned also in 2 Pet. 2:4–5 and Jude 1:6) whose stories are told in 1 Enoch and Jubilees. It may even be of some significance here that these infuriatingly enigmatic verses seem to echo the account of Enoch's visit to the abode of these spirits in order to proclaim God's condemnation upon them (1 Enoch 12–15). Who can say? It is certainly of considerable significance, however, that this passage seems to say that the risen Christ was able to make his journey to those hidden regions precisely because he was no longer hindered by a carnal frame but instead now possessed the boundless liberty of spirit.

It is just such liberty, incidentally, that for the New Testament appears to constitute much of the substance of salvation. If we fail to notice this, it is only because, again, the words and concepts we rely upon lead us instinctively to draw an absolute qualitative division between physical and spiritual reality. The authors of scripture inhabited a very different universe, one in which the cosmological and the metaphysical were not separated from one another, much less the natural and the supernatural. For them, Christ's descent into this world was at once genuinely a movement from transcendence into immanence but also a movement through space from the unchanging divine aeon or realm above the heavens, down through the concentric spheres of the planetary and lunar heavens, into the realm of generation, alteration, and decay. Conversely, our ascent to God in and through Christ was understood as at once a sacramental, mystical, and gracious passage from death to new life but also an ascent in and with Christ through the heavens into God's eternity above. Both Christ and those saved by him traverse the spiritual and moral chasm of estrangement between God's empyrean and this cosmos but also (in some sense) the actual space between them. Or, at any rate, it was believed that the intervening heavens, in the wake of Christ's conquest of the hostile powers reigning over them and governing the world below, will no longer be barriers between God's heaven and the world of the Age to come.

It is hard for us, admittedly, to imagine in any but metaphorical colorations the great religious anxiety of late antiquity: that we are imprisoned in the "here below," in the realm of transience, of birth and death, below the sphere of the moon in the region of "air" with all its fleeting volatility, under the impenetrable, turning, and sentineled spheres of the heavens above. Some of us may be aware that, in the early centuries of the church, there were mystery religions or "gnostic" sects or Orphic cults or Hermetic wisdoms (and so on) that promised salvation precisely in the form of escape from—and through the midst of—the hostile celestial agencies that imprison us. Very nearly the oldest stratum of Christian apologetics records the fact. Irenaeus's *Adversus haereses* abounds in curious descriptions of "gnostic" variants of the tale. Especially amusing to us, perhaps, are its reports of sects that thought it necessary for the elect to memorize certain secret words or phrases that would win them passage through the spheres of the archons, or for the faithful to impart such words to the spirits of the dead as they began their ascent (see, for instance, *AH* 121.5). And we find the idea confirmed in various of the "gnostic" literary remains, such as the *Second Book of Jeu* (52) in the Berlin Codex, or *The Apocryphon of James* in the Nag Hammadi Corpus (*NHC* 5.3.32.29–35.25). We know from Origen, in fact, that a number of sects (the Ophites, for example) believed that such secret knowledge permitted the enlightened *pneumatikos* to slip past the "gatekeepers" of the planetary realms and the "everlastingly chained gates of the archons" (*Contra Celsum* 6.30ff; 7.40). But, setting aside the perhaps vaguely comic notion of a the liberated spirit traversing the heavens like a Prohibition-era tippler whispering passwords through a series of speakeasies' doors, the essential picture of this world as a prison and of salvation as escape through its encircling walls was very nearly universal. "Orphic" mysteries had long taught that the Dionysian "daemon" within each initiate must ascend back through the celestial spheres through which it had originally fallen into this world, successively shedding each of the encumbering "Titanic" layers it had acquired along the course of that immemorial descent. We find much the same picture in the *Corpus hermeticum* (1.23–26). Mithraism too promised that the saved would rise through the seven planetary heavens and past the hostile powers guarding them. The Sethian treatise *Zostrianos* depicts these seven spheres as "places of penitential suffering" (*NHC* 8.1), as do the Mandaean *Diwan Abithur* and *Left Ginza*. For this last tradition, salvation lies in the divine regions of light above the seven *martatâs* confining us to this world. We deceive ourselves, however, if we imagine that it was only the marginal, eccentric, and "heterodox" sects of the early centuries that thought in such terms.

Most Jews, from well before to well after the time of Christ, as well as most Christians of those early centuries, thought of the cosmos and of salvation in just these terms. Hence the New Testament tells of a cosmic dispensation under the reign of the god of this aeon (2 Cor. 4:4) or the Archon of this cosmos (John 14:30; Eph. 2:2), and of spiritual beings hopelessly immured within heavenly spheres thronged by hostile archons and powers and principalities and daemons (Rom. 8:3, 39; 1 Cor. 10:20–21; 15:24; Eph. 1:21; etc.), bound under and cursed by a law that was in fact ordained by lesser, merely angelic powers (Gal. 3:10–11, 19–20). Into this prison, this darkness that knows nothing of the true light (John 1:5), a divine savior descends from the divine realm above (John 3:31; 8:23; etc.), bringing with him a secret truth that has been hidden from before the ages (Rom. 16:25–26; Gal. 1:12; Eph. 3:3–9; Col. 1:26), a wisdom unknown even to "the archons of this cosmos" (1 Cor. 2:7–8) that has the power to liberate fallen spirits (John 8:31–32, etc.). The letter to the Ephesians is practically a primer in this sort of cosmic soteriology: Christ has been seated at God's right hand in the heavenly places, "far above every Rule and Authority and Power and Lordship" with "all things ordered under his feet" (1:20–22), having taken the hostile powers captive as he ascended through the heavens (4:8–10); he has, moreover, emancipated us from the "Archon of the Power of the Air" (2:2), and set us alongside himself in the heavenly places (2:6); and even now he is revealing God's plan to these celestial archons and powers through his church (3:10); nevertheless, until the consummation of all things, Christians must continue to wrestle "not against blood and flesh, but against the Archons, against the Powers, against the Cosmic Rulers of this darkness, against the spiritual forces of wickedness in the celestial places" (6:12). The language is perfectly clear. Nor should we doubt for a moment how very literally these images were meant to be taken. This might seem to some of us today, of course, to reduce much of the soteriology of the New Testament to little more than naive mythology or bad science; but that would be a thoroughly parochial judgment. Persons of every age are constrained to think and speak within the image of reality they know; but that does not mean that the truths they attempt to enunciate are exhausted by those conceptual forms. The language of salvation in Christ as it appears in the earliest Christian documents reflects the presuppositions of its time, but perhaps its revolutionary import has the power to shatter all presuppositions without losing its force. It may even long outlive the tacit (and, sadly, mechanistic) metaphysics and cosmology of reality that forms the dominant cosmic mythology of the modern age. Whatever the case, the fact remains that, for Paul (as for others of his time), Christ's triumph over and subjugation of the cosmic Principalities and Authorities and Powers (1 Cor. 15:24–28) has literally opened a path through the planetary spheres, the encompassing heavens, the armies of the air and the potentates on high, all the way to God. This is a claim made in intonations at once both physical and spiritual. And, even if now most of us can hear only the latter as having any genuinely compelling or credible force, we should nevertheless—just for understanding's sake—let ourselves occasionally hear the former as well. We should, that is, let ourselves recognize the integral unity of the natural and the supernatural, the cosmic and the divine, in Paul's joyous proclamation that "neither death nor life nor angels nor Archons nor things present nor things imminent nor Powers nor height nor depth nor any other creature will be able to separate us from the love of God" (Rom. 8:38–39).

VI: Tunics

There is no need further to belabor the point. One last observation, however, and this a thoroughly speculative one. I have complained with monotonous regularity in the past about how certain established conventions of translation have often had the effect of entirely hiding from view two vital conceptual oppositions that pervade the books of the New Testament: that between flesh and spirit, and that between the psychical and the spiritual. They do this in a number of quite predictable but also quite effective ways. At certain crucial junctures, for instance, words having to do with the principle of soul—ψυχή or ψυχικός—are rendered in vague and misleading fashions, as references to nature or natural life, or as describing sensual and irrational characters, or something else of the sort. In certain intrusively tendentious translations, like the New International Version, words related to flesh—σάρξ or σαρκικός—become references to sinful nature or carnal-mindedness or something like that. And, most appalling (but also most common) of all, almost every use of a word having to do with spirit—πνεῦμα or πνευματικός—is turned into some kind of reference to the Holy Spirit, although practically none of them actually is. As a consequence, a whole host of the New Testament's most essential theological, cosmological, anthropological, moral, and religious concepts are suppressed, subverted, belied, forgotten, and finally replaced by alternative concepts. As I have mentioned before, elsewhere, I tend to regard Jude 19 as an especially poignant example of these practices. The Greek reads: Οὗτοί εἰσιν οἱ ἀποδιορίζοντες, ψυχικοί, πνεῦμα μὴ ἔχοντες, which literally means "These are those who cause divisions, psychical men, not possessing spirit." Any rendering much different from this—and especially one that fails to give any indication of the original's invocation of "soul" while transforming the mention of "spirit" into a mention of "*the* Spirit [of God]"—has utterly misrepresented the Greek, to the point of either saying something quite different from what the original text says, or of saying absolutely nothing at all.

Another verse from the same epistle, however, raises a question of another sort. I suspect that it too may contain a reference to the opposition of soul and spirit in the thinking of the early church; but, if so, it is precisely by rendering it accurately and clearly that a translation is likely to make its meaning impenetrable. The verse is Jude 23: οὒς δὲ σῴζετε ἐκ πυρὸς ἁρπάζοντες, οὒς δὲ ἐλεᾶτε ἐν φόβῳ μισοῦντες καὶ τὸν ἀπὸ τῆς σαρκὸς ἐσπιλωμένον χιτῶνα, which I have rendered as "Yet also save them by seizing them out of fire; but have mercy on them in fear, hating even the inner tunic stained by flesh." This part of the epistle (this verse and the one just preceding it) is notoriously difficult to translate lucidly, and different ancient textual exemplars give us quite a few variants, all of which are somewhat confusing. But this last image of the tunic stained by flesh is common to all versions, and I cannot help but suspect that it has a greater significance than it might at first seem to have. On its face, it appears to be no more than a homely metaphor for something probably quite ordinary—precisely what, it is hard to say: putting off our lustful natures, perhaps, and putting on God's likeness instead (as in Eph. 4:22–24). There is, of course, the opprobrious reference to flesh, as something that defiles or stains; that is only to be expected. But is the tunic—the χιτών—really only a tunic? And in what sense is flesh so loathsome that it is a virtue to despise even the garments that come into direct contact with it? Perhaps it is only an oblique baptismal image and refers to the removal of a catechumen's old clothes before he or she descended into the water and then, on ascending from the font again, donned a new garment of pure linen. In all likelihood, it is. On the other hand, one should not ignore the long tradition of the use of the word *tunics* (χιτῶνες) or, more rarely, *garments* (ἱμάτια) as an image for different

kinds of malign accretions to the soul or spirit within us. In some parts
of that tradition, these accretions were moral flaws or corruptions of temperament or the ill effects of the world upon personal character. In the
Gorgias (523b-e), for instance, Plato speaks of the need for the philosophical soul to strip off the habiliments of high birth, personal wealth,
and the well-formed body of the aristocrat in order to achieve purity; and,
according to Dioscurides, he spoke of δόξα—in the sense of "personal
glory" or "false opinion"—as the very last of these χιτῶνες that must be
shed when one dies. For most of antique tradition, though, the "tunics"
that garb our inner natures are more than mere metaphors for personal
failings or worldly emotional attachments. When Philo of Alexandria
speaks in his *Allegory of the Law* (2.56–59) of this same δόξα as a kind of
psychic involucrum wrapped around the rational faculty within us, he
seems to be speaking of more than the bad habits and improper desires
that we cultivate during the courses of our lives. Throughout late antiquity, it was a trope not only of the Neoplatonists but apparently of
various of the more popular systems of belief and devotion—the so-called
"gnostic" churches, or Orphic sects, or hermetic schools—that the spirit
or intellectual principle within us, in descending into this cosmos, acquired layers of "soul" or psychical substance, and that it is these "tunics"
or "garments" that must be removed if we are to ascend again to the divine. Plotinus, for instance, in offering his interpretation of the ancient
mystery religions, treated the disrobing of initiates as symbolic of the
decortication of those ἱμάτια that come to envelop the νοῦς when it
descends through the heavens and enters this world (*Enneads* 1.6.7). Proclus, in both his *Commentary on the Alcibiades* and his *On the Subsistence
of Evils* (at least, in a fragment of the original Greek text quoted by Michael Psellus), also speaks of the enveloping χιτῶνες that we acquire in
coming hither and that we must shed again in going hence; and he uses
the image in a way that is simultaneously moral and, so to speak, physical.
For late Platonism in general, the rational spirit or intellect within us is
wrapped in the seven "tunics" it successively donned as it passed through
the seven planetary spheres, as well perhaps as additional layers gathered
from the elements of the sublunary world. Each of these "souls" constitutes a kind of vehicle or support, an ὄχημα, which allows the spiritual
principle at each stage of its descent to enter into the next lower sphere,
until finally it is able to enter into the prison of the mortal material

body. With each garment assumed, the oblivion of the spirit's true home and nature deepens. This same metaphysical and mystical imagery was shared also by any number of the less respectable spiritualities and mysteries of late antiquity, though with variations (the Valentinians, for instance, may have imagined a similar scheme of seven celestial soul-tunics, while the Basilideans may have thought that there are in fact 365).

All of which causes me to wonder whether Jude 23 is saying something rather different from what we might expect. Perhaps the inner tunic in question is not meant to be—or not meant *merely* to be—a reference to humankind's vices and frailties, or to the external tunic that lies upon the skin, beneath one's outer garments, that must be removed before one descends into the baptismal waters. Perhaps it is a reference to the psychical vehicle that mediates between the spirit deep within us and the mortal body of flesh and blood in which it lives. Perhaps it is an "inner tunic" in a deeper sense, one "stained by the flesh" from the inside, so to speak. One could no doubt have thought of this condition, not in terms of a prenatal descent through the heavens, but only as the consequence of life in a fallen world. Then again, who can say what Jude thought regarding the origins of the spirit in human beings (or, at least, in those among them actually "possessing spirit")? Whatever the case, given the language of verse 19 and given the theology of resurrection found elsewhere in the New Testament, this idea of a psychical vehicle could very well explain the image. Again, I am not suggesting that I have any firm convictions on the matter; but, for me, the mere plausibility of the question is, by itself, significant. It causes me to remember, I hope with at least something like a slight pang of humility, that the more we know of the intellectual and spiritual world in which Christianity and its scriptures took shape, the more perplexing the language and imagery of the texts become. The more successful we are in departing from the prejudices and preconceptions of the present and in making our way back into that age, the more we find ourselves confused by the variety, complexity, and sheer wildness of its vision of reality. The more we know, the less we understand; and, conversely, the more we understand, the more we discover what we do not know. And so, after two millennia of theological and hermeneutical tradition—and, indeed, to a very great extent, *because* of tradition—we find ourselves ever anew confronted by these texts as mysteries yet to be penetrated . . . worlds yet to be discovered.

INDEX

Photo by Nicole Waldron

DAVID BENTLEY HART is an Eastern Orthodox scholar of religion and a philosopher, writer, and cultural commentator. He is the author and translator of fifteen books, including *That All Shall Be Saved: Heaven, Hell, and Universal Salvation.*

Lightning Source UK Ltd.
Milton Keynes UK
UKHW010951131220
375109UK00001B/82